International Management Behavior

Happy Journeys!

Martha Maznevski

[signature]

International Management Behavior
Leading with a Global Mindset

Sixth Edition

Henry W. Lane
Darla and Frederick Brodsky Trustee Professor in Global Business, Northeastern University, and Professor Emeritus, Richard Ivey School of Business, University of Western Ontario

Martha L. Maznevski
Professor of Organizational Behavior and International Management, IMD, Lausanne, Switzerland

Joseph J. DiStefano
Professor Emeritus, IMD, Lausanne, Switzerland, and Richard Ivey School of Business, University of Western Ontario

Joerg Dietz
Professor of Organizational Behavior, Faculty of Business and Economics, University of Lausanne

A John Wiley and Sons, Ltd, Publication

This edition first published 2009

© 2009 Henry W. Lane, Martha L. Maznevski, Joseph J. DiStefano & Joerg Dietz

Registered office
John Wiley & Sons Ltd, The Atrium, Southern Gate, Chichester, West Sussex, PO19 8SQ, United Kingdom

For details of our global editorial offices, for customer services and for information about how to apply for permission to reuse the copyright material in this book please see our website at www.wiley.com

A catalogue record for this book is available from the British Library.

ISBN 978-0-470-71412-6 (P/B)

Set in 10/12pt Baskerville by Macmillan Publishing Solutions, Chennai, India.

Printed in Great Britain by CPI Antony Rowe, Chippenham, Wiltshire.

Dedication

To all the friends who have helped me learn about their cultures, and my own.

Henry (Harry) W. Lane

To Katie and Julianna, to help them inspire the next generation.

Martha L. Maznevski

To my parents and grandparents, whose combined legacy of deep pride in our Old World roots and openness to New World diversity has provided me with a wonderfully rich cultural life.

Joseph J. DiStefano

To Maura for her unwavering love and support in our adventures far away from home.

Joerg Dietz

Contents

Acknowledgments

The sixth edition of this book has involved a major revision of material from previous editions as well as additional new chapters, new cases, a new format, and a new co-author.

Professor DiStefano retired from IMD but is still active professionally and was very much involved with this edition of the text. We also welcome Professor Joerg Dietz to the team with this 6th edition. As will be seen from these acknowledgments the authors probably more closely resemble a family than just a team.

With Professor DiStefano's retirement, Professor Lane has to acknowledge his historical contribution to this book and to Professor Lane's career. Professor DiStefano interviewed Professor Lane who was doctoral candidate at the Harvard Business School and recruited him to Canada. He became a colleague, co-author, and friend. Professor DiStefano also started one the first cross-cultural courses anywhere in 1974 at the Ivey Business School (at the time the Western Business School) which was the genesis of this book. Another person at the University of Western Ontario who became a colleague, co-author, and friend, Don Simpson, deserves special recognition for introducing Professor Lane to Africa and helping him begin his "voyage of discovery" into the reality of functioning in other cultures and doing business internationally.

Professors Lane and DiStefano appreciate the support for their work on international business shown by their colleagues and research associates over the years at the Ivey Business School. Professor Maznevski, who graduated from Ivey's PhD program and who has collaborated with Professors Lane and DiStefano since that time, also acknowledges the broad support and assistance from the Ivey Business School, financial and otherwise, that contributed to her development and to this book.

All of us owe a special debt to our professors, colleagues, and friends who shaped our interests and knowledge at that institution. We are grateful to: Deans J. J. (Jack) Wettlaufer, C. B. (Bud) Johnston, Adrian Ryans, and Larry Tapp; Professors Jim Hatch,

Terry Deutscher, and Ken Hardy; the directors of Research and Publications at the Ivey Business School; and especially the donors of the Donald F. Hunter professorship (a Maclean Hunter endowment) and the Royal Bank professorship, which provided extra time for Professors Lane and DiStefano to undertake much of the initial work in developing this text. The Donald F. Hunter Professorship recently also supported Professor Dietz. We all also recognize the special contribution and mentorship of the late Professor Al Mikalachki who taught us so much about change.

After the third edition Professor DiStefano moved to Hong Kong to launch the Ivey EMBA program there and acknowledges with thanks Ivey alumnus, Dr Henry Cheng, whose financial and personal support were so critical to the success of this effort and to the deepening of Professor DiStefano's understanding of Hong Kong and China. In particular this made possible the addition of new Asian cases. In this regard we must also recognize the Richard and Jean Ivey fund of London, Ontario, for funding the development of Asian case studies, some of which appear in this new edition.

In 1994, Professor Lane assumed responsibility for Ivey's Americas Program and is grateful to Ivey for the support that made possible the development of many Latin American cases, including ones in this edition. That same year he also began work-ing with IPADE in Mexico and is very appreciative of the wonderful colleagues and friends he has made there over 15 years who not only have contributed to his educa-tion about Mexico and Latin America, but made it enjoyable to spend time there learn-ing. In September 1999, Professor Lane moved to Northeastern University where he is the Darla and Frederick Brodsky Trustee Professor in Global Business. The generous endowment of Darla and Frederick Brodsky has contributed to making this sixth edition possible and Professor Lane is grateful for their support and friendship.

In 1994, Professor Maznevski moved from Ivey to the McIntire School of Commerce. She thanks her colleagues there, in particular Dean Carl Zeithaml. The commitment of the school to making its programs global provided substantial support for her involve-ment in developing material for this book. Dean Zeithmal sponsored, both financially and with his enthusiasm, the first ION conferences and the genesis of a great network of colleagues.

In January 2000, Professor DiStefano joined IMD in Lausanne, Switzerland, and in 2001 Professor Maznevski followed him there. They would like to thank President Peter Lorange and the IMD research directors for their support in writing the sixth edition.

In 1999, Professor Lane helped to recruit Professor Dietz to Ivey where he was until 2009 when he joined the University of Lausanne. Professor Dietz is grateful to his co-authors for the invitation to join the team. He is particularly indebted to Harry Lane who has been a wonderful and patient mentor during the writing process and, more importantly, ever since Professor Dietz's academic career started.

To this list of acknowledgments we need to add a large number of people and insti-tutions from around the world who have broadened and informed our experience: managers in both the public and private sectors; colleagues at other universities and institutes; companies who have provided access to their operations for the purpose of writing cases; and a number of former students and research assistants who worked with us to develop material for this and previous editions. Among the former research assistants, a special note of thanks is due to Professor Bill Blake of Queen's University and to Professor Lorna Wright of York University. We would also like to thank Professor David Ager of Harvard University, Dan Campbell, David Wesley, and Karsten Jonsen for their substantial contributions. Other previous doctoral students who contributed to the intellectual tradition in international business at Ivey and to our learning included Paul Beamish, Neil Abramson, Shawna O'Grady, Terry Hildebrand, Iris Berdrow, Sing Chee Ling, and Jonathan Calof.

The restructuring that has taken place in the publishing industry adds considerably to this list of acknowledgments. A series of acquisitions and reorganizations has led to our experience with six publishers and five editors during the writing of the six editions. Our sincere thanks go to Joerg Klauck who was at Methuen, Ric Kitowski who was at Nelson Canada, Rolf Janke who was at PWS-Kent and then Blackwell, and Catriona King at Blackwell. All were strong believers in, and advocates for, this book. Additionally, Rosemary Nixon who was at Blackwell also has been a strong supporter of our work in this and other books. When Wiley acquired Blackwell, Rosemary moved to Wiley and we are delighted to be continuing our relationship with her now at Wiley. We also express our appreciation to colleagues who have provided the publishers, and us, with helpful critiques. To Nick Athanassiou, Bert Spector. Chris Robertson, and Jeanne McNett, we say a special thanks for the reviews, suggestions, and editing, which shaped this and earlier, editions.

Students and managers who have worked with our materials, and colleagues who have adopted our book and have written to us with thanks and suggestions, all have helped us and others learn. To them we also add our gratitude. Professor Lane would acknowledge, in particular, Professors Nick Athanassiou, Sheila Puffer, Alexandra Roth, and Tricia McConville who use this book at Northeastern and the executives who have shared their experiences with us or have facilitated access to case situations: Ken Clark, Gail Ellement, Ted English, Charles Forsgard, Astrid Nielsen, Philipp Röh, and Ron Zitlow. Professors Maznevski and DiStefano thank all the many executives in programs at IMD that have shared their stories and challenges. In particular, for this edition, specific contributions from the following have been invaluable: Emad Al-Dughaither, Arie Baan, Magdi Batato, Lars Björklund, Petter Eiken, Hischam El-Agamy, Mads Ingholt, Rafiq Kalam Id-din, Mona Kamal, Roland Kleve, Reinhard Krickl, Miz Kusairi, Sebastien Lize, Poul Madsen, Jemilah Mahmoud, David Meek, Dermot O'Gorman, Omar Safey El-Din, Jill Szekely, Lijong Tjang a Tjoi, Christine Wall-Pilgrenroeder, and Sean Westcott.

We all warmly thank our friends and colleagues at ION, the International Organizations Network. This group has greatly facilitated and inspired our work, helped us make new friends and create new knowledge, and is always fun.

Last, but hardly least, we thank our families who have supported our learning and the publishing of what we have learned. This has meant time away from home, time spent alone writing, and time and energy devoted to the many visitors and friends from around the world who have shared our homes. All have been critical to our development. Our spouses, Anne, Brian, Lynne, and Maura have been more than patient; they have contributed significantly to our understanding and commitment, as have all our children. We thank them all for their love and assistance. Notwithstanding this lengthy list of personal acknowledgments, we close with the usual caveat that we alone remain responsible for the contents of this book.

H. W. Lane
Boston, MA

M. L. Maznevski
Lausanne, Switzerland

J. J. DiStefano
Lausanne, Switzerland

Joerg Dietz
Lausanne, Switzerland

January 2009

INTRODUCTION

The real voyage of discovery consists not in seeking new landscapes, but in having new eyes.

—*Marcel Proust*

This book is different. It is not just another book about global business. It is about people who conduct business globally. It discusses and explores typical situations that managers encounter: the problems and opportunities; the frustrations and rewards; the successes and failures; and the decisions they must make.

Global business is not an impersonal activity, so international business should not be studied solely in an impersonal way. It is important, for example, to understand trade theories; to be able to weigh the pros and cons of exporting versus licensing; or to understand the advantages of a joint venture versus a wholly-owned subsidiary. But eventually, theory must give way to practice and strategizing and debating alternatives must give way to action. Working globally means interacting with colleagues, customers, and suppliers from other countries to achieve a specific business outcome. We focus on these interactions, on getting things done with and through other people in a global context.

This book is intended to help develop the knowledge, perspective, and skills that global managers need to function effectively in different cultural environments and to work effectively with people from other cultures. Our desire is to develop, to the extent possible using this medium, an appreciation of what it is like to work with people from other cultures and to work in other countries. In short, we want to help the reader develop a global mindset and global leadership competencies so that he or she can create value in international settings.

This sixth edition is also different from the previous five. As a result of our research, teaching and consulting activities, and discussing the concepts and frameworks in the context of global business with practicing managers, we have expanded each section to provide a more comprehensive view of what it is like to work globally. What has not changed, however, is our orientation to the topic.

ORIENTATIONS TO TEACHING INTERNATIONAL MANAGEMENT BEHAVIOR

These orientations describe perspectives that have been developed, refined, and tested for over 40 years with undergraduates, graduate students, and practicing executives around the world. The combination of conceptual knowledge and contextually based skill building opportunities offered in this book provide an effective learning package. In addition to drawing on the research of others, we have conducted our own research on the issues and skills relevant to international management, and also on how best to train global managers.

Management orientation   This book presents a problem-solving approach to international business. International business activities are complex situations in which both business and cultural factors are often simultaneously embedded. The skills needed to cross boundaries cannot be isolated from business realities and an appreciation of various and multiple influences on behavior can make a difference in outcome and performance.

Behavioral orientation   The human element in managing effectively across cultures is just as important as, and sometimes more important than, the technical or functional elements. However, interpersonal and cultural skills are likely to be less developed in managers than technical or business skills. People chosen to work in the international side of business generally have already developed a basic set of business or technical skills as a prerequisite for the assignment. They need to complement these capabilities with people and cultural skills; if they don't, they may never get the opportunity to use the business or technical skills.

Process orientation   Related to the behavioral orientation is a process orientation – behaving, interacting, learning, and moving forward to meet objectives. We think this perspective is an important contributor to success in a global market.

Richard Pascale contrasted the Japanese "proceeding" with the American "deciding" mentality. "The process of 'proceeding' in turn generates further information; you move toward your goal through a sequence of tentative steps rather than bold-stroke actions. The distinction is between having enough data to decide and having enough data to proceed."[1] Conducting business in other countries and cultures is an activity that is filled with ambiguity and uncertainty. In this type of situation, "proceeding" is often the appropriate mode of operation. Too often the focus is on quick decisions and end results rather than on the activities necessary to achieve the end results. An orientation that moves someone closer to his or her objectives is needed, accomplished through "process," or a series of interactions with other people.

The term "process" conjures up words that are active and interactive: words like exporting, managing, trading, negotiating, licensing, and joint-venturing or partnering; selecting, training, entering, leaving, and relating. The interactions and relationships with other people in other organizations in other countries are necessary in order to be a successful exporter, manager, trader, or negotiator. The cases in this book have a process orientation. Often, the reader will not be able to "find a solution" or "come to a decision," but will have to suggest and outline a process. This reflects the reality of international management.

Intercultural orientation   The material in this text focuses primarily on the interaction between people of different cultures in work settings. This intercultural orientation is distinct from a comparative approach, in which management practices of individual countries or cultures are examined and compared. The intercultural perspective has been chosen because it is in the interaction of cultures that managers experience difficulties.

Culture-general orientation   This book is intended for general managers (meaning management generalists rather than the specific position) and international staff who must function effectively in a realm of cultural diversity. This book is also useful to people who aspire to such positions in global management and staff of multinational or transnational corporations. A culture-general perspective provides a framework within which country-specific learning can take place more rapidly as necessary. It helps the reader know what questions to ask and how to interpret the answers received when conducting business globally or helping others to do the same. It helps the learner become more effective at learning and adapting to other cultures. As such, the book does not deal extensively with a particular culture, country, or region: the reader will not become an expert in any one culture or be able to operate in a given culture flawlessly. This is not to say that culture-specific learning will not take place. The cases and text will convey information and knowledge specific to certain cultures. In-depth culture-specific training is more appropriate when someone is assigned to a specific country, and may also be appropriate for staff specialists concentrating on a particular country or a limited regional area. But any kind of culture-specific training is strongly enhanced by this culture-general orientation.

OUTLINE OF THE BOOK

The book has four parts.

Part 1 is a single chapter, The Global Manager. This chapter introduces the global mindset, a way of organizing knowledge, and describes the capabilities needed to be an effective global leader.

Part 2 consists of three chapters that look at the individual and interpersonal sides of global management. Chapter 2 discusses culture and its effect on people and their behavior, Chapter 3 describes a model for interacting effectively across cultures, and Chapter 4, a new addition to this book, focuses on global teams and networks.

Part 3 moves the discussion from the individual to the organizational level. Chapter 5 focuses on strategy execution in a global context. Chapter 6 examines the challenge of complexity facing global managers and issues in recruiting and developing the people in this talent pool. Chapter 7 also is a new addition to the book and provides a perspective on managing change in global organizations.

Part 4 has two chapters on competing with integrity in global business. Chapter 8 focuses on ethics at an individual level and Chapter 9 looks at organizational and corporate social responsibility issues.

Each section contains text and cases. The text is a capsule view of the main cultural knowledge required by global managers. It is drawn from our own research and experience and that of many others. The cases put the reader in the position of a manager interacting with people from other cultures. Of course, studying a few cases in a book is not a substitute for experience. However, cases provide initial practice, and a mechanism for comparing previous experiences to others' experiences. In taking a manager's role, a reader psychologically puts himself or herself into another person's place and situation, sorts out the issues involved in that situation, and plans action. In this way, a reader can simulate experience. A combination of the knowledge and the experience gained from immersion in the case situations improves the judgment and skills of managers.

We have been involved in writing many of the cases for this book. We have lived in, or traveled to, the locations in the cases while working as teachers, consultants, or managers, or have traveled to the sites specifically for case writing. We have worked with the managers described in the cases and have tried to bring the flavor, feeling, and tempo of these people and the countries in which they live into the classroom and to the readers of this book.

Some cases may seem like unusual and, possibly, improbable dilemmas to a reader with no international business experience. However, before jumping too quickly to say "I'll never go to those countries" or "I will never find myself in these situations," consider these experiences of managers who said something similar. One person was completing a management training program and, as part of that program, a speaker came from the operation in Germany to address the class. As the speaker discussed the challenges associated with the operation, the listener was thinking, "I'm glad I'll never be sent there." He was quite surprised when, soon afterwards, he actually was sent to Germany as a manager. He wished he had listened more carefully to the speaker.

Another manager dismissed as irrelevant a cross-cultural case taught at an executive development session. But on his first day back at the office he faced a very similar situation. He called one of the authors that same afternoon saying, "I should have paid more attention to that class discussion that I complained about!" He then offered to work with us to write a case about his experience.[2]

Globalization means that one does not have to travel to another country to be exposed to situations of cultural diversity. For example, consider a manager in Boston who works for Reebok. This well-known athletic shoe company that was founded outside of Boston was acquired by Adidas AG from Germany in 2006. Now the American manager may be travelling to Germany frequently or interacting with German managers when they come to Boston. This same manager possibly interacts with a number of other local Boston companies that are also now foreign-owned. He or she may have an account with Citizen's Bank (owned by the Royal Bank of Scotland Group); purchase insurance from John Hancock (owned by Manulife Financial of Canada); and buy groceries from Stop & Shop (owned by Royal Ahold of the Netherlands). And managers from these companies also are likely to be experiencing working with their Scottish, Canadian, and Dutch counterparts.

In countries with long histories of open immigration, such as Canada and the United States, there is considerable diversity within the domestic workforce and many managers experience working with cultural diversity as part of their daily routine. Many managers in both of these countries have told us that the material in this book is also applicable in these situations and has been useful – without their ever having to leave their home base. More recently, countries in Europe also have experienced increasing diversity as a result of guest worker programs, immigration from former colonies, and European Union agreements lowering immigration barriers.

A FINAL NOTE

This book is based on the philosophy that learning is a lifelong, continuous process. Rather than provide an illusion of mastery, we hope it stimulates and facilitates even more learning about other cultures and how to work effectively with others. For some readers, the material in this book may represent a first encounter with different cultures. Other readers may have been exposed to different cultures through previous courses or personal experience. For those with prior exposure to other people and places, the journey continues with a new level of insight. For those without prior experiences, welcome to an interesting journey!

Notes

1   Pascale, R. T., "Zen and the art of management," *Harvard Business Review* 56(2) (1978).
2   The result was two cases about the same experience, but from two different points of view – his and his subordinate's. These cases are David Shorter and Bob Chen Ivey, cases 9-91-C004 and 9-91-C005, respectively.

PART 1

CHAPTER **1**

The Global Manager

It has become cliché to say that today's managers, wherever they are, must be internationally minded. We have been saying it since the first edition of this book in 1988, and it seems to be more imperative with each year. In the twenty-first century, being a global leader is no longer a nice-to-have capability, it is a must-have for those who want to create value for their organizations. Recently we asked a group of executives from several countries, "How important is it for you to be a global leader – a leader who has expertise working effectively across countries?" Here are some typical responses.

David, CFO in an American paper manufacturing firm: "We're a small firm in our industry, and we're trying to fuel our growth through some acquisitions. The best acquisitions aren't in the US, though. Right now we'll operate them as a holding company so we don't really need to manage them, but I still need to know a lot about working in these other countries to get the best deal. I need to assess the potential acquisition and its ability to do business in its own market. I need to develop the kind of relationship with the current owners that will help us get a fair price for the acquisition. I need to set up the kind of relationship that ensures they manage it for us well, and talk with us openly when things aren't going well before it's a crisis. And I need to establish the connections that help us learn together in the future. We may not manage our company as an integrated multinational, but we all have to be good at leading across these cultures."

Christine, head of a key product division in an industrial product firm's largest country market, Germany: "My customers are all in Germany and so is my team, so you would think my job is all in Germany. But our company is headquartered in Scandinavia and our plants are in several different locations around Europe. When we have challenges serving our customers, the people I need to work with are mostly outside of Germany. And those are the interactions that make the biggest difference in my business. Maybe even more important, my new ideas come from outside of Germany. The German market is mature, saturated, we and the customers all know what to expect. It's when I work with people in the international arena that I learn how to build my business better within Germany."

Ho Yin, corporate director of human resources of a Singapore-based conglomerate's utility businesses: "You might think that a business involved in generating, distributing and retailing electrical power is fundamentally local. But as we extend our reach to Australia, India, Southeast Asia and China, it is clear that we need to identify and adopt the best practices in the industry worldwide. Regulators across the region are clear about their expectations that we provide reliable service at competitive prices. To do this we need managers and executives beyond our solid base of technical experts; we require people who are experienced at dealing with ideas and people from many countries and cultures, and who can lead in demanding circumstances in many different countries. Finding and developing such people is a major challenge, perhaps our biggest one."

Leading internationally is more complex today than it was a generation ago. At that time, "international managers" were a relatively small subset of managers, those who journeyed away from home as expatriates to do exciting important things. They experienced hardship from (sometimes unexpected) foreign conditions, and rewards from generous expatriate compensation packages as well as fulfilling their need for growth and adventure. With changes in areas such as technology, finance, political systems, business models, air travel, and the media, most managers today work across national borders. There are more managers who have to work across countries, and they must do so in a wider variety of situations. Having a successful management career in any kind of business today requires some level of international management. Second, international management today is rarely about just going from one culture to another. Typical international managers, like the executives quoted above, may travel to many different countries in any year, and frequently work with people from many different cultures at the same time. To be successful, they cannot simply learn about another culture and adapt. The dynamics are much more complex.

In this chapter we discuss how the forces in the international political economy are shaping the characteristics needed by global leaders and explore what it means to have a global mindset – the capacity to work effectively across cultures and other types of boundaries. We describe how to develop as a global leader, and conclude by showing how the different sections of this book can help you on your personal development journey.

> *As we stand at the dawn of the twenty-first century, we must ask ourselves if we can truly manage ourselves cross-culturally. This is the principal question. A decade ago, culture was not a particular issue, but the more we advance, the more managing people of different cultures and beliefs becomes the benchmark of an efficient company.*
>
> **Carlos Ghosn, President and CEO of Nissan Motor Company**
> **and President and CEO of Renault[1]**

MANAGING GLOBALIZATION = MANAGING COMPLEXITY[2]

As we write this edition of the book, the markets are highly volatile in the worst global financial crisis in a century, and the effect on industry is uncertain. The only thing that is clear is that there will be an effect, and a large one. Some observers claim, "This is a completely unpredictable outcome of the financial boom of recent years." Others call out, "This was inevitable, the only question was when." Who's right? It is not a simple question.

A few years ago we were trying to learn from managers what globalization meant to them. Economists tend to define globalization in terms of flows of goods or money or people across borders, compared to the flow within borders. We spoke with managers who were working outside their home country or inside their home country, traveling a lot, or traveling little. When we asked them, "What is the effect of globalization on your management role?" the answer they shared was one that surprised us. They all responded: "It's exhausting." When we probed further, we found that whatever level of cross-border transactions a single manager actually dealt with, the effect of a more globalized economy and society meant increased complexity in the management role. This increased complexity meant that the traditional way of managing – often one learned in business school – was not adequate. Managers were working harder and harder to try and understand the complex forces, in order to plan and execute with any kind of predictability. The result was a feeling of being overwhelmed and, yes, exhausted. Our experience with managers today suggests that this trend has continued unabated.

Globalization has increased the **interdependency** between countries and people in those countries. We are all now more connected to each other and therefore influencing each other in a reciprocal way. With the fall (or at least permeability) of barriers to cross-border flow of goods and money, events and decisions in one company or in one part of the world affect others who may be distant and seemingly unconnected with the initial event or decision. The recent financial crisis, for example, which was triggered by the subprime mortgage crash in the United States and the derivatives based on it, affected the ability of businesses as far away as South Africa to invest in improvements in manufacturing productivity. China's hunger for basic resources such as steel and wood affects the price of those commodities for all manufacturers, and affects environmental issues in countries relying on mining in South America. With such high levels of interdependence, it is impossible for a manager to predict the impact of a specific action. This makes effective managerial decision-making extremely difficult.

Executives face more **variety** than ever before. In many countries, the domestic workforce is more diverse. For example, in Toronto, Canada, only eleven per cent of the population identifies its ethnic origin as "Canadian," and only 28 % as "European." Almost half the population was born outside of Canada, and the most recent census reports more than 200 ethnic origins among the citizens of the metropolitan area.[3] But workforce diversity is just one aspect of the increased variety that managers face today. With modern media and technology, both businesses and consumers have become more discerning customers, and companies must define customer segments much more carefully. Competitors, too, come with more variety in products and services. In the voice communications industry, the competitors today include mobile phone companies like Nokia and Motorola, computer and consumer electronics firms like Apple, and internet providers and services such as Skype. Companies that operate in many countries face many different legal and economic environments. Developing consistent compensation policies worldwide for a company like Royal-Dutch Shell, for example, is almost impossible. Making decisions and taking action as a manager are much more complicated when there are so many variables to consider.

Managers also face more **ambiguity**, or lack of clarity. First, interconnectedness and variety make it much more difficult to see cause–effect relations. What is cause and what is effect is not always clear. Did the 2008 financial crisis result simply from a decline in the housing market or were there other reasons such as United States government sponsored enterprises like Fannie Mae and Freddie Mac securitizing questionable mortgages and aggressively selling them; over-leveraged banks and greedy financiers; people buying houses they could not afford and defaulting; unscrupulous mortgage brokers recommending loans for unqualified buyers; or was it a result of a Congress that did not oversee the mortgage giants Fannie Mae and Freddie Mac; or that encouraged extreme deregulation; or that was interested in increasing affordable housing? Was it a result of the Bush administration's interest in promoting the "ownership society," or did it go back to the Clinton administration and Henry Cisneros, Secretary of Housing and Urban Development, who was interested in making home ownership a reality for low-income families? Maybe the culprit was Alan Greenspan, who did not see the housing bubble as dangerous and who was strongly against regulation of the financial industry. It could also have been the European and Asian banks who enjoyed the riches of the derivatives based on these mortgages without, they thought, the potential for downside risk. Undoubtedly they all played a role and as some observer said there is plenty of blame to go around. However, simple cause and effect is difficult to establish.

Second, although we have more information available to us today than at any time in the past, the reliability of this information is not always clear, and we cannot always turn it into meaningful knowledge. Financial analysts give us ratings of particular companies – how do we know what information they've based those ratings on, and what should we do with the information? Customers complain to us through a web site – how representative are they of all our customers? How much impact will their public complaints have on potential new customers? Again, decision-making and action are much more challenging when we are not sure about the cause–effect relations or the clarity of our information.

As if that weren't enough, the configuration of our complex environment is always shifting and changing. Even if you could take a snapshot today of the interdependence, variety, and information available and study it enough to understand and make clear decisions, tomorrow would be different. Decisions you made yesterday may not be ideal today or tomorrow. We call this "**fast flux**" because it represents rapid unpredictable change in many directions, not predictable change in a few dimensions.

It is no wonder that managers feel overwhelmed by globalization, whether or not they are directly involved in cross-border transactions!

How do you manage this level of complexity in the environment? The way to manage the complexity of globalization is by using the capacity that is in people to manage it themselves. The most complex thing in any organization is people: human brains and the relationships among people. When managers simplify a few key control processes, such as the organizational structure, the company values, goals and strategy, and some key performance indicators, they can "let go" and empower people to manage complexity. We call the technique "Hercules meets Buddha."[4]

Hercules used his strength and power to overcome obstacles. This model, which pits Hercules against external forces, originates in Greece, the cradle of Western rational thought. It is a control model that encourages the use of comparison, measurement, categorization, and analysis in understanding the world around us.[5] Such an analytic, strength-based, control mode of thinking and acting may not be sufficient to respond to globalization pressures since not everything is under our control. The Eastern way of "seeing and understanding" as presented in Buddhism and Taoism seeks to achieve understanding of a world in which all things and events are interrelated and in which change is constant and natural. Understanding and using the natural processes that exist, a flow mode of operating, will make dealing with complexity more manageable. Global managers could benefit from understanding both Hercules and Buddha.

The combination of airlines Air France and KLM provides an interesting example. The combination remains short of a merger for legal and cultural reasons – also, executives felt a full merger was not necessary and would be too complex to implement. The companies have a single short document outlining their structure and the areas in which they will act as one company (such as cargo and networks), the areas in which they will coordinate but not necessarily act as one company (such as maintenance, purchasing, and branding), and the areas in which they encourage best-practice sharing but will have no formal coordination (such as human resources). AF-KLM has made strong efforts to coordinate formally only where it makes most business sense. This represents the "control" part of managing complexity. But they have also strongly encouraged building networks and informal coordination across the two companies, for example, through joint executive learning programs and professional meetings, encouraging the "flow" part of managing complexity by connecting and empowering people. Actual coordination across the companies is at a much higher level than the formalized, regulated coordination, as managers get together with their counterparts to learn and share, thus both streamlining the business and taking advantage of various opportunities.

Managers, especially those from the West, tend to have well-developed knowledge and skills about organization and control. The management of people in a complex setting like globalization presents much more of a challenge; however, as we have seen in our research on complexity, it is absolutely critical to the success of organizations today. By focusing on working with people for effective results, we hope to help you combine this knowledge and skill set with your other business skills to become more effective.

We equate the terms "global" and "international" in this book. Traditionally, an "international" perspective focuses on two or a few countries at a time and relatively straightforward interactions between them. A "global" perspective looks at the whole world at once and does not see national borders as being contiguous with business borders. For example, a global company such as Renault-Nissan produces components for its European cars in a wide range of countries, conducts subassembly processes in a few countries, and does final assembly in various parts of Europe, depending on the model, for final delivery to customers in specific markets. The fact is, as we found in our research on complexity, the strictly "international" perspective is disappearing from managers' minds and actions (even if not from economists' definitions), and the difference between global and international is not normally meaningful to managers.

We also use "leadership" with "management" interchangeably. This is a bit more controversial. Management usually refers to coordinating, decision-making, organizing, and controlling aspects of a manager's job, while leadership more often refers to visioning and direction-setting, motivating, aligning, and empowering people. Although these roles are two distinct aspects of the job, the reality is that, in order to achieve results in complex settings, an executive must both manage and lead. The chapters and cases in this book combine managing and leading into the role of the Manager or Executive, and when we need to refer to specific aspects of the job, we will do so.

GLOBAL MANAGING STARTS WITH A GLOBAL MINDSET[6]

Executives today do not have to be just more capable than in the past, they also have to be differently capable.[7] The global mindset is not just an additional capability; it is a different capability.

As the global economy continues to develop, managers must learn how to function as effectively in other contexts as they do in their own country, and to build bridges across the world by leveraging both similarities and differences. In the broadest terms, this means reorganizing the way one thinks as a manager. As one executive put it, "to think globally really requires an alteration of our mind-set."[8] Thinking globally means extending concepts and models from one-to-one relationships (we to them) to holding multiple realities and relationships in mind simultaneously, and then acting skillfully on this more complex reality.

At the heart of the global mindset is the ability to see and understand the world differently than one has been conditioned to see and understand it. It is a meta-capability that permits an individual to function successfully in new and unknown situations and to integrate this new understanding with other existing skills and knowledge bases.

A global mindset enables a person to adapt to the changing needs of global business. It is not simply a set of facts, which is useful in the present but perhaps not in the long-term future. It is a way of organizing a set of attitudes and skills for developing and acting on knowledge in a dynamic world. A global mindset incorporates knowledge and openness about working across cultures, and about implementing business across strategic complexity.[9] With a global mindset, a manager can function successfully in new and unknown situations and integrate this new understanding with other existing skills and knowledge bases. We define a global mindset like this:

> A global mindset is the capacity to develop and interpret criteria for personal and business performance that are independent from the assumptions of a single context; and to implement those criteria appropriately in different contexts.

For example, we know a company that was implementing self-managed teams throughout the organization for its new modular-based production facilities. In its dynamic and interdependent environment, the company believed it was important to have decision-making authority with the people who had the most immediate information to make the decisions, and who had to implement the decisions. The company developed a model of how self-managed teams should work; pilot-tested it in their home country; then rolled out the new structure around the world. However, it met with resistance. In many parts of the world, the idea of teams managing themselves, without a specific boss to lead them, is completely unheard of. Some plant managers pushed through the self-managed teams program to greater and greater dissatisfaction; others gave up and just kept the more rigid and hierarchical teams.

Some managers, however, did something a bit different. They looked at the two most important criteria for identifying who should make a decision in this new manufacturing context: the people who have the information, and the people who have to implement it. They also realized that manufacturing would not achieve its potential unless there was more interdependence among the various parts of the process. Then they questioned whether the only way to accomplish this was the self-managed team model that head-quarters dictated. They met with their managers and teams, and developed a way to achieve the required working relationships and decision processes that fit with the local teams' preferences and context. In some cases this had more hierarchy, in others it had fewer specific roles and more fluidity, and still others had more individual responsibility. In all cases, it achieved the performance goals.

These last managers were working with a global mindset. They were able to separate performance criteria, like "people with the information make the decisions," from culturally influenced contextual preferences, like "self-managed teams." Then they found a way to achieve the performance criteria in different contexts.

COMPONENTS AND DOMAINS OF A GLOBAL MINDSET

In a detailed literature review, researchers have identified two constructs that comprise a global mindset: cognitive complexity and cosmopolitanism.[10]

- Cognitive complexity. This is an ability to perceive multiple aspects of complex issues from multiple perspectives and to be able to see competing interpretations (differentiation); and to see interactions and interactive effects and to synthesize new and more complex understandings (integration).
- Cosmopolitanism. This is not just passive "tolerance" but actively valuing and seeking out diversity which is seen as an asset. It is openness to different cultural experiences and a willingness to explore, learn, and change.

In addition to the competencies of cognitive complexity and cosmopolitanism there are four types of knowledge in the domains in which a global mindset operates. The crux of developing a global mindset is achieving self-awareness and other-awareness, and more specifically the relationship between context – institutions, cultures, professions – and characteristics of the self and others. It is important for managers to see themselves and others both as individuals and as members of collective units, and to develop insights about individual and social behavior in these contexts.

The two dimensions or contexts in which the global mindset finds expression are the context of individuals within groups and organizations and the context of self compared with others. These two dimensions result in four domains of knowledge, as shown in Figure 1.1. To be effective globally, a manager must develop the type of knowledge appropriate to each of the quadrants, and the ability to act on that knowledge.

FIGURE 1.1   Domains of a global mindset

	Individual	Organizational
Self	**Type 1: Myself** Understand myself and how who I am is associated with the context I am in.	**Type 3: Own organizations** Understand my own organizations and how their characteristics and effectiveness are associated with the context we are in.
Other	**Type 2: Others** Understand how characteristics of people from other countries, cultures, and contexts are associated with the context they are in.	**Type 4: Other organizations** Understand how characteristics and effectiveness of organizations from other countries, cultures, and contexts are associated with the context they are in.

Type 1: Knowledge about Self

A global mindset incorporates a concept of self, both as an individual and as part of an organization. Understanding how context shapes individuals requires acknowledging and understanding what it is about our mindset that has been shaped by our own context.

A critical part of context that influences self is culture, and a global mindset should include sophisticated knowledge about culture. Culture is an implicit agreement among a group of people concerning what people's actions mean. It is their list of "shoulds" and "oughts" for life or, as Hofstede described it, the collective programming of the mind that distinguishes one group from another. This conceptualization allows numerous cultures to be identified other than national culture. As Brannen has pointed out, we should not use "nation as a cognate for culture."[11] Gender, age, religion, or region of a country, for example, can be considered cultures, and a person can be a member of many cultures simultaneously. Culture is often hidden from members of the culture: we rarely examine our own values or context in the normal course of doing things – it is there, taken for granted as the foundation. To paraphrase Edward T. Hall, culture is like air to us, all around and necessary for survival but usually not noticed. Hall observed:

> [Culture] is a mold in which we are all cast, and it controls our daily lives in many unsuspected ways . . . Culture hides much more than it reveals, and strangely enough what it hides, it hides most effectively from its own participants. Years of study have convinced me that the real job is not to understand foreign culture but to understand our own.[12]

Becoming aware of the influence of culture on oneself can be both uncomfortable and difficult. But the ability to "see" it and to examine it is critical to developing an effective global mindset.

Type 2: Knowledge about Others

Since culture is a set of shared, deep-level assumptions and values that influence thoughts and behavior and come from the social environment or contexts in which people are raised, different contexts create different assumption and value systems that influence people to perceive the same situation differently; interpret what they notice differently; evaluate the situation differently; and take different actions. A global mindset facilitates understanding these differences.

Type 3: Knowledge about Own Organization

Similarly, understanding how context influences organizations requires understanding how the organizations of which we are a part (families, peer groups, institutions, companies) are influenced by their context. Most companies have a particular administrative heritage that has evolved within the culture of their home countries. This means that a potential cultural bias may exist in their strategy, systems, and practices – "the way things are done in the headquarters' home country."

Geert Hofstede has reminded us that "theories reflect the cultural environment in which they were written."[13] Management concepts and practices are explained by theories regarding organization, motivation, and leadership. Therefore, theories of management systems and management practices may work well in the culture that developed them because they are based on local cultural assumptions and paradigms about the right way to manage.

Type 4: Knowledge about Other Organizations

A mindset that is structured around continually adapting to business and contextual contingencies will always serve an executive well. To illustrate, it is possible to identify criteria for performance that can be universally applied, rather than focused on today's cultural differences. For example, a human resource system that provides collective performance bonuses in Mexico and individual performance bonuses in the United States might fit with cultural preferences in those countries and encourage high performance today. However, a human resource system dedicated to "motivating all employees to perform well, whatever their background or preferences" will always be subject to adaptation and will encourage high performance into the future.[14]

DEVELOPING GLOBAL MINDSETS IN THEORY AND PRACTICE

Is a global mindset something that one was born with, or can it be learned? We do not believe it is innate. If it were, there would be no point to trying to develop one! However, we also don't believe it can be developed by simply reading a book on an airplane or by being lectured about it in a classroom. It has to be shaped or developed, which implies that changes have to take place.

A global mindset is a specific type of mental framework, or cognitive schema, for organizing information, in other words, a worldview. Schemas influence what we notice and what meaning we attribute to perceptions and guide the actions in the world around us.[15]

Schemas are simple at first and become more complex with greater experience.[16] This development of more complex schemas allows a person to process enormous amounts of information and to see patterns without getting lost in the detail. According to Bird and Osland, there is a difference in the way that expert and novice global managers think.

> When entering into a new situation [experts] notice more and different types of cues, they interpret those cues differently, they choose from a different, wider range of appropriate actions than do novices, and then they execute/implement their chosen course of action at higher levels than do novices. In the case of global managers, these differences between novices and experts are magnified . . .
>
> [As] they become more competent, they recognize complexity and a larger set of cues. They are able to discern which cues are the most important and are able to move beyond strict adherence to rules and to think in terms of trade-offs. On attaining the expert stage, they can read situations without rational thought – they diagnose the situation unconsciously and respond intuitively because over the years they have developed the holistic recognition or mental maps that allow for effortless framing and reframing of strategies and quick adaptation.[17]

Once a schema, or mindset, exists, it changes through one of two processes – *assimilation* or *accommodation*.[18] In assimilation, new information is seen to be consistent with the schema and is incorporated readily, perhaps refining the details of the schema. In accommodation, new information contradicts the schema to the extent that the schema itself is changed. In organizational learning, these processes have been referred to as single-loop and double-loop learning[19] and evolutionary and revolutionary change.[20]

When perceptions are consistent with assumptions, people don't question assumptions. When they encounter something that contradicts existing assumptions, theories of good management or a preferred course of action, for example, these encounters set up "cognitive dissonance," an uncomfortable feeling of imbalance. People are motivated to reduce the imbalance to achieve consistency again by either changing perceptions of the evidence to match the assumptions (call into question the other), or by changing assumptions to match the evidence (call into question ourselves). People are more inclined to invoke the first method than the second; it requires a great deal less energy, is reinforced by others who hold the same assumptions, and is less confusing. The other option, altering one's own assumptions, unfortunately is usually a less chosen alternative.

A key characteristic of accommodation is the ability to articulate the current schema accurately. Without a realization that a current schema exists to shape information processing, its limits cannot be identified and its inadequacy cannot be addressed with a new structure.

Another characteristic of accommodation is the importance of feedback. A learner can only judge the appropriateness of a schema if the effects of the schema are made clear.[21] This is why experiential learning is generally so much more effective than passive knowledge acquisition: the experience usually provides immediate feedback.[22]

For example, if a schema leads an American shopper to believe that US dollars are welcomed anywhere, and that shopper pays for a purchase in Canada with American cash (which the shopper can do in virtually any Canadian store), then quickly exits the store, he or she will never learn that most Canadians perceive the behavior as demonstrating an attitude of arrogance and inflexibility. Even telling the American that Canadians resent the behavior might not change the schema. The effects of the shopper's behavior, which were consistent with the currently-held schema, did not confirm this new information. In order to change a schema, the learner must see from concrete feedback that the effects of his or her current schema are not appropriate. A process of active learning must be followed with experience combined with feedback and reflection in a continuous development of new knowledge that is actionable.

How do you, the reader of this book, develop a global mindset? First, it requires active learning. You have to engage problems where you have to assess the situation, see options, make decisions, and receive feedback. Our experience suggests that managers and students have "theories" or frameworks about what are successful and unsuccessful management techniques or courses of action. When presented with a problem, they make their analysis and suggest a corrective course of action. It is necessary to engage in a process of questioning existing narrow frameworks or worldviews and replacing them with new, more inclusive ones.

You will become aware of how your assumptions and frameworks shape perceptions, values, and behavior only as you confront different sets of assumptions guiding the views and practices of others. If you are exposed to new experiences under the right circumstances, part of your response may include an examination of your own guiding values and theories of management – the beginning of developing a global mindset. You may find that your existing frameworks are incomplete or are disconfirmed because you did not see the whole picture or could only see it from a narrow point of view. The use of case studies, experiential exercises, and the facilitation of personal experiences in group settings are useful tools and techniques. The educational experience is also richer and can have a greater impact if it also includes a diverse set of participants.

The text and cases in this book have been written and selected to help readers develop knowledge in each of the quadrants and to practice applying it to specific business situations. As you go through the material, focus both on building awareness of yourself in your own context, as well as learning about others in their contexts. Question your assumptions and those of others, and test the application of your knowledge in different contexts. These actions will help you build a global mindset. They will extend your repertoire of behaviors and enrich your personal experience of the world.

GLOBAL LEADERSHIP COMPETENCIES: FROM FOUNDATION KNOWLEDGE TO SYSTEM SKILLS

Research on global leadership has skyrocketed in the last decade, and many studies have been published identifying the skills that global leaders need. In fact, the lists are so long, it seems that only a superhuman can be a global leader. However, there are ways of sorting out the most important criteria, and we will share a framework here that we think best captures the most important capabilities. The Global Leadership Competencies model developed by Bird and Osland[23] summarizes the most important skills and knowledge, and illustrates how they build on each other.

Global managers also need certain personal traits, attitudes, and skills in addition to a global mindset. In reviewing studies about what makes a successful expatriate or global leader, Bird and Osland found that the various approaches to answering this question identified anywhere from 11 to 250 different competencies. They decided to take a different approach to the topic.

One striking characteristic of both the expatriate and global leadership competency research is that it has, for the most part, taken a *content* approach. There is an unspoken assumption that effective managerial action will flow from an appropriate *content* of competencies. We adopted a different perspective, choosing to focus on the *process* of global managing.[24]

In their view, global managerial expertise is a constellation of traits, attitudes, and skills or what they call "global competencies." Their model of global competencies is shown in Figure 1.2 and Table 1.1 contains a brief summary of the elements in the model.

The foundational level is **Global Business Knowledge**. This is knowledge about the business a manager is in, and how that business creates value. It also includes knowledge about the political, economic, social, and technical environment. This foundational knowledge does not necessarily presume that the manager can apply it to the components of a global mindset, but the knowledge is necessary before any of the next steps.

The next level identifies **Threshold Personality Traits**. Among the myriad of personality traits associated with effectiveness, four stand out as differentiating people who are effective in global settings from those who are less effective: integrity, humility, curiosity, and hardiness or resilience. Integrity is having a firm set of values associated with honesty and transparency, and being true to those values. Humility is recognizing that knowledge and skills are widely distributed, and that others know and can do things that you, yourself, may not. Humility opens one to accept differences and different ways of doing things. Curiosity is active motivation to know things one does not already know. While humility creates openness, curiosity drives action to learn more, and to experiment with different ways of creating value. Finally, hardiness or resilience is the ability to persevere in the face of challenges and difficulties. This resides partly in the manager's own personality, and partly in the extent to which the manager has a support network of family, friends, and/or colleagues.

FIGURE 1.2 Global Competencies

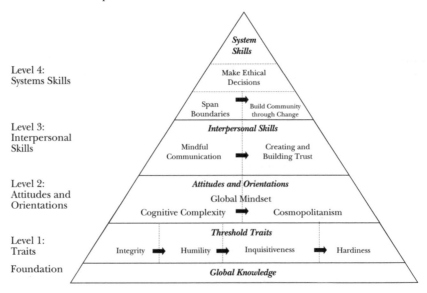

TABLE 1.1   Global Competencies – Brief Definitions and Descriptions[a]

Competency	Description
Integrity	Adherence to moral and ethical principles; soundness of moral character; honesty
Humility	A willingness to learn from others and not assume that one has all the answers
Inquisitiveness	An interest in learning; questioning; curious about other people and cultures
Hardiness	Capable of surviving under unfavorable conditions; resistance to stress; emotionally resilient
Cognitive complexity	Ability to balance contradictions and ambiguities; a differentiated (number of dimensions to view a situation) and integrated (number of links between constructs) cognitive capacity
Cosmopolitanism	External orientation; free from local, provincial, or national ideas or prejudices; at home everywhere
Mindful communication	Culturally appropriate and skillful communication
Creating and building trust	Ability to inspire confidence in the certainty of future actions
Boundary spanning	Creation of linkages that integrate and coordinate across organizational boundaries
Building community through change	Ability to bring the members of heterogeneous groups together to act in concert
Making ethical decisions	Adherence to accepted standards of behavior; decisions with all stakeholders in mind

[a]The definitions come from http://dictionary.reference.com and from Henry W. Lane, Martha L. Maznevski, Mark Mendenhall and Jeanne McNett, *The Blackwell Handbook of Global Management: A Guide to Managing Complexity*, Blackwell Publishers, 2004. For a more in-depth discussion of global competencies please see the *Handbook* and in particular Chapter 3, "Global Competencies: An Introduction," Alan Bird and Joyce Osland; pp. 57–80.

Bird and Osland suggest that components of a **Global Mindset** build on these threshold personality traits. As we described above, the mindset is a way of organizing information to use it for global leadership effectiveness. The two leadership competencies associated with building a global mindset are cognitive complexity and cosmopolitanism. These are the ability to see a situation from multiple perspectives, to see connections among the perspectives, and to build new connections with existing and new information, as well as having a positive attitude towards people, things, and perspectives from other parts of the world. For example, people who are cosmopolitan are more likely to have close friends who are from countries other than their own. As we mentioned earlier, the text and cases in this book are designed to help readers develop the kind of knowledge required for a global mindset, inputs for cognitive complexity and cosmopolitanism.

The two most important **Interpersonal Skills** for global leaders are mindful communication and building trust. Mindful communication is paying attention to how you communicate with others, especially those who are different, and adapting your communication as necessary in order to ensure that meaning is transmitted the way people intend. This includes both sending messages (speaking, writing, and nonverbal acts) and receiving them (listening, reading, and observing the behavior of others).

Building trust is creating a relationship where both (or all) parties believe that the other(s) will act with good intentions for the relationship, and can make decisions on each others' behalf. Many other interpersonal skills are of course important to global leadership effectiveness, such as negotiation and conflict resolution. However, if a manager is adept at mindful communication and building trust, then generally these other skills will follow. The reverse is not necessarily true – one can negotiate solutions and resolve conflicts without increasing trust, for example. Managers who prioritize mindful communication and building trust are more likely to be effective in diverse situations. The next two chapters of this book focus on interpersonal skills, especially mindful communication and building trust.

Finally, a set of three **Systems Skills** are critical for global leaders: spanning boundaries, building communities through effective change management, and ethical decision-making. Boundary-spanning is working effectively across countries, organizations, divisions within organizations, and so on. It involves using all of the skills and attitudes identified in lower parts of the model to create insights and synergies across different perspectives. Building communities through effective change management is more than "just" managing organizations through change. It is about managing change such that the organization creates an internal culture of support and cohesiveness. Ethical decision-making is about making and implementing decisions that take into account the long-term benefit of society. Sometimes this means making difficult and counterintuitive decisions in the short run. This book prioritizes these three systems skills throughout. Moreover, Chapter 3 dives deeply into managing across cultural boundaries, Chapter 7 focuses on managing change in global organizations, and Chapters 8 and 9 examine ethical decision-making.

OPPORTUNITIES FOR GLOBAL MANAGERS

Poul, a Danish senior executive in charge of integrating a Chinese acquisition into his company, told us:

> Global leadership isn't just about overcoming the challenges. There are lots of those of course. More importantly it's about the opportunities. The global environment creates more opportunities than a domestic one – opportunities for growth, innovation, learning. My motivation for becoming a better global leader is to be able to find and take advantage of those opportunities.

For example, Poul's company is facing a shortage of engineers in its European operations. He believes that the acquisition in China might open the door to a new source of talent – engineers from China coming to Europe. But he is not sure his organization is ready for that yet, and he is working on developing ways to increase his company's global leadership even in its home country.

In this chapter, we have acknowledged that today's business environment is highly complex, and the trends creating the complexity are accelerating. Global leadership is about leading across countries, and it is also about leading for opportunities related to globalization within a single country. Success in such an environment means leading people to achieve results. Global leaders must have a global mindset – a way of organizing knowledge to create openness to new ways of thinking and acting about personal and business effectiveness. Global leaders must also have a set of competencies, including interpersonal and systems skills. The remaining chapters of this book help to develop these global mindset and leadership skills.

Notes

1 Ghosn, C. 2007. Khazanah Global Lecture Series, March 21, 2007. *Khazanah Merdeka Series: A Year in Pictures 2007–2008*, published by Khazanah Nasional (Malaysia), at 102.
2 Lane, H. W., Maznevski, M. L., and Mendenhall, M., "Globalization: Hercules meets Buddha". In Lane, H. W., Maznevski, M. L., Mendenhall, M. and McNett, J. M. (eds), *Blackwell Handbook of Global Management: A Guide to Managing Complexity* (Blackwell Publishers, 2004).
3 City of Toronto, 2006 Census Information, released April 2008. http://www.toronto.ca/demographics/pdf/2006_ethnic_origin_visible_minorities_backgrounder.pdf.
4 For a more in-depth discussion of this see "Globalization: Hercules Meets Buddha," in Lane, H. W., Maznevski, M. L., Mendenhall, M. and McNett, J. M. (eds), *Blackwell Handbook of Global Management: A Guide to Managing Global Complexity*, n. 2 above.
5 Capra, F., *The Tao of Physics* (Bantam Books, 1984).
6 This section is based on the book chapter: Maznevski, M. L. and Lane, H. W. "Shaping the global mindset: Designing Educational Experiences for Effective Global Thinking and Action," in Boyacigiller, N., Goodman, R., and Phillips, M. (eds), *Crossing Cultures: Insights from Master Teachers* (Routledge) 343–371.
7 Wilson, M., Personal communication with Meena Wilson at the Center for Creative Leadership (1998).
8 Bernard Daniel, Secretary-General, Nestlé, Vevey, Switzerland. Personal communication.
9 Levy, O., Beechler, S., Taylor, S., and Boyacigiller, N. What do we talk about when we talk about 'global mindset': Managerial cognition in multinational corporations. *Journal of International Business Studies*, 38 (2007) 231–258.
10 Ibid. See also Boyacigiller, N., Beechler, S., Taylor, S., and Levy, O., "The Crucial Yet Illusive Global Mindset," in Lane, H. W., Maznevski, M. L., Mendenhall, M. and McNett, J. M. (eds) *Blackwell Handbook of Global Management: A Guide to Managing Complexity* (Blackwell Publishers, 2004).
11 Brannen, M. Y., The Many Faces of Cultural Data. *AIB Newsletter*, First Quarter 1999.
12 Hall, E. T., *The Silent Language* (Garden City, NY: Doubleday & Company, 1959; Anchor Books paperback edition, 1973).
13 Hofstede, G. H., "Motivation, Leadership, and Organization: Do American Theories Apply Abroad?" Organizational Dynamics, vol. 8, no. 2, Summer (1980): 50.
14 Lane, H. W., DiStefano, J. J., and Maznevski, M. L., *International management behavior*, 5th edn (Oxford, UK: Blackwell, 2006).
15 Lord, R. G. and Foti, R. J., "Schema theories, information processing, and organizational behavior." In Sims Jr, H. P. and Gioia, D. A., *The thinking organization* (San Francisco: Jossey-Bass Publishers, 1986) 20–48. See also Rhinesmith, S. H., "Global mindsets for global managers," *Training & Development* 46(10) (1992) 63–69.
16 Lord and Foti, n. 15 above. See also Salancik, G. R. and Porac, J. F., "Distilled ideologies: Values derived from causal reasoning in complex environments." In Sims Jr, H. P. and Gioia, D. A. *The thinking organization* (San Francisco: Jossey-Bass Publishers, 1986) 75–101.

17   *The Blackwell Handbook of Global Management: A Guide to Managing Complexity*, n. 2 above, at 58.

18   Furth, H. G., *Piaget for Teachers* (Englewood Cliffs, NJ: Prentice Hall, 1970).

19   Argyris, C. and Schon, D. A. *Organizational learning: A theory of action perspective* (Reading, MA: Addison-Wesley, 1978).

20   Gersick, C. J. G., "Revolutionary change theories: A multi-level exploration of the punctuated equilibrium paradigm," *Academy of Management Review*, 16(1) (1991) 10–36.

21   Argyris and Schon, n. 19 above. See also Woolfolk, A. E., *Educational psychology*, 7th edn (Boston: Allyn & Bacon, 1998).

22   Kolb, D. A., *Experiential learning: Experience as the source of learning and development* (NJ: Prentice Hall, 1983).

23   Bird, A. and Osland, J. 2004. "Global Competencies," in Lane, H. W., Maznevski, M. L. Mendenhall, M., and McNett, J. M. (eds), *Blackwell Handbook of Global Management: A Guide to Managing Complexity* (Blackwell Publishers, 2004).

24   *The Blackwell Handbook of Global Management: A Guide to Managing Complexity*, n. 2 above, at 65.

PART **2**

CHAPTER **2**

Intercultural Effectiveness in International Management

A generation ago, when international managers tended to go from one country to another one, the best advice they could get was to learn about that other country's culture and to adapt as much as possible. However, today's complexity, as we discussed in Chapter 1, makes that advice naïve. Instead, recent research and practice focus on the idea of Cultural Intelligence (CQ). Cultural intelligence is the capacity to act effectively in multiple cultural environments. It is a system of interacting knowledge and skills, linked by mindfulness, or the tendency to be thoughtful and deliberate about one's actions and the reactions to them.[1] One of the hallmarks of CQ is the ability to adapt and work effectively and respectfully with people from other cultures, while simultaneously maintaining your own identity. CQ is related to Emotional Intelligence (EQ),[2] but adds the condition of working across boundaries. One can have high Emotional Intelligence within one culture, but not necessarily be able to apply it across cultures.

CQ is a critical part of the global mindset. The global mindset, as we defined it in Chapter 1, consists of four different knowledge components, each associated with a different aspect of self and context. CQ gives us the cultural context of self- and other-awareness. This chapter focuses on the knowledge component of CQ, and Chapter 3 looks closely at skills. The book as a whole is intended to increase mindfulness, both for CQ and for the global mindset.

Two categories of knowledge are critical for cultural intelligence. *General* cultural knowledge is an understanding of how culture works and how to observe and gain insights about the effect of culture in different settings. *Specific* cultural knowledge is the set of facts and information about a particular culture, such as China or Nigeria or the Southwest US. In the first part of this chapter we examine culture in general, and in the second part we introduce a framework for Mapping, or describing, characteristics of specific cultures.

CULTURE: EASIER TO IDENTIFY THAN DEFINE

Think about the following examples of cultures: Nigerian, Japanese, Québécois, soccer (football) fans, golfers, snowboarders, wine connoisseurs, Generation Y, engineers, artists, Nestlé Corporation, and Matsushita Electric. What other examples have you come across? What do they have in common? What makes each a culture?

Culture is the set of assumptions and values that are shared by a group of people and that guide that group of people's interaction with each other. To paraphrase Kluckhohn and Strodtbeck, culture consists of a shared, commonly held body of general beliefs and values that define the "shoulds" and the "oughts" of life. These beliefs and values are taught to people so early and so unobtrusively that they are usually unaware of their influence. In a similar way, Hofstede defines culture as "the collective programming of the mind which distinguishes one group or category of people from another."[3]

Culture is most readily seen in norms and practices, such as language, clothing, and behavior; however, its meaning and important influence are much deeper than these surface manifestations. Speaking French and eating poutine do not make one automatically Québécois; watching the World Cup and wearing a football jersey do not make one automatically part of the soccer (football) culture. A new employee at either Nestlé or Matsushita becomes part of the culture slowly.

The assumptions and values that define culture – the ones that are held by members of the culture – are those that identify what is successful and what isn't, what is to be prioritized, and how people should behave in the world and towards each other. These assumptions and values are learned by passing them on from one generation to the next in both formal ways, such as school or orientation programs, and informal ways, such as story telling and social reinforcement.

All Groups Have Cultures

Culture serves two important functions for groups. First, it makes action more simple and efficient. When people know what to prioritize and how to interact with each other, business and social interactions take place quickly and easily. There is no need to question each action. Members of the Japanese culture can produce and interpret each level of bowing without conscious thought; engineers can easily proceed together using standardized work methods and mathematics. Think about the last time you were in a new culture, working or as a tourist. How did you feel at the end of the first day? Some people say excited or exhilarated, some say frustrated, but most people say they were exhausted. This exhaustion comes from spending the day wondering what is meaningful and what is not. Should I tip the driver? How much? The receptionist didn't smile at me. Is that normal or was I rude? Or was the receptionist rude? Which side of the sidewalk should I walk on? What are others doing? Oops I just used my left hand – is that impolite here, or is it okay? Or should I have used both hands? Even if you have read all the guide books, questions like these arise. When you are interacting across cultures, you lose the efficiency that comes from shared meaning and values within a culture.

Second, culture provides an important source of social identity for its members. Humans have a basic need to belong to social groups. Belonging to a culture – as demonstrated by acting in accordance with the norms and values – brings safety and security from the group, and separates the group from outsiders who are different and perhaps even threatening. Interestingly, most people feel this identity even more strongly when they are outside their own culture than when they are in it. Foreign students or expatriates from the same country often choose to socialize more closely than the same individuals might when in their own country.

Culture and individuals interact in many ways. Culture is a characteristic of groups, and is defined in terms of what group members share. However, individuals within the culture are all different and subscribe to the culture's assumptions and values to a greater or lesser degree. We are all members of many cultures – cultures related to our national, regional, professional, organizational, age, gender, hobby, and other identities.[4] The culture we identify with most closely in a given situation influences which set of assumptions and values we prioritize in that situation. When a Nigerian oil engineer is working at the company's Norwegian headquarters office as an internal consultant, she may identify most closely with her professional and corporate cultures and act with the priorities and assumptions of a corporate engineer. When she is working in her home country on the oil rig supervising local employees, she may identify more with her national culture and interpret events and act according to Nigerian cultural assumptions.

Culture is an important context for people's behavior together. We often use Edward Hall's analogy that says culture is to people like water is to fish. Water is all around the fish and is critical to a fish's survival, but the fish does not notice it or know what water is. It is simply the context in which the fish lives. However, a fish out of water could not function normally. Most people are unaware of their own culture; it is simply a set of unquestioned assumptions that create a context for their interactions together. People become much more aware of their own cultures when they visit other cultures. This awareness, however it is gained, is critical to leading effectively in an international context and overcoming the "fish out of water" syndrome.

Is Culture Becoming Less Important?

A basic premise of this book is that working across cultures is one of the two fundamental characteristics that distinguish international management from "normal" domestic management (strategic complexity is the other). It is worth taking a moment here to reflect on this assumption, since many people argue that this perspective is misleading. They assert that cultures around the world are converging, that business is business everywhere, and that people are basically the same all over. Of course, there is some truth to all these statements, and when we present them to groups of managers, they provide quick examples to support the case. People around the world wear jeans and carry European bags and pens, eat at McDonald's, talk on Nokia phones, listen to iPods, and play games and DVDs on their Nintendo or Sony devices. Currencies are traded globally every moment, and there are global infrastructures and norms for conducting business. Accounting standards are becoming more and more global. Everyone has the same basic physiological and psychological needs.

However, as we argued above, leading effectively in the complexity of globalization means empowering people to make decisions and implement them in ways that are consistent with the important priorities for the company. This means understanding the relationship between people and organizations, on the one hand, and their context on the other. This is an underlying component of the global mindset. And one of the most important elements of the context – especially for understanding people and their behavior – is culture.

Take another look at the converging cultures examples. We think McDonald's is an interesting example to analyze. Yes, the golden arches and basic format are recognizable everywhere, as are some of the menu items. Kids all over the world love the Happy Meal, and, in fact, McDonald's is the world's single largest toy distributor. The Big Mac is such a universal item that the magazine *The Economist* has selected it as the best example of a world consumer commodity, and bases its purchasing power parity (PPP) index on the price of a Big Mac in different countries.[5]

However, look a bit deeper. McDonald's has different menu items in different countries. Beer is served in Germany and some other countries, a McArabia is on the menu in the Middle East, and there is no beef in Indian McDonald's. Corn is an alternative to fries in many Asian countries, and it is very hard to find a VeggieMac in Italy. Consumer Reports recently found McDonald's premium coffee in the US to taste better than Starbucks,[6] but this would come as no surprise to Australians who have McCafé shops in almost all McDonald's outlets, complete with a whole menu of specialty coffee drinks and high end cakes and pastries.

Look a bit deeper still: watch the people, learn to see the norms about McDonald's. In North America, a large proportion of revenues comes from drive-through. This proportion is increasing elsewhere, but nowhere else does it reach the same level as in North America. What might this indicate about North American culture? The importance of efficiency, of being on the go, of moving from one place to another? The *un*importance of eating as a social event, where people sit down for a meal together? In Delhi, India, outside the expatriate areas McDonald's is frequented by small, wealthy families. It is more of a luxury family experience than a commodity eating experience. In downtown Cairo, Egypt, many McDonald's customers are businesspeople holding meetings, and the restaurant layout caters to this with bright lighting, photos of dynamic places in the city, and tables far enough apart to encourage conversation. McDonald's is a symbol of progressive capitalism while encouraging socialization and business discussions around meals. In Saudi Arabia, McDonald's has two sections which are completely separated from the front door to the service to the eating areas: one for singles (men), the other for families (women or mixed groups). In the family section, the booths can be closed with a curtain so women can eat in privacy and remove their veils if they choose. In southern Norway, McDonald's is the place families go on rainy Sunday afternoons. Why? It has the only indoor playground in town, and both family time and activity are important in Norwegian culture. In Malaysia, McDonald's has an all-you-can-eat event during Ramadan. Ramadan is the traditional month of fasting in the Islamic calendar, and adherents must fast during the day but may eat in the evening. More and more people in Kuala Lumpur take advantage of McDonald's one price evening ticket. This creates some controversy in the city, with some appreciating McDonald's adaptation to their culture, and others decrying a degeneration of Ramadan that focuses on consumerism rather than discipline. This is an ongoing debate in Malaysia and other countries, and it is played out even at McDonald's.

In short, McDonald's, one of the icons of globalization, represents the complexities of culture and the debate on cultural convergence and divergence. Cultures are *both* converging and diverging. The convergence allows us to do business together. It allows mergers and acquisitions to be negotiated, money and goods to be traded, and employees to stay briefly in foreign countries without too much trouble. It allows us to work together, at least on the surface. However, deeper level differences become apparent when people have to interact more intensively with each other on a day-to-day basis. As a Chinese student said to her American peers, "To say that we're becoming Westernized because McDonald's does well in Shanghai, is like saying that the U.S. is becoming Easternized because there are a lot of Chinese restaurants." Naïve assumptions about convergence can cause problems or disappointments such as when the synergy anticipated from a merger or acquisition is more elusive than expected or when goods purchased don't arrive on time or are not as expected.

Incidentally, the McDonald's story also shows the opportunities of globalization. For example, when McDonald's entered Europe, most countries, and France in particular, protested the low nutritional value. As a response, McDonald's developed a wide range of healthy food (salads, sandwiches, drinks, alternatives for Happy Meals, etc.) for Europe, much more extensive than the range in the US. When US consumers started decreasing their McDonald's intake due to health concerns, McDonald's was ready, and they took their learning from Europe back to the US. This kind of synergy from understanding cultural differences is one of the sources of opportunity from international management.

In short, managers must understand the context of the people they are working with in order to lead them well, and one of the most important elements of context is culture. As long as people live and work in groups, managers will need to work effectively across cultures.

Why Focus on Country Cultures?

Although we defined culture above as the set of values and assumptions shared by any group of people, in international management we tend to focus on the role of country cultures. There is a good reason for this. The institutions that carry culture tend to be very powerful and consistent within a country. For example, most countries have one *official* language which is the language of most families, is taught in all state schools, is the language of regional- and country-level government, and is the language of official and most unofficial media. Most countries have a single basic legal system (e.g., constitutional or civil or Islamic law), a system of government that is relatively consistent across regions (e.g., representative democracy in different states or cantons, or a monarchy that reigns throughout the country), a single relationship between church and state (e.g., there is a strong relationship or there is officially no relationship). These practices and relationships are often different from those in the country next door. The beliefs and values associated with these institutions are taught to people so early and so unobtrusively through family norms and institutional practices that most people are unaware of their influence.

There are some important exceptions, such as Canada, Belgium, Switzerland, and India, which have two or more official languages and cultures. However, the generalization is true for most countries. Country is therefore a very important type of culture to account for in international business. For most of this chapter, and indeed the book, we will focus, therefore, on country-based cultures. However, towards the end of the chapter we turn to some important caveats around this notion, and throughout the book we will acknowledge the important influence of other cultures.

THROUGH THE LOOKING GLASS: CULTURE INFLUENCES HOW WE SEE THE WORLD

To understand culture's influence, we need to understand first the basic role of *assumptions* and *perceptions* in influencing our own thoughts and actions. This allows us to see our own culture's influence on us, and why cross-cultural encounters are both so difficult to understand and so interesting.[7]

An assumption is an unquestioned, taken-for-granted belief about the world and how it works. Assumptions help create our world view, or the cognitive environment in which we operate. They come in many different varieties. Some are so deeply ingrained and unquestioned that it is difficult ever to surface them, and even when surfaced, they are not testable. For example, assumptions about the basic nature of humans are normally surfaced and questioned only by philosophers and religious leaders, and even they cannot test them in an unambiguous way. Culture incorporates many of these deep assumptions, and we will elaborate on more of them presently.

Other assumptions are learned at various stages of our lives, and, once learned, are taken for granted without further questioning. A child comes into the world with no knowledge of it, yet in the first few years learns to take so much for granted: day and night follow each other; manipulating switches makes things work or turns them off; things that move are either alive or powered by something; living things need nourishment; and, when in doubt, look on the Internet. As we develop through life, we learn more and more, and each lesson becomes a basic building block for adding new skills and competencies. A financial analyst valuing companies takes for granted certain assumptions about efficient markets and develops analyses that affect the companies' ability to obtain resources. An advertising account manager takes for granted certain assumptions about human motivations and produces advertising campaigns that play to those motivations and invoke them.

Assumptions influence the process of perception, or what we notice and how we interpret events and behaviors. Assumptions influence our perceptions themselves, our interpretations of events and behaviors, or the meaning that the events and behaviors have for us. The expression "we see what we want to see and hear what we want to hear" is a reflection of how our assumptions affect our perceptions. Karl Weick, a social psychologist, suggests "I'll see it when I believe it" is more accurate than proclaiming "I'll believe it when I see it." [8]

The financial analyst focuses on financial ratios, earnings growth, or dividends but may not notice programs with long lead-times that may enhance the company's reputation for social responsibility. If she did notice this information, she would likely interpret it as something admirable but nothing that should influence stock price or ability to borrow money today. The boundary conditions for such financial assumptions became abundantly clear in 2008 when they failed to hold, and banks around the world collapsed.

The advertising account manager will likely notice only product features that fit into his framework of assumptions about motivation for the target audience and miss other implications of those features. The first marketing campaigns for cellular phones focused exclusively on the business audience. The next generation of campaigns realized that the same features were equally important for families involved in multiple activities and attractive to teenagers wanting to stay in touch with their friends. If marketers' assumptions had not focused exclusively on business, they may have tapped this broader consumer market much earlier. Today's telecommunications industry includes a wide variety of competitors, from Internet providers to handset manufacturers to content developers, all vying to create the next set of assumptions.

Assumptions are necessary. If we did not make innumerable assumptions about the world, we would be paralyzed by the constant need to inquire about the meaning of events and the motives of others. The more others share our assumptions, the more easily we can interact and communicate effectively with each other. It is not surprising that our assumptions are generally effective when we operate within our own culture.

Clearer Vision with D-I-E

A simple way to remember this process of social perception is captured by the acronym D-I-E, which stands for *Describe, Interpret,* and *Evaluate.* We observe something and take note of its characteristics, or describe it. In describing something we stay with the objective facts. What we are inclined to notice is influenced in part by our assumptions of what is important. We then interpret those facts, or give them meaning, again based on our assumptions. Finally, we evaluate the facts and take action based upon our evaluation.

When selecting a potential supplier for specialty chemicals, a purchasing agent may notice that different companies offer different prices for the same grade of chemical. The purchasing agent will build a table comparing the different suppliers, describing their price ranges. The purchasing agent may not notice that the suppliers offer different types of technical assistance or compound customization, because his assumptions about priorities do not include this. Although price is sometimes an indicator of quality, the purchasing agent may interpret the chemical grade as the quality information. As long as prices are identified for the same chemical grade, the purchasing agent interprets that he is comparing them on an equal basis. Finally, the purchasing agent evaluates the lowest price compound as good for the company. He takes action and buys this compound.

Just like the purchasing agent, we all act based on the world we perceive, the world we see through the *Describe, Interpret, Evaluate* sequence. Since the sequence builds so heavily on our assumptions of the world and how it works, those assumptions end up influencing our own actions and what we think of others' actions. Therefore, when we cross cultural boundaries we need to be especially careful in our tendency to interpret and evaluate from our own perspective. Our "rule of thumb" regarding the D-I-E model is to spend more time on description, treat interpretations as hypotheses, and defer evaluation until we have explored multiple possible interpretations.

Culture Influences our Lenses

Figure 2.1 shows the influence pattern of culture on assumptions, perceptions, and management behavior, and demonstrates why culture and assumptions play such a large role in cross-cultural encounters.

A good way to identify someone's cultural assumptions is to ask a series of "why" questions. For example, consider the following conversation:

Colleague: We should adjust our incentive scheme for salespeople so they have more commission.
You: Why?
Colleague: That way they'll be more motivated to sell the products.
You: Why will it work?
Colleague: Because they'll see that if they sell more products, they'll get more money.
You: Why will they change their behavior?
Colleague (getting frustrated with you):   Because everyone wants more money!
You: Why?
Colleague (not believing he is part of this conversation):   Just because!

When you get to this response – "just because" – you have reached the level of assumptions. These assumptions are often provided by the person's culture. You can also identify assumptions by giving people examples of situations that involve the assumption and asking them how they would respond. For example, people may not be conscious enough about their basic belief about human nature to articulate it. However, ask someone "What do you expect someone to do if she found a large amount of money in an unidentified package on the street?" and "What type of system should be put in place to prevent dishonest employees from stealing money?" Your respondent would probably be able to reply easily, and this will give you clues about his assumptions regarding human nature. In general, people are more consciously aware of how they ought to behave in situations that are specific and concrete; but people are not usually aware of where those "oughts" originate. Often, they come from culture.

FIGURE 2.1   Culture's Influence on Individual Behavior

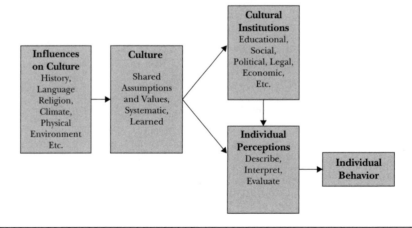

When Cultures Meet – Question the Other or Question Ourselves?

If culture is a set of shared deep-level assumptions and values, and these assumptions and values influence thoughts and behavior, what happens when people from two or more different cultures meet or work together? Their assumptions and value systems (cultures) may direct them to perceive the same situation differently, interpret what they notice differently, evaluate the situation differently, and take different actions.

This sets up a potential conflict situation. From our own point of view, the other person is thinking and behaving in a way that is inconsistent with our assumptions about the world (assumptions which we are not conscious of holding). When assumptions are consistent with perceptions, we experience a neutral feeling, or perhaps comfort or harmony. We are able to function, to get our work done, to produce. But what happens when we encounter something that contradicts our assumptions? What if the purchasing agent assumes that all compounds within the same chemical grade are equal, then the chemical engineer tells him they are not? These encounters set up a condition described by psychologists as "cognitive dissonance." It is an uncomfortable feeling of imbalance. Because we seek pleasure and avoid pain, we are motivated to reduce the imbalance to achieve consistency again.

There are two ways to regain consistency: change our perceptions of the evidence to match the assumptions (question the other), or change our assumptions to match the evidence (question ourselves). We are much more inclined to invoke the first method than the second; it requires a great deal less energy, is reinforced by others who hold the same assumptions, and is less confusing. We usually do this by distorting what we've perceived to make it consistent with our assumptions. The purchasing agent tells the engineer that she is just seeing the engineering point of view and doesn't understand the strategic picture.

Although the usual mode of reducing the gap between assumptions and perceptions is to distort perceptions, there is another option: altering one's own assumptions. The purchasing agent we met above may question the engineer about time and other costs related to technical assistance for new product development associated with different suppliers, and shift his assumptions about purchasing priorities to include such investment. Unfortunately, this is usually an unexamined alternative. Furthermore, the closer the relationship between the assumptions in question and one's identity or concept of self, the less likely one is to consider changing assumptions.

This tendency to make perceptions congruent with assumptions is often a source of misunderstanding between people in the same cultural milieu. It is an even bigger problem in an intercultural context where there is a lack of shared assumptions. Recall that definitions of how one ought to behave and, therefore, the explanations of why a person is behaving in a particular way, often differ from one culture to another. People get into difficulty by making inaccurate assumptions about a person or situation in a different culture. Consider this short exchange:

Susan (British):	Pablo, the company has decided to transfer you to the regional headquarters in Sao Paulo.
Pablo (Chilean):	That will be very difficult. I think I'll stay here.

There is an awkward pause. What are both thinking? If each is thinking from their own assumption set, Susan is probably wondering whether Pablo is really interested in developing his career: "A transfer to regional headquarters is an important promotion. Maybe he's not as ambitious as I thought. It's too bad to waste such talent." Pablo may wonder why Susan or the company would transfer him: "My family and my life is here. Why would I want to go to Brazil? I don't speak Portuguese; I could not have a life there. How can the company do this to me?"

With this interpretation, both are making assumptions about the other's motivations and values, based on their own assumption set. Moreover, because we make interpretations from our own assumption set, we are prone to ethnocentric error. Ethnocentrism is the evaluation of differences between groups, seeing "us" as better and "them" as worse. We have a strong tendency to use our own group's assumptions as the benchmark when viewing other groups, placing our group at the top of a hierarchy, and ranking all others as lower.[9] Remember that our advice at the end of the D-I-E model section above was to defer evaluation and to explore multiple interpretations. Susan's thoughts may continue with, "No wonder the Chilean economy is still struggling." Pablo might think, "This is just another example of Anglo values colonizing the rest of the world – and we'll end up as robots without heart and loyalty to our families."

The dynamics of what happens when cultures meet are shown in Figure 2.2. The same perceptual process occurs as described earlier and shown in Figure 2.1, but in this case two different people are acting based on two different sets of cultural assumptions. The resulting different decisions or behaviors set up the conditions for conflict – or synergy, as discussed below.

In intercultural situations, people from the "other" culture say things and behave in ways that are not at all familiar to us, and we may even stereotype the other culture as

FIGURE 2.2   Cross-Cultural Encounters

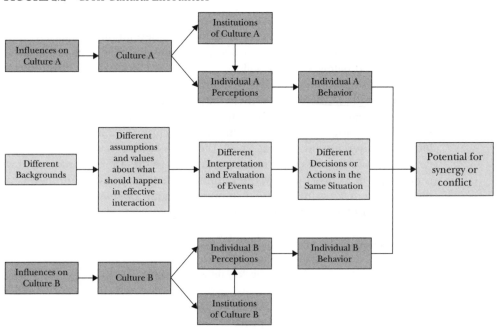

"primitive," "lazy," or some other negative stereotype. Again, notice that this process is an example of negative evaluation, just what the D-I-E model warns us to avoid.

People tend to become aware of how their assumptions shape perceptions, values, and behavior only as they confront a different set of assumptions guiding the views and practices of other people. If people are exposed to new experiences under the right circumstances (including the person's own motivation), part of their response will include an examination of their own guiding values. The next stage of Susan and Pablo's hypothetical conversation could easily have been one of open dialogue about reasons for moving or not, and how those were related to different values. Both could be enriched by the conversation.

Culture Creates Efficiency and Identity

In the above section, we focused mostly on the cognitive aspect of culture: our shared values and assumptions influence how we perceive the world and the people in it, how we make choices, and how we act. For the mechanics of doing business, this cognitive aspect is important. Furthermore, it is the aspect of culture that managers misinterpret most, leading to conflict more often than synergy in intercultural interactions.

It is equally important to respect the identity that culture provides. This seems so basic that we should not need to say it; however, we can all forget to respect such identities, especially when we are uncertain or in a new situation ourselves. Managers have a tendency to downplay cultural identity: "We are all part of a global business culture." But remember that identity becomes more important to the extent that it is threatened. If you disrespect someone's identity – for example by behaving in a way that is considered rude in his culture, by serving food that is unacceptable in her country, by not accommodating requirements of their culture – you set up a situation in which the other person becomes more locked into his or her cultural identity in order to defend it. This makes conflict even more likely, and makes it even more difficult to achieve synergies.

MAPPING CULTURES

The second type of knowledge important for cultural intelligence is culture-specific knowledge, or a set of facts and information about a particular culture. It is outside the scope of this book to provide such specific information about any one culture; we suggest readers turn to any of a myriad of guides for tourists, traveling businesspeople, or expatriates in various countries and cultures. Instead, we provide a powerful tool for Mapping specific cultures – for comparing cultures with each other, and for developing expectations about how to work with people from different cultures. This kind of tool is invaluable for managers who work across multiple cultures, especially when the cultures are also complex and changing.

We use the metaphor of Mapping quite deliberately. A map is a tool for navigating in a new territory. The map is useful to the extent that it is accurate, provides just the right level of detail and scale, and shows reference points. It should help you develop a guess about how to get from one place to another. A "you are here" point makes a map even more practical.

Maps of social features are less common than maps of geographical ones, and Mapping social features of groups is difficult because it is hard to verify the data against an unchanging reality. However, social maps that are carefully constructed help people enter new cultural territories as much as geographical maps help people enter new physical territories.

Just as a geographer uses different types of maps for different purposes, an international manager has access to several cultural maps. Each map shows different dimensions of culture, and allows different types of cultural comparisons. For example, Edward T. Hall has written several books and articles describing elements of culture that are relevant to business. In his classic article, "The Silent Language in Overseas Business," he describes cultural differences and their impact on international behavior, relating to the five dimensions of Time, Space, Things, Friendships, and Agreements.[10]

Geert Hofstede has developed the most extensively researched framework or cultural map.[11] By examining the satisfaction surveys of employees in a multinational, he identified four basic value patterns of cultures around the world: Individualism, Power Distance, Uncertainty Avoidance, and Masculinity. He also linked these dimensions to management theories and practice. Later, with colleague Michael Bond, he identified a fifth value of Confucian Dynamism, or Long-term Orientation.[12] Hofstede's framework was recently validated across multiple organizations and countries and updated by House *et al* in the GLOBE project.[13]

Following Hofstede, but incorporating more dimensions developed in sociology and anthropology, Trompenaars developed a map of seven dimensions: Universalism versus Particularism, Collectivism versus Individualism, Affective versus Neutral Relationships, Specificity versus Diffusiveness, Achievement versus Ascription, Orientation towards Time, Internal versus External.[14] He assesses a country's positioning on these dimensions by asking managers to respond to a series of short, often amusing, dilemmas and summarizing patterns among responses.

Schwartz developed a framework of values, specifically focusing on the values that are related to an individual's interaction with society.[15] Schwartz found that cultures differ in terms of valuing mastery versus harmony with the environment, embedded versus autonomous relations, and hierarchical versus egalitarian control.

All of these Mapping tools have different strengths. Hofstede's, for example, provided the earliest comprehensive set of data and has been used extensively to guide interactions since its publication in 1980. Trompenaars' vignettes provide vivid and interesting applications of cultural maps, and his focus on bipolar (either/or) dimensions supports his process of resolving cultural dilemmas. Schwartz's dimensions allow a translation from country to individual level values.

When we map cultures, we prefer when possible to use one of the longest established frameworks in anthropology, the Cultural Orientations Framework of Kluckhohn and Strodtbeck.[16] We find it to have the most comprehensive set of dimensions that are relevant for comparing cultures, even today. To reflect the complexity of the real world, we appreciate that it allows us to examine variations between cultures by measuring individual values and cultural values. As a result of our own research using this framework over the past 20 years, we have adapted the description here slightly from the original to reflect the dimensions and comparisons most relevant to management, but it retains its important characteristics.[17] The next section describes the Cultural Orientations Framework and presents a set of maps based on the Cultural Perspectives Questionnaire.

The Cultural Orientations Framework

Kluckhohn and Strodtbeck found that there are common themes in the issues or problems that different societies have faced throughout time, and these universal issues provide a way of viewing culture objectively. Kluckhohn and Strodtbeck produced their Cultural Orientations Framework by analyzing hundreds of ethnographic descriptions of cultures from around the world, conducted by researchers from many different backgrounds. They identified six problems or challenges that all societies throughout recorded history face. Different societies have developed and continue to develop different ways of coping with these challenges, but there tends to be a basic pattern of response configurations. The six issues are referred to as *cultural orientations*, and the different responses to each issue are called *variations*. The six issues are:

1 Relation to the environment
2 Relationships among people
3 Mode of normal activity
4 Belief about basic human nature
5 Orientation to time
6 Use of space.

For all of these orientations, there is no possible "proof" that one variation is better or worse. In fact, all variations exist because they are useful in particular situations that are relevant to the group. What is important is that members of a culture agree on a set of values and priorities related to one or more of the variations, then behave as if that is the best way of believing and doing things. This agreement brings the efficiency and identity we discussed earlier. The different types of agreement give us different cultures.

Our research suggests that the first three of these issues are most related to the cultural differences important for business, so we will focus on these and give only a short discussion of the last three.

We measure individuals' variations of the Cultural Orientations Framework using the Cultural Perspectives Questionnaire (CPQ), which we developed. The discussion in this chapter is based on our analysis of responses to our previous and current versions of the survey. All respondents are business students, practicing businesspeople, or people working in other types of organizations. We analyzed over 5000 responses (from over 60 countries) to previous versions of the survey, and over 10 000 responses (from almost 200 countries) to the current version.

The graphs which follow are based on our most recent version of the survey, with a sample of over 10 000 respondents. *Remember that all our respondents are business students and people working mostly in business organizations, and may not be representative of the general population.* About one third of our respondents are business students, mostly MBA but some undergraduate. The other two thirds are practicing managers with an average age of about 40, and with an average of 15 years of full-time work experience.

To create the country comparisons, we included data only from respondents who represent the culture. Either they were born in the country, have always lived there, and identify most closely with that country's culture; or they were born in the country, lived there longer than in any other country, and identify most closely with that country's culture. For example, someone who was born in the country but lived in other countries equally as long or longer, was not included in the country sample.

The number of respondents for each country sample is included after the country's name in the graph. Smaller sample sizes can be less representative of the culture (however, we only included sample sizes smaller than 100 if the sample had relatively low variance among individual respondents). When you are looking at the graphs, a good rule of thumb to keep in mind is that a difference of 0.4 is almost always both statistically significant and meaningful. In other words, a difference between two countries' scores that is 0.4 or greater is enough to create quite different patterns in members' expectations of how to respond to challenges related to that graph.[18]

Relation to the Environment The issue of people's relationship to the environment reflects how people in a society orient themselves to the world around them and to the supernatural. What do people direct their attention to, and what do they see as their role in the environment? There are three main variations of responses.

Harmony Harmony is a belief that we are not separated from the world – that we and the "world around us" are all part of the same system. Furthermore, it is a belief that the system must be kept in balance for things to go well, for life to progress and grow. In cultures with a high orientation towards harmony, people believe that our role as humans is to keep this system in balance and, when things are out of balance, we should nudge the system to realign it. Most aboriginal cultures are strongly harmony-oriented. Native Americans, for example, are traditionally hunters as well as gatherers, but their traditions for hunting incorporate strong norms of studying the ecosystem to ensure that no more game is hunted than the system can tolerate without becoming unbalanced, and utilizing every single part of the hunted animal without any waste. Their social traditions also encourage harmony within the tribe. Today's Chinese cultures tend to have a strong emphasis on harmony. In these cultures, managers prefer look at all aspects of a business system and engage in small actions to affect various parts of the system and bring it into alignment. They also tend to encourage harmony among people in the social system. This can be frustrating for members of other cultures who would like to see direct action on a particular issue, but it has enabled China to develop a powerful economy and social force.

Mastery Mastery is a belief that humans are separated from the world around us, and that our role is to influence and control our environment. An example of mastery is the goal to land a person on the moon when the technology did not exist for accomplishing the task. The audacity of announcing that this mission was to be achieved by the end of the 1960s reflected, among other things, a profound belief that if enough time, money, and brains are applied to a goal, nearly anything is achievable. Western cultures, especially Anglo and Northern European ones, tend to be highest on mastery orientation. This is reflected in the Anglo business emphasis on direct consequences for individual managers who do or do not achieve their goals. It is commonplace to pay top managers seemingly exorbitant amounts for (short-term) company success, and to change the CEO when a company is not doing well. Today, people are questioning such rewards and consequences focused on the assumption that the CEO has direct influence on results. This is a tacit questioning of the mastery assumption which has guided these cultures for generations.

Subjugation   Subjugation is a belief that the environment is dominated by something other than humans, typically God, fate, or a supernatural force. Life in this context is viewed as predetermined or preordained, or, less often, an exercise in chance. One should not try to alter the inevitable, for such actions will be futile at best and blasphemous at worst. To a devout Muslim, the expression "Insh'allah," which means "God willing," reflects a worldview that plans can be made, but will only take place according to the will of God. Although Islam is a religion and not a country culture, many countries have Islam as their official faith, and the religion strongly influences business practices.

People who do not come from societies with an appreciation for subjugation often view it as a variant of fatalism: why bother working hard, for example, if everything is preordained anyway? This quotation from a Muslim friend of one of the authors helps explain subjugation as active submission:

> Through meditation and prayer, I am to understand what it is that Allah has planned for me – what role I am to play in His plan. Then it is my own responsibility to fulfill that role as well as I can. If I understand my role well and work hard to be effective in it, then if something happens to prevent me from doing it well, I know that act was meant to happen and is part of Allah's larger plan. If I do not understand my role – which may be because I have not communicated well with Allah – and something happens to prevent me from doing it well, that act might be predetermined to help me understand my role better. If I do understand my role but I am lazy and don't work well towards it, and something happens to prevent me from fulfilling my role, that act may be my own responsibility. So it's a lot more complicated than "God determines everything," meaning every detail.

Country comparisons   It is important to note that all three of harmony, mastery, and subjugation are in all cultures all the time. Cultures differ in the extent to which they prefer one variation or another – or some combination – across situations. Figure 2.3 shows our research for mastery and harmony. The graph was created by subtracting a country's harmony score from its mastery score, so countries above the zero line prefer mastery over harmony, while those below the line prefer harmony over mastery. Those hovering around the zero line score the same on both, suggesting they differentiate between situations and maximize harmony in some and mastery in others.

Figure 2.3 mostly confirms the pattern we described above, with Anglo and Northern European cultures on the left (more mastery-oriented) and Chinese and other Asian cultures on the right (more harmony-oriented). Japan may appear to be an anomoly, with a slightly higher mastery than harmony score. Many people expect Japan to be further

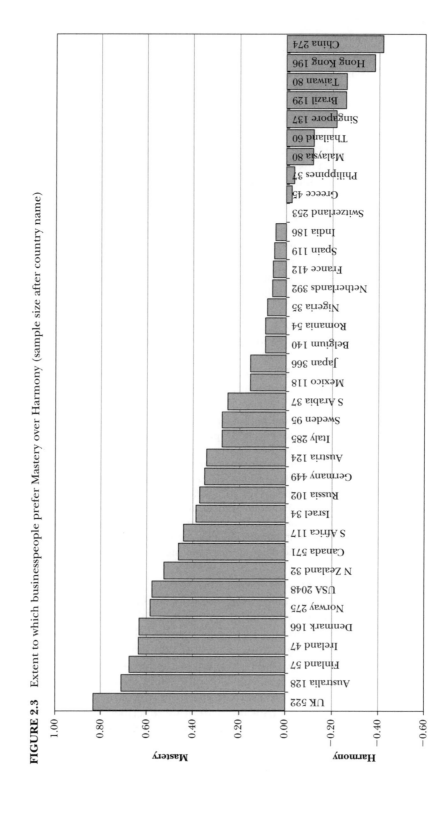

FIGURE 2.3 Extent to which businesspeople prefer Mastery over Harmony (sample size after country name)

to the right with its focus on *wa*, or harmony. This is seen, for example, in Japanese gardens and scripted social relationships, and the popular Japanese saying that "the nail that sticks up gets hammered down." However, a closer look at Japanese culture shows that such harmony is achieved through strong mastery. The Japanese garden must be tended every day, and would never achieve such a state naturally. Japanese companies are much more likely than those from other parts of Asia to send their own managers to control operations abroad, rather than promote local managers. Even the Japanese nail is "hammered" down. This example illustrates the importance of Mapping with data whenever possible, rather than relying on stereotypical descriptions of cultures. Managers from other cultures will be more able to avoid conflicts and create synergies with Japanese companies if they recognize the importance of mastery in addition to harmony in that culture.

We have found that in all countries we've measured, mastery and harmony are both higher than subjugation. Some groups certainly have a stronger belief in subjugation than others: managers in our research from Thailand, the Philippines, Malaysia, and Saudi Arabia, for example, have subjugation scores on average much higher than managers from Australia, New Zealand, Mexico, and Brazil. However, even the countries with higher subjugation scores do not prefer it over the other orientations. Managers moving from a very low subjugation culture, such as Australia, to a higher subjugation culture, such as Thailand, may notice the subjugation simply because of the difference. However, placing too much emphasis on this may lead to misleading conclusions. An Australian manager from a shipping company assumed, for example, that managers in Thailand were unlikely to take charge of situations or take initiative to influence them. He learned his mistake three years after arriving in Thailand, when he decided to try a pilot test with empowerment practices. To his surprise, the Thai managers responded very well and service improved dramatically. The Australian manager wished he had questioned his assumptions earlier.

Environment dilemmas in real life A global chemicals company we worked with had quality control units at different sites around the globe. According to the Cultural Perspectives Questionnaire, employees at the quality control sites in the US and Canada shared a strong mastery orientation, while those at the sites in Europe shared a strong harmony orientation. At one point there was a quality problem at a site outside these two continents, which had no established quality control unit. The plant was still producing, but the quality was lower and the output would have to be sold at a lower price. Members from Europe and the US were sent to this other site to address the problem. Serious conflict erupted immediately! The Europeans wanted to understand the entire system – upstream, downstream, all possible causes in technology systems, and so on – before proposing a solution. They wanted to ensure that anything they did would not cause other problems, and in fact would prevent other problems that might be waiting to happen. The Americans wanted to pinpoint the one place where the problem was happening and fix that. Days went by while the team argued about which approach was correct, each group blaming the other for lack of progress. Of course, from the company's perspective, both approaches were valuable. The mastery approach would have resolved the immediate issue, while the harmony approach would have prevented it from occurring again and perhaps improved quality overall. However, this time the company stumbled to a mediocre solution.

After the crisis was over, the different quality control units decided to map their cultural differences, to see if they could understand what had gone wrong. They discovered their profound split in terms of mastery and harmony, and realized that this was the cause of their inability to work together. They discussed the importance of each, and agreed to use each others' strengths in the future. Shortly afterwards, the company built a new plant in yet another location. The team that had failed in the improvement operation were given a chance to redeem themselves by planning for and implementing the quality control systems at the new plant. That plant set a record for the company, operating at its target quality and production levels well ahead of time and under budget, in large part due to the teamwork of the quality control group who this time combined the harmony systems approach with the mastery control approach.

Differences in expectations about relationship to the environment are evident in many other spheres of organizational life. For example, goal-setting is a cornerstone of most business management. But managers in mastery-oriented cultures tend to set goals to identify specific achievements, while managers in harmony-oriented cultures tend to set goals related to entire systems, and to link goals to each other. Budgeting is another managerial activity affected by relation to the environment. In stronger mastery-oriented cultures, the budget is assumed to be a tool that influences people to control its different aspects. In more harmony-oriented cultures, the budgeting exercise is often seen as a way of analyzing the entire business system and the relationships among the parts, and the process of creating a common language for this system is more important than accountability for specific results.[19]

Summary   While assumptions about mastery over, harmony with, and subjugation to the environment are present in all cultures, most cultures prefer one over the others in most situations. People are expected to act according to that preference, and actions are interpreted from that perspective. All of these variations offer important value, and none of them is "correct" across all situations. Managers who can interpret others' perspectives according to this Mapping dimension are more likely to be able to combine them for synergies.

Relationships among People
This orientation is concerned with issues of power and responsibility. What responsibility do people have for the welfare of others? Who has power over us, and over whom do we have power?

Collectivism   In a culture that is collective, the group is dominant. Members of the group look after each other, and subordinate their own wishes to those of the group. This does not mean complete conformity; it simply means that on issues that are related to maintaining the group, the group has power over its members.

An important corollary in collective cultures is the notion of in-group and out-group. The rules and privileges of the group apply only to members of the group, and there is no obligation to help or care for people outside the group (they are assumed to have their own groups). This complexity of collectivism can give rise to many misunderstandings. They are exemplified by the apocryphal story of an American who assisted a pedestrian brushed by a passing car in a busy street in an Asian city. Appalled by the lack of attention to the injured stranger, the American yelled at a nearby police officer, provided first aid, and insisted on hailing and paying for a taxi to take the person to a hospital. Afterward, the American muttered about the inhumanity of the local population. Meanwhile, the police officer's family listened, horrified, as the officer told about the American who treated a stranger like a family member, then was so indifferent as to send the person off in a taxi, rather than accompany the injured to the hospital personally and to attend to the victim properly afterwards.

A related question that is critical to ask in collective cultures is: "What is the group?" The dominant group could be based on extended family, on companies, on communities, on society as a whole, or any other collectivity. As we will see later when we compare countries, cultures that are equally collective may prioritize different types of groups.

Individualism   Whose welfare is primary? This variation's answer is the "individual." Individualism is a belief that if people look after themselves and if no one has absolute power over anyone else then we will all be better off. Individuals should make their own decisions, and live with the consequences of them. In individualistic cultures status usually is based on personal achievements, and these cultures also tend to be egalitarian. However, even with regards to egalitarianism, there are subtle differences. One of the authors, an American, lived in Canada for over 20 years. He observed that egalitarianism to Canadians usually meant equality of outcomes while to Americans it meant equal opportunity but not necessarily equal outcomes.

This attitude is dominant in North America, Australia and New Zealand, and parts of Europe. The nuclear family tends to be the outer limit of formal responsibility, and even that changes after children reach the age of majority. Independence is valued, and "Stand on your own two feet!" is the injunction. Except in unusual circumstances, such as the current economic crisis, parents whose adult children are still living with them would be seen to have failed to instill this independence and sense of rugged individualism.

Another country that is very individualistic according to our research is Switzerland. The Swiss system of democracy is almost truly representative at the individual level. Many important decisions are made at the level of small villages, and most federal laws are passed by means of whole-population referenda.

Hierarchy   In hierarchical cultures, relationships of power and responsibility are arranged such that those higher in the hierarchy have power over those lower in the hierarchy. All cultures have hierarchies; however, those with a lower hierarchical value tend to have fewer layers whose boundaries are more flexible. In return, they are expected to look after and provide for those lower in the hierarchy. In strongly hierarchical cultures the hierarchy tends to be stable over time, such that most people remain in the same general level throughout their lives. Perhaps more important for multinational businesses, preference for hierarchy is usually associated with patterns in information-sharing. While individualistic cultures share information broadly – sometimes attaching a price to it, but making it accessible to everyone – and collective cultures share information within groups but not across groups, hierarchical cultures tend to share information freely only up and down the vertical lines.

In a small Malaysian services organization, all 30 members of headquarters (four departments) sit in the same large room, and eat lunch together in groups that are unrelated to department. However, members of the staff discuss work only with their bosses and direct reports (sometimes not even openly within the same department), and blame their managers when they do not know what is going on in other departments. After attending a management course, the president saw the need for cross-fertilization and interdependence below the management level, so she tried to encourage and facilitate cross-department communication. Her attempts failed miserably; people simply could not understand what she was getting at. Finally, she used her hierarchical authority to insist that each department post an information board describing all the activities they were currently working on, the involvement of different department members, progress towards goals, and so on, and she insisted that the boards be updated once a week. The boards were posted in heavy traffic areas so everyone would walk by them. Through this action, departments slowly started noticing each others' board and activities, and, over time, information became shared across hierarchical levels without losing the comfort of the hierarchy.

Country comparisons   All cultures have all three types of power and responsibility patterns: collectivism, individualism, and hierarchy; cultures simply differ in their prioritization. Figure 2.4 shows the relative preference for collectivism and individualism (the individualism score subtracted from the collectivism score) for the countries in our research. The further a country is to the left, the more strongly it prefers collectivism over individualism. The first thing to notice in Figure 2.4 is that no country in our sample strongly prefers individualism over collectivism – the most extremely "individualistic" cultures prioritize individualism and collectivism about the same.

Most people expect that the United States would be far to the right, rather than in the middle. This is because previous research and popular culture highlights the stereotype of individualistic Americans, including the "lone cowboy." However, the US shows strong collectivism within communities, churches, teams (particularly team sports), and in patriotism for the country as a whole. There is less collectivism among extended families or the workplace than in other cultures, which is partly why people from those other cultures do not notice the collectivism. Moreover, with the multicultural nature of the US, many people come from countries or cultures that do have high collectivism around the family. This pattern of collectivism is evident in our research in all regions of the US, although it is possible that different regions focus on different groups. Managers from other countries going to the US should remember how important these groups are to Americans. We have worked with many managers from other parts of the world who were confused in the first years in the US – pleased (even if overwhelmed) with the warm welcome given to strangers, but sometimes offended when the welcome didn't translate to deep friendship the way such a welcome would in other places (although the welcome would be rarer in the first place). For most of them, the cultural breakthrough came from joining and being active in a church community and/or a team sport, especially with their children. By integrating into the collective, expatriates created a place for themselves in the group, and their management became more productive afterwards.

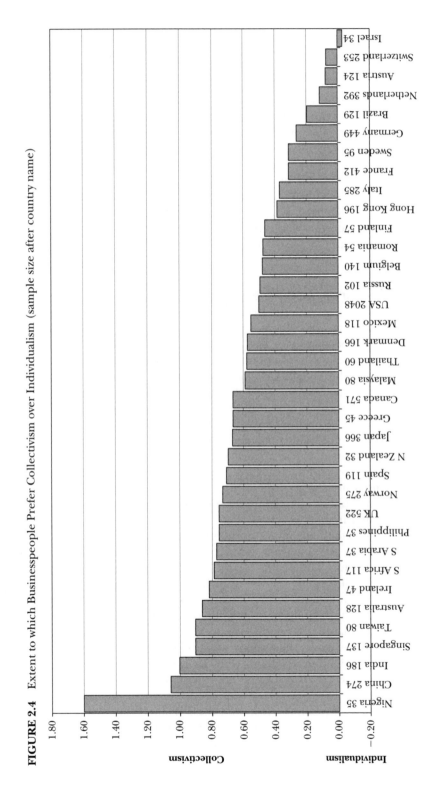

FIGURE 2.4 Extent to which Businesspeople Prefer Collectivism over Individualism (sample size after country name)

The relative preference for hierarchy is shown in Figure 2.5, where the higher a score is above 0.0, the higher the culture's preference for hierarchy. Interesting here is the highly negative score for Sweden. In Sweden, a boss who tells others what to do is a bad boss. What does a Swedish boss do, then? Most Swedes say that the role of a boss is to facilitate the performance of others – to guide subordinates to develop their own way of doing things. This works very well for commitment and innovation, and Swedes were instrumental in developing such high-performance work practices as self-managed teams. But there is a "dark side" as well, as we explored with a number of senior Swedish executives recently. Such negative hierarchy is extremely inefficient, and this inefficiency can be costly or even deadly in a crisis. After some chagrin, this group of highly successful executives admitted to each other that in crises they had learned to manage in an "un-Swedish" way, deliberately stepping out of character, then apologizing later. Swedish managers who work abroad often have a difficult time being taken seriously by their new direct reports, until they learn to adapt and step into a more hierarchical role, at least sometimes. This situation is explored further in Chapter 3.

Relations among people dilemmas in real life   It is a common misconception that collective cultures engage in more teamwork than individualistic cultures do. In fact, all cultures work in teams; they just do it differently.[20] The more individualistic a culture is, the more team members prefer to have specific roles and responsibilities and the ability to identify individual team contributions. Their commitment is to the task, rather than to the team. The leadership role may change depending on which part of the task needs to be emphasized, and membership may change frequently depending on the needs of the task or of the individuals on the team with respect to other tasks. In collective cultures, roles are more fluid, and commitment is to the team itself. Each person is responsible for his or her own contribution, but also for the success of the team itself. Membership is less likely to change. In hierarchical cultures, team members have specific levels and roles in the hierarchy, and the team is directed clearly by the leader. People contribute to meetings and discussions in accordance with their place in the hierarchy.

What happens when all these cultures get together in the same team? Lijong, a Global Account Director from a global computer firm, was in charge of one of the largest accounts in the company – a global financial services firm headquartered in the Netherlands. The global account team consisted of a small core of three regional representatives, each of whom liaised with up to 40 local representatives in the customer's different markets. All members of the team had strong relationships with customers. Because of the different cultures involved, managing relationships in the team presented difficulties. Local account managers from some countries responded better to global coordination if Lijong played a strong hierarchical role and dictated the orders; others responded better if he made suggestions and listened to their responses, letting them decide. Some identified more closely with the customer than they did with their own company (defined the group as local relations) while others had fierce loyalty to the company at the expense of the customer (defined the group as the company). Some preferred clear roles within the team (more individualistic); others expected flexible roles (more collective). Lijong came from a Chinese family of immigrants in Latin America, and had moved to the Netherlands as a young adult. He had developed a high level of cultural intelligence through careful reflection on his experiences. He found that to be successful with this

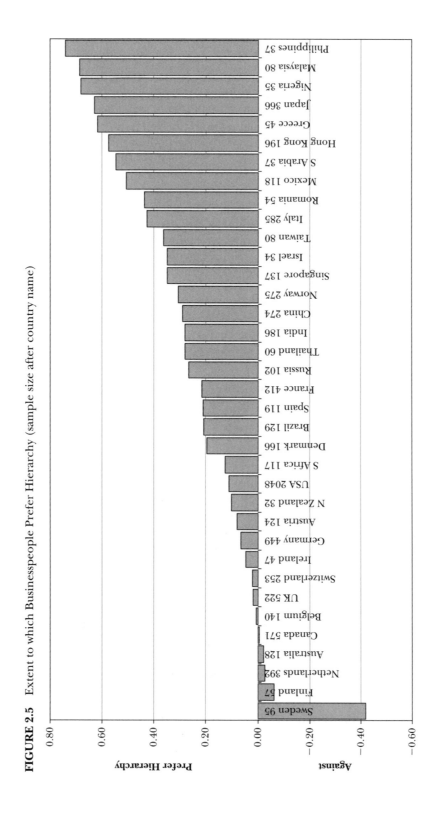

FIGURE 2.5 Extent to which Businesspeople Prefer Hierarchy (sample size after country name)

team, he was constantly shifting roles and behaviors. He got to know team members from their own perspectives, and appreciated how each contributed something important to the customer experience. He led the team towards the common goal of serving the global customer, learning from each other and developing best practices. Lijong's ability to read (map) the cultural differences and adjust his behavior according to them created great synergies in the team. It also made it easier for the team to face its greatest challenge – merging with another team when the client acquired another one of the company's customers.

Summary   All cultures are collective, individualistic, and hierarchical, but they emphasize the different types of relationships to different degrees. As should be evident from the discussions above, high-performing teams and organizations in fact incorporate all three sets of relationships, depending on the situation. Multicultural organizations, therefore, have an opportunity for higher performance, if they can capture these synergies.

Basic Mode of Activity   The activity orientation does not refer to a state of activity or passivity, but rather, the desirable focus of activity. There are two variations of activity found across business cultures: doing and thinking.

Doing   Doing is akin to the story of Prometheus from Greek mythology. Prometheus stole fire from Olympus and gave it to humans to use. As punishment, he was chained to a rock and tormented by vultures. Throughout eternity, he strained to break free of his chains, but new chains constantly reappeared when he was successful. The relentless striving to achieve and compulsive attempts to accomplish are the core of the doing variation. This is often associated with the Protestant work ethic, which dictates that hard work is pure, and it is seen in many western European and Anglo cultures. Marxism, too, argues that work is part of humans' identity, and goes so far as to say that the problem with capitalism is a separation of the identity of work from the person through management ownership.

   In doing cultures, "when in doubt, take action." This action may be to fix or resolve an issue, as tends to be the case in pragmatic Finland, or it may be to do something to get feedback – to learn more – as in process-oriented Japan.

Thinking   Thinking is closer to the Apollonian mode, in which the senses are moderated by thought, and mind and body are balanced. Thinking-oriented cultures place a high value on being rational and carefully thinking everything through before taking action. In thinking cultures, "when in doubt, get more information and plan more." At the extreme, they may value the beauty of an elegant argument at least as much as the results it creates. Most academic and research institutions have thinking-oriented cultures, and countries with a strong focus on careful engineering often have thinking-oriented cultures.

Being   Kluckhohn and Strodtbeck also identified a mode they called being, which is characterized by spontaneity. This is the Dionysian mode (the Greek god of wine and celebrations). In being-oriented cultures, the present is experienced to its fullest, and people are expected to act out their feelings as they experience them.

Latin American cultures are often associated with being, where emotion is expressed openly and punctuality is less important than paying attention to the present. However, in our research we found that country business management cultures are not very different on this dimension – many managers and some organizations in Brazil and Mexico are not so being-oriented, while many organizations in other parts of the world, such as some software and research companies, are more being-oriented than other companies within their cultures. In general, organizations and cultures with only a strong being orientation (not thinking or doing) would have a hard time coordinating in an interdependent world. The orientation of the Latin American cultures, which seems to combine "doing things in their own time" with emotional expression, is better captured by a polychronic time orientation, as discussed below in the section on Time.

Country comparisons   Figure 2.6 shows the results for our respondents with respect to doing and thinking in the activity orientation. The graph was created by subtracting the doing score from the thinking score. Countries with scores below the zero line and to the left prefer doing over thinking, whereas countries with scores above the zero line and to the right prefer thinking over doing.

People from other countries are often surprised to see the Nordic countries on the left of this graph. In the words of an Italian manager in a Norwegian multinational, "Those Scandinavians talk and talk forever before getting anything done! How can you say they're doing oriented?" Once again, though, the data help us examine underlying assumptions and question them. Managers in the Scandinavian countries of Denmark, Sweden, and Norway do engage in long discussions with each other before making decisions (in the fourth Nordic country of Finland, the long "conversations" happen at least as much with signals and nonverbal language as with talking). However, from a Nordic point of view this is not so much *planning* as it is *aligning*. Remember that the Nordic countries are moderately collective and relatively (or very) low on hierarchy. To make a decision, management teams need to discuss an issue to ensure that everyone is committed and aligned before going ahead. To outsiders, these discussions look like planning. But to Nordics there is a crucial difference. Once agreement is made, it is not agreement to a particular plan (a process or sequence), but commitment to a set of ideas and roles. In fact, Nordic managers assume that once commitment is made, the individuals or team involved will figure out how to implement it – in other words, the plan has not been made. Non-Nordic managers, especially those from thinking-oriented cultures, are often left confused once the decision has been made and the Nordic members of the team just start implementing, without discussing specific plans. Managers from other countries going to the Nordic countries or working in a Nordic firm should understand this distinction. In the "pre-decision" phase, they can learn to focus on aligning roles and commitment, rather than making specific plans that may be futile later. The implications of this dynamic are explored further in Chapter 3.

Activity dilemmas in real life   A Swiss firm that makes precision components for manufacturing processes, such as those used in the making of clothing and sporting goods, was working with a large US customer. The manager for new products, Tomas, was developing a new version of the components that had potential to decrease manufacturing

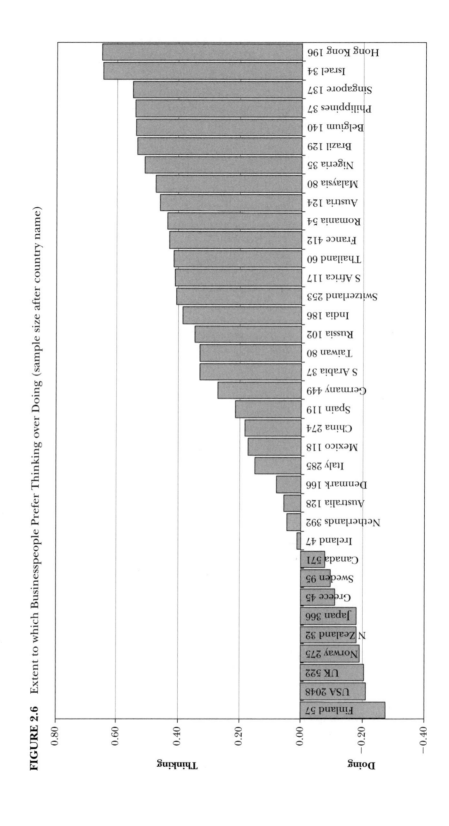

FIGURE 2.6 Extent to which Businesspeople Prefer Thinking over Doing (sample size after country name)

costs dramatically, but it was not yet ready for use. He described all the features and the testing process so far enthusiastically (thinking) to his counterpart at the US customer, with the intention of getting the customer excited about future possibilities. However, the US customer was so impressed he wanted it now (doing) for his factories in China. When Tomas said it wouldn't be ready for at least another year, the American replied, "You Swiss always over-engineer everything [are so thinking-oriented], I'm sure it's good enough to go and make a difference to us [we are doing-oriented]." Tomas finally agreed to try. But the implementation had to be done through the Singapore office of the Swiss company, which was its Asian headquarters. The Singapore office was even more reluctant than Tomas, because the component wasn't ready (Singapore is even more strongly thinking-oriented). "What if they put it in place, and it creates more problems than it solves? Besides, we still haven't got the extra functionality worked out. It needs more development before we let it out." The customer reiterated, "We don't want that extra functionality. If it has these basic functions, that's great for now." Problems also arose around the contract. The US customer wanted a contract based on cost savings achieved, but the Swiss firm was used to charging prices based on features and technical standards, plus a maintenance contract. In the end, the customer waited for the product but was frustrated enough to negotiate much more difficult contracts afterwards. Tomas was frustrated and knew he had missed something, but wasn't sure what he could have done to convince the customer. If both had realized the nature of the cultural difference – the US doing and the Swiss and Singaporean thinking – then they might have been able to arrange something beneficial for everyone. For example, the US company could have been heavily involved in beta tests of the technology, paying for a technician from the Swiss company to be on-site at the factories, rather than paying for the technology itself.

In doing-oriented cultures, decisions tend to be made with pragmatic criteria, reward systems are results-based, and there is a compulsive concern for achieving tangible performance measures. These are the cultures that invented "to do" lists and extensive personal calendars that allow people to track their activities and accomplishments. In work and team settings, meetings are used to make decisions, and they close with everyone committing to action points. In cultures with a dominant thinking orientation, decisions are more likely to be made based on rational criteria, rewards are distributed logically with complex formulae, and output is measured against balanced objectives such as long- and short-term profitability, quality as well as quantity of production, and so on. While companies from all cultures use Balanced Scorecards to assess performance, companies with thinking-oriented cultures excel at them. They spend more time designing the process to identify what goes into the scorecard, tracking indicators with detailed measures, assessing the extent to which indicators relate to other dimensions of performance, and designing reward systems that fit the performance shown by the indicators.

Summary Doing and thinking orientations are strong in all cultures, at least in the business and management aspects of the cultures. Things are planned, and actions are taken. However, different cultures tend to prioritize the doing or the thinking mode. They agree that in most situations it is better either to act more, or to plan more. Since business situations themselves are complex, international organizations that encompass both types of culture have opportunities to leverage these differences.

The Other Orientations Kluckhohn and Strodtbeck's framework identified three other orientations that describe issues cultures need to address. According to our research, although they are intuitively appealing and describe aspects of cultures we notice, they are not particularly reliable at differentiating country cultures. We describe them here briefly since they are often helpful in describing company or department cultures.

Belief about basic human nature The belief about basic human nature does not reflect how one thinks about individuals, but rather one's belief about the inherent character of the human species. What is the fundamental nature of infants before they are affected by their environment? What would humans be like if they all had the "right" environment? Can you trust strangers? This orientation asks two basic questions. First, are humans primarily *evil, good, neutral* (neither good nor evil), or *mixed* (a combination of good and evil)? Note that this is not a question about *behavior*, but about the basic nature. For example, in Christian faiths the story of Adam and Eve in the Garden of Eden is pertinent. Adam's eating of forbidden fruit symbolizes the "fall of man," as Adam gave in to the devil. This incident shows (to Christians) that the basic nature of humans is evil. However, the main task of a Christian is to overcome this basic nature, to resist temptation, and to *behave* according to the model of Christ, who was good. Some of today's more secular Christian perspectives tend to hold a more neutral or mixed orientation – "there is good in everyone." Our own understanding of Muslim and Shinto faiths and personal communications from Arab and Japanese proponents suggest that orientations emerging from these traditions are closer to the "good" end of the spectrum. The Baha'i view "begins with the notion that human beings are essentially good, and that evil is a corruption of our true human nature."[21] According to a Taiwanese friend, this same orientation is the main theme of a very popular Chinese children's story.

The second question is whether the fundamental nature of people is *changeable or unchangeable*. For example, in Christianity men and women are perfectible if they follow and worship God.[22] We see this debate frequently around political campaigns, foreign affairs discussions, and criminal litigation: can someone who has shown his or her nature to be bad change and become good? Note that we cannot "prove" either answer except through faith or argument; these are assumptions we make that affect our thoughts and behaviors.

These are interesting and clearly important questions that today are linked more closely with personal predispositions or religions than with country cultures per se.[23] For example, we could predict that in cultures with an assumption that humans are evil, there would be more control systems to prevent theft and fraud. However, given the effect of even one or a few people engaging in such behavior on the system, and the role of insurance companies in regulating companies' behavior, even in countries where the religion suggests that people's human nature is good, we see strong control systems.

Orientation to time There are two ways to think about time. The first involves a general orientation toward time; the second relates to how people think about or use specific units of time.[24]

A culture's general orientation to time reflects the time-related criteria used to make decisions, interpret events, or prioritize actions. For example, in a *past*-oriented culture, people respond to a new challenge by looking to tradition and wondering: "How have others dealt with this kind of problem before?" If people primarily consider the immediate effects of an action, then the dominant orientation is more likely to be *present*-oriented. If the chief concern is "What are the long-term consequences of this choice?" then the dominant orientation can be described as *future*-oriented.

One author of this text remembers vividly his Sicilian grandfather's answers to questions. The grandfather would invariably frame his answers in the form of vignettes and start with: "Well, I remember that my father would always tell me. . . ." In contrast, the author's father, who had been born in the United States, almost always answered: "What is it that you want to accomplish?" Then he would give his advice, usually in the form of alternatives rather than answers. This example also illustrates that generations within a culture often subscribe to different subcultures!

Our research suggests that this general time orientation is more related to company cultures than to country cultures. In this way, country cultures are shifting. While it used to be the case that Japanese companies, for example, were very long-term focused, with lifetime employment and long planning horizons (such as Konsuke Matsushita's famous 250-year corporate plan[25]), today they are shifting, and many companies are losing these traditions in the interests of efficiency. On the other hand, it used to be the case that American companies were focused only on tomorrow's returns. While most US-based companies still look first to the current quarter's results, the assumption that this is the best indicator of performance is being questioned. Within a given country, some companies are much more focused on longer planning horizons and reward systems, which tend to be associated with a combination of past and future orientations; while others are focused on short planning horizons and reward systems, more associated with a present orientation.

Another aspect of time orientation that strongly influences behavior asks the questions: What are the most important units of time, and how does time flow? In some cultures, time is broken up into small, specific, equal units, and it is assumed to flow in a linear fashion. These cultures are called *monochronic* cultures. In these cultures, such as most Anglo cultures, time is a valuable commodity. People save, spend, and waste time. People live by their schedules, and punctuality is valued. In Switzerland, the famous Swiss railway system apologizes publicly if a train is more than one minute late, which is a very rare occurrence; in Japan there is no need to apologize – the trains are always exactly on time! Punctuality is defined by the most natural division of time. Pay attention to when people start to explain why they are late, or offer an apology for their tardiness, and you will have a clue to what is the natural division of time for that society.

In *polychronic* cultures, time is seen as elastic. Units may be small or large, depending on what is being done or experienced at the time. Several timelines flow in parallel, and people believe it is natural to be doing many things at the same time. Arab and Latin cultures are typical polychronic cultures. In these cultures, time schedules are less critical. It might be 45 minutes to an hour before an apology or explanation for being late is expected, and among friends no explanation is ever needed. In polychronic cultures, individuals who are driven to meet schedules and deadlines are seen as lacking patience, tact, or perseverance. Polychronic cultures are often also collective, and they use the parallel modes as a way to build relationships. Someone from a monochronic, less collective culture may want to "get down to business" quickly, which prevents taking the time to develop relationships. Many Americans and western Europeans have stories of how they have destroyed opportunities to conduct business or negotiate contracts by underestimating the combination of collectivism and polychronic time orientation!

Monochronic and polychronic time is related to country cultures, but it is in the midst of a transition related to globalization. The increase in global interdependence we discussed in Chapter 1 has led to an increase in coordination, and coordination requires both a monochronic base for planning and a polychronic approach for dealing with inevitable changes. So although countries tend to prefer a monochronic or polychronic approach, global businesspeople have developed an appreciation for the necessity of both. Moreover, the formal global business culture is probably shifting more towards monochronic. However, if one is doing business with people from another culture beyond basic transactions, then one will encounter the monochronic-polychronic difference in the rest of the culture. Managers will be able to perform more effectively if they can navigate this dimension well, regardless of what happens on the surface.

One of the authors recently went on a trip to Saudi Arabia, as a guest of a large multinational there. The author received a four-day agenda two weeks in advance, and it was meticulously planned to the 15-minute interval. The agenda included many non-company meetings and locations, in order to help the author learn to understand the complexity of the culture. The company had planned according to monochronic time, and this was greatly appreciated. Once the author arrived in Saudi Arabia, about half of the agenda happened in ways other than what was planned, with often quite dramatic changes in events, timings, or people involved. The implementation of the event was more polychronic, and this was also appreciated since the guides took advantage of whatever would work best at the time. In this way, the author was able to see much more of the culture and appreciate the people who have created success there.

Use of space   The variable in space orientation has to do with how one is oriented towards surrounding space.[26] How does one view its use, especially the sense of "ownership" of space relative to others? This dimension is also related to ownership of whatever is in the space, including information and resources. The *private* perspective holds that space is for the exclusive use of an occupant, and that information and resources are privately owned. Space is for an occupant's benefit, and it defines a large area surrounding the occupant as part of that person's territory. Protective action is taken if this larger area is "invaded" by others. In contrast, the *public* orientation sees space as available for anyone's use. The sense of territory is small, and defensive action to guard against invasion is taken only in the immediate area around the occupant. The *mixed* orientation is a blend of the private and public perspectives – an intermediate position.

The spatial dimension can have an impact on communication, influence, and interaction patterns and on physical realities such as office and building layout. On one hand, managers operating in a culture dominated by a private orientation are more likely to find themselves communicating on a one-to-one basis in a closed, serial pattern. Physically, these managers are most comfortable having a fair amount of distance between them when talking directly to each other. On the other hand, managers interacting in a culture dominated by a public orientation are more likely to engage in a wide variety of interactions using an open style. Their conversations may involve several people simultaneously, and physically close relations will not be uncommon. Gestures will be broad and will use space expansively. Cultures with a mixed orientation influence managers to be more selective in their communications, with moderately separated space between people and somewhat more organized, semiprivate arrangements.

As with the human nature and general time orientation, we find that space is more associated with company cultures than with country cultures. It is important to understand how the company and managers you are working with think about space, but we cannot create country-based maps for this orientation.

Cultural Orientations Framework Summary   The framework is summarized in Figure 2.7, which gives brief definitions of each dimension. The chart is helpful to refer to when you are entering into or trying to understand new cultures. Use the chart to develop ideas about what aspects of the culture to observe, and which questions to ask. It is particularly helpful if you understand your own perspectives, through either self-reflection or perhaps doing the survey yourself.[27]

The Discipline of Cartography

Being able to map involves more than the knowledge of the framework. It requires *using* the framework to understand, explain, and predict others' attitudes and behavior. Mapping creates awareness and appreciation of differences and their implications in a structured and consistent way. It begins a conversation about similarities and differences using a common language and framework, and allows the conversation to move quickly and constructively to individual and situational differences. Like cartographers, managers need to combine various sources of information to create their own dynamic maps and use them to navigate complex territories. Just like any other skill, managers can practice Mapping and improve their ability to map. With practice, they begin to see patterns in the values and actions of other people and to understand those patterns from the other people's own perspectives.

The Limits of Maps   Mapping is a good first step to cross-cultural understanding, but it is important to recognize its limits. We describe the four most important ones here.

The first is that *individuals do not always conform to their cultures.* Variety and unpredictability are both the beauty and the complexity of human nature. We are all different, and we do not always behave as predicted! Within cultures, some people hold more strongly to the cultural norms than others. Personality and environmental factors influence individual behavior. Even people who are strong proponents of their culture's values do not always behave in a way that is consistent with those values.[28] This limitation is called the *ecological fallacy*: by knowing the culture (ecological level) you cannot always predict individuals; by knowing an individual, you cannot automatically predict the culture. Figure 2.8 illustrates this principle with data from our research, showing distributions of mastery scores in the US and Taiwan. In this figure you can see that there are individuals who are *atypical* of their cultural group, and others who cluster around the norm. You can see that there are differences between the two cultural groups: on average, Americans

FIGURE 2.7 Summary of the Cultural Orientations Framework

Orientation	Variations			
Relation to the Environment How do we relate to the world around us? This includes the physical world but also the economic and social world.	**Harmony** The environment is a complex system of which we are one part. Our actions should keep the system in balance, then everything will work well.	**Mastery** The environment is separate from us, and something to be managed. Our actions should influence and control the environment to get things to work well.	**Subjugation** The environment and ourselves within it are influenced or controlled by some other force, such as God or fate. Our actions should be consistent with that other force, and should implement the plans.	
Relations among People How do we think about relationships of power and responsibility among people?	**Collective** People in the group should be responsible for each other, and everyone is responsible to fulfill the group's needs. The group may be the extended family, the community, or any other large group.	**Individual** Each of us should be responsible for him- or herself alone, and perhaps the immediate family if necessary. Society works better if everyone looks after him- or herself.	**Hierarchy** Power and responsibility are arranged such that those above have power over those below, and responsibility for them. Those below should obey the wishes of those above.	
Mode of Activity What is the basic sequence of activity we agree to use together?	**Doing** We agree it is important to jump into action. When in doubt, do something.	**Thinking** We agree it is important to plan carefully, before taking action. When in doubt, plan and analyze.	**Being** We agree it is important to do things in their own time, to express spontaneity. When in doubt, do what feels right.	
Nature of Humans What is the basic, underlying nature of the human condition?	**Good** The underlying nature of people is basically good; when people do bad things it is the environment that is influencing them.	**Neutral** The underlying nature of people is mixed or neutral; the environment influences whether they become bad or good.	**Evil** The underlying nature of people is basically evil; people should try to overcome this nature and do good things.	**Changeable/ Unchangeable** People's underlying nature can be changed: good people can turn bad, and vice versa.
Time How do we use time horizons in decision-making?	**Past** We agree it's best to make decisions based on tradition or past precedent.	**Present** We agree it's best to make decisions based on present needs.	**Future** We agree it's best to make decisions based on long-term future needs.	
How do we measure and use time in an ongoing way?	**Monochronic** We measure time in linear, equal units. We prefer to do one thing at a time, then move to the next. Punctuality is important.	**Polychronic** We think of time as flexible, and we do many things at a time. Punctuality is less important than doing things in their time.		
Space How do we see and use physical space?	**Private** Space and the things in it belong to people; privacy and ownership are important.	**Public** Space and the things in it belong to everyone; sharing is important.	**Mixed** We use public space for some things, private for others.	

Note: Although these are presented in rows, there is no correspondence or correlation. For example, a culture that is harmony-oriented is not necessarily also collective-oriented. Every combination is possible.

FIGURE 2.8 Individual Distributions of Mastery Scores in Taiwan and the United States

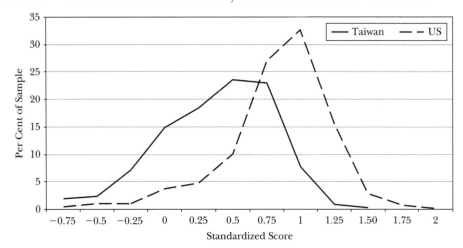

score higher on mastery than Taiwanese, but there are overlaps, too. Some individuals in each cultural group are more like those in the *other cultural group*! On the Cultural Perspectives Questionnaire, most people are close to their country's norm on most variations, and quite different on at least some variations. However, most people perceive of themselves as atypical of their culture. Think about yourself; are you more or less typical of the cultural group you identify yourself with?

Second, *all individuals belong to multiple cultures, and types of cultures, simultaneously.* Jemilah, for example, considers herself part of the Malaysian, Malay, Chinese, medical doctor, Muslim, female, mother, humanitarian aid, and global business cultures, and she articulates clearly what it means to be part of each of those cultures. Which culture she draws upon to guide her perceptions and behaviors depends on her context. She is always guided by her religious culture, covering her hair with a scarf in public, observing prayers and other disciplines, and reflecting in her behavior the lessons of the Prophet and the Koran. She is proud of her Malaysian culture and a strong advocate of Malaysians worldwide. She also celebrates Chinese holidays and traditions, and has close ties with her Chinese family. When delivering babies at the hospital, she behaves according to the norms and values of the medical doctor culture. When providing medical aid in an emergency situation, such as after natural disasters in Indonesia or Myanmar or as a result of conflict in Iraq or Gaza, she disregards some of the procedures typical of the hospital culture and behaves according to the emergency (for example, doing surgery outside her area of specialization), consistent with the humanitarian aid culture. When negotiating for resources with corporate sponsors for her humanitarian organization, Mercy Malaysia,[29] or when gaining access to emergency situations, she acts according to the global business culture, and she is well-respected as a tough player. She does not always choose to act according to a single culture, because she carries all these cultures in her, and often uses several at the same time to guide her behavior. For example, when trying to get emergency supplies to a conflict site, she uses both the humanitarian aid and the global business culture, and leverages her identity and expertise as a doctor to establish her credibility.

Jemilah's set of cultural identities is more complex than many people's. She is one of a growing minority of people in the world who are considered bicultural by having two (or more) ethnic cultures. Research on biculturalism shows that people who grow up with two or more cultures, such as children of immigrants or children whose parents come from two cultures, face unique challenges in developing their identity but also can develop advantages such as flexibility and cognitive complexity.[30] They manage these identities in different ways, for example they may prioritize one identity over another, they may separate them and draw on each in different situations, or they may combine them in various ways.[31] Although Jemilah is an extreme example, it is important to remember that the pattern is common to everyone, and we all identify with multiple cultures.[32]

Third, cultures are much more *complex* than can be described simply by these orientations with their aggregate variations. The configuration of preferences themselves leads to complex differences. Mastery combined with doing, for example, looks different from mastery combined with thinking. Mastery-doing is associated with obsessive task activity for accomplishment; mastery-thinking is associated with more depth in analysis before controlling. More importantly, the dimensions cannot ever capture the richness of cultures. We have provided examples to illustrate some of the principles, but the art, music, literature, traditions, practices, and beliefs of cultures go far beyond these dimensions. As we discussed earlier, multiple cultures exist in the same social "space" simultaneously. The existence of subcultures and complementary cultures also adds to the complexity of culture.

Finally, cultures are *dynamic*, always changing. In fact, Kluckhohn and Strodtbeck argued that cultures must change or they will stagnate and die, and that change is made possible by the variation of individuals within cultures and the existence of subcultures.[33] Usually change is quite slow, but sometimes external and internal events combine to create fast change. For example, when we look at some cultures in transition, we see differences between people 35 and younger versus people 36 and older. In Japan, Singapore, and China, the younger group is significantly lower on hierarchy and on thinking than the older group. In Russia, China, and Italy, the younger group scores higher on individualism than the older group. Generational differences can be seen as creating both conflicts and social movements within the countries, and it will be interesting to see the dynamics in another generation. In the Anglo and northern European countries, in contrast, there are no differences between younger and older respondents.

The Map is Not the Territory To summarize the main lesson in the second part of this chapter: maps are critical tools for navigation, but it is important to remember that the map is not the territory. In its most basic form, Mapping is sophisticated stereotyping. Sophisticated stereotyping is describing cultures using objective, nonevaluative data to predict thinking and behavior patterns of the culture's members.[34] As we illustrated above, sophisticated stereotyping is extremely helpful when we enter new situations or try to understand unexpected events. People who go into new countries and cultures without sophisticated stereotypes, saying "I have no expectations, I have an open mind," are really assuming "I think they will be like me." This is due to the basic human processes related to the assumptions and perceptions described earlier in this chapter.

As research has shown, when people go into a new situation with a map of expectations concerning how the others are likely to be different from oneself – sophisticated stereotypes – they are more prepared for differences in thinking and behavior, and they manage those differences much better.[35]

CULTURE IS THE CONTEXT OF INTERNATIONAL MANAGEMENT

Knowledge about culture is one of the most important foundations of both cultural intelligence and the broader global mindset. Culture is the context in which international management is conducted. Culture provides guidance for how to decide and behave, and provides an important source of identity for its members. To build towards cultural intelligence and the global mindset, we discussed culture-general knowledge in depth: knowledge about how culture influences its members. We also provided a framework for developing and using culture-specific knowledge that managers should find useful for organizing their interpretations of cultures with which they operate.

It is possible to ignore cultural difference for a short time or for basic transactions – that is, to operate without cultural intelligence or a global mindset – especially if you have power or other resources. However, it is impossible to create high performance or sustain performance over time in a multinational business world without a sophisticated understanding of culture, and an ability to draw on the strengths of different cultures in different situations. Moreover, all international managers we know agree that cultural differences create the most interesting, dynamic, and ever-enjoyable canvas possible on which to paint a management career!

Notes

1   Thomas, D., Maznevski, M., *et al* "Cultural Intelligence: Domain and Assessment," *International Journal of Cross Cultural Management, 8* (2008); Thomas, D. C. and Inkson, K., *Cultural Intelligence* (San Francisco: Berrett Koehler, 2004).

2   Goleman, D., *Emotional Intelligence* (Bantam Publishers, 1995).

3   Kluckhohn, F. and Strodtbeck, F., *Variations in Value Orientations* (New York: Row, Peterson & Company, 1961). Hofstede, G. H., *Cultures and organizations: Software of the mind* (Maidenhead, Berkshire, England: McGraw-Hill Book Company Europe, 1991).

4   For an elegant and powerful work on the risks of defining oneself with only a single identity (or allowing others to define you as having only one identity) see Maalouf, A., *In the Name of Identity* (New York: Penguin Books, 2000).

5   http://www.economist.com/markets/bigmac/index.cfm. Accessed November 1, 2008.

6   http://www.consumerreports.org/cro/food/beverages/coffee-tea/coffee-taste-test-3-07/overview/0307_coffee_ov_1.htm. Accessed November 1, 2008.

7   Erez, M. and Earley, P. C. (1993) *Culture, Self-Identity, and Work* (Oxford: Oxford University Press: 1993).

8   Weick, K., *The Social Psychology of Organizing* (Reading MA, Addison-Wesley Publishing Co., 1979).

9   Berry, J. *et al, Cross Cultural Psychology: Research and Applications* (Cambridge, UK; Cambridge University Press, 1992) 8.

10 Hall, E. T., "The silent language in overseas business," *Harvard Business Review,* 38(3) (1960) 87–96.

11 Hofstede, G. H., *Culture's consequences: International differences in work related values* (La Jolla, CA: Sage Publications, 1980). Also in 1980: "Motivation, leadership and organization: Do American theories apply abroad?" *Organizational Dynamics*, 9(1) (1980) 42–63. Hofstede, G. H., *Culture's consequences: comparing values, behaviors, institutions, and organizations across nations*, 2nd edn (Thousand Oaks, Calif.: Sage Publications, 2001).

12 Chinese Culture Connection, "Chinese values and the search for culture-free dimensions of culture," *Journal of Cross-Cultural Psychology*, 18(2) (1987) 143–164. Hofstede, G. H., *Cultures and organizations: Software of the mind* (rev. edn) (New York: McGraw-Hill, 1997).

13 House R. J., Hanges, P. J., Javidan, M., Dorfman, P., and Gupta, V. (eds), *GLOBE, Cultures, Leadership, and Organizations: GLOBE Study Of 62 Societies* (Sage Publications: Newbury Park, CA, 2003).

14 Hampden-Turner, C. and Trompenaars, F., *The seven cultures of capitalism* (New York: Currency Doubleday, 1993). Also Trompenaars, F. and Hampden-Turner, C. *Riding the waves of culture: Understanding cultural diversity in global business*, 2nd edn (New York: Irwin Professional Publications, 1998).

15 Schwartz, S. H. (1994) "Beyond individualism/collectivism: New cultural dimensions of values," in Kim, U., Triandis, H. C., Kagitcibasi, C., Choi, S., and Yoon, G. (eds), *Individualism and collectivism: Theory, method, and applications* (Thousand Oaks, CA: Sage, 1994) 85–119. Schwartz (1999); Sagiv and Schwartz (2000). Schwartz, S. H. (1999) "A theory of cultural values and some implications for work," *Applied Psychology-an International Review-Psychologie Appliquee-Revue Internationale*, 48(1) (1999) 23–47. Sagiv. L., and Schwartz. S. H., "A new look at national culture: Illustrative applications to role stress and managerial behavior," in Ashkenasy, N. M., Wilderom, C. P. M., and Peterson, M. F. (eds), *The Handbook of Organizational Culture and Climate* (Newbury Park, CA: Sage, 2000) 417–435.

16 Kluckhohn, F. R. and Strodtbeck, F. L., *Variations in value orientations* (New York: Row, Peterson & Company, 1961).

17 Maznevski, M. L., DiStefano, J. J., Gomez, C. B., Noorderhaven, N. G., and Wu, P.-C., "Cultural Dimensions at the Individual Level of Analysis: The Cultural Orientations Framework," *International Journal of Cross-Cultural Management*, 2(3) (2002) 275–295.

18 To take the survey yourself and obtain your scores (the "you are here" point on the map), please go to www.imd.ch/research/cpq.

19 Perret, M. S., *The Impact of Cultural Differences on Budgeting.* (unpublished doctoral dissertation, London, Canada: The University of Western Ontario, 1982).

20 Gibson, C. B. and Zellmer-Bruhn, M. "Metaphor and Meaning: An intercultural Analysis of the Concept of Teamwork," *Administrative Science Quarterly*, 46 (2001) 274–303.

21 "Introduction," *To the Peoples of the World – A Statement on Peace* (Thornhill, Ontario: The Baha'i Council of Canada, 1990).

22 Note that if one believes that by following the religious tenets only the *behavior* of people changes but not the fundamental *nature* (which remains marked by original sin), then the orientation would be evil/unchangeable.

23 Whitener, E. M., Maznevski, M. L., Sæbo, S., and Ekelund, B., *Testing the Cultural Boundaries of a Model of Trust: Subordinate-Manager Relationships in Norway and the United States.* Presented at Academy of Management Annual Meetings, Chicago, August 1999.

24 For a more complete treatment of the time variable, see Hall, E. T., *The silent language* (New York: Doubleday and Co, 1959).

25 Lightfoot, R. W. and Bartlett, C. A., "Philips and Matsushita: A portrait of two evolving companies," in *Transnational management: Text, cases and readings in cross-border management*, edited by Bartlett, C. A. and Ghoshal, S. (Homewood, IL: Richard D. Irwin, 1992) 82.

26 Hall, E. T. "The silent language," in Hall, E. T., *The hidden dimension* (Garden City, NY: Doubleday, 1966), where the subject of space is even more fully developed.

27   To take the survey yourself and obtain your scores (the "you are here" point on the map), please go to www.imd.ch/research/cpq.

28   Gibson, C. B., Maznevski, M. L., and Kirkman, B. L., "When Does Culture Matter?" Bhagat, R. S. and Steers, R. M. (eds), *Handbook of Culture, Organizations, and Work.* Cambridge University Press, 2009).

29   Dr Jemilah Mahmoud, President of Mercy Malaysia, personal communications. www.mercy.org.my

30   Thomas, D. C., "Biculturalism pays," *National Post,* November 11, 2008, Toronto, Canada. *Multiple Modes of Biculturalism: Antecedents and Outcomes,* Fitzsimmons, S. R., unpublished Ph.D. dissertation, Simon Fraser University, Canada; 2009. Brannen, M., Thomas, D., Roth, K., Cheng, C., Locke, G., Garcia, D., Lee, F., and Fitzsimmons, S., "Biculturalism in the global marketplace: Integrating research and practice," Symposium presented at the Academy of Management Meetings, August 2008, Anaheim, CA. Cheng, C., Lee, F., and Benet-Martinez, V. "Assimilation and Contrast Effects in Cultural Frame Switching (CFS): Bicultural Identity Integration (BII) and Valence of Cultural Cues," *Journal of Cross Cultural Psychology* 37(6) (2006) 1–19. Brannen, M. Y. and Salk, J., "Partnering across borders: Negotiating organizational culture in a German-Japanese joint venture," *Human Relations,* Vol. 53, No. 4, 451–487 (2000). Leu, J., Benet-Martinez, V., and Lee, F., "Bicultural identities: Dynamics, individual differences, and socio-cognitive correlates," *International Journal of Psychology* 35 (2000). Brannen, M. Y., "Organizational Culture in a Bi-national Context: A Model of Negotiated Culture," *Anthropology of Work Review,* Vol. 13, No. 2, 1992.

31   Fitzsimmons, S. R. (August 2007), "Multiple modes of being bicultural," in Brannen, M. Y. (Chair), *Neither/nor or both/and? Understanding, nurturing and leveraging biculturalism as a strategic human resource.* Symposium conducted at the meeting of AoM, Anaheim, California.

32   Phillips, M. E. and Sackmann, S. A., "Managing in an Era of Multiple Cultures" Finding synergies instead of conflict" *Graziadio Business Report,* Pepperdine University, 2002, Volume 5, Issue 4. http://gbr.pepperdine.edu/024/multi-cultural.html, accessed January 9, 2009. This article was excerpted and adapted from Boyacigiller, N. A., Kleinberg, M. J., Phillips, M. E., and Sackmann, S. A., "Conceptualizing Culture: Elucidating the Streams of Research in International Cross-Cultural Research," in Punnett, B. J. and Shenkar, O. (eds), *Handbook of International Management Research* 2nd edn, (Ann Arbor: University of Michigan Press, 2004).

33   Kluckhohn and Strodtbeck, n. 16 above.

34   Adler, N. J., *International Dimensions of Organizational Behavior, 3rd edn,* (South-Western College Publishing, Cincinnati Ohio, 1997). Bird, A. and Osland, J., "Beyond sophisticated stereotyping: Cultural sense-making in context," *Academy of Management Executive,* 14 (2000) 65 –79.

35   Ratiu, I., "Thinking internationally: A comparison of how international executives learn," *International Studies of Management and Organization,* 13(1-2) (1983) 139–150.

CHAPTER **3**

The MBI Model for High Performance

Which performs better – a diverse team or a homogeneous team? It's a trick question of course, and the answer is the same as the answer to any management question: "It depends." Let's take a closer look.

First, it depends on what we mean by *diverse*. There is, of course, no such thing as a completely homogeneous team. Everyone on a team is different from each other. But some teams are more diverse than others. For example, a team of six people who are men and women from different countries and ethnic cultures, professions, and organizations, is more diverse than a team of six men or women from the same country and culture, profession, and organization. In today's organizations, teams are more diverse than they were in the past. With increased workforce diversity, more organizational structures with units that reach across professional and country borders, and with more alliances across organizations, teams inevitably are composed of people from more diverse backgrounds. As we discussed in the previous chapter, cultural differences, and in particular, country-based cultural differences, are an important source of difference in perspectives and values.

Second, it depends on what we mean by *performance*. A diverse team brings many different perspectives to a task. This diversity increases divergent processes in teams – processes related to creativity and questioning of assumptions to develop new ideas.[1] If the task is a routine, structured task, such as calculating the best combination of production runs, then this diversity may not bring any advantages, and in fact the group may have difficulty becoming aligned around a solution. But if the task is an unstructured, ambiguous task, such as developing a strategy for a new market, then the diversity may bring helpful perspectives. Furthermore, because diverse groups tend to have broader sets of networks than homogeneous groups do, diverse groups can be better set up to implement change effectively.

Third, and most importantly, *it depends on how you manage the interactions in the team.* Some teams use their diversity effectively, combining ideas and building on them to create new and better ways of doing business. We call these teams "creators." Other teams we refer to as "destroyers;" they let the differences lead to destructive conflict and personal disputes, ending up with poor solutions. Most teams do something safer – they suppress differences and pretend the differences don't exist. These "equalizer" teams focus on similarities among team members.[2] This is usually done for noble reasons ("it's what we have in common that matters"), but the strategy has two problems. The obvious shortfall is that it does not realize the potential of the team. It leaves unused resources on the table, and suboptimizes decision quality and implementation. "Okay," some managers respond, "maybe it's not worth the effort or the risk of conflict. It could be a good rational decision not to invest in the diversity." Yes, in the short term.

But the second problem is both more subtle and more damaging. Have you ever worked on a team where you felt like you couldn't be yourself? Where you had to work, for a sustained period of time, in a way that was not comfortable for you? When people's perspectives and ways of working are suppressed over time, they act through a filter and are constantly spending energy thinking about *how* to present their ideas and *how* to participate, rather than on creating and presenting ideas and reflecting on others' ideas in the first place. Most people in this situation eventually become frustrated and disengaged. They may even initiate serious conflicts or, more likely, simply leave the team. The "equalizer" strategy reduces the challenges of diversity in the short term, but over time it ends up sliding into the "destroyer" strategy.

Diverse teams can perform better than homogeneous teams, and multicultural teams can perform particularly well, if they manage the diversity constructively. Our research shows that performance in diverse teams, especially multicultural ones, derives from a basic set of interactions we call Map-Bridge-Integrate, or MBI.[3] *MBI processes are so fundamental that they are necessary not only for teams to perform well, but for effective and constructive interaction among any people who have different backgrounds and related perspectives and values, whether they are leader–subordinate, co-workers, partners in a customer–supplier alliance, or managers adapting business practices from one place to another.* In this chapter we focus on the MBI processes themselves, and in the next, we add other layers of complexity associated with global teams.

Mapping is about understanding cultural and other differences among each other. Bridging is communicating effectively, taking those differences into account. Integrating is bringing the different perspectives together and building on them. When these three skills are executed well, interactions between individuals or among team members result in high performance. The basic model is shown in Figure 3.1. Integrating leads directly to effectiveness, but Bridging accounts for more than two-thirds of the variance in Integrating. In other words, if Bridging is done well, Integrating almost follows naturally; if Bridging is not done well, there is likely to be no Integrating. Moreover, Bridging cannot be done without good Mapping, no matter how skilled or well-intentioned are the people involved. Below, we discuss and illustrate each of these skills.

FIGURE 3.1   The MBI Model in Brief

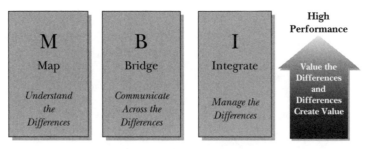

MAPPING TO UNDERSTAND AND DESCRIBE DIFFERENCES

In Chapter 2, "Intercultural Effectiveness in International Management," we introduced the metaphor of mapping culture. Mapping is systematically and objectively describing characteristics of people and identifying similarities and differences that can be used to help each other perform. The most useful Mapping uses data and summaries of facts, organized with frameworks that help compare the data and facts across groups and individuals. In Chapter 2 we described the results of our research with the Cultural Perspectives Questionnaire, which maps culture. It is possible – and often desirable – to map other characteristics such as personality, profession, or gender.

Most people are afraid of Mapping because they worry it will lead to stereotyping. They resist being put into a box as an unthinking representative of a group, and do not want to categorize others that way. This is a healthy fear and resistance, and we encourage it. Like any tool, Mapping can be misused. However, Mapping is such a powerful tool that it is worth using. Maps are objective descriptions of characteristics that are relevant to an interaction. They help people respect each others' values and perspectives, and give people suggestions about how to use each others' ideas better. Maps are revised whenever new data are available, and are constantly tested as hypotheses rather than taken for granted as truths. Maps should be seen as windows to the complex territory of human beings, ways of entering the different perspectives and really seeing the person inside.

Stereotypes, on the other hand, are subjective descriptions of groups of people that are usually used to judge those people, often in a negative way. Stereotypes are assumed to be true and are neither tested nor changed with new information. They usually lead people to close doors – making assumptions about how people will behave – rather than open windows. The differences between Mapping and stereotyping are subtle, but important. Mapping leads to healthy dynamics among individuals, with people casting aside the maps as they develop more insight into the territory.

Above we described "equalizer" teams, those that focus only on similarities. Research shows that without explicit intervention, teams tend to spend most of their time discussing information that all team members share, and only a small portion of the time discussing information that only one or a few team members have.[4] This dynamic is not conducive to high performance, especially if the task is complex and multidimensional. Explicit Mapping is an excellent way to avoid this dynamic. If team members are aware

FIGURE 3.2   MBI: Mapping

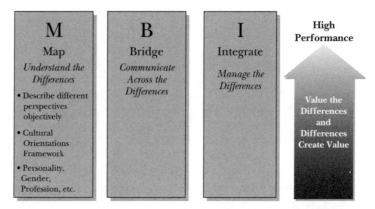

of the different perspectives – the different points on the map – and of the potential contributions, they are more likely to bring them into team discussions and to create better solutions. Among individuals, such as between a leader and a subordinate or between a customer and a supplier, Mapping helps prevent conflict and aids in seeing opportunities. The more the people involved understand the nature of each other's different perspectives, the more they can use those differences to achieve high performance. Mapping is summarized in Figure 3.2

Mapping in Action – A New Team

We are often asked, "How important is it to sit down and create detailed maps, for example, with survey data about individuals involved, or can you just know the general patterns and map from there?" As a manager, you must make a trade-off between investment and results. Explicit Mapping does take time, but it pays off in more ideas coming into the group, more comprehensive examination and analysis of the ideas, and more possibility of building on ideas in innovative ways. The more important the task and/ or the more diverse the people involved, the more critical Mapping is. In our experience, it is best for a group, such as a team or a leader and his or her subordinates, to go into detailed Mapping on two dimensions that are important to the group's work, such as culture and personality or gender, then use those discussions to access Mapping on any other relevant dimensions. The use of an outside facilitator to help with Mapping is not necessary, but some managers prefer it (by "outside," we mean outside the team or group of people, not necessarily outside the organization). If the leader is not comfortable with Mapping but knows it is important, or if the leader would prefer to be a neutral participant rather than lead the process, then an outside facilitator may be a good idea. Some maps, such as many personality surveys, must be administered and facilitated by a certified professional, so if you want to use these maps and no one in the group is certified, then an outside facilitator is necessary. On the other hand, a leader may want to have the team lead and facilitate the process themselves to empower the group.

As long as the process is facilitated to bring out and value individuals' contributions and perspectives, this is also constructive.

A New Team

Recently, Reinhard was appointed to lead the global marketing group for a new, highly innovative medical product. The product was based on a combination of robotic, bionic, wireless, and biologic technologies, and had the potential to revolutionize the treatment of debilitating diseases. It could be the "next big thing" for the company, and everyone involved was excited about the impact. Reinhard knew he needed a diverse team of professionals to tap into different ideas and different aspects of the task and the market, so he deliberately recruited his 10 direct reports to reflect a scope of organizational veterans and newcomers, medical professionals, engineers and social scientists, young and experienced people, and people from multiple country cultures and with different personality types.

Shortly after the team launched, Reinhard brought the team together for a Mapping exercise. Given the importance of the product launch, the sensitivity of the product, and the diversity of the team, he decided to work with an outside facilitator although he remained very active in the Mapping process and often took the lead. He first used an exercise called the Diversity Icebreaker, which uses a short survey and a specific process to get people to explore the different team roles they prefer to contribute and the implications for the team. The Diversity Icebreaker creates a positive environment for discussions about diversity, opening people up to Mapping and the entire MBI process.[5]

Reinhard had the team map personality and culture, the former using the Myers-Briggs Type Indicator (MBTI), the latter using the Cultural Perspectives Questionnaire. For each of these maps, the team discussed patterns associated with different dimensions, such as the examples we described for culture in Chapter 2, and identified each individual's position on the Map. Who prefers extraversion and who prefers introversion as a personality dimension? Who prefers mastery and who prefers harmony as a cultural dimension? In this Mapping discussion, people identified specific potential contributions of individual team members. For example, the mastery-oriented members will help us remember to take charge of the market, and identify what we can control; the harmony-oriented members will help us remember to keep in mind the whole medical system and all the different players, and how we can work through the system.

After these discussions, the team created a large grid on the wall, with team members' names down the left as rows and dimensions of diversity across the top as columns. The first columns were the Diversity Icebreaker, MBTI, and Cultural dimensions. Then they added professional background, generation (some were Baby Boomers, others were Generation X and Y), gender, organizational experience, family experience, and other life experiences, which consisted of travel, hobbies, and anything else they could think of. By the end of the process, team members were even more excited about working together, learning from each other, and using the different perspectives and some newly discovered commonalities to create a great product launch. As this book went to press, they were moving into planning the launch, so the results are not yet available, but all team members felt they were better prepared to manage challenges and achieve results than they would have been without the Mapping.

BRIDGING DIFFERENCES THROUGH COMMUNICATION

Mapping to understand the lens through which others see the world is an enormous aid to intercultural effectiveness. But this understanding provides little benefit as long as it remains latent. It must be put into use to help the flow of ideas among people in a conversation, a team, or an organization. The goal of these interpersonal flows is effective communication, or the transfer of meaning from one person to another as it was intended by the first person. Most managers recognize that effective communication within one's own culture is difficult enough. Interactions with people from different cultures are even more difficult. The challenge is to interpret correctly what a person from a different culture means by his or her words and actions. Even if interaction is aided by slowing speech, speaking more distinctly, listening more carefully, or asking more questions, there still remains the problem of interpreting the message. Resolving miscommunication depends, in large part, on a manager's willingness to explain the problem rather than to blame the other person. And the quality of the explanation depends, in large part, on the manager's ability to map the other person's culture or background with respect to his or her own.

Although language is an important part of communication, communication is not simply a matter of understanding and speaking a language. Communication is broader than language alone. Someone who is able to speak five different languages still may not be able to understand the issues from the viewpoint of those from another culture. Or put more eloquently by an Eastern European manager to the Australians in an English-speaking executive program, "I can speak to you in your language, but I can't always tell you what I am thinking in my own language."

There are three skills important to effective communication in a cross-cultural setting: Preparing, Decentering, and Recentering.[6] While it is true that these three skills help improve all communication, in interactions within a single culture the parties can generally assume the same set of background assumptions, so the steps can be conducted implicitly. The more culturally diverse the setting, though, the more difficult it is to accomplish these steps, and the more explicit they should be. But they also result in bigger payoffs. This Bridging component of the MBI model is summarized in Figure 3.3.

FIGURE 3.3   MBI: Bridging

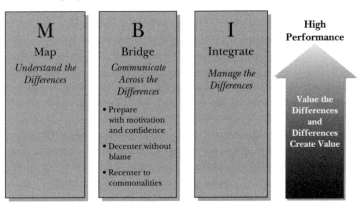

Prepare

Preparing is about setting the ground for communication. The most important place to set the ground is in one's own mind. Two attitudes are especially predictive of effective communication: motivation and confidence. Motivation is having the will to communicate across a cultural boundary both to be understood and to understand others. We are usually very good at the former, but not as good at the latter. The confidence part of preparing is to believe that it is possible to overcome any barriers and communicate effectively. Ironically, people with little cross-cultural experience and those who have never tried to understand others from the others' perspective tend to have high confidence, but that confidence often decreases with initial experiences and the realization of the complexity of the undertaking. However, with practice and success – as aided, for example, by the tools described here – confidence increases rapidly, and this later confidence has a much more realistic foundation.

These attitudes may sound simple to control, but their manifestation is complicated by some psychological tendencies we all have. They are inherent to our nature and normally serve us well, but tend to slip us up in cross-cultural interaction. More specifically, we tend to assume:[7]

1 The other person sees the situation the same way we do.
2 The other person is making the same assumptions we are.
3 The other person is (or should be) experiencing the same feelings as we are.
4 The communication situation has no relationship to past events.
5 The other person's understanding is (or should be) based on our own logic, not their feelings.
6 If a problem occurs, it is the other person who has the "problem" or does not understand the logic of the situation.
7 Other cultures are changing and becoming, or want to become, more like our culture and, therefore, the other person is becoming more like us.

While reading a book it may seem easy to keep these in mind, but in the rush and pressure of making decisions, we often forget to withhold judgment. There are some simple things to do that can facilitate the process, aside from just trying to remember to be motivated and confident. For example, expatriates who spend most of their time in the company of other expatriates often have little motivation to bridge the cultural communication gaps with locals. When they do run into difficulties at work, they have little practice at resolving them in more relaxed, nonwork settings. A more positive sign of motivation to communicate cross-culturally is learning the language of those with whom one is working. Nothing is more likely to signal your motivation for cross-cultural communication than such an effort. Of course, having confidence that you can learn the language and that, in doing so, you will be more effective, is in itself a boost to the motivation to learn. These two elements create a positive, reinforcing circle, since having the motivation to learn also boosts confidence in the possibility of improving cross-cultural communication.

Even without language training, there are ways of developing motivation and confidence in cross-cultural skills. Reading and studying about other countries' cultures, meeting people from the culture and asking them to help you immerse in the culture, watching their movies, and learning to apply other parts of this model are examples of how to increase confidence in your cross-cultural communication ability and how to demonstrate the motivation to do so. Mastering a cultural framework or "map," such as the one described in Chapter 2, is another way. This gives you the motivation and confidence to ask questions that will be especially helpful in preparing yourself for future understanding. Our research shows that it is possible to learn enough about the MBI model in a two-day training program to improve performance. There is ample reason for managers to feel both motivated and confident that preparing to bridge cultures can make a difference.

Decenter

Decentering is actively pushing yourself away from your own "center." It involves moving into the mind of the other person to send messages in a way the other will understand, and to listen in a way that allows you to understand them from their own point of view. In effect, one has a bicultural tongue and bicultural ears. The fundamental idea of decentering is empathy: feeling and understanding as another person does. But in the context of the communication model, decentering requires going beyond empathy, *using* one's empathy in hearing and speaking. A child sees two cookies on the table and is about to take both. The mother says, "Now, if you take both cookies, how will your sister feel?" The child knows her sister will feel terrible (strong empathy), but goes ahead and takes both cookies anyway (not decentering). This interaction happens all the time in cross-cultural situations. The Canadian manager says, "I know that as a Chinese it's hard for you to disagree openly with your boss, but I want you to know it's okay to do that with me. I don't mind when you disagree with me, in fact I expect you to." Or the Brazilian manager, "I know that in your [Scandinavian] culture it's not good to be open about feelings, but I am Brazilian and in my culture it's fine. So when I express my anger, don't worry, it's okay." We all know people who understand exactly how we feel, but nevertheless go ahead and say or do something awkward or hurtful anyway. This is practicing empathy without decentering.

There are two main elements to decentering. The first is perspective taking, which is the skill of being able to see things from the other person's point of view to the extent that you can speak and listen that way. The second is explaining without blame. When problems in communication do occur, and they inevitably will, it is critical that no one blames the other in a personal way, but that all parties seek an explanation in the situation: the differences in initial starting assumptions. *This last point cannot be emphasized enough. In our research this emerged as the single best predictor of effective cross-cultural interaction. People who withhold blame and search for situation-based explanations of miscommunication almost inevitably have more effective interaction.* Does this mean that all you have to do is explain without blame? No. But look at the sequence of events initiated when blame is suspended. This simple act leads a group into a positive cycle of decentering, exploring alternatives to build a shared reality, developing trust and common rules, and building confidence in the group's ability to use different perspectives productively. This conversation not only resolves the present miscommunication, but also prevents some further ones and provides ideas for creative synergy.

Good decentering is largely dependent on good Mapping. The map warns you that surprises and problems may have different explanations, and also provides you with some alternatives to explore. The describe-interpret-evaluate framework identified in Chapter 2 is also very helpful here. When differences are encountered, the people involved should try to come to a point where they can agree on a description: what are the tangible, concrete facts we are talking about? Next they should explore their different interpretations: what do those facts mean to each person, and why? This is where the map provides a common language for sharing the analysis of interpretations. Finally, they should try to understand the different evaluations of the facts: why do some people see something as an opportunity and others as a threat? In cross-cultural situations, the greater the tendency to judge events, the greater the probability of making errors. Resisting the interpretive and evaluative modes while maintaining a descriptive posture for as long as possible is the best protection against cultural gaffes.

Decentering in Action – Scandinavian Managers Abroad During our culture research studies, we developed a dialogue called "the Dark Side of Scandinavian Management." Scandinavian (the collective name that usually encompasses Norway, Sweden, and Denmark, sometimes Iceland, but not Finland, which is Nordic but not Scandinavian) management has often been described as unique, and several groups of Scandinavian managers asked us to help them understand the challenges they were facing when they worked with people from other cultures.[8] Based on our Cultural Perspectives Questionnaire study and work done by Smith *et al*,[9] we developed a data-based picture of the generic Scandinavian management style (Mapping). Although all organizations and all leaders are different, and the Scandinavian country cultures differ from each other, Scandinavian managers and those from other cultures who work with Scandinavians agreed that the picture was generally accurate. We mapped Scandinavian management style as (see Chapter 2 for more details):

- **Strongly collective** – the group is important, it is critical to get everyone aligned and on board, opinions of co-workers and subordinates are very important.
- **Strongly anti-hierarchical** – power and influence come not from your position but from your ideas and values and contributions to the group; considering your co-workers' and subordinates' ideas is often more important than considering your boss's ideas.
- **Action-oriented and pragmatic** – take control of situations, influence them, get things done, task focus, change actions as necessary to achieve the goals.
- **Not necessarily slow** – the stereotype of Scandinavian management style is that things move very slowly; however, the bias towards action is strong, and once the decision is made from group alignment, action is quick.

Based on this Mapping exercise, we created a typical conversation between a Scandinavian manager and his or her non-Scandinavian subordinates, probably outside Scandinavia. This hypothetical conversation brought tears of laughter to Scandinavian executives who recognized themselves in the middle of it:

1. Scandinavian manager . . . Asks subordinates and co-workers for their opinions, tries to negotiate alignment.

2. The others . . . Don't understand why the Scandinavian boss can't just decide. May want to make decision quickly so planning phase can begin.

3. Scandinavian manager . . . Responds to the requests and anxiety for decisions by asking more questions to get ideas and create alignment.

4. The others . . . Become even more frustrated with the lack of decision-making, complain that decision-making is SLOW, we'll never get to planning.

5. Scandinavian manager . . . Becomes paralyzed by not wanting to act in an authoritarian way. Not sure what to do.

6. The others . . . Become convinced that the process is SLOW, lose respect for the business capability of the Scandinavians.

7. Scandinavian manager . . . Finally, in frustration, makes and announces a decision.

8. The others . . . Relieved, voice agreement with the boss.

9. Scandinavian manager . . . Assumes agreement = alignment and signals readiness for action, moves onto considering other things.

10. The others . . . Either wait for further directions for action, or act in unaligned ways.

11. Scandinavian manager . . . Becomes frustrated by lack of action or unaligned action, waits for it to improve.

12. The others . . . Continue to wait or to act in many different directions.

13. Scandinavian manager. . . Becomes frustrated with unenlightened subsidiaries.

14. The others . . . Under-perform according to standards or expectations.

15. Scandinavian manager . . . "Knows" (assumes) that everyone will contribute to their potential for the group, and will self-correct performance. Does nothing.

16. The others . . . "Know" (assume) everything is fine because the boss has not said anything. Nothing changes.

17. Scandinavian manager . . . Waits patiently for performance to self-correct; perhaps manages the environment to make it easier for people to self-correct.

18. The others . . . Start to recognize performance problem but see that boss doesn't "care" about it. Nothing changes.

19. Scandinavian manager . . . Becomes frustrated with unenlightened, unempowered subsidiaries.

20. The others . . . Become convinced that Scandinavians avoid conflict and are weak managers.

This conversation shows what happens when decentering is *not* practiced by anyone involved. Notice the evolution to blaming on both sides – Scandinavian managers assuming the others are unenlightened, the others assuming Scandinavian managers are weak – that comes from not understanding each others' starting point. Scandinavian managers who are effective in other cultures say that they adapt this process through decentering in several ways. For example, although they believe that in most situations getting ideas from subordinates and developing alignment is the best way to make decisions and implement change, when they first go to a new culture where hierarchy is stronger, they are more likely to use their position as boss to manage explicitly a process of getting ideas from others – explaining the importance and "commanding" people to take part, contributing their own ideas directly (in Scandinavia they would more likely do so indirectly, for example, by expressing agreement with some subordinates), and using the hierarchy to dictate each part of the process. They are also more likely to incorporate specific planning into the early discussions, recognizing others' need to make firm plans.

On the other hand, the executives in these workshops volunteered that the real "dark side of Scandinavian management" emerges in crises. Precious time can be lost getting alignment and assuming people will act in a unified way, when what is really important is taking a single decision and clarifying a set of actions for everyone to follow together. These executives admitted that they had learned to manage in an "un-Scandinavian way" when crises arose, even within Scandinavia.

Recenter

The final step to effective communication is Recentering, or establishing a common reality and agreeing on common rules. Like the other elements, establishing a common reality is easier said than done. But it is much easier to see the need to do so, if one is aware of the types of differences between your own values and those of others. For example, the implicit definition and purpose of "a meeting" varies from one culture to the next, with some cultures using meetings to discuss perspectives and come to a joint decision, and other cultures using meetings to publicly formalize decisions that were discussed informally among smaller subgroups of a team. A multicultural team that has not addressed even this basic definition is bound to find at least some members very frustrated with the first meeting. Again, good mapping helps to find a common definition and give the team a point of leverage. For example, members of a multisite global R&D team differed enormously on Relationships and Environment orientations, but virtually all preferred thinking strongly over any other mode of activity. They were able to use their common ground of the need to plan and be rational to discuss their differences and work together. A team managing a strategic alliance in a manufacturing technology firm consisted of members from all over Europe, North America, and Asia. Like the team of R&D scientists, they had strong differences on many cultural orientations. Coincidentally, though, all were engineers for at least some part of their career, and they shared the same mastery orientation to the environment. Their common reality was based on what had to be done (changed and controlled), and they used this point to launch discussions about how to divide the work and what task processes to use.

Common norms for interacting must also be established. However, what is critical here is not necessarily agreeing on the same norms for everyone, but rather, agreeing what the acceptable norms are to be. It is futile to expect someone to behave in a way that is uncomfortable to them, yet still expect them to participate to their full potential. Asking someone with a predominantly thinking orientation to constantly jump in and "do" because that is the dominant mode and "you'll just have to adapt," is tantamount to asking that person not to bother contributing his or her best ideas to the group. The most effective groups find ways of allowing different members to work with the group differently. Finding these norms is a creative process. It takes time and relies on strong relationships and trust within the group. But, like good preparing and decentering, the effort is well worth it. When the processes are not explored or discussed to find common ground, serious misunderstandings can occur, even when the cultures are not dramatically different.

For this example we look at the subtle differences among Nordic cultures, rather than Scandinavian management as a generic whole. The following exchange took place between the Finnish operating head and a senior Swedish executive of a software company grown by a series of acquisitions across the Nordic countries.

The Senior Vice President Finn was explaining the decision process in the company:

> We reach our decisions by informal consultation "feeling out" positions, evolving into a common view of what should be done – what is possible, what alterations to each others' views are necessary, etc. This all occurs during the "feeling-out" process. Then when I think everything is clear I put the issue on the agenda of a meeting that ratifies the result of this process.

His Swedish colleague, who had been working as part of the senior executive team for nearly two years, interrupted and exclaimed heatedly:

> This is exactly the problem with you Finns! It [annoys] me very much when I don't have the opportunity to contribute . . . or even worse, I come to the meeting expecting it to be the first of a series of discussions and after I talk, you Finns give a PowerPoint presentation with the decision already included!! Don't insult me by pretending to ask for my involvement and opinion when you've already made up your mind!!

When he calmed down he explained more mildly:

> We Swedes expect a series of meetings, each an opportunity for extensive discussion among the participants, with all involved, until a consensus is achieved or an *explicit* decision is taken. Since Finns occupy many of the senior posts at headquarters, we often find ourselves really annoyed by the process. Now I know why!!

Recentering in Action – A Multicultural Team We captured a classic example of cross-cultural communication when we videotaped a group of executives discussing the possibility of their company acquiring another firm. The group consisted of five senior managers from the United States (two members), United Kingdom, Japan, and Uruguay, and we videotaped them at their request to help them develop their Bridging skills. After studying various aspects of the potential deal, they had come together to make a recommendation.

The discussion was dominated by the American and the British managers, who were concerned about the lack of compatible strategies and financial problems in the negotiations. In the first hour, two key incidents happened which showed the need for recentering. First, the Uruguayan manager tried three times to introduce the issue of who would constitute the top executive team should the deal be struck. Would the buying company or the acquired organization supply the key executives for the merged entity? But each time he tried to raise the issue, the three others brushed his comments aside. Soon their dominance in the discussion extinguished the South American's view of what was important. Second, after 40 minutes of discussion, the British manager stood up in the room and went to the flip chart and wrote: "Do Nothing!" He punctuated his writing by saying, "I don't usually entertain this option, which is always raised as a 'straw man' by business school professors, but I really think in this situation it is our best choice. The deal is far from being ready to make for a whole host of reasons." There was a moment of silence, then the Japanese manager cleared his throat and quietly said, "Wait." The others thought that he was asking for a chance to discuss the "Do Nothing" option, but only a silence ensued. After a barely discernible pause, the British manager crossed out "Do Nothing" and wrote next to it, "Wait," and then he proceeded with his next point.

After one hour of discussion, the group stopped and looked at the video before continuing on. They analyzed the two incidents above. Regarding the Uruguayan's concerns, the group learned that, for him, relationships were fundamental and, in fact, were related to the financial and strategic analysis of the deal. If certain members of the acquired organization were maintained, the price could be lower and returns could be more certain than if those individuals were not part of the deal. The Anglo-American managers were more focused on quantitative and product-market issues and missed the potential link. Through this discussion, the group recentered around a new common objective. Their original goal was simply to evaluate the deal, but they realized they were all using different criteria to evaluate, so this was not as common as it seemed. Their new goal was to identify combinations of factors that could create a positive investment outcome, then to analyze the extent to which it was possible to create those combinations of factors. This was a more complex goal, but one that the group members all agreed to and that eventually led to better value creation for the company.

The group then explored the British "Do Nothing" vs. the Japanese suggestion to "Wait." The British executive literally meant "Don't do anything more; proceed to look for other deals unless the other party indicates a change in the conditions." In contrast, the Japanese executive's "Wait" was filled with subtle actions including continuing to get to know the other parties, extending attempts to get more information about their business, and so on. Both wanted action, but in the British manager's mind, "waiting" was a passive mode and to be avoided. It was better to do nothing on this deal, and move on with other things. In the Japanese manager's mind, "waiting" was a very active mode and would help create the conditions for a good deal. The group members realized that the two actions could be complementary and recentered around a more comprehensive strategy of concerted dialogue and extended research, including into alternative deals.

Finally, the group discussed some of the norms they saw, such as the dominance of three of the members. They realized after watching the video that the Uruguayan had posed his ideas in the form of questions ("Don't you think we should explore from which company the top officers will be drawn?"). The Anglo-Americans were much more definite and assertive in their phrasing ("That's irrelevant until we get the financials and strategy agreed to!"). The Uruguayan was not really asking questions, he was using the phrasing of questions to demonstrate his respect for the collegial relationships in the group. But in the Anglo-American cultures phrasing something as a question signals uncertainty. In their mind, this was not a time for uncertainty in the analysis; it was time to be assertive. The team learned to recenter on norms by picking up the Uruguayan's cues about his opinions and learned to listen and take him seriously, even when he phrased his ideas as questions. It was also quite evident from the video that the Japanese manager rarely spoke unless someone asked him a question directly. All the others knew that this was a characteristic of Japanese culture, but they had not developed a set of norms that would constructively encourage the Japanese member's participation. Moreover, the manager from Uruguay waited until there was a brief pause in the conversation before speaking; in contrast, the American and British managers often interrupted each other. They recentered with an agreement that in the future, at the beginning of every new stage of the discussion, they would go around the table and have each person make a two-minute statement. They would assign a facilitator (a rotating role) to ensure this happened with discipline, and that facilitator also had the responsibility of ensuring balanced contributions afterwards.

By recentering around a common view of the task and situation and around specific norms that facilitated participation, the team enhanced their Bridging and were able to provide much more valuable advice to the company.

INTEGRATING TO MANAGE AND BUILD ON THE DIFFERENCES

The final component of the MBI model is integrating the differences. It is not sufficient to have a way of understanding cultural differences and bridging the gaps by effective communication. One also needs to manage the differences effectively if they are to result in higher performance of the people who are working together. As shown in Figure 3.4, there are three main integration skills: generating participation, resolving conflicts, and building on ideas.

FIGURE 3.4   MBI: Integrating

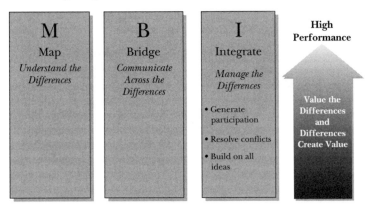

Generating Participation

To realize the benefits of different perspectives and ideas, it is necessary to express the ideas in the first place! Not all cultures are equally predisposed to offer their ideas openly. People from cultures with a strong hierarchical orientation, for example, are not likely to put forth their ideas in a group in which their direct superior or a higher status person is also a member. In contrast, people from individualistic cultures are more likely to assert their ideas. The first challenge for a multicultural group, then, is to ensure that all the ideas are heard.

As foreshadowed by our multicultural team that focused on Recentering, it is especially helpful if someone on the team monitors participation to notice whether there are systematic differences in participation rates. Figure 3.5 shows the pattern of participation in two meetings of multicultural teams, first in proportion of contributions by number, then in percentage of time. If there were no differences in the rates of participation, each shaded area would be equal in size. Aggregating the UK and US data shows a clear dominance of executives from these countries in both groups for both percentages of inputs and time. This pattern is especially clear in the second group.

There are ways of engaging all group members and facilitating their participation. In the example given earlier, the Japanese manager hardly spoke in the first half hour; his "Wait" was his lone contribution during the first 45 minutes. Yet, after the break to analyze the video and recenter, one of the Americans in the group noticed his silence and invited participation by saying, "If I recall, Sugano-san, a couple of years ago you had some experience in a merger similar to the one we are discussing. What do you think about this situation?" What followed was a highly relevant discourse, fluidly expressed, which had a big impact on the shape of the group's recommendation. When his involvement was sought, this otherwise infrequent participant made an important contribution.

To avoid relying solely on the serendipitous observation of a group member to notice the absence of participation, the group can set up routines to facilitate everyone's participation. For example, the group can use a process of going around the table to produce as many ideas as possible before discussion starts, as did the group above. Or one person

FIGURE 3.5   Participation by Individuals in Two Group Discussions

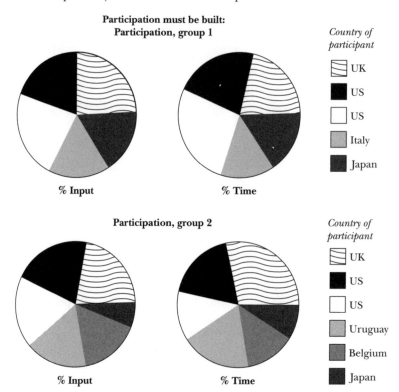

can be charged with ensuring that all members have been included before an important decision is made. Another way of facilitating participation is to vary the modes of input. It might be easier, for example, for a member to provide written input than to appear to be dominating or advancing his or her own interest by speaking in the group. Circulating written agendas well in advance of a meeting can help members prepare themselves this way and submit written responses before the meeting. Or it might be easier to provide ideas outside the context of formal meetings: in a private, face-to-face setting instead of a group meeting where the status issues may inhibit easy communication. Once they accept the possibility of having different norms for group members, most groups find creative ways to get everyone's input.

Resolving Disagreements   As more ideas from various viewpoints are expressed, there is an increasing likelihood that there will be disagreements. The way these conflicts are handled, then, becomes the next cross-cultural challenge. Even the way conflict is expressed, quite apart from how it gets resolved, varies in different cultural traditions. In many cultures it is deemed inappropriate to express conflict openly. So for a manager from a culture where open expression of disagreement is valued, the first problem becomes detecting the existence of the conflict. In high-context cultures, a disagreement may be expressed very subtly or indirectly through a third party. In low-context cultures, conflict is more likely to be stated bluntly, in words of little ambiguity. When these norms are not understood, frustration or anger is likely to be the result. If I express conflict more directly, I may be frustrated by behavior that I read as sending "mixed signals" or conclude the other person is confused or cannot make up his or her mind. If I expect indirect expression of conflict, I might feel insulted by what I experience as impolite or crass comments from the other person who feels she or he is "just putting the issue on the table."

One way to deal with these issues is to use the Mapping and Bridging components of the model noted in the previous sections. Mapping provides a way to anticipate when the conflict gaps may occur; the Bridging techniques (prepare, decenter, recenter) give tools for reaching a common understanding and a common set of rules or norms for resolving the conflicts and avoiding them in the future. Effective communication is more than half of effective conflict resolution. The map of cultural differences may provide clues as to the other person's preferred ways of dealing with conflict. By decentering, you can adapt to the other's perspective without falling into the ethnocentric trap of blaming the other person or misinterpreting the meaning of actions by referencing your own cultural codes.

Building on Ideas   Even if the mapping framework is well understood, the communication skills are well developed, and participation and conflict issues are managed effectively, there is still a key component to realizing the potential in cross-cultural encounters, namely, moving forward and building on the ideas. There are cultural barriers in this phase of activity, too. As mentioned earlier, some cultural preferences would lead a person to push their ideas (individualism), while another orientation (hierarchical) is more likely to lead to deference to authority. If you are in a group with several cultures, there might be an agreement (common rules of interaction) to surface ideas without attributing them to individuals or using an individual's ideas as a starting point for discussion. The main idea is to encourage the exploration of ideas with the conscious attempt to invent new ideas, to build on the ideas initially surfaced. A real stimulus to innovation is to try to do more than combine ideas and to avoid compromises. Finally, striving to find solutions to issues or problems that are acceptable to all (another rule for interaction or norm for behavior) is another way to increase the probability of getting synergy from the diversity in the group. Trying to invent new ideas from those available and reaching for solutions to which everyone can agree are ideals that are difficult to accomplish. But even setting them as objectives will help a multicultural team achieve its potential for high performance.

MBI CREATES RESULTS

The complete MBI model is summarized in Figure 3.6. It is helpful to categorize six types of situations that managers face, each of which requires a different application of the fundamental MBI principles (see Figure 3.7). In each of these situations, decisions must be made and implemented across cultural boundaries. At the individual level

FIGURES 3.6   MBI: The Complete Model

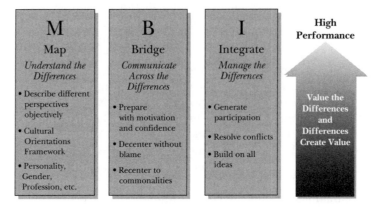

FIGURE 3.7   Six Arenas for Synergy in Cross-Cultural Interaction

	One-Way	**Multi-Way**
Individual Level	Arena 1: *Expatriate* ▪ Individual manager going to another country to manage a business unit or perform a specialist job.	Arena 2: *Multicultural team* ▪ Group from many countries, often cross-functional, managing across units or a multi-country project.
Organizational Level	Arena 3: *Export or import system* ▪ Take human resources, information systems, or other practice or strategy from one country into another.	Arena 4: *Global system* ▪ Develop human resources systems, organizational structures or strategies, to be implemented in many countries.
External to Organization	Arena 5: *External relationships* ▪ Customer, supplier, marketing, or other information developed in one market, adapt to another market.	Arena 6: *Multilateral systems* ▪ Conglomerates, lobbying or trade agreements, professional organizations.

(Arenas 1 and 2), managers must interact effectively with individuals from other cultures. People from different cultures will bring with them diverse expectations about the interaction, and effectiveness depends on understanding and building on these differences. At the organizational level (Arenas 3 and 4), managers must design systems of interaction that guide the coordinated behavior of many people. It is important for managers to know whether these systems will be consistent or contradictory with the cultural system in place. External to the organization (Arenas 5 and 6), managers work with customers, suppliers, and other stakeholders in partnerships, complex negotiations, and indirectly through marketing and advertising efforts. In one-way transactions (Arenas 1, 3, and 5), managers need to take something that has been developed in one culture and put it into another one. Successful execution is based on an understanding of how things will be interpreted in the new context. In multi-way transactions (Arenas 2, 4, and 6), managers must take into account many cultural and contextual systems at the same time. Unless the differences are understood, conflict and division will characterize the situation.

We will illustrate two arenas here to focus on the MBI fundamentals. The remaining arenas will be illustrated throughout the rest of the book in different contexts.

Arena 2: A Broad Scope of Multicultural Teams

In our research, we have worked with a wide variety of multicultural teams from different industries and parts of the world, different levels of the organization, and doing different tasks. To examine the importance of MBI, we identified the teams for which we had the most reliable data on their membership characteristics and their Mapping, Bridging, and Integrating applications, and final performance defined as the extent to which they met the mandate assigned to them by the organization. This gave us a total of 17 very different team situations. We compiled a matrix of the team composition and process data, ranking the teams by quality of processes, then compared it with a separate ranking of performance. The two sets of rankings are very similar, with the teams who engaged in the most MBI behaviors also being the highest performing.[10] The teams and the data are summarized in Figure 3.8.

Five of the 17 team situations were classified as having high to very high performance; eight had medium to medium high performance, and four were classified as having low to very low performance. The high performing teams all exhibited high motivation, almost all also demonstrated high confidence. They engaged in medium to high decentering with low blame, and medium to high Recentering behavior. In terms of the Integrating elements in the model, all of the high performing teams had high participation, widely distributed over the members. They also demonstrated medium to high conflict resolution (though one had very little conflict to resolve!). They were all medium to high in behaviors that helped them to build on each other's ideas.

In contrast, the low performing teams showed the opposite kinds of behaviors. Almost all exhibited high levels of blaming behavior. Their overall decentering was low in most cases, and most also had low motivation and confidence. Their Recentering was either low in frequency or in quality; for example two of the teams displayed a façade of Recentering but were not sincere in their efforts. Their participation patterns were either mixed or skewed one-way in the direction of the dominant person or subgroup. Three had low conflict resolution and the fourth team had trouble even detecting the conflict that was bubbling beneath the surface. None of the four systematically built on the ideas expressed by their members.

It is interesting to see that the mode of interaction was not related to performance. Teams could achieve high levels of MBI and performance whether they were working

FIGURE 3.8 Seventeen Multicultural Team Situations: MBI leads to high performance.

Type of Team	Level of Diversity	Mapping	Bridging Function	Integrating Function	Mode	Performance*
Special Task Forces (4 teams)	High Culture & Personality	Culture & Personality	High Motivation & Confidence, Medium Decentering, Low Blame, Medium-High Recentering	High Participation, Medium Conflict Resolution, High Building on Ideas	Face to Face daily	Very High
Bank Back Office Team (self-managed)	High Culture & Personality	Culture only	High Motivation & Confidence, High Decentering, Low Blame, Hi Rec	High Participation, Low Conflict so Resolution not relevant, High Building on Ideas	Face to Face	Very High
Research & Development (self-managed)	High Culture & Personality (large team)	Culture only	High Motivation & Confidence, High Decentering, Low Blame, Hi Rec	All elements high	F2F 2 × per year, Virtual often	High
National Account Teams	High Personality	Personality only	High Motivation & Confidence, Medium Decentering, Low Blame, High Recentering	High Participation, Medium Conflict Resolution, Medium Building on Ideas	F2F for 1 week & 2 ×/yr + Virtual as needed	High
Executive Team	High Culture & Personality	Culture & Personality	High Motivation & Medium Confidence, Medium Low Blame, Medium Decentering & Recentering	High Participation, Medium Conflict Resolution, High Building on Ideas	Face to Face daily	High
Task Force for Merger & Acquisitions	High Culture & Personality	Culture & Leadership Styles	Medium Motivation & Confidence, High & Low Decentering, Low Blame, Medium Recentering	High Participation, Medium Conflict Resolution, Medium Building on Ideas	Face to Face daily for 2 wks	Medium High
Global Account Team (MNC)	High Culture	Culture only	Medium Motivation, Low Confidence, Medium Decentering, Low Blame, Medium Recentering	Medium Participation, Medium Conflict Resolution, Medium-High Building on Ideas	Face to Face, 1/yr. Virtual often	Medium High
Executive Team (Regional Company)	Medium (2 local, 2 from region, 1 expat from headquarters country)	Intuitive Mapping *post facto*	Medium Motivation & Confidence, Medium Decentering, Medium Blame, Medium Recentering (Expat exception)	High Participation, Medium Conflict Resolution, Low Building on Ideas	Face to Face Weekly	Medium (expat executive resigned)
Executive Team + Regional Team (MNC)	Low in Top Executive Team, High in Regional Team	Culture only	High Motivation & Confidence, Medium Decentering, Low Blame, Medium Recentering	High Participation, Medium Conflict Resolution, Medium High Building on Ideas	Exec Team F2F often, Reg Team F2F 1/yr. Low Virtual	Medium
Executive Team (Domestic)	Low Culture, Medium Personality	Culture & Personality	Medium Motivation & Confidence, Medium Decentering, Medium Blame, Medium Recentering	High Participation, Medium Conflict Resolution, Medium Building on Ideas	Face to Face, 1/week	Medium

Team	Culture/Personality	Measures	Elements	Participation	Communication	Performance*
Executive Team (Global Reach, Headquarters Expats Dominate)	Medium (14 local Culture, 2 from largest market)	Culture only	High Motivation & Confidence, Medium Decentering, Low Blame, High Recentering	Mixed Participation (Heaquarters culture is High Context Culture), Medium Conflict Resolution, Medium Building on Ideas	Face to Face for 2 days each month	Medium
Executive Team + Direct Reports (Multi Domestic)	Ethnic Diversity within Domestic Culture	Culture & Personality	High Motivation & Medium Confidence, Medium Decentering, Medium Blame, Medium Recentering	High Participation, Medium Conflict Resolution, Medium High Building on Ideas	Exec Team F2F Daily, Dir Reports F2F 1/Quarter	Medium
Executive Team & Multi-Functional Teams (2)	High Culture & Personality	Culture & Personality	All elements	All elements	F2F & Virtual	Medium (met expectations)
Executive Board (Multi-Domestic firm)	Very Low	Personality only	Low Motivation and Confidence, Low Decentering, High Blame, Facade of Recentering	Mixed Part, Low Conflict Resolution, Low Building on Ideas	Weekly Face to Face, frequent informal	Low
Executive Team (Regional team of MNC)	Medium (Top positions all expats, rest of team from region)	Culture only	Low Motivation and Confidence, Medium Decentering, Medium Blame, Recentering on Expat culture	Skewed Participation, Low Conflict Resolution, Low Building on Ideas	Face to Face bimonthly	Low
Global Account Team (MNC)	High Culture, Moderate Personality	No Formal Measures	Low Motivation, Low Decentering, High Blame, Low Recentering	One way Participation, Low Conflict Resolution, Low Building on Ideas	Virtual only, using low richness technology	Low
Financial Services Team	High Culture & Personality	Inaccurate stereotyping for culture & personality	High Motivation, Low Confidence, Low Decentering, High Blame Low Recentering	1-sided Participation, Low Detection of Conflict, Low Building on Ideas	Face to Face, but infrequent	Very Low (Critical Person Quit)

* Performance Scale: High = Exceeded mandate and expectations, Medium = Met mandate and expectations, Low = Fell below mandate and expectations.

face-to-face (F2F) or virtually. We address these modes in more depth in Chapter 4; for now we simply emphasize that the underlying processes of MBI are more important than which modality is used.

By comparing the experiences across such a wide variety of teams, we highlight the flexibility of the MBI processes and their application to a wide scope of situations.

Arena 3: Exporting or Importing Systems

MBI processes are critical when adopting best practices from one context to another. This is illustrated by Omar, an Egyptian proud of his humble peasant origins and founder and CEO of Smarthome Superior Plumbing Solutions. Omar developed his plumbing supplies company from nothing to become one of the main suppliers of plumbing infrastructure such as pipes and drains in the country. "It is not an exciting industry," he admits, but in a country where bringing water and taking away waste make an enormous difference to people's lives, the business creates exciting opportunities.

He was looking for tools to help take his company even further. Omar read everything he could find about management from Western sources, and realized that one tool he could use was to create a vision or mission statement. This kind of framework would help all the employees align together around a set of common ideas. With a common vision and mission, people would make better decisions and act in a way that helped the whole business. For inspiration, he read every vision and mission statement he could find, mostly on multinationals' web sites from the US and Western Europe (Mapping). All of them left him cold – they would not work to align his managers. So he stepped back from the process and asked himself what vision and mission statements really need to do (Bridging). Then he thought about how to accomplish that within his own culture and with his employees (Bridging). Finally, he developed a vision based on applying the teachings of the Koran to his business, and a set of guidelines about how employees should implement Muslim values at work (Integrating). Posted on the walls of every manager's office and every meeting room is a set of statements about the importance of creating infrastructure to help do God's work on earth (Integrating). Every meeting must start with a set of reflections on how, since the previous meeting, managers and employees had helped others (Integrating).

After implementing the vision and related practices, Omar saw an increase in motivation, commitment, and initiative from employees, and a concomitant increase in sales and production. He adopted some other best practices, for example, performance appraisals. His company now supplies 80 % of the plumbing infrastructure products in Egypt, and he exports products to Europe. The vision also helped him make and easily justify his decision to invest a significant portion of profits in infrastructure and microfinancing projects in Egypt, to help the country progress. "I can only increase my business if the country is also becoming more healthy economically."

Omar's vision and mission statements helped him align people to make and implement decisions that advance the company, and furthermore, hold people accountable for their actions and results – what any vision and mission statement is intended to do. But the four pages of his vision and mission statements are very different from those that would inspire people in most Western-origin companies. In adapting the standard management practice to his own Egyptian-Muslim context, Omar used his strong MBI skills and achieved very high results.

Who Should Adapt?

The MBI process assumes that at least some people involved in an interaction are adapting to the others. But who should adapt? This is a difficult question.

A number of factors influence the answer. As a general rule, the onus for adaptation usually rests with the party who is seen as the foreigner. The sheer force of numbers probably influences this. But this rule of the majority also misses significant opportunities for learning and inventing, as we saw in the example of the culturally mixed team of managers discussing the acquisition.

Location is another strong factor. Everything else being equal (which is rarely the case), the guest is expected to adapt to the host. Technological dependence may alter this equation. A German joint venture in Beijing may choose to emphasize German cultural values and management practice in spite of the location and overwhelming majority of Chinese population, simply as a recognition of the need to acquire information. In fact, the power of resources in general has a strong influence on who is expected to adapt. The buyer almost always expects the seller to adapt, unless the seller has something extremely rare for which there are many willing buyers.

Individual preference may also enter the equation. An expatriate dealing with Chinese in Hong Kong may attempt to adapt to Chinese traditions, even though there is no expectation from the Hong Kong staff to do so. The motives for adaptation in this situation may range from showing courtesy to a desire to learn and to increase one's own repertoire of behavior. Furthermore, no matter where a company is operating, an attempt to adapt to others' customs will be appreciated and will have a positive influence on relations.

We usually give a different but quick and easy answer to the question "Who should adapt?": "Whoever cares about performance." There are a lot of contingencies that influence who *tends to* adapt and who is *expected to* adapt. But as our description of the MBI process should emphasize, the more all parties adapt, the more potential there is for performance to improve. If one party adapts, there is higher performance than if neither adapts. However, if both adapt, performance can be even higher. Discussing "who should adapt" often becomes a negotiation of power; discussing "how can we perform together" puts the perspective in the right place.

Back to Mindfulness: Continuous Learning for Development and Effectiveness

As we discussed under the section above on Preparing – Confidence, managers often feel discouraged when they realize the complexity and depth of skills needed for working effectively across cultures. However, there is good news. A little bit of skill goes a long way. The relationship between the MBI processes and performance is not a one-time linear equation. You don't "check the box" and get all of MBI right, then hit the button and, "ka-ching," automatically get performance. It is a much more iterative process.

Doing a bit of Mapping will help you ask a couple of questions differently in Bridging. You'll get different answers, which will lead you to avoid or manage a conflict differently, and you'll see yourself on the way to higher performance. This gives you and others more motivation and confidence, you ask more Mapping questions, engage in more Bridging, and people will volunteer some ideas you hadn't heard before. Performance looks even better. And so on.

Being able to learn continuously comes from mindfulness, which we discussed in Chapter 2 in the section on Cultural Intelligence. Mindfulness is paying attention to your actions, selecting your behaviors carefully, paying attention to the results, managing the impact, and learning to prepare yourself for the next set of actions. Along the way there will be some blips and dips. Experienced managers love sharing stories about these incidents with each other. All of the authors have experienced many of them, even recently, and we research and teach these processes! Much more important than avoiding mistakes completely (because it is impossible) is learning. Ask questions about what you should have done. Ask them in a way that's appropriate to the culture. Provide "what if" scenarios and ask for people's reactions. Experiment when it feels safe. Then learn the new information and incorporate it into your Maps for next time.

A businesswoman we know, Susan, when in Saudi Arabia, was invited by a Saudi woman to remove her headscarf, even though there were men present. Normally Susan would have declined immediately and left the headscarf on, but there were several aspects of the situation that made it ambiguous, and she was not sure what to do. She made a decision which seemed to be appropriate, since the Saudi woman continued the meeting as before with genuine warmth, but the most important part of the learning came afterwards. Susan asked a mixed group of Saudi men and women what she should have done (without telling them what she had done). The spirited discussion lasted for half an hour, and there was no consensus. All agreed that either action would have been fine, but they disagreed about what messages would be sent by leaving the scarf on or taking it off, with arguments for both being "better" or "less offensive." The group offered many examples of factors that should be taken into account – Did she see you as an expert or as a peer? How covered was her own hair? What does she do with her relatives and outside her business context (some of them knew the woman)? What kind of statement would she have wanted you to make? Who were the men in the room? Did you get the sense she was offering this to you as a gift? And so on. They also agreed that they were fairly liberal as a group, there would be many people in the country who would disagree with them that either option was fine, and that there might be different answers if only men or only women were asked, rather than a mixed group. This led to a discussion about dynamics in different parts of the country. Susan knew when she made her decision about the headscarf that either leaving it on or taking it off could be a mistake. But the learning from the situation was invaluable and became input for the next set of interactions.

Perhaps most importantly, if you offend people or create a negative impact you didn't intend, make sure you manage that impact. That means first of all, you must be watching for these impacts with mindfulness. Become sensitive to the cues that you have inadvertently created offense, such as the other person switching the type of pronoun to a more formal one, or using more structured language and actions. If you see the signs, first apologize sincerely. A genuine and respectful apology goes a long way to creating the conditions for turning it into a learning situation. Then, using your mindfulness and

MBI skills, learn for next time. If you are sincere in your attempts to learn and improve, you almost always get at least one more chance and people willing to help you learn.

In the remaining chapters of the book, we look at many different contexts for international management. Sometimes we draw on the MBI model explicitly; often we incorporate other lenses to focus on other aspects of the situation. But MBI is always assumed to be a foundation underneath the other processes, to be drawn upon in all situations.

Notes

1 Stahl, G. K., Maznevski, M., Voigt, A., and Jonsen, K., "Unraveling the diversity-performance link in multicultural teams: A meta-analysis of studies on the impact of cultural diversity in teams." Paper presented at the Academy of International Business Annual Meeting, Milan, August 2008. Published in the conference proceedings. See also Earley, P. C. and Gibson, C. B., *Multinational work teams: A new perspective* (Lawrence Erlbaum Associates, 2002).

2 DiStefano, J. and Maznevski, M., "Creating value with diverse teams in global management," *Organizational Dynamics* 29 (2000) 45–63.

3 Maznevski, M., *Synergy and performance in multicultural teams* (unpublished doctoral dissertation, London, Canada: The University of Western Ontario, 1994); Maznevski, M. "Understanding our differences: Performance in decision-making groups with diverse members," *Human Relations*, 47 (1994) 531–552. DiStefano, J. and Maznevski, M., "Creating value with diverse teams in global management," n. 2 above.

4 Stasser has conducted many insightful studies exploring the dynamics of sharing distributed information in teams. They are reviewed well in Stasser, G., "The uncertain role of unshared information in collective choice," in Thompson, L. L., Levine, J. M., and Messick, D. M. (eds), *Shared cognition in organizations: The management of knowledge* (Mahwah, NJ: Erlbaum, 1999) 49–69.

5 Ekelund, B. Z., *Diversity Icebreaker*. This instrument and process were based on research on dynamics around diversity and how to create positive acceptance. The exercise is excellent for introducing Mapping. The instrument, background research, and other information can be found at www.diversityicebreaker.com.

6 This scheme was adapted from the work of Rolv M. Blakar. See Blakar, R. M., "Towards a theory of communication in terms of preconditions: A conceptual framework and some empirical explorations," in Giles, H. and St. Clair, R. N., *Recent advances in language, communication, and social psychology* (eds) (London: Lawrence Erlbaum Associates, Ltd., Publishers, 1985) 10–40.

7 The first five of these are drawn from Porter, R. E. and Samovar, L. A., "Approaching intercultural communication," in Samovar, L. A. and Porter, R. E. (eds), *Intercultural communications: A reader*, 5th edn (Belmont, CA: Wadsworth Publishing Company, 1988) 15–30. The last two are corollaries of the first five, which, according to our observations, are particularly critical to cross-cultural communication.

8 Originally discussed in an Executive Dialogue at the ION conference in Aarhus, February 2005, then followed up in several forums through Scandinavia and with Scandinavians throughout the world.

9 Smith, P. B., Peterson, M.F., and Schwartz, S. H., *Journal of Cross-Cultural Psychology*, 2002; Smith, P. B., Andersen, J. A., Ekelund, B., Graversen, G., and Ropo, A., *Scandinavian Journal of Management*, 2002.

10 This is obviously not a closely controlled or measured set of studies. But we did attempt to avoid bias in our estimates of performance. For example, we did the descriptions and assessments by similar types of groups (e.g. project teams, executive teams, etc.) and ordered the groups from high to low performance only after all the data had been assembled.

CHAPTER 4

Managing Global Teams and Networks

Shawna moved from her native Ireland to continental Europe to take a job leading a special innovation team for a consumer goods firm. The team's mandate was to help the company spread innovations more systematically and efficiently throughout the international network of subsidiaries. The team was performing fine – each of its projects was well-received – but the company thought somehow the team could do more. Shawna quickly perceived that although projects were done well, each project was a standalone, and there were many missed opportunities to build innovation systems and knowledge sharing. The team had worked more as a group of individuals assigned in different configurations to projects; in order to build integration, the team would have to work more together in an interdependent way.

The challenges Shawna faced were significant. The team of 25 was highly diverse in terms of nationality, function, and types of experience – this was considered important for innovation but made it difficult to bring integration. Moreover, assignment to the team was considered a three-year development experience for high potentials, so about one third of the team turned over each year. Team members worked in subgroups on projects, and the subgroups did not have much opportunity to interact.

Shawna started by interviewing all the team members and some important external stakeholders, both to get to know them and also to understand the issues. Her first actions in the team were based on this initial feedback. She structured roles more clearly within the team, including the leadership role, and implemented a comprehensive set of performance expectations and an assessment system combining team priorities and stakeholder input. She brought the team together more often to develop common ways of working and joint priorities. She shifted the agenda of the biannual week-long workshops. In the past they had focused more on reporting and administrative issues as well as general team-building; instead, she had the entire team work together to create joint knowledge books around key competency areas, which they could all then deploy. Identifying the priorities and key competency areas was the toughest part; it meant bringing together and analyzing all the projects and potential projects and matching them against the company strategy. Once those were identified, team members could finish the competency books when working apart from each other and share them virtually. Another topic was to explore the challenges of driving multimarket innovation. The workshops also included significant team-building activities to increase trust and communication among team members when they weren't together.

The second area Shawna started to work on was related to working across boundaries. She put in place a clear recruitment and succession plan so the team could become more stable in terms of skills and capabilities. This also facilitated a transfer of knowledge in the team with the turnovers, and increased the chances of retaining these individuals in the organization after their "tour" with the team. The team implemented a very structured orientation program, an important and novel part of which was helping newcomers to the team develop their networks and relationships in the team and among key stakeholder groups. They developed an alumni group to leverage the relationships of people who had "graduated" from the team and help make innovation more systematic throughout the firm.

As we will see in this chapter, Shawna addressed all the areas important to complex teams in international organizations. She checked the basic dynamics of the structure, task, and social processes, and built more complex dynamics including trust and boundary-spanning in addition to the team's already well-developed innovation processes. She set up the team to manage its dispersion well, and leveraged the team's networks. The team really began to achieve its higher mandate of spreading innovation more systematically.

Most work in organizations today is done in some configuration of teams. A team is a group of people who must work together to achieve a particular outcome. There are many different kinds of teams, each with different tasks, structures, and other characteristics. For example, Royal-Dutch Shell identified the following categories:[1]

- *Project teams:* Teams with defined duration, clear deliverables, core membership but relying on networking with experts and other stakeholders outside; e.g., exploration team for a new potential drilling site.
- *Management teams:* Teams with indefinite duration, clear membership representing different departments, high-level deliverables; coordination and communication are key to the mandate; e.g., global lubricants management team.
- *Production/work teams:* Teams with indefinite duration, clear membership, specific and clear deliverables; team does regular and on-going work together; e.g. production team operating a refinery.
- *Service teams:* Teams with indefinite duration, clear membership, deliverable depends on serving other people's and teams' deliverables; team members provide regular and on-going support to others; e.g., IT or HR support for a global business unit.
- *Action teams:* Teams with defined duration, clear deliverables, created as needed from a network of potential members; team members work together in a fast and fluid way; e.g., emergency response team for a refinery fire.

Like everything in management, teams have become more complex in today's international, interdependent, and fast-moving economy, and there is no simple "how to" guide that fits all teams. With the wide variety of tasks that groups of people work on jointly, managers must develop a sophisticated view of contingencies.[2] Different situations call for different configurations of people. Even the same group of people will sometimes need to work in different ways, depending on which phase of the task they are in. In this chapter we use the terms "group" and "team" interchangeably, as we explore the principles and complexities of people working together on joint outcomes.

We start by describing the basic processes that all teams must accomplish, as well as the processes that are necessary for teams doing more complex tasks. Then we examine the special case of virtual teams, or teams whose members are distributed across different locations, since many teams in international management are virtual teams. The final section of this chapter looks at network structures, or different combinations of connections among people for collaboration. Looking at teams and organizations as networks helps managers leverage relationships more effectively and efficiently.

EFFECTIVE TEAMS[3]

Although every team is a unique combination of people, tasks, processes, and environment, there are some characteristics that effective teams share no matter what their configuration. First, some basic conditions are necessary for all teams even to get started on the road to performance. In addition to these basic conditions, teams in more complex settings must address another set of advanced dynamics in order to perform well. Although these basic conditions and advanced dynamics are important to managing teams anywhere and not just in international management, we highlight both sets of ideas in this book. Within a culture, it is often possible to remain unaware of the rules without sacrificing performance, since most people have similar enough assumptions and experience about how to work in teams. But in the international context, they cannot be taken for granted and even basic conditions must be developed carefully. To optimize performance, teams can develop further characteristics and processes that manage complexity.[4] The relationship between Basic Conditions and Advanced Dynamics is shown in Figure 4.1.

Basic Conditions of Team Performance: OST

For teams to meet their basic objectives, certain conditions must be met, which we often refer to as the OST model: the team must be Organized around certain principles, and the team must manage the Social and Task processes.[5] These conditions can be managed in many different ways, depending on the team, the task, the environment, and the leader, but all are necessary for even a minimum level of performance.[6]

Ost: Organize Many aspects of teamwork require organization, and it can get overwhelming. But teams that focus on three important aspects find they are well on their way to performing well: the definition of the task and objectives, team composition, and team roles.

FIGURE 4.1 OST Basic Conditions and Advanced Team Dynamics for Team Effectiveness.

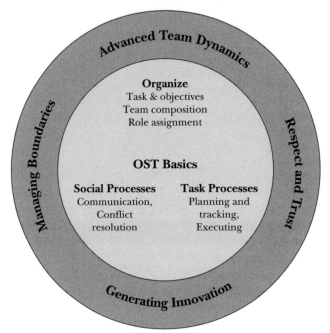

Defined task and objectives Team members must know clearly what their task and objectives are, in order to achieve them reliably. For example, the "savory flavors R&D team" at a fragrance and flavors company has the mandate of developing new flavors for salty (rather than sweet) foods, such as soups and sauces. The account sales team at an Internet bank has the objective of selling new accounts. This sounds simple, but many teams do not understand their objectives well or do not agree on them. Sometimes this is due to lack of clear communication from the leader. The leader presents a set of objectives that are clear to him- or herself but are difficult or ambiguous from the point of view of the team.

For example, a CFO we know said clearly to the team of country finance managers that the goal was to achieve 11 % EBITDA (Earnings before Interest, Taxes, Depreciation, and Amortization). In his mind, this was a clear goal. However, the country finance managers thought their mandate was ambiguous. There were many ways of achieving the goal, and it was evident to them that how to achieve it should be an important aspect of the team's financial mandate (lower costs, more revenue, which combination of new product areas). They had no idea how to interact with each other, for example, on transfer pricing, nor with their own country organizations, based on this goal. And some countries were ahead of the goal while others were behind. Was it okay if the average met 11 % or did everyone need to meet 11 %?

Often, team members have different interpretations of the task and objectives. For example, the same organization launched a new industrial product, with a multifunctional team guiding the launch. Their mandate from the CEO was to launch the product successfully.

The VP of marketing on the team defined a successful product launch by high market share, while the financial director defined it by profitability. These two objectives are potentially conflicting, and this team unfortunately did not discuss or resolve their different ideas until well into execution phase, when they had already created unaligned actions.

The simple lesson here is: make sure the team has a clear mandate, and don't take clarity for granted. In complex teams such as those in international settings, you will have to revisit the goals and objectives many times. People may think they agree and are clear at the beginning, but as they interact with each other, they will discover differences, and it is important to clarify these as the team goes along.

Team composition Teams need the right combination of skills among members. Of course, the right combination depends on the task, and usually includes technical skills, functional and geographical knowledge, and skills important for managing the organizational, social, and task processes defined below. It is often helpful to have diversity in personal characteristics among team members to boost innovation and increase the quality of decision-making, as we discussed in Chapter 3. However, teams are often composed based on convenience – who is available – rather than careful assignment, and sometimes the necessary skill combination is not available. As a result, teams frequently have significant skill or knowledge gaps which should be addressed by adding members or developing the necessary knowledge or skills.

Roles Roles are sets of specific responsibilities within a group for interacting with others to complete the task. The number and diversity of processes that teams must manage (see next two subsections) are high, and no one person can manage them all for the team. Therefore, teams function best when different members take responsibility for different aspects. Should roles be explicitly assigned, or should they emerge? We have heard managers of teams argue strongly for both: "Our team worked well because we assigned and followed clear roles," and another team: "Our team worked well because we let each person's role in the team emerge in a fluid way, shifting as necessary." Which is really best? In fact, teams can perform well in either case. It is safer to assign roles, especially in a team of people who have not worked together before, or in a task that is new, or in complex situations like international teams. The best teams usually use some combination of assigning roles and adjusting them as necessary.

oSt: Manage Social Processes Social processes are those that facilitate interaction, commitment, and motivation within the group. The most important social processes are communication and conflict management. These were discussed in detail in Chapter 3, so will only be outlined briefly here.

Communication Effective communication is transmitting meaning from one person to another or others as it was intended by the sender.[7] To achieve effective communication, senders must phrase their messages carefully so that receivers will understand, and receivers must listen or read carefully to try and understand from the sender's point of view. This kind of communication is a very active process, requiring extensive questioning, checking, and paraphrasing from everyone involved. The challenges are described in detail in the section on Bridging in Chapter 3, referring to cross-cultural communication. Team performance is higher when team members understand each others' perspectives and the information brought to the team. Communication is also important in ensuring that all members are kept informed of progress in the team in a continuous way. Many teams find that having a member responsible for facilitating communication (a team role) is extremely helpful in ensuring effective communication.

Conflict resolution   Conflict is the expression of differences in opinion or priority due to opposing needs or demands.[8] The effect of conflict on teams is complex, with conflict sometimes helping performance and sometimes hurting it.[9] Task-related conflict – disagreement and discussion about facts and priorities directly related to the task – tends to enhance team performance. Teams need a certain amount of task-related conflict in order to question their assumptions and ensure they are bringing in all relevant perspectives, but the conflict does not need to "feel" negative. For example, some teams assign a formal role of "devil's advocate" to prevent groupthink. In one highly successful team we worked with in a chemicals company, this role was rotated for each meeting, and, as a result, individual team members also developed the capacity to see the team's task from many points of view. Social or person-related conflict – disagreement about people in the team and their motivations or capabilities – on the other hand, tends to decrease team performance. This is related to our discussion in Chapter 3 in Bridging, on the importance of not blaming each other when problems arise in cross-cultural communication. Conflict that prevents a group from moving forward in a coordinated way with an acceptable solution is harmful to a team, whatever the type of conflict. Some teams find it necessary to assign someone on the team, generally someone who is trusted to be neutral, a role of facilitating or mediating conflict.

osT: Manage Task Processes   Task processes are those that are directly related to accomplishing the team's task. This is often thought of as "doing the work." The two main types of task processes are planning and tracking, and executing.

Planning and tracking   Planning and tracking are often referred to as "project management" and are the subject of many books, articles, guides, and software packages. Simply put, teams are more likely to achieve results if they plan clear processes with activities, milestones, and deliverables, if work and subtasks are allocated clearly to members, and if the team tracks progress compared to plan, adapting the plan when necessary. Planning and tracking is enhanced if communication and conflict management – two social processes – are effective. Without good communication and conflict management, plans are unlikely to be complete or comprehensive, and tracking is likely to be inaccurate.

Executing   Executing is about individual team members accomplishing their own parts of the task – whether it is data gathering, analysis, report-writing, or other things – and the group as a whole combining the individual outputs to create a joint deliverable. This requires individual discipline – team members need to finish their own parts on time and come prepared to meetings – as well as group commitment, with team members helping each other out as unexpected challenges arise. For some team tasks, executing also involves actually implementing. For example, an equipment purchasing team formed after two companies merged was charged with identifying the best few suppliers from among the two companies' previous relationships. Then the team negotiated new contracts with these suppliers and worked with the suppliers and individual purchasing departments to adjust volumes and delivery conditions until new routines had been established.

OST: The Basics are Just the Beginning One of the most effective examples we have seen of OST principles was a set of production teams in a factory in Southeast Asia, part of a global foods company. Each production team of about 10 people had its own small planning room, with one glass wall facing the factory. On two walls were highly organized displays of quantity and quality goals and performance-against-goals. Both of these walls linked the team's goals to plant goals and tracked plant progress, as well. The third wall displayed other team goals and events, such as innovation, training, team roles, and social information, such as the factory soccer league standings and team member family news. These team rooms facilitated all of the Organization, Social, and Task processes. But they went further, and facilitated factory performance in a synergistic way: the performance of the plant was better than the sum of the performance of the teams. Because all teams had the same type of room, organizational OST processes were enhanced across the factory. People from one team were able to interface with other teams and help each perform better, relatively easily. People could move from one team to another as needed for production, with little adjustment. This production site became one of a handful of best-practice sites for the global organization.

The OST principles are necessary for performance in any team, whether it is in Russia or India, a production team or a top management team, a short-term emergency action team or a multiyear development team. Whenever a team is underperforming, it is useful to check these basic conditions first; they are too often taken for granted. For teams with simple, routine, or stable tasks, these OST principles are usually sufficient for performance that meets expectations and fulfills the team mandate. However, teams that face more challenging tasks or environments must address a further set of dynamics.

Advanced Dynamics for More Complex Teams

To perform well in more complex situations, teams must develop three characteristics in addition to the basic OST conditions. They must have respect and trust, innovation and creativity, and effective boundary-spanning outside the team.

Building Respect and Trust

Respect Respect in a team is recognizing the legitimacy of each others' contributions to the team and valuing the importance of those contributions. When people feel respected, they give more of themselves to the team, contributing with greater motivation and commitment. When a team is characterized by respect, more ideas are considered and combined, resulting in higher quality decisions.

Respect is easier to develop within a culture where individuals have a relatively common understanding of the different types of experience and knowledge associated with different backgrounds, and can more easily anticipate each others' contributions. In multinational teams, people have less context in which to understand each others' knowledge and skills, and often devalue each other. This is often felt acutely by people coming from developing and emerging countries, who are frequently thought by managers from the West to have experienced less sophisticated and complex business environments and less formal business training, and who therefore have less to contribute. They are respected for knowledge of their own markets, but not valued as much for their professional expertise, which could help the overall mandate of a team. But managers from developing and emerging economies often manage businesses that are equally sophisticated and have high levels of formal training. Moreover, they learn in their markets to meet customer needs creatively with scarce resources, to adapt to changing and politically challenging conditions, to work in culturally complex interactions, and to implement change pragmatically – things that are more difficult to learn in stable Western environments. The skills developed in these markets provide potentially valuable contributions to any global team.

Trust Trust in a team is a belief that any team member would make decisions that optimize the team's interests, even in the absence of other team members. Trust, like respect, increases motivation and commitment to the team, and thus the quality of contributions and communication processes. In addition, trust makes teamwork more efficient.[10] If team members can act on behalf of the team without always going back to check with the team first, more progress can be made in a shorter time than when trust is absent or weak. Respect is a prerequisite for building trust, but trust goes further.

Trust is particularly important when the task is impossible for team members to achieve individually, when each member is truly expected to contribute something unique, and members do not have the knowledge or expertise to supervise each other. In a global account team, representatives of the supplier in each country must work with local subsidiaries of the customer in such a way that the global brand is maintained and enhanced. From time to time, that may mean particular country representatives making exceptions. If country representatives feel committed to the team so they make the best decisions possible and if team members trust each other to be committed, then the account team will get the best combination of customer service and profitable value creation.

Trust cannot be switched on (although it can be lost quickly), and many teams are disappointed when they come away from their team launch without complete trust. Trust must be generated through a series of experiences, building from predictability and reliability (I know I can rely on you to do what you committed to do) to deep-level personal trust (I can rely on you to make big decisions for me). Ironically, to build trust, members must take risks. Team members can only demonstrate to each other that they will act in the team's interests if other team members let them take unsupervised actions. This is something worth bearing in mind, especially if you are leading a team; it is a good idea to set up a series of minor tasks in the beginning of a team's life together that will help create trust that the team can rely on later.

Building trust in a multicultural team is a challenge. Research shows that members of multicultural teams are more motivated to work with the team and enjoy the interaction together, but have lower general cohesion than single-culture teams.[11] It seems that members of multicultural teams enter the team situation with good intentions, but often encounter challenges due to the different values and perspectives of team members. However, using the MBI processes from Chapter 3 has been shown to help multicultural teams develop strong and sustainable trust.

Generating Innovation Innovation is developing something new that creates value. Product innovations come most quickly to mind, with the iPod being the most frequently cited example in recent years. However, process innovations are equally important. Many argue that to the technology company Apple, the value of the iPod, which is really just a disk drive with an innovative user interface, comes less from the device itself and more from the linking of the device to iTunes, a complete solution for managing and downloading music. The latter innovation is more of a process innovation than a product innovation. Consistent innovation requires a combination of creativity and deep understanding of the challenge the innovation is trying to address.[12] Creativity is the consideration of a wide variety of alternatives and criteria for evaluating alternatives, as well as the building of novel and useful ideas that were not originally part of the consideration set.

Many group techniques combine creativity with structured problem-solving to achieve high quality innovation. These techniques begin with a set of ideas about the problem, generate more, then assess and combine ideas to create new ones. For example, Ideo, the world's most award-winning design firm, uses a process called the "Deep Dive" to create innovative solutions to design challenges: anything from developing a new toothbrush to revising the way insurance claims are processed.[13] The first step is a deep and careful examination of the challenge from all points of view, paying particular attention to features the end users need. The second step is a structured brainstorming exercise to generate as many ideas as possible. Third, the team creates prototype solutions to the challenge and tests them in a variety of contexts. The results of the prototypes are combined and built upon, and a final solution is created and implemented. In all steps, diversity of perspectives is encouraged and assumptions are questioned, but the team maintains discipline in its focus on the problem and on a timeline and structure. Since the membership of the design teams often consists of people from many different backgrounds and specialties, there usually are many perspectives.

Research has shown clearly that multicultural teams have higher creativity and innovation than single-culture teams.[14] The diversity of perspectives leads to more idea generation, and better potential quality in idea analysis and building. Whether the diverse team turns the innovation into final implementable performance depends on the quality of interaction processes in the team, particularly the social processes covered in the MBI model in Chapter 3.

Managing Boundaries and Stakeholders For a simple, routine, stable task, a team can sometimes take the task mandate and fulfill it without looking outside the team. However, most team tasks require extensive interaction between members and various parties outside the team.[15] Specifically, teams usually need to interact with external stakeholders to obtain resources for the team, to gather information both from within the organization and from sources outside, and to implement solutions.

Many teams assume they have a "right" to the resources, information, and response from people outside the team. They expect a budget that includes travel and that business units and other sources will provide information freely; and managers outside the team will pay attention to the team's suggestions and implement them. However, external stakeholders usually have different priorities, some of which may even conflict with those of the team. A global product team developing a new brand approach for a mobile phone company found that country managers, who had built their own markets autonomously in entrepreneurial ways, were unwilling to provide detailed information about their markets or to engage in pilot studies, even when mandated by top management.

If these interactions are anticipated and the relationships are developed, the team's access to these stakeholders increases, as does the cooperation from the stakeholders.[16] Effective teams map out the external relationships they need and strategically assign members to be responsible for different relationships on behalf of the team. By building the relationships, teams increase their social capital, or the resources that can be drawn upon from relationships. We return to this topic later in the chapter in the section on Networks.

One challenge teams typically face in boundary-spanning is interpreting and incorporating external perspectives into the team.[17] Such perspectives rarely come in a form that is tailored to the team's needs. For example, a team in a global construction firm was assessing the potential market in several countries for contracts to build and upgrade hospitals and medical facilities; they had developed a strong reputation for this in two countries and wanted to build on this in other parts of the world as part of a growth strategy. However, different countries report health-related data differently and have very different types of health management, so the data were extremely difficult to compare across countries, and it was hard to assess the potential in many countries. The team had to develop some common indicators and assess each country on an individual basis to calculate the indicator. In the end, they were able to successfully prioritize an international strategy, which they are now executing.

Multicultural teams usually have a broader set of external connections than do single-cultural teams, giving them access to more perspectives and resources. This is one of the potential competitive advantages of a multicultural team. However, because the information and resources must all be managed differently, there are often higher costs to maintaining the relationships in multicultural teams.

Advanced Dynamics are Fluid   Trust is probably the most fundamental of the three advanced dynamics. With strong trust among each other, team members are more likely to offer innovative ideas, to examine and question each others' ideas with a constructive spirit, and to build new ideas together. Strong trust also facilitates working well with external stakeholders. Team members are more willing to build and use external connections on behalf of a team they feel committed to and whose members they trust.

In order to achieve trust, innovation, and boundary-spanning, highly effective teams manage the basic OST principles in a fluid and flexible way. For example, a global airline cargo management team, created from a merger of two airlines, started off with clear roles and a set of task processes for first merging the two sets of operations, then developing and implementing a plan to win a larger share of the cargo market. As the nine team members from six countries and four different functions began to work together, they managed all the OST basics well. They defined the different parts of their mandate and revisited the definition as they worked on the task. They assigned roles and developed and followed a task plan. The early part of the task, integrating the operations, had some relatively simple aspects, and they tackled those first, as "low hanging fruits." As they worked on the integration, they learned more about each others' knowledge and cultural backgrounds. They implemented parts of the integration in their own divisions and saw the good results. At this point, they started experimenting with shifting roles, diving more deeply into innovation and unexpected solutions. In the next stages, which were more difficult, they hit some problems, such as market resistance to the merger and challenges with customer alliances. But the trust and knowledge they had built up earlier helped them support each other and find good solutions to these challenges. Once every few meetings, they took time to examine their processes, both basic OST principles and advanced dynamics, and took action to correct the course if necessary. The team exceeded their market share goals and began setting their sights on the next targets.

Managing Faultlines: A Challenge Specific to Diverse Teams

Above we have examined processes important to all teams, while highlighting their roles in international teams. In Chapter 3 on the Map-Bridge-Integrate principles, we described a set of processes that help create performance in intercultural interactions. Recent research has highlighted one further challenge to take into consideration for multicultural teams – the management of faultlines. Faultlines are rifts in teams that are created by alignment of different types of diversity.[18] For example, a global team may consist of two production engineers, two marketers, and two R&D scientists, from the US, Japan, and Germany. If the engineers are from the US, the marketers from Japan, and the scientists from Germany, then the functional and cultural divisions are aligned and there are likely to be three subgroups within the team who find it very difficult to collaborate. On the other hand, if each of the functions is represented by people from different countries, the subgroups will be less evident and differences will be easier to bridge.

Groups with faultlines can provide real depth and expertise by having more than one person representing each point of view. However, there is a clear risk of being unable to integrate. Furthermore, the faultlines can create power bases that hinder team processes. For example, on a team that was developing a new global pricing strategy for the company's service offerings, all the finance expertise on the team came from the headquarters country. The other members of the team assumed that whatever the finance people suggested represented the headquarters' point of view, so the others on the team were unwilling to question the finance members, in fear of losing power for their subsidiaries. When composing the team, the company had not anticipated such a reaction; the finance directors were selected for the team from headquarters simply because there were more of them there, they were more available for project work, and they had the knowledge of the global perspective. The company eventually took one of the headquarters people out and brought in a finance director from a moderate-sized subsidiary on a different continent, and this changed the dynamics significantly in a positive way.

When a team has such faultlines, it is more important than ever to find similarities that bind the subgroups together and facilitate communication among them. It is best not to ignore the faultlines. Everyone knows they are there, so the team should at least discuss them and their potential implications. Leaders of such teams can help by encouraging team members to voice ideas and questions that are not necessarily aligned with the groups they seem to represent, even through role-playing, and rewarding such contributions by considering them further.

Effective Teams Adapt to the Situation

Although there is no easy formula for team performance, teams that fulfill the basic OST principles are well on their way to at least fulfilling their mandates. Teams with more complex tasks must also pay attention to going beyond the basics with respect and trust, and to create value by innovating and interacting well with stakeholders outside the team. Effective teams adjust each of these dynamics according to the needs of the team. This need for adjustment means that managers and members of teams must take the responsibility to monitor and discuss the team's progress on a regular basis, rather than just ride along for the team journey.

VIRTUAL TEAMS: OVERCOMING THE BARRIERS TO CREATE PERFORMANCE

A virtual team is one whose members, usually based in different locations, work together more over technology than face-to-face. Most professionals are members of at least one virtual team and around half the managers of international companies are in two or more virtual teams. Although virtual teams are ubiquitous today, they are still quite new to the landscape. Some teams perform well, some fail miserably; most get something done but underperform against expectations. As a result, most managers are unsure about how to lead such teams across situations. In this section, we describe what makes virtual teams so difficult to manage, the dynamics these teams should focus on, and how to turn those dynamics into high performance. Some of the advice re-emphasizes aspects of team effectiveness in general from the section above; these are points that are particularly important for virtual teams. Other parts of the advice are specific to virtual teams.[19]

Virtual Teams: Just What Are We Dealing With?

Because virtual teams communicate through technology, many virtual teams focus on the technology challenges. But the characteristics that really challenge virtual teams are more difficult to see: dispersed configuration and diverse composition.

Dispersed configuration Virtual team members are distributed widely, often around the globe. Some of the consequences of dispersion are obvious. You may be familiar with the Tokyo-Berlin-Rio conference call scheduling dilemma! A more subtle challenge is that different regions have different infrastructures, and communicating seamlessly over different network types or with the same mobile phone in different parts of the world is often impossible. Moreover, team members are embedded in different contexts. They deal with different legal and political infrastructures, social relations, and climates. Even explaining to co-workers in the "real world" what the virtual team is doing will be different for team members, based on their different working context.

Team dispersion creates high needs for coordination and conscious processes. If the team is not well organized, members cannot work interdependently. And if team members do not explain their infrastructures and contexts to each other, communication will not be effective. On the other hand, high-performing virtual teams use dispersion to their advantage. For example, by overcoming the barriers, team members can use the 24-hour clock to develop tasks asynchronously and use the discipline of coordination to move the task forward steadily.

Diverse composition   Members of virtual teams are usually assigned because of their geographic, functional, experiential, or some other type of expertise. This assignment inevitably creates high levels of diversity on characteristics like culture and language, personality, values, and perspectives. As we discussed in Chapter 2, team members therefore bring different expectations to the team regarding how to interact with each other and how to engage in the task. For example, team members from Japan or Brazil may prefer a clear hierarchy in the team, with a specific leader who manages the team's actions, takes final decisions, and represents the team outside. Team members from Sweden or Canada, though, will likely be more comfortable with a fluid leadership structure and different people taking the lead for different parts of the task.

As we discussed in Chapter 3, unless these diverse perspectives are managed continuously, the team will likely experience conflict that can destroy it. But the high level of diversity also presents opportunities for applying expertise and creating innovation, and teams that work effectively capture this synergy and turn it into performance.

Three challenging conditions   Dispersed configuration and diverse composition combine to create three challenges for virtual teams: complexity, invisibility, and restricted channels (see Figure 4.2). With many more dynamics to manage at the same time and high levels of ambiguity, virtual teams are much more complex than face-to-face teams. They obviously face physical invisibility – team members cannot see each other, and nonverbal communication is therefore missing. But they also face mental and emotional invisibility. Being apart from each other creates blocks to perception, and it is much harder to practice the empathy or perspective-sharing needed for Bridging (see Chapter 3). Finally, communication channels are highly restricted. They are physically restricted: members must choose among a limited number of technologies and coordinate their choices. But they are also mentally and emotionally restricted. Members often work in second (or third . . .) languages and translate ideas across cultures or into unknown contexts, sometimes stripping those ideas of their richness.

Most teams focus on how to use technology to overcome the challenges of the conditions. However, successful teams first focus on a particular set of dynamics that are based on

FIGURE 4.2   Challenging conditions in virtual teams.

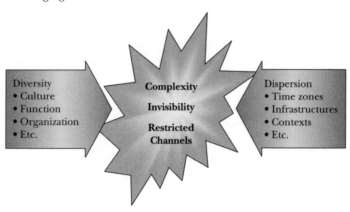

the Team Effectiveness principles identified above, as applied to the specific context of virtual teams.

Virtual Team Dynamics: What Do We Need to Accomplish?

Virtual teams *must* focus on three dynamics: shared understanding, trust, and ongoing communication. These are difficult to accomplish, but teams that do so create cycles of effectiveness. Virtual teams usually begin with a basic level of each of these dynamics. Then they either build on the dynamics or destroy them, as shown in Figure 4.3. In this section we distinguish the positive cycles from the negative ones; in the next we describe the tools for influencing the dynamics positively.

FIGURE 4.3   Dynamics of shared understanding, trust, and ongoing communication.
FIGURE 4.3a   Base level dynamics.

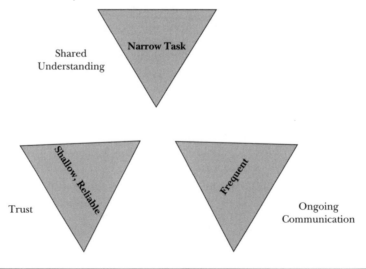

FIGURE 4.3b   Potential positive dynamics.

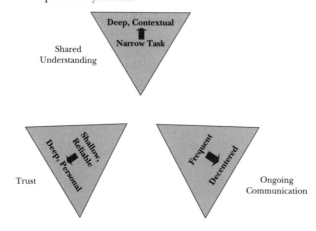

FIGURE 4.3c   Potential negative dynamics.

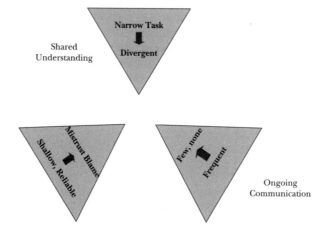

FIGURE 4.3d   Virtuous cycle.

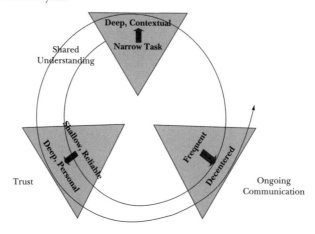

Shared understanding   Most teams start with a basic level of shared understanding. This includes agreement on the Organizing principles, such as a set of goals or objectives, often from a mandate given to the team, and general knowledge about others' potential contributions to the task, perhaps from their job titles, types of formal expertise, or reputations. High-performing teams take this shared understanding and build on it, using trust and ongoing communication. They use diversity and dispersion to develop shared contextual knowledge of the issue, learning about how it is interpreted in different contexts. They create a deep understanding of multiple causes of the issue they are working on, and a rich picture of implications of possible solutions. Low-performing teams do not build trust or communicate in an ongoing way, so they don't test their shared understanding past the first basics. Inevitably, when members are working in their own places, they encounter different interpretations of the task and develop different ideas of what to prioritize. Because they do not share these evolving interpretations with each other, misunderstandings arise and lead to serious conflicts.

Trust   We discussed the importance of trust above; in virtual teams it is even more critical. Most virtual teams start with a basic type of reliability. People are willing to give each other the benefit of the doubt. This shallow trust can either grow into something stronger or can degenerate into lack of trust. High-performing virtual teams, who use ongoing communication to build deeper shared understanding, can build personal trust, a belief that each member's priorities and values coincide with those of the team and that individual members can make good decisions on behalf of the team. In low-performing teams, who are not engaging in ongoing communication or building deeper shared knowledge, members make decisions and take actions that create a culture of blaming and mistrust within the team. Members begin to believe that others are not motivated to act on behalf of the team and are incapable of making good decisions.

Ongoing communication   Again, most teams start out fine on this dynamic. After the team launch there is a flurry of emails, postings, phone calls, and so on. High-performing teams use trust and shared understanding to create communication that is *decentered* – focused on the receiver's perspective and ensuring that the receiver really does understand and is invited to question, clarify, and reply (see Chapter 3 on Bridging). Such teams might tell stories about customers to illustrate what they suggest for the team, and share visual information like photographs or videos. Low-performing teams, on the other hand, do not develop such rich communication. In combination with their lower trust and lack of shared understanding, their messages to each other become less and less frequent. When they do communicate, it is usually minimal information, such as spreadsheets or PowerPoint reports, and not combined with contextual explanations.

As shown in Figure 4.3, the three dynamics of shared understanding, trust, and ongoing communication work together. Teams cannot develop or ignore one or the other without affecting the rest.

Managing Virtual Teams: How Do We Create Virtuous Cycles?

Advice to virtual teams is often confusing, and even outdated when a new technology emerges. We've identified three principles that apply to virtual teams whatever their technology, configuration, or task: organize and discipline, match technology to process, and create a heartbeat.

Organize and discipline   We identified this above as a basic principle for any team, but it is important to re-emphasize here because it is absolutely critical for virtual teams and is too often neglected. Face-to-face teams can get away with being unorganized and undisciplined. When members see each other, they catch up on the task; when they meet, they muddle through an agenda, even if there is no clear process and members are unprepared. For virtual teams, lack of organization and discipline is deadly. Complexity, invisibility, and restricted channels make this principle more difficult, but without it the team simply cannot progress.

High-performing virtual teams set up their norms for organizing and disciplining early in the team's life, but they also understand that the definitions, milestones, norms, and roles will change as the team and the task evolve. Such teams *use* the organization and discipline to build shared understanding, trust, and ongoing communication so they can revise the team's structure as necessary.

Match technology to process   Virtual teams are faced with a wide array of technologies and applications. However, there is actually no correlation between specific technologies and performance across teams and situations. Some good teams use only email and telephone calls, others use high-tech voice and video over Internet and shared live web sites. Overall, high-performing teams use a menu of technologies and select the right one for the team process at a given time.

The more you are *building trust and shared understanding*, the more you need *rich media* that allow communication using multiple modes at the same time, such as voice, text, and visual. This includes face-to-face or web-based videos. High quality videoconferencing is not always necessary; what's important is capturing context and some personal contact. On the other hand, the more you are engaging in *routine work*, the more you can rely on *less rich media*. Tracking progress and sharing routine reports can be done with email or shared web sites that are checked regularly.

High-performing teams also select technologies depending on infrastructure availability, members' skills, and personal preferences. They shift technologies over time, both as the phases of their task change and as their relationship as a team develops. Ongoing communication, trust, and shared knowledge help high-performing virtual teams select their technologies appropriately.

Create a heartbeat   When should we get together in person? It is often assumed that high-performing teams get together whenever things become complex, for example, a situation of intense conflict or ambiguity. Our research[20] and experience, however, suggest otherwise. Quite simply, high-performing virtual teams get together on a regular schedule, creating a heartbeat for the team.

Teams should set a schedule of regular meetings, perhaps once a quarter or twice a year. These team meetings can be planned in advance to coincide with other events such as professional conferences or large management meetings. Heartbeat meetings should focus on the major dynamics: building shared knowledge, trust, and ongoing communication.

A two-day agenda of presentations sharing PowerPoint results from the last quarter will do nothing to help the team. But a two-day agenda of customer visits, site visits, and discussion of difficult cases to share knowledge and advice will pump the equivalent of high quality oxygen into the team's circulatory system. Learning together and discussing situations through dialogue will enhance the team's shared knowledge, and sharing advice will increase the team's level of trust.

The heartbeat rhythm does not need to coincide with major decision points or milestones. This is often easier, but a high-performing team can handle intense conflict and heavy deliverables in virtual mode if it has developed shared knowledge, trust, and ongoing communication. Rhythm is critical. Like a human heartbeat, a team's heartbeat should be adjusted depending on the situation. If the team is less fit – for example, if there are new members or if trust has been damaged through a difficult situation – then the heart should beat faster than if the team is highly fit. If the team's task is more difficult – includes more ambiguity, more strategic importance, or the environment changes unexpectedly – then the heart should beat faster than if the team's task is simpler or more predictable.

Ideally, heartbeat meetings are in person. A well-developed team may have a slow face-to-face heartbeat supplemented with "interim virtual heartbeats," but it is important for the interim heartbeats to focus on keeping the team in a high-performing mode and not degenerate into round-robin reporting. We also have worked with successful teams that cannot meet face-to-face, who develop strong heartbeats using virtual technologies. These teams consciously use ongoing communication to develop shared knowledge and trust. For example, they use simple multimedia technologies – digital cameras and webcams – to share what is going on in their separate worlds, and they explicitly develop social relationships by sharing family and personal information as they increase their trust.

Virtual Teams are Complex, but Can Create Great Value

We are often asked "What's the secret?" as if there is some simple key that will unlock virtual team performance. Unfortunately, there is no such key. Collaborating across dispersion and diversity brings challenges. But it also brings opportunities that are worth the investment. Virtual teams can do things that face-to-face teams simply could not do: they expand our possibilities. In addition, most professionals find the work of a virtual team motivating, even if it is challenging. In today's flat organizations, well-managed virtual teams create development experiences with exposure to other cultures and situations. When virtual teams try to replicate their face-to-face team experiences, they are usually frustrated and disappointed. But when they develop new skills to address the challenges discussed here, they achieve high performance and create competences that the organization as a whole can benefit from.

MANAGING NETWORKS AND SOCIAL CAPITAL[21]

Often when we are discussing global teams, managers ask us "how big can a global team be?" and "How can I manage my reality of having teams within teams?" A global brand manager for a large consumer electronics group said, "My team has 100 people; that is probably too much, but that's the real group of people who need to work together on this." A global supply chain manager for an industrial parts manufacturing group said, "I have purchasing teams, production teams, logistics teams, and integration teams, and they all need to work together at different times. Which sets of teams should I apply these principles to, and how, when they are always shifting?"

The idea of "team" tends to limit us to thinking about "a group of people" (as noted in our definition that started the chapter) that is relatively stable over time, doing a single task. However, most collaborations in international organizations are not really that stable or unidimensional.[22] We discussed boundary-spanning above, but for many teams the term "boundary" – identifying who is internal and who is external to the team – is difficult. It is helpful for international managers also to think in terms of a relatively new field of social science: social networks and the social capital they carry.

Describing Networks

A network is simply a set of relationships among people. We visualize networks by drawing them as a set of points representing people (or organizations, or teams, or other social entities), with lines or arrows linking them to represent existing relationships. Figure 4.4 shows the network of a small 10-person account team for a marketing and advertising firm.[23] In the centre of the diagram are the 10 core members, from the US, Europe, and Asia. Team member number 1 is the Managing Director, number 2 is the Assistant Director, and the others are relatively equal in the team hierarchy. The arrows among them show two-way information relationships – among the core members of the team, who goes to whom for advice about the client and the task? The second layer of relationships, shown with dotted-line circles, adds one-way information relationships between team members and others in the firm – who do the core team members go to, outside the team but within the firm, for advice about the client and the task? The third layer of relationships, shown with dashed-line circles, adds one-way information relationships between the team members and people in the client firm – who do the core team members go to at the client firm for advice about the client and the task?

This network view shows many things about managing the team that a simple team perspective cannot and helps the team manage themselves more effectively. For example, the managing director of the account does not interact with the account team members as much as many would expect, and it may look as though she is a negligent team leader. However, as we see by the network diagram, she does interact frequently with the most senior people at the client, and this helps in the success of the team. Another pattern that becomes evident from the network diagram is related to team members 9 and 10 in Asia, the most recently added location for this account. The assistant director goes to them whenever he needs information from them. But until they saw this network diagram, the two most senior account managers did not realize how little members 9 and 10 were integrated into the core team. The two Asian representatives went only to people in their own office and in the client's local offices to work on the account, but their contacts at the client don't overlap with anyone else's, so if they were to leave the team, the contacts would be gone and the team would have to start again. Clearly, learning

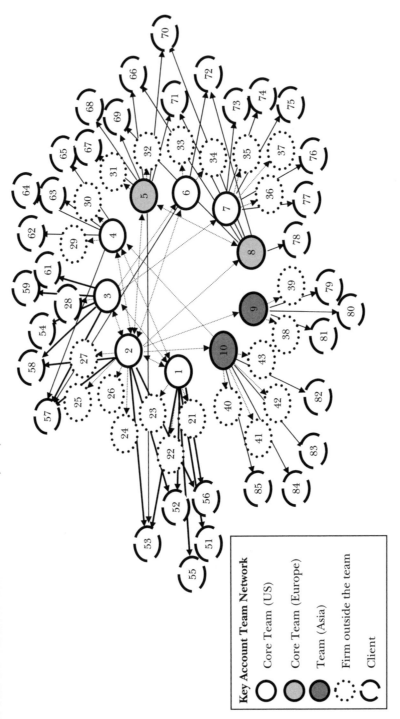

FIGURE 4.4 An account team's networks: team, firm, and client.

Key Account Team Network

◯ Core Team (US)

◯ Core Team (Europe)

◯ Team (Asia)

⟳ Firm outside the team

⟳ Client

and synergy opportunities are also being missed, and the assistant director started incorporating the two Asian members into more team meetings, encouraging them to visit the others and vice versa.

Assessing Social Capital

Relationships are important for many aspects of business performance, and different types of relationships help with different business elements. To sort out all these relationships, it is useful to draw on the notion of *social capital*, the set of assets in networks of personal relationships that can be valuable to achieve specific objectives.[24] Like other assets, building social capital requires investing, and the payoff may be immediate or long-term. Social capital can be more or less accessible and convertible to a useful purpose. Furthermore, one must "use it or lose it." Using it can increase it, and not using it can decrease it. Unlike other assets, though, social capital exists entirely in a relationship between parties. One person cannot own social capital by him- or herself, it exists only as a result of a link between people. If one party breaks the link, the social capital disappears completely. Social networks, like the structure shown in Figure 4.4 for the marketing account team, are holders and carriers of social capital. Social capital flows along the connections to and through people to other parts of the network, to get things done. Lin[25] identified four ways in which social capital moves through social networks: a social network facilitates flow of useful *information*; a person's network ties wield *influence* on others who play a critical role in decisions; people develop a reputation and related *credentials* by their ability to access resources through their networks; and, networks reinforce people's *identity* and their recognition in a network. Relationships that increase information flow, provide influence, clarify credentials, and reinforce identity enable the actor to access and use social capital to access, influence, and ultimately perform.

A large audit team from one of the Big Four multinational public accounting firms was auditing a large multinational client.[26] The audit was very comprehensive, and the client also wanted the firm to provide recommendations for improving the client's worldwide profitability. The audit team members had to gather information about the client and the industry, and combine it among themselves in a way that fulfilled the legal reporting obligations of the market and helped the client.

To the audit firm, the team is a unit with a network relationship with the team's managing partner. This partner assembled and supervised the team, and treated it as a single entity for administrative purposes. He assigned the team a mandate, provided access to key resources, and assessed its outcome with respect to the client firm's strategic expectations and the audit firm's own standards. The core audit team itself was composed of members from the audit firm's branches from several cities around the world to capture diverse functional and geographic experiences related to the client. As with the marketing team in Figure 4.4, each audit team member had relationships within his or her own network in the audit firm's worldwide organization. Also, each core team member had relationships outside the team, within the client's organization in various overseas operations, and in the broader communities around the world within which these operations are embedded. The collective external relationships of the audit team members created the external network within which the team was embedded. These relationships potentially could be used to facilitate the team's work in completing the audit.

Internally, the team coordinated its members to leverage their external network relationships and create a thorough personal understanding of the client's worldwide activities. Then the audit team members combined their individual understanding of audit information to compose a comprehensive report, which was presented to, accepted by, and acted upon by senior partners and the client's senior management.

In this complex global team, all four aspects of social capital – information, influence, credibility, and identity – were facilitated by social networks. Team members used their relationships to *influence* people whose cooperation they needed, and to facilitate *information* flow. Relationships with the client were important for obtaining the *information* and detecting its validity; auditors used strong relationships to *influence* people within the firm and at the firm's customers and suppliers to provide complete and comprehensive information. Relationships among team members were important for sharing *information* and creating a comprehensive picture of the client firm's activities; team members with strong *influence* encouraged other team members to increase their commitment to the client and the team, providing better solutions for the client. Relationships with the client were also used to *influence* the client's propensity to accept the audit firm's advice. Auditors' relationships with their professional organizations influence their *credibility*, and the senior partner in this team derived enormous *credibility* from the quality of his relationships with other senior partners and senior managers at client firms. Finally, auditors' *identity* as professionals was enhanced when the team produced a report that helped clarify and make transparent information to shareholders and the market, and at the same time, helped the firm identify areas in which to improve. This *identity* facilitated cooperation in further audits.

Network Structure and Social Capital

The two most important structural properties of networks are strength of ties and density. Connections between people, or ties, can be weaker or stronger.[27] *Weak ties* are those among people who have met briefly, perhaps exchanged business cards, and connect with each other infrequently; or, they may have connected more frequently and have to work together but do not have a close personal relationship. Weak ties are good for access to information, such as learning about new products or customers, or for looking for job candidates or jobs. They are relatively easy to maintain. *Strong ties* are those among people who have known each other longer, have a personal relationship, maybe even deep trust in each other. Strong ties are good for getting in-depth information, scarce resources, and commitment to new ventures. Strong ties are relatively difficult to maintain.

Internet social networking sites such as MySpace, Facebook, and LinkedIn[28] show connections among people. To be useful in connecting people with each other, they have developed innovative ways to indicate and leverage strength of ties. A main objective of MySpace is to promote musicians and other artists. People linked to each other through MySpace have a common interest in a particular band or artist, but do not tend to explore other aspects of the relationships. These large numbers of weak relationships are excellent for distribution of music and information about the music. Facebook, on the other hand, is aimed at linking together social networks of friends. On Facebook, when you accept someone as a friend, he or she can add personal things to your site that others can see, so most Facebook users tend to accept as friends only people with moderately strong relationships or who have moderately strong relationships with others they know. When two users have a number of connections in common, Facebook provides the possibility of connecting with others in the network. LinkedIn was developed to build networks of professionals, especially in business. LinkedIn emphasizes that you should only accept as connections people you know and trust, since others who can see your network will be able to see and possibly leverage those connections. LinkedIn provide a mechanism for recommendations, which is another way to indicate strength of ties. If I recommend you, our relationship is likely stronger than if I do not recommend you.

Density is a measure of how closely connected people in the network are to each other. The more everyone is connected to everyone else, the higher the density. In high density networks, information is passed quickly. There also tends to be redundancy in information, as everyone is talking to the same sources. In low density networks, information is passed less efficiently and may miss many members of the network. However, low density networks tend to access a broader set of resources and information, with less overlap.

The two basic structural properties combine to create many different types of networks. Two important patterns we call fishing nets and safety nets, and all teams should have both kinds of net. *Fishing nets* are lower density structures with many relatively weak ties.[29] Like "real" fishing nets, they can be cast in the right place to cover an area and catch things in the area. Fishing nets catch ideas, job candidates, customers, suppliers, and other opportunities. They can work when the network owner is not actively involved, but they must be checked from time to time in order to bring in the catch. These nets must also be maintained at regular intervals, checking that the connections are still in place and replacing those that have ripped. A real fishing net that is too dense brings in too many fish that are too small; not dense enough and it doesn't catch anything. Likewise, a fishing social network that is too dense – in which everyone is connected to everyone else – brings in too much of the same kind of information. One that is not dense enough – in which there are no connections or the connections are spread too broadly – brings in too little information or resources.

Figure 4.5 shows a global engineering company's fishing net. In general, this company has good fishing nets, with connections broadly distributed across all geographies and specialties. But this diagram highlighted the fact that two members from Latin America, "She" and "Bab," were not connected to the rest of the company. The Latin American operations these two were involved in had developed expertise in mining and other heavy operations that would have been very valuable to the rest of the company, but it was not being "caught" by anyone else. After they saw this diagram, managers in Latin America and other parts of the company worked to repair these holes and transfer more information. As we discussed above under "boundary-spanning," global teams should assess their fishing net to ensure it is catching and holding the right resources, and build fishing nets where necessary. In fact, this is good advice for all managers.

Safety nets are higher density structures with relatively strong and flexible ties. Like "real" safety nets, they catch people when they fall, and bounce them back up again. They are rarely used for this purpose, but they must be carefully maintained in case they are needed. Human safety nets usually include family members and a few close colleagues.

FIGURE 4.5 An international engineering company's cross-business unit, cross-geography fishing net.

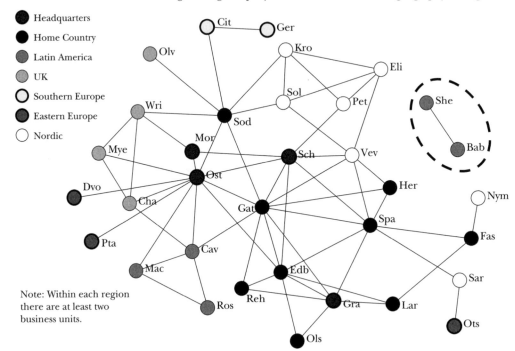

Some people say it is best never to use a safety net, but we disagree. In fact, when one is training in arts like trapeze and tightrope, the first instructions are always about how to use the safety net, and experts say that if you are not using your safety net during training, you are not improving your skill.[30] Figure 4.6 shows one manager's business execution network, which is clearly structured as a safety net. This manager is an investment banker in a highly volatile country, and he believes that structuring his business network in this way is critical to achieving success in the business.[31] One of the more peripheral members of the network is his golf instructor, whom he is carefully introducing to everyone else in his network in order to facilitate interaction among network members during a leisure activity. All teams should have safety nets, as well as fishing nets. In many complex teams, the core team itself is a safety net. One top management team of a global company we worked with realized that members' divisional roles left them feeling isolated and frustrated, with nowhere to turn for advice. Once they realized this, they deliberately began to create relationships among themselves to become the safety net for each other, and explicitly used the relationships that way, in order to help the company take some bold but important steps in a coordinated way. Although the company is in an industry that has been hit hard by the current global turmoil, they are much better positioned than their competitors in terms of coordination and strategy to weather the storm.

There are many other ways of looking at social networks and social capital that are very useful, and we encourage such teams to consult the many good references on this topic.[32]

FIGURE 4.6 One investment banker's business execution safety net.

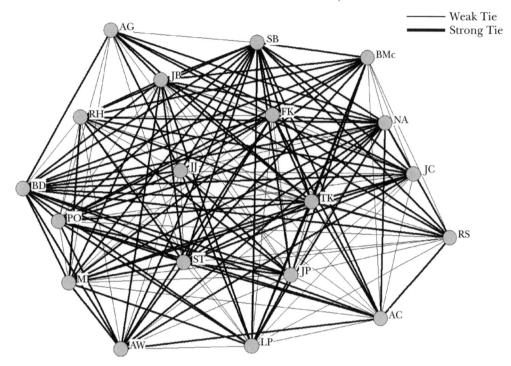

Putting Networks and Social Capital into Practice in Complex, Distributed Global Teams

Many managers facing complex global team situations find the ideas of networks and social capital appealing but aren't sure how to use them to help manage the teams. We share this example to illustrate. The situation is in the area of development, and the organization coordinates research and implementation projects to improve sustainable agriculture around the world. More than two hundred local projects are distributed on all continents, with the majority in Asia, Africa, and South America. There is a team of people at headquarters who oversee the projects and funding. There is also a representative of the organization in each region, who coordinates and monitors local projects. The headquarters team wanted to create more impact than would a simple selection and monitoring of projects. They thought there was more potential for learning across projects, and even for coordinating projects to achieve joint outcomes across regions that shared waterways and climate. However, creating multiple teams and adding the burden of coordination to those teams might take away effort from the immediate challenge of better farming in local projects.

Together with them, we combined the principles for managing virtual teams with the principles for managing teams and networks, and created the following suggestion, which is currently being implemented. First, members of the core team decided to spend more time in the field, learning from local and regional projects. They now meet only twice a year as a whole group in person for a week each time. They meet monthly for a half-day scheduled conference call as a whole team (sometimes they are able to do these meetings in person), and ad hoc in subgroups to share ideas and follow up on particular aspects of projects. Each of the members of the core team meets with their regional team twice a year, for two full days. These meetings are scheduled for the opposite quarters of the core team. They are held at a different site within the region each time, and regional team members learn about each others' countries and projects. Once a year, related to one of the core team meetings, a group of 20 representatives from various local projects meets for three days. The 20 representatives are selected to highlight a diverse spectrum of projects in different stages who can learn from each other. Attendees are also selected for having high levels of social capital within their local areas, and are likely to pass on what they have learned and to motivate others to collaborate. Once every three or four years, the organization plans to have a large conference with representatives from as many projects as possible, as well as external experts, suppliers, and other parties who can learn from and help the projects. Finally, the organization has set aside a travel fund to finance members of individual projects to visit projects in other parts of the world to learn and share knowledge.

The implementation of this interaction strategy is complex. But so is the goal, and ambitions are high. By managing both the various levels and types of teams and the entire network in a strategic way, the goal is more likely to be achieved. And once routines are in place, it is actually easier to manage – with discipline and focus – than it is to describe. Most people in the network do not need to see the whole network of teams. The role of the core team shifted from assessing, funding, and monitoring projects to managing the relationships among projects, and this was a difficult shift for some of the members of the core team. In the future, selection to the core team will reflect the new criteria. But the organization is beginning to see the results of the efforts in new innovations in sustainable agriculture, combining ideas from unlikely places.

Managers facing complex international coordination appreciate the combination of the team and network perspective since it helps them find and manage patterns in the complexity of their task. They know the task is difficult and that simple solutions and principles will only go part of the way. Even if the perspectives here are not simple to apply, they are systematic, and they provide ways of working towards performance and assessing progress.

TEAMS IN INTERNATIONAL MANAGEMENT COMBINE THE OLD AND THE NEW

As work in international firms becomes more interdependent, the need for coordination is increased. And the most common mechanism for coordination is the team. Most managers are part of multiple teams of different configurations, with at least some of those teams with members distributed across space. Before all else, managers must remember the OST basics of team management: Organize, manage Social processes, and manage Task processes. These principles have always been part of good managers' repertoire, and if a team is not performing as well as it should, this is the place to start. The next layer is the advanced dynamics of building trust, generating innovation, and spanning boundaries. These have also always been important, but with needs created by increased competition and speed in the marketplace, we have only recently systematized them. Virtual teams are a more recent phenomenon and our knowledge about them is still emerging. They will certainly be different a generation from now, when today's Internet-raised generation will be running international organizations. We expect the principles of organize and discipline, matching technology to the task, and creating heartbeats will always be important, though. Finally, today's managers must develop the capacity to see networks of relationships, not just sets of bounded teams. Using this perspective, they can manage complex coordination for synergistic results.

Notes

1   Baan, A. Personal communication.
2   Maznevski, M.L. and Athanassiou, N.A., "A New Direction for Global Teams Research: Introduction to Special Issue," *Management International Review* (2007).
3   This section draws from the chapter "Leading Global Teams," in Mendenhall, M.E., Osland, J.S., Bird, A., Oddou, G.R., and Maznevski, M.L., *Global Leadership: Research, practice, and development* (London: Routledge, 2008).
4   Maznevski, M.L. and Jonsen, K. "The value of different perspectives," *Financial Times, Mastering Uncertainty*, March 24, 2006, at 11.
5   Govindarajan and Gupta, 2001 (n. 10 below); Canney Davidson, 1994; Bettenhausen, 1991.
6   Often these conditions are referred to by the handy rhyme: "forming, storming, norming, performing;" however, not all effective teams experience the so-called stages the same way and it is more important to understand the underlying processes. "Forming" comprises task definition and team composition; "storming" is usually strongest during role assignment; "norming" is a condition of smooth team processes; and "performing" puts together roles and processes to achieve performance.
7   Maznevski, M., "Understanding our differences: Performance in decision-making groups with diverse members," *Human Relations*, 47 (1994) 531–552.
8   Tjosvold, D., *Working together to get things done: Managing for organizational productivity* (Lexington Books: Lexington, MA, 1986).
9   Jehn, K. A. "A multimethod examination of the benefits and detriments of intragroup conflict," *Administrative Science Quarterly* 40 (1995) 256–282. Jehn, K.A., "Enhancing effectiveness: An investigation of advantages and disadvantages of value-based intragroup conflict," *International Journal of Conflict Management* 5 (1994) 223–238. De Dreu, C. K. W. and Weingart, L. R. "Task versus relationship conflict, team performance, and team member satisfaction: A meta-analysis," *Journal of Applied Psychology* 88 (2003) 741–749.
10 Govindarajan, V. and Gupta, A.K., "Building an effective global business team. *MIT Sloan Management Review*, Summer (2001) 63–71.
11 Stahl, G. K., Maznevski, M., Voigt, A., and Jonsen, K., "Unraveling the diversity-performance link in multicultural teams: A meta-analysis of studies on the impact of cultural diversity in teams." Paper presented at the Academy of International Business Annual Meeting, Milan, August 2008. Published in the conference proceedings. Rohn, A., "Melting pot or tossed salad? Implications for designing effective multicultural workgroups from a coupling perspective," *Management International Review* (2007).
12 O'Reilly, C. A., Williams, K. Y., and Barsade, S. 1998. "Group demography and innovation: Does diversity help?" *Research on Managing Groups and Teams* 1 (1998) 183–207.
13 Kelley, T., Littman, J., and Peters, T. *The art of innovation: Lessons in creativity from Ideo, America's leading design firm* (Doubleday, 2001).
14 Stahl *et al*, (2008) n. 11 above.

15 Ancona, D. G. and Caldwell, D. F., "Bridging the boundary: External activity and performance in organizational teams," *Administrative Science Quarterly*, 37 (1992) 634–661.

16 Freeman, R.E. "The stakeholder approach revisited," *Zeitschrift für wirtschafts- und unternehmensethik* 5 (2004) 228–241. Driskat, V. U. and Wheeler, J. V. "Managing from the boundary: The effective leadership of self-managing work teams," *Academy of Management Journal* 46 (2003) 435–457.

17 Maznevski, M. L. and Athanassiou, N. A., "Bringing the outside in: Learning and knowledge management through external networks," in Nonaka, I. and Ichijo, K. (eds), *Knowledge creation and management: New challenges for managers* (Oxford: Oxford University Press, 2006).

18 Lau, D. C. and Murnighan, J. K., "Demographic diversity and faultlines: The compositional dynamics of organizational groups," *Academy of Management Review*, 23 (1998) 325–340. Maloney, M. M. and Zellmer-Bruhn, M., "Building bridges, windows and cultures: Mediating mechanisms between heterogeneity and performance in global teams," *Management International Review* (2007).

19 This section is based on research conducted by M. Maznevski with A. Baan, Arie Baan Consulting.

20 Maznevski, M. L. and Chudoba, K. M., "Bridging space over time: Global virtual team dynamics and effectiveness," *Organization Science* 11(5) (2000) 473–492.

21 This section draws on research conducted by the authors with N. Athanassiou, Northeastern University.

22 Maznevski and Athanassiou (2007) n. 2 above.

23 Athanassiou, N. A., Maznevski, M. L., and Walker, P. Unpublished study.

24 Adler, P. S. and Kwon, S. "Social capital: Prospects for a new concept," *Academy of Management Review* 27 (2002) 17–40; Lin, N., "Building a Network Theory of Social Capital," *Connections* 22 (1999) 28–51.

25 Lin (1999) n. 24 above.

26 This example was first introduced in Maznevski, M., Athanassiou, N., and Zander, L., *Global Teams in a Multinational Enterprise: A Social Capital and Social Networks Perspective*. Paper presented at the Organization Science Winter Conference, 2000.

27 Granovetter, M. S., "Economic action and social structure: The problem of embeddedness," *American Journal of Sociology* 91(3) (1985) 481–510.

28 www.myspace.com, www.facebook.com, www.linkedin.com. Accessed January 15, 2009.

29 Also referred to as networks with structural holes, Burt, R. S., *Structural Holes: The Social Structure of Competition* (Cambridge, MA: Harvard University Press, 1992).

30 Various circus school participants, personal communications.

31 Research by Shaner shows that foreign direct investments in stable and predictable environments perform better if the business unit has a fishing net type of network with customers, suppliers, and others in the business environment. However, in unstable and unpredictable environments, the business unit performs better with a safety net type of network. Shaner, J., *The relation between external business networks and performance in foreign investments*. Unpublished doctoral dissertation, University of Lausanne, 2005.

32 We particularly recommend Cross, R. and Parker, A., *The hidden power of social networks: Understanding how work really gets done in organizations* (Harvard Business School Press, 2004). Cross, R., Borgatti, S., and Parker, A., "Making invisible work visible: Using social network analysis to support strategic collaboration," *California Management Review* 44(2) (2002) 25–46. Cross, R., Nohria, N., and Parker, A., "Six myths about informal networks and how to overcome them," *MIT Sloan Management Review* 43(3) (2002) 67–75. Cross, R., Ehrlich, K., Dawson, R., and Helferich, J. "Managing collaboration: Improving team effectiveness through a network perspective," *California Management Review* 50(4) (2008) 74–98. Narasimhan, A. and Conger, J. Capabilities of the consummate networker, *Organizational Dynamics* 36(1) (2007) 13–27.

CASE **1**

Monsanto Europe (A)[1]

We should diligently explore the possibilities of non-chemical methods [of pest control]. . . . Until a large-scale conversion to these methods has been made, we shall have little relief from a situation that, by any common-sense standards, is intolerable.[2]

Environmentalist Rachel Carson, author of Silent Spring

On November 5, 1996, the captain of *Ideal Progress* piloted the large freighter into the calm waters of Hamburg harbor. Suddenly the still autumn air was pierced by a shrill noise and large floodlights momentarily blinded the captain. The engines ground to a halt as some of the deck crew gathered around the bow to listen to the chants of their strange assailants. The captain was one of the few who understood what the commotion was about; a Greenpeace ship had come to protest the arrival of the first shipment of genetically modified soybeans from the United States.

Richard Ivey School of Business
The University of Western Ontario

Northeastern
U N I V E R S I T Y

David Wesley, Professors Francis Spital and Henry W. Lane prepared this case solely to provide material for class discussion. The authors do not intend to illustrate either effective or ineffective handling of a managerial situation. The authors may have disguised certain names and other identifying information to protect confidentiality.

The protesters delayed the freighter's arrival as harbor authorities guided it to the pier. For most of the crew, the event was an entertaining delay to their anticipated shore leave, but to Monsanto it had deeper implications. Nobody really knew whether *Ideal Progress* carried any genetically modified soybeans in its 67,000-ton cargo hold since the soybeans were mixed with conventional crops during and after harvest. Still, for Greenpeace it was an opportunity to warn Europeans that genetically modified (GM) foods were beginning to arrive on a scale hitherto unknown in Europe.

To Monsanto, *Ideal Progress* was not only the name of a ship, but also closely reflected the aspiration of the company. "Sustainable Development" through the use of genetic engineering promised to reduce the use of pesticides and curtail world hunger, two laudable goals that should have garnered support, rather than opposition. Therefore, the success of environmental agitators in Germany (where the German subsidiaries of Unilever and Nestlé, among others, pledged to avoid GM foods for the foreseeable future) was difficult to understand. Robert Shapiro, a former Northeastern University law professor and chief executive officer (CEO) of Monsanto, explained:

> New technology is the only alternative to one of two disasters: not feeding people — letting the Malthusian process work its magic on the population[3] — or ecological catastrophe. We don't have 100 years to figure that out; at best, we have decades. In that time frame, I know of only two viable candidates: biotechnology and information technology[4]

Although other European countries remained relatively silent on the issue, Germany was one of the world's top five importers of U.S. soybeans, and therefore a market that could not be ignored.[5] Many at Monsanto believed that the negative reaction was simply a result of incomplete information and that "once the public is informed . . . there will be widespread acceptance."[6] The next task would be to decide how best to quell opposition, while educating Germans on the benefits of GM products.

MONSANTO HISTORY

In 1901, Monsanto was founded in St. Louis, Missouri, as a part-time venture to produce artificial sweetener. From the outset, the company had a multinational element. Founder John F. Queeny, an Irish immigrant without the know-how to produce the company's sole product, imported Swiss scientists and began production in direct competition with large German producers, thereby challenging their previously held worldwide monopoly.

It was not long before the company learned the importance of managing the political challenges of running a chemical company. Under pressure from the sugar industry, the U.S. Department of Agriculture decided to investigate Monsanto Chemical Works, as it was then known, to ensure that its artificial sweetener was not poisonous. In 1911, the company sought and received the support of then president Teddy Roosevelt, who stated that he had been using the product for years "without feeling the slightest bad effects."[7]

When a trade war with Germany nearly bankrupted Monsanto, Queeny decided to diversify into other food additives. By 1916, Monsanto's catalog included such well-known products as caffeine and Aspirin. The First World War proved to be a boon to Monsanto, as its German competitors were unable to transport their products to international markets.

In the postwar years, Monsanto began to expand rapidly, purchasing other chemical producers that had not fared so well during the war. With the company's success, bank financing was easily obtained until the company's debt level well exceeded equity. When foreign competitors finally went back on line in the early 1920s, Monsanto had difficulty meeting its debt obligations. Queeny assuaged bankers with promises of a turnaround, but was barely able to forestall bankruptcy. From then on, Monsanto adopted a very conservative approach to debt financing, instead preferring to use internal funds or equity to finance growth.

Shortly after its initial listing on the New York Stock Exchange in 1927, Monsanto moved to acquire two chemical companies that specialized in rubber. Other chemicals were added in later years, including detergents. Monsanto quickly became one of the world's largest producers of commodity chemicals.

The company began to redefine itself in 1960, with the creation of the agricultural products division, the purpose of which was to produce and market pesticides developed within the company's various chemical divisions. By consolidating Monsanto's research and development efforts in this field, the company hoped to improve the level of new product development and marketing.

The sixties also spawned what some in the company referred to as "Eco-nuts." Environmental activists were becoming especially critical of Monsanto and its catalog of toxic chemicals such as DDT (a pesticide), PCBs, Agent Orange and organic phosphates. All of these had been shown to have a direct negative impact on the environment and human health, but pesticides in particular had come under heavy criticism in the early 1960s.

Monsanto's chairman of the board at the time responded to these concerns:

> Pesticides involve the matter of tradeoffs. Their benefits far outweigh their perils. We in the pesticides business should continue to keep increasing their benefits and keep minimizing their risks.[8]

In subsequent public communications, Monsanto would argue that pesticides offered a potential solution to world hunger. "The world could never produce sufficient food without chemicals," they argued.

By the 1970s, the impact pesticides were having on the environment and human health had been well documented. Many countries, including the United States, either severely restricted or banned the use of pesticides. A new approach to pest control, known as integrated control, involved more restricted use of pesticides, along with the development of pest-resistant crops through selective breeding and the use of natural predators.

Roundup Herbicide

In 1970, a glyphosate herbicide called Roundup was developed in Monsanto's research laboratories. This became the world's leading herbicide and was used on more than 100 different crops around the world. Roundup had the effect of exterminating all vegetation without discrimination. Therefore, farmers applied the herbicide to fields before crops were planted.

One advantage to farmers was that fields did not need to be plowed every year in order to remove the stubble from the previous harvest. Instead, after spraying the field with Roundup, a farmer could plant between the rows, thereby reducing labor and conserving topsoil. Roundup was also less toxic than many herbicides, largely biodegradable and would bind to soil, thereby eliminating the risk of groundwater contamination.

Roundup quickly became the company's largest contributor to agricultural sales, accounting for 40 per cent of total company operating earnings. However, in many countries, the patent for Roundup expired in 1991 and was due to expire in 2000 in the United States. As a result, Monsanto sought ways to extend the life of this highly successful product.

Genetic Engineering

It was not long after the invention of Roundup herbicide that Monsanto undertook research efforts to develop genetically modified crops that could resist the herbicide in hope of increasing the value of Roundup to farmers. By the time the U.S. Supreme Court ruled, in 1979, that genetically modified living organisms could be patented,[9] Monsanto had already begun to take a leading role in the field.[10]

The Supreme Court decision only served to increase the incentive for companies to undertake research and development (R&D) investment in this new technology. New competitors quickly began to appear on the scene, ranging from small biotech firms specializing in niche products to giants, such as DuPont. Genetically engineered produce started to reach the consumer market in the early-1980s in the form of GM potatoes and tomatoes.[11]

Biotechnology presented potential solutions to a number of problems faced by farmers. In addition to herbicide resistance, genetic engineering could make crops resistant to insects and disease, increase the nutritional content, produce crops capable of growing in less hospitable environments (such as deserts) and increase the shelf life of fruits and vegetables. Theoretically, the increased yields offered by such technologies could also help alleviate hunger in developing countries, where some 1.5 billion people lived in abject poverty.[12]

Pest-resistant crops, in particular, were held up as a solution to the *Silent Spring* scenario. Since the book's introduction in the 1960s, *Silent Spring* had become the battle cry of naturalists and environmentalists who protested the widespread and indiscriminate destruction of plant and animal life, as a result of the increased use of pesticides. Monsanto maintained that genetic engineering could become the basis for the integrated approach to pest control, since crops could be made selectively resistant to predators and disease without harming other life.

By 1984, Monsanto had begun to divest itself of commodity chemicals in order to focus more on life sciences, including biotechnology and pharmaceuticals. This was reflected in the 1985 purchase of pharmaceutical manufacturer G.D. Searle & Co., maker of the highly successful artificial sweetener known as Nutrasweet. The following year, Monsanto sold its petrochemical, paper chemical, and plastics divisions, among others.

Dick Mahoney, who was Monsanto's CEO at the time, developed a three-pronged strategy that was to carry Monsanto into the next millennium.

First, the profitability of Roundup herbicide could be sustained at least through the 1990s.

Second, agricultural biotechnology would work, would reach the market and would potentially transform agriculture.

Third, sustained research investment in [the] Searle pharmaceutical business, at a scale larger than that which Searle's revenues could support, would pay off in new products.[13]

Although Monsanto had yet to bring a single GM product to market, the company fully expected to derive nearly a third of its revenue from genetically engineered products within the next 15 years.[14] At the same time, financial analysts were wary of the new technology, citing concerns about regulatory approval and consumer acceptance, and warned investors to steer clear of biotech companies that focused on genetic engineering.[15] Philip Needleman, Monsanto's vice-president in charge of research and development, seemed unconcerned. He believed that consumer acceptance was simply a matter of getting more GM products into the hands of consumers, and that once GM foods became commonplace, people would wonder what all the fuss was about.[16]

The company's first commercial application of agricultural biotechnology was a growth hormone that stimulated milk production in cows. The hormone, known as BST, was developed in 1984, and was expected to be available to farmers in 1988. However, because of concerns about hormones entering the food supply, and the fact that world milk production already well exceeded demand, the FDA delayed approval of the product for several years while it conducted further studies. When the product finally reached the market, Needleman was proven correct, as the anticipated consumer backlash never materialized. In 1996 alone, sales of BST increased by 48 per cent.

The BST case made it clear to Monsanto that regulatory bodies, not consumer acceptance, would be the greatest hindrance to the ultimate success of biotechnology products. Monsanto therefore sought to improve its understanding of, and influence with, such bodies, and to that end successfully attracted the former EPA director and the former U.S. Secretary of Commerce to its Board of Directors.

In addition to the potential of stand-alone products, such as BST, genetic engineering also promised to extend the life of the company's most successful agricultural product, Roundup herbicides. By inserting a particular gene into seeds, crops were made resistant to the herbicide. Since Roundup Ready crops could be planted before fields were sprayed, farmers would be able to selectively spray crops when needed, and thereby reduce the amount of herbicide needed. Through "the introduction of Roundup Ready crops," noted Shapiro, Monsanto could "expect Roundup to continue generating substantial cash and earnings in the years ahead."[17]

The main factor that allowed Monsanto to capitalize on food biotechnology was a very significant drop in the cost of genetic sequencing.[18] For example, in 1974, the cost to Monsanto of sequencing only one gene approached $2.5 million. Given that a typical agricultural product, such as rice, contained approximately 40,000 genes, sequencing costs became the company's most significant barrier to developing genetically engineered products. However, in subsequent years, advances in computers and other technologies helped to significantly reduce the cost of genetic sequencing to a mere $150 per gene. Company scientists viewed this as a very significant breakthrough.

A Bountiful Harvest

The initial reception of GM foods in the United States was very promising. About two-thirds of all manufactured food products contained soybeans, and as more of these products began to incorporate Roundup Ready varieties, there was little or no protest. Marketing studies conducted in the United States and Japan showed overwhelming consumer approval of the high-tech foods, and it appeared that earlier concerns over public acceptance were once again unfounded (see Exhibit 1). In fact, as far as the typical U.S. consumer was concerned, the GM issue was not an issue at all. Professor Thomas Hoban, a sociologist who conducted the U.S. Department of Agriculture's consumer research on biotechnology, concluded:

> Biotechnology has not (and likely will not) become an issue for the vast majority of consumers. When asked either to report the greatest threat to food safety or to rate a series of food safety hazards, biotechnology is seen as the least significant issue or concern.[19]

Under the assumption that "life sciences" would give Monsanto its strategic advantage, in 1996 the company's board of directors decided to spinoff the chemical products division into a separate wholly owned subsidiary known as Solutia. Shapiro planned to recreate Monsanto's image in the public mind by disassociating the company from environmental conflict, in favor of what he called "sustainable development." Shapiro explained:

> We became a life sciences company because we were engaged in three historically separate businesses — agriculture, food ingredients and pharmaceuticals — that now have begun to share common technologies and common goals . . . the intersection of these technologies and goals defines an extraordinary set of business opportunities. . . . Few people understand the size and scope of the opportunities we're pursuing.[20]

EXHIBIT 1   1995 Survey Of U.S. And Japanese Consumers[1]

Consumer Support for Agricultural Biotechnology			
	Support	*Oppose*	*Don't Know*
Japan	82%	16%	2%
United States	66%	26%	5%
Consumer Willingness to Purchase			
	Very Likely	*Somewhat Likely*	*Not Too Likely*	*Not at All Likely*
Insect Protected				
Japan	5%	54%	28%	3%
United States	31%	42%	15%	9%
Taste Better or Fresher				
Japan	4%	59%	34%	3%
United States	20%	42%	23%	14%

1 "How Japanese Consumers View Biotechnology." *Food Technology*, July 1996.

Investors took a positive view of Monsanto's new focus, as the company's stock price more than tripled in less than two years. In 1996 alone, Monsanto shareholders were rewarded with a 62 per cent return on their investment.

By 1997, some 30 million acres of farmland, mostly in the United States and Canada, had been planted with Monsanto's genetically modified seed. Monsanto quickly engaged itself in a buying spree, acquiring biotech companies and seed distributors. In one well-publicized purchase, Monsanto paid $1 billion (23 times sales) for an Iowa-based seed company. In 1998 alone, Monsanto more than tripled its long-term liabilities to a total of $6.2 billion, outstripping equity by approximately $1.5 billion. Monsanto had clearly staked its future on biotechnology, and most investors continued to display a very high level of optimism.

EUROPEAN REACTION

> *[Biotechnology] makes me remember the first trains which crawled along the countryside. People at that time were concerned that their cows would drop dead and worse still, they were convinced that man could not survive at such high speed. They were proven wrong and now we can go from Paris to Lyon in two hours, and nobody complains about it. But from time to time a dramatic train crash will remind us that there is no such thing as zero risk.*
>
> **Emma Bonino, European Commissioner in Charge of Consumer Policy and Health Protection**

Despite the fact that the U.S. Food and Drug Administration (FDA) and the European Union (E.U.) had approved the product for sale, some in the European press likened the introduction of GM foods to a number of other food safety concerns, the foremost being mad cow disease.[21] When a link was made between BSE and a similar fatal neurological disease in humans, the British government downplayed the risk and insisted that British beef was safe. This position was later reversed, but not before nearly every British consumer had been exposed.[22] "Why should these same authorities now be trusted?" some asked.

> Will the public wish to eat such genetic simulacra, knowing that they are foodstuffs that have been tinkered with by scientists, refashioned according to a relatively new technology and usually for the benefit of biochemical companies and farmers rather than consumers who will buy and eat the results?[23]

Germans, and other northern Europeans, in particular, placed more importance on food purity than most other cultures. Many still shopped at bakeries and delicatessens, where mainly traditional products were sold. Even processed foods were more pure than equivalent products elsewhere in the world.[24] They did not want to see their food contaminated with genetically engineered ingredients.

Risk-Averse Culture

Many Americans viewed the problem of European resistance as one of risk aversion. While acknowledging the importance of the mad cow crisis in hypersensitizing consumers to food safety issues, the real issue, they argued, had more to do with culture. One top U.S. official commented:

> I joke with some of my European friends saying that the definition of an American is a risk-taking European. We immigrated here. We had faith in the future. Those who stayed behind had a little less faith in the future. They were more risk-averse.[25]

The same sentiment was echoed by advocates of GM foods in Europe. Gordon Conway, a British ecologist and president of the Rockefeller Foundation, a philanthropic organization that funded $100 million in biotech research, noted:

> The U.S. is a very hazardous place. You have hurricanes. You have tornadoes. You have rattlesnakes. You have all kinds of tick-borne fevers. You have 250 million guns. In contrast, the sole hazard in Britain is one very rare poisonous snake. That's it. Period. It's a well-manicured country. So the American population is used to living with hazards. Most Americans are more worried about getting shot than the remote chance that some GM ingredient in food going to affect their health.[26]

In the United Kingdom, for instance, this cautious attitude was reflected in the lack of entrepreneurial optimism. Whereas in the United States, where "public attitudes encourage risk-taking," more than half of the American population was optimistic about opportunities to start a business, in the United Kingdom only 16 per cent thought that good opportunities existed, despite significant government incentives.[27]

Risk Versus Benefit

For British consumers, the issue boiled down to one fact, that the technology had so far not produced any benefits to the consumer, but was perceived to pose a variety of risks. While Monsanto had developed products that provided consumer benefits, such as higher vitamin content or lower cholesterol, these were still being tested and were years away from commercial applications. One such product was vitamin A-enhanced rapeseed oil, one teaspoon of which provided the recommended daily intake for an average adult. This product was "designed to address the specific nutritional needs in particular areas of the world," where some 800 million people suffered from serious illnesses related to vitamin A deficiency.[28]

One Monsanto director noted, "It would have been nice if the first products could have had health benefits for the consumer instead of cost benefits to the food industry."[29]

Product Labeling

Months before *Ideal Progress* left U.S. shores, Henrik Kroner, secretary general of Eurocommerce (the official E.U. retail and trade association) warned Monsanto of the developing negative sentiment and requested a delay of one year to educate and prepare consumers.[30] He notes that European consumers' confidence in food safety was already at an all-time low, as a result of Mad Cow disease. His message to Monsanto was this, "If you are wise, don't ship those soybeans to Europe because you may trigger a lasting reaction. And if you must, separate and label them."[31]

Labeling advocates were also quick to point out that British biotech firm Zeneca Plant Science had earlier in the year voluntarily labeled their Flavr Savr tomatoes,[32] and consumers seemed to be responding favorably to the product.

While labeling appeared to be an easy way to calm anxiety over the new soybeans, that would have entailed separating the beans at their source. The U.S. agricultural industry claimed to have neither the infrastructure for such an undertaking, nor the desire to incur the considerable expense required to develop that infrastructure. Instead, Roundup Ready soybeans were often mixed with conventional beans during harvest, storage and shipping. As a result, nobody could tell which were modified and which were conventional. Furthermore, as stated by Monsanto (see Exhibit 2) separating and labeling genetically modified produce would have implied that these products were different from conventional products and perhaps unsafe.

EXHIBIT 2   Monsanto Reply to Labeling Request[1]

December 16, 1996

To the Editor, Financial Times, London

Sir,

Joe Rogaly's article "Beans and genes" did not contribute very much to the genetic engineering debate. I'm not referring to his name-calling – "mad scientist soybeans", "futuristic corporation", "Big M" - to which I won't respond, nor to his self-acknowledged cynicism (which somewhat ruined his humour just as it was starting to amuse).

I'm just disappointed that he only gave a passing reference to the fact that experts and government agencies around the world, including the US, Europe/UK, Japan, Canada, Mexico and Argentina, have concluded unconditionally that Roundup Ready soybeans (RRS) are as safe as other soybeans.

Mr. Rogaly says there would be no problem if only customers could be given the option through labelling of not buying products containing RRS. However, mandatory labelling of products such as these beans, which are unchanged in composition, nutrition, function and safety, would imply that these products are different from their unmodified counterparts when they are not. Again, the same regulatory authorities as mentioned above have concluded that there is no need for special handling or labelling because these soybeans are as safe as other soybeans and because they are substantially equivalent to other soybeans. All this was reaffirmed again by the Ministry of Agriculture Fisheries and Food's food advisory committee on December 12.

We are fully aware and accept that some may have concerns and questions about RRS, which is why we and others have opened consumer hotlines and produced information leaflets to address the issues. We remain at anyone's disposal to discuss the matter.

Michael A. Scharf,
Monsanto Services International
Avenue de Tervuren 270-272, B-l1150
Brussels, Belgium

1 "Experts Say Genetic Soybeans are Safe," Financial Times, December 18, 1996.

Misguided Concern

Monsanto had heard all this before. Scaremongers had warned the company many times in the 1980s that U.S. consumers would not buy milk from hormone-fed cows, and again that they would be reluctant to buy GM produce. Each time these dire warnings failed to materialize. Monsanto simply needed to "convince people that this is a good useful technology," Shapiro noted, and those who opposed GM foods were "at best misguided."[33]

Shapiro did not seem too concerned:

> The multinational corporation is an impressive invention for dealing with the tension between the application of broadly interesting ideas on the one hand and cultural differences on the other. Companies like ours have gotten pretty good at figuring out how to operate in places where we can make a living while remaining true to some fundamental rules. As more countries enter the world economy, they are accepting — with greater or lesser enthusiasm — that they are going to have to play by some rules that are new for them.[34]

In the company's annual report, Shapiro devoted a scant two sentences to the topic. "In some European countries," he wrote, "questions remain about the labeling and public acceptance of food products with genetically modified crops. We'll continue to work with interested parties to help resolve those questions."[35]

Growing Opposition

On the other side of the Atlantic however, opposition to GM foods continued to grow. A 1997 E.U.-wide survey revealed that food safety had become the most important issue for European consumers, with some 68 per cent of those surveyed expressing concerns about the safety of their food. As a result of such concern, the European commission "decided to place consumer health and food safety at the center of a new political initiative." The commissioner responsible for implementing this initiative noted:

> Consumers are increasingly aware of the importance of safe food and the impact certain products have on health. They resist the idea of a passive role and are more and more conscious of their ability to shape the market with their buying power. They have decided to use their right of choice and quite rightly so; they demand adequate information, they want to know what they eat, what it is derived from and where it is produced.[36]

Genetically modified foods, in particular, became a focus of concern. German and Austrian consumers, while having the highest levels of awareness of food biotechnology in the world (90 per cent awareness), were among the least willing to purchase GM produce (30 per cent and 22 per cent, respectively). In contrast, awareness in the United States had declined to 55 per cent, while willingness to purchase had increased to 73 per cent.[37]

Some European governments began responding to the public concerns about GM food safety by banning their import and sale (Austria and Luxembourg), while other countries imposed various restrictions. An increasingly skittish European parliament, having felt the sting of various food scandals, tried to assure Europeans that food safety was being taken seriously. Although the European Union had opposed labeling of GM foods, a new proposal known as the "Novel Foods Law," would require it, if passed. Some industry observers were skeptical of the whole notion. "Because the altered foodstuffs look exactly like the natural ones and, in most cases, will be less expensive," commented one, "many consumers don't see what the big fuss is about."[38]

THE ADVERTISING CAMPAIGN

By 1997, German opposition was well entrenched, while in the United Kingdom, most consumers were still willing to purchase modified produce. However, consumer acceptance in the United Kingdom was declining in the wake of environmental activism and negative press reports, which questioned the safety of modified produce.

Monsanto hoped to allay public fears through education. As early as 1996, the company employed targeted advertising and toll-free hotlines in both the United Kingdom and Germany, but these seemed to have little effect.

Other efforts to educate the public proved equally ineffective. An industry association known as the Familiarization and Acceptance of Crops Incorporating Transgenic Technology (FACTT) was formed by 21 European organizations with interests in biotechnology, and set out to educate British farmers and consumers about the benefits of genetically engineered crops. However, two public education events scheduled for April 1998 had to be cancelled due to a "lack of interest." A third seminar in May was also cancelled when activists threatened to vandalize trial crops and thereby disrupt the event.[39]

Field Trials

More radical opponents were becoming frustrated that the British government had not taken steps to ban GM foods and began to take matters into their own hands. In one incident, the biotech industry tried to engage environmentalists in an open dialogue and invited one group (Friends of the Earth) to inspect field trials. Without authorization, Friends of the Earth published the field trial locations on the Internet. Shortly afterward, a number of environmentalists showed up at the farm dressed in white radiation suits. After a brief confrontation with a local farmer, the white hooded invaders took to burning and uprooting crops. This, and other similar actions, hampered efforts to educate the public and resulted in the loss of valuable research data intended to address environmental and safety concerns.

While the U.K. government had approved applications for 152 trial crops, farmers, fearing violence and retribution at the hands of "Eco-warriors," were hesitant to co-operate with Monsanto and other biotechnology companies. Some farmers noted that GM opponents had raised "genuine concerns" and wanted these concerns answered before planting trial crops (see Exhibit 3 for a summary of environmentalist concerns).[40]

Public opposition frustrated many European biotech scientists. As a result of what appeared to be an increasing lack of opportunity in Europe, they began leaving for better paid and more respected positions in the United States.

EXHIBIT 3   Summary of Concerns by Opponents of Gm Crops[1]

1. **Harm to wildlife:** Bacillus thuringiensis is a naturally occurring bacteria that organic growers use to control caterpillars and other pests. New genetically engineered plants have a toxin produced by the Bt bacterium in each and every cell, from the roots to the pollen to the chaff plowed under after harvest. Cornell University researchers made headlines when they announced laboratory research showing that monarch butterfly larvae died after eating milkweed dusted with genetically engineered corn pollen containing the BT pesticide. Milkweed, the monarch's primary food source, commonly grows alongside corn. Researchers in Europe have made similar discoveries involving ladybugs and green lacewings, both beneficial insects. Yet another study, reported in 1997 in the British publication New Scientist, indicates that honeybees may be harmed by feeding on proteins found in genetically engineered Canola flowers.
2. **Harm to soil:** Microbiologists at New York University have found that the BT toxin in residues of genetically altered corn and rice crops persists in soils for up to 8 months and depresses microbial activity. And in another study, scientists in Oregon tested an experimental genetically engineered soil microbe in the laboratory and found it killed wheat plants when it was added to the soil in which they were grown.
3. **Harm to humans:** A growing body of evidence indicates that genetic engineering can cause unintended changes to our food, making it less nutritious or even harmful.
4. **Hidden Allergens:** DNA, the cell formations from which genes are composed, directs the production of proteins. Proteins are also common sources of human allergies. When DNA from one organism is spliced into another, can it turn a non-allergenic food into one that will cause an allergic reaction in some people? The Iowa-based biotech seed company Pioneer Hi-Bred International tried to change the protein content of soybeans by adding a gene from the Brazil nut. When researchers tested the modified soybean on people with sensitivity to Brazil nuts (but no sensitivity to soybeans), they found it triggered an allergic reaction. (Based on those findings, the company shelved development of the soybean.)
5. **Antibiotic resistance:** Genetic engineers use antibiotic marker genes to help them transfer genetic coding from one life-form to another. But some scientists worry that this process could compound the increasingly serious problem of antibiotic resistant bacteria. The concern is that bacteria living in the gut of humans or animals could acquire antibiotic resistance from GMO foods eaten by the human or animal, possibly rendering treatments for such infections as meningitis and gonorrhea ineffective.
6. **Religious and Moral Considerations:** People who choose not to eat animals for religious or moral reasons face an almost impossible task with many genetically engineered foods. When genes from flounder are spliced into tomatoes or genes from chickens are added to potatoes for increased disease resistance, are those vegetables still, purely speaking, vegetables? And without mandatory labeling, how can people who object to eating any trace of meat know what they are getting?
7. **Super bugs:** With Bt constantly present in millions of acres of crops, Bt-resistant insect strains will evolve-in as little as 3 to 5 years, the biotech industry's own scientists acknowledge.
8. **Super weeds:** Plants engineered to survive herbicides, such as Canola (oilseed rape), are cross-pollinating with wild cousins, which could create herbicide-resistant weeds. Which will defeat the purpose of engineering the plants and may coax farmers into using more powerful poisons to kill weeds.
9. **Indentured farmers:** The corporations committed to genetic engineering research—many of the same companies that produce chemical pesticides—are rapidly buying up seed companies and gaining control of entire food-production systems and educational-research facilities. Farmers who use this patented technology, meanwhile, are prohibited from the self-sufficiency of saving seed and instead are forced into a costly cycle of corporate dependency.
10. **Pollen drift:** Organic farmers could lose their certification and face financial ruin if their fields are contaminated by wind-borne pollen from nearby genetically modified crops. Even non-organic farmers are at risk for problems.

[1] "Ten Reasons Organic Farming is Concerned About Genetically Engineered Plants," Organic Gardening, January 2000.

Turning Back the Tide

As Monsanto's position in the United Kingdom became increasingly precarious, the company decided that something had to be done to turn back the swelling tide of public opposition. Professor Thomas Hoban, the leading industry consultant on consumer opinion, suggested that educational efforts would be the best means to "facilitate acceptance." He recommended:

EXHIBIT 4   Monsanto Advertisements

WORRYING ABOUT STARVING

FUTURE GENERATIONS

WON'T FEED THEM.

FOOD BIOTECHNOLOGY WILL.

THE WORLD'S population is growing rapidly, adding the equivalent of a China to the globe every ten years. To feed these billion more mouths, we can try extending our farming land or squeezing greater harvests out of existing cultivation.

With the planet set to double in numbers around 2030, this heavy dependency on land can only become heavier. Soil erosion and mineral depletion will exhaust the ground. Lands such as rainforests will be forced into cultivation. Fertiliser, insecticide and herbicide use will increase globally.

At Monsanto, we now believe food biotechnology is a better way forward. Our biotech seeds have naturally occuring beneficial genes inserted into their genetic structure to produce, say, insect- or pest-resistant crops.

The implications for the sustainable development of food production are massive: Less chemical use in farming, saving scarce resources. More productive yields. Disease-resistant crops. While we'd never claim to have solved world hunger at a stroke, biotechnology provides one means to feed the world more effectively.

Of course, we are primarily a business. We aim to make profits, acknowledging that there are other views of biotechnology than ours. That said, 20 government regulatory agencies around the world have approved crops grown from our seeds as safe.

Food biotechnology is too great a subject to leave there. Ask for a leaflet at your local supermarket, write to us, call us free on 0800 092 0401 or visit our online Comments & Questions

WE BELIEVE FOOD SHOULD

BE GROWN WITH

LESS PESTICIDE.

Monsanto is a leading biotechnology company. We believe biotechnology is one way to cut down on the amount of pesticides used in agriculture. For instance, the tomato here is grown by fusing a naturally-occurring beneficial gene into the tomato plant, making it insect resistant. As a result, the farmer can spray substantially less insecticide onto his fields.

Some biotech crops need no insecticides at all. For others, their use is reduced by a third or more. The result is food grown in a more environmentally sustainable way, less dependent on the earth's scarce mineral resources. (We also want you to know that we produce the world's best-selling herbicide, Roundup.)

Our food crops have been approved by government regulatory agencies in over 20 countries, including Switzerland, Denmark, the Netherlands, the U.S.A. and Great Britain.

Obviously we believe in the benefits of plant biotechnology, both for the environment and for everyone who eats food grown from our seeds.

If you'd like to find out more about this subject, please ask for a leaflet at your local supermarket, call us free on 0800 092 0401 or use our online Comments & Questions form.

(THE INSECT RESISTANT TOMATO HAS NOT BEEN APPROVED IN MORE THAN 20 COUNTRIES AND IS NOT YET COMMERCIALLY AVAILABLE)

Source: Monsanto UK

The best way to reach consumers is by educating opinion leaders, including scientists and health experts, government officials, the media and food industry officials. Key messages should include the benefits and uses of biotechnology as well as the government regulations that are in place to ensure safety.[41]

On June 6, 1998, Monsanto launched an advertising campaign in the United Kingdom with the stated aim of providing consumers with "the information they need to make informed decisions," and included newspaper advertisements, a toll-free hotline, leaf-lets, and a consumer Web site.[42] Issues of safety and nutrition, as well as feeding the world's hungry, were central to the campaign (see Exhibit 4).

The British weeklies in which the ads appeared were those typically read by better-educated individuals from higher socio-economic backgrounds, such as government ministers, senior bureaucrats and business leaders; the "state elites," as Monsanto referred to them. In accordance with Professor Hoban's recommendations, Monsanto hoped to influence political decision makers as a way to achieve wider acceptance of genetic engineering.

Opponents of GM foods were not impressed and reacted with campaigns of their own. Other, sometimes better respected, opponents, such as His Royal Highness, the Prince of Wales, joined traditional opponents such as Greenpeace. Two days after Monsanto's advertising campaign was announced, Prince Charles released an essay on GM crops in a leading newspaper, in which he likened modified crops to mad cow disease "and other entirely man-made disasters in the cause of cheap food."[43]

This case was made possible through the generous support of Darla and Frederick Brodsky through their endowment of the Darla and Frederick Brodsky Trustee Professorship in International Business.

Notes

1   This case has been written on the basis of published sources only. Consequently, the inter-pretation and perspectives presented in this case are not necessarily those of Monsanto Corporation or any of its employees.

2   Rachel Carson, *Silent Spring*. Riverside Press, Cambridge, 1962.

3   Malthusian Principle: A population theory advanced by Thomas Malthus in his *Essay on the Principle of Population* (1798, First Edition). Malthus criticized Britain's social welfare pro-grams as promoting unsustainable population increases because they prevented "checks to population," such as "the want of proper and sufficient food."

4   Growth Through global Sustainability, *Harvard Business Review,* January – February 1997.

5   Greenpeace Campaigns Against Altered Soybeans, *Journal of Commerce,* November 7, 1996.

6   Genetic Soybeans Alarm Europeans, *New York Times.* November 7, 1996.

7   Forestal, D.J., *Faith. Hope and $5000. The Story of Monsanto.* Simon and Schuster, New York, 1977.

8   Forestal, D.J., *Faith. Hope and $5000. The Story of Monsanto.* Simon and Schuster, New York, 1977.

9   The Supreme Court, 1979 Term: Patentability of Living Microorganisms, *Harvard Law Review,* November 1980.

10   Genetic Markets Tempt More Firms, *Industry Week,* July 7, 1980

11   Test-Tube Plants Hit Pay Dirt, *Fortune,* September 2, 1985.

12   Growth Through Global Sustainability, *Harvard Business Review.* January–February 1997.

13   Letter to Shareowners, *Monsanto Annual Report,* 1996.

14   Splicing Together a Regulatory Body for Biotechnology, *Business Week,* January 14, 1985.

15   Agritech on the Move, *Financial World,* April 3–16, 1985.

16   Next Term He's in Business, *Chemical Week,* December 21, 1988.

17   Letter to Shareowners, *Monsanto Annual Report.* 1996.

18   Sequencing refers to the process by which geneticists determine the chemical structure and characteristics of a gene.

19   "Consumer Acceptance of Biotechnology in the United States and Japan," *Food Technology,* 1998.

20   Letter to Shareowners, *Monsanto Annual Report,* 1997.

21   In 1986, British livestock became contaminated with bovine spongiform encephalopathy (BSE), also known as "mad cow disease."

22   "How to Lasso a Mad Cow," *Canadian Business,* December 1996.

23   "Look What's Coming to Dinner . . . Scrambled Gene Cuisine," *The Observer,* October 6, 1996.

24   Chocolate bars were a typical example. Belgium, France, Germany, Italy, Luxembourg, the Netherlands and Spain all banned the use of cocoa substitutes in chocolate bars, while American and British chocolates regularly contained no cocoa at all, and many contained a significant number of chemical substitutes and preservatives.

25   House of Representatives Subcommittee on Risk Management, Research, and Specialty Crops, Committee on Agriculture, March 3, 1999.

26   "The Voice of Reason in the Global Food Fight, "*Fortune,* February 21, 2000.

27   Report of the Director, *Annual Report of the Scottish Crop Research Institute,* 1998–1999.

28   Enhanced Rape Seed Oil Could Supply Vitamin A, *Irish Times,* September 14, 1998.

29   Firm in Pounds 1m Campaign for Genetically Altered Food, *The Daily Telegraph,* June 6, 1998.

30   Call for a Ban on Biotech Beans, *Financial Times,* October 8, 1996.

31   Genetic Soybeans Alarm Europeans, *New York Times,* November 7, 1996.

32   Flavr Savr tomatoes were modified to resist spoilage, stick better to pasta, and mix easier into sauces. Flavr Savr products were also sold for approximately 10 per cent less than average price. "Future in the Can," *The Scotsman,* February 9, 1996.

33   Address to Greenpeace Business Conference, Monsanto Company Document, October 6, 1999.

34   "Growth Through Global Sustainability," *Harvard Business Review,* January–February 1997.

35   Letter to Shareowners, *Monsanto Annual Report,* 1996.

36   Speech by Commissioner Emma Bonino at the Opening Ceremony of EuropaBio'98 in Brussels, *Commission of the European Communities,* October 28, 1998.

37   "Consumer Acceptance of Biotechnology: An International Perspective," Nature Biotechnology, March 15, 1997.

38   "The Hamburg Soybean Party," *Journal of Commerce,* December 24, 1996.

39   "Threats Halt GMO Trials Open Day." *Farmers Guardian,* May 22, 1998.

40   "Monsanto Apologises Over GM Soya Bean." *Farmers Guardian.* May 22, 1998.

41   Consumer Acceptance of Biotechnology: An International Perspective, *Nature Biotechnology,* March 15, 1997.

42   Monsanto Company Announces Major U.K. Information Programme on Food Biotechnology, *Monsanto Press Release,* June 5, 1998.

43   Seeds of Disaster, *The Daily Telegraph,* June 8, 1998.

Johannes Van Den Bosch Sends An Email

After having had several email exchanges with his Mexican counterpart over several weeks without getting the expected actions and results, Johannes van den Bosch was getting a tongue-lashing from his British MNC client, who was furious at the lack of progress. Van den Bosch, in the Rotterdam office of BigFourFirm, and his colleague in the Mexico City office, Pablo Menendez, were both seasoned veterans, and van den Bosch couldn't understand the lack of responsiveness.

A week earlier, the client, Malcolm Smythe-Jones, had visited his office to express his mounting frustration. But this morning he had called with a stream of verbal abuse. His patience was exhausted.

Feeling angry himself, van den Bosch composed a strongly worded message to Menendez, and then decided to cool off. A half hour later, he edited it to "stick to the facts" while still communicating the appropriate level of urgency. As he clicked to send the message, he hoped that it would finally provoke some action to assuage his client with the reports he had been waiting for.

Professor Joe DiStefano prepared this mini-case as a basis for class discussion rather than to illustrate either effective or ineffective handling of a business situation.

The mini-case reports events as they occurred. The email exchanges in both cases are reported verbatim, except for the names and dates, which have been changed. Professor DiStefano acknowledges with thanks the cooperation of "Johannes van den Bosch" in providing this information and his generous permission to use the material for executive development.

IMD
INTERNATIONAL

He reread the email, and as he saved it to the mounting record in Smythe-Jones's file, he thought, "I'm going to be happy when this project is over for another year!"

Message for Pablo Menendez

Subject: *IAS 2007 Financial statements*

Author: *Johannes van den Bosch (Rotterdam)*

Date: *11/12/08 1:51 p.m.*

Dear Pablo,

This morning I had a conversation with Mr. Smythe-Jones (CFO) and Mr. Parker (Controller) re the finalization of certain 2007 financial statements. Mr. Smythe-Jones was not in a very good mood.

He told me that he was very unpleased by the fact that the 2007 IAS financial statements of the Mexican subsidiary still have not been finalized. At the moment he holds us responsible for this process. Although he recognizes that local management is responsible for such financial statements, he blames us for not being responsive on this matter and inform him about the process adequately. I believe he also recognizes that we have been instructed by Mr. Whyte (CEO) not to do any handholding, but that should not keep us from monitoring the process and inform him about the progress.

He asked me to provide him tomorrow with an update on the status of the IAS report and other reports pending.

Therefore I would like to get the following information from you today:

- *What has to be done to finalize the Mexican subsidiary's IAS financials;*
- *Who has to do it (local management, B&FF Mexico, client headquarters, B&FF Rotterdam)*
- *A timetable when things have to be done in order to finalize within a couple of weeks or sooner;*
- *A brief overview why it takes so long to prepare and audit the IAS f/s*
- *Are there any other reports for 2007 pending (local gaap, tax), if so the above is also applicable for those reports.*

As of today I would like to receive an update of the status every week. If any major problems arise during the finalization process I would like to be informed immediately. The next status update is due January 12, 2009.

Mr. Smythe-Jones also indicated that in the future all reports (US GAAP, local GAAP and IAS) should be normally finalized within 60 days after the balance sheet date. He will hold local auditors responsible for monitoring this process.

Best regards and best wishes for 2009.

Johannes

CASE **3**

Disneyland Resort Paris: Mickey Goes to Europe

Globalization in the positive sense is like a mosaic of cultures where identities remain visible and where we can play freely with the interaction in between. Where people can project themselves in something that is created elsewhere but is not perceived foreign. We are contributing to something important here. We need to help Disney become global in this positive sense. It is a long journey but we now understand the magnitude of globalization and can use this learning elsewhere.

Dominique Cocquet, Executive VP, Development & External Relations

Dominique Cocquet was legendary among Disneyland Resort Paris managers for his vision. He was part of the senior management team determined to turn the vision into reality. "We create magic," explained Roland Kleve, director of parks & resort operations support, "Mickey is a great boss."

Disneyland Resort Paris opened its gates in April 1992 amidst enormous controversy as a bastion of American cultural imperialism in Europe. By 2006 it was the most visited tourist site in Europe with over 12 million annual visitors. In spite of a difficult tourist industry in the early 2000s, Disneyland Resort Paris's attendance remained stable: 60% of its visitors were repeat visitors, and guest satisfaction was extremely high. The operation had created 43,000 jobs, invested more than 5 billion and contributed to the development of a new region. "You cannot say this is not a success!" exclaimed Cocquet.

Research Associate Karsten Jonsen prepared this case under the supervision of Professor Martha Maznevski as a basis for class discussion rather than to illustrate either effective or ineffective handling of a business situation.

As the leaders developed their execution plans, they wondered what principles should guide them and how to interpret Disney in multicultural Europe. Guests from different parts of Europe wanted different things from a vacation: how could they keep the classic Disney magic yet successfully appeal to European consumers? After 15 years of switching between French and American leadership, the answers were still not obvious. The leaders agreed that the 2007 celebrations of its 15th anniversary should set the scene for Disney's recognition as a well-established experience in the heart of Europe, and a long-term financial success. But what would it look like and what path would take them there?

THE WALT DISNEY COMPANY: A 20TH CENTURY FAIRYTALE

The Walt Disney Company was founded in 1923 by Walter Elias Disney and his brother Roy, as Disney Brothers Studio. In the early years, Disney created classic cartoons such as Mickey Mouse and Donald Duck. In 1937 they bet the company and created the first – and perhaps most successful ever in the company's history – full-length animated color film: *Snow White and the Seven Dwarfs*.

The company was known early on for professional marketing as well as creativity, and continued to make animated movies. It has remained the world leader in animation ever since. Disney added live productions in 1950 with a television program called *Disneyland*. Movies and television would later prove to be long-term pillars for the Walt Disney Company. In 1995 Disney acquired ABC to become the largest entertainment company in the US, the year after the revolutionary animated film *The Lion King* had broken all box office records.

Walt, always the visionary, wanted to create a "real" world of fantasy that families could immerse themselves in to get away from the trials of the real world and to have fun, *together*. In 1955 he bet the company for the second time and opened the first Disney theme park, Disneyland, in Anaheim, Southern California – inspired by Tivoli Gardens in Copenhagen. Disneyland was an instant success, and other parks followed. Walt Disney World opened near Orlando, Florida in 1971 and quickly became the world's largest resort area with several Disney parks and many other attractions. Tokyo Disneyland, the first Disney Park outside the US, opened in 1983. Euro Disneyland (now Disneyland Resort Paris) the first *multicultural* park, opened in 1992. Hong Kong Disneyland opened in September 2005.

By 2005, the Walt Disney Company was a large diversified organization with yearly revenues of more than US$30 billion, a film library of almost 1,000 theatrical releases and a market capitalization of almost $60 billion. Most revenues came from theme park resorts, films and the media-network business. Although the company was more than 80 years old, the strong voice of the founding father still provided guidance for decision making: *How would Walt have done it?*

THE MAGIC OF STORIES

Disney believed in magic. And the essence of Disney magic was storytelling. The excitement of great adventures, the challenge of impossible tasks, the loneliness of being among strangers, the shame of guilt, the terror of evil, the warmth of good, the pride of accomplishment, the love of a family. All of these themes were evoked by Disney stories.

Disney told its purest stories in animated films, many of which won Academy Awards. From the classics like *Snow White*, the *Jungle Book* and *Cinderella* to more recent releases like *The Lion King, Beauty and the Beast, Finding Nemo* and *The Incredibles,*[1] millions of people around the world were drawn to the powerful stories. They related to the characters, quoted the dialogue, told the stories and sang the songs. Would the youngsters of the 21st century continue this admiration for animated characters? Disney believed so and acquired Pixar Animation Studios – their partner in many successful films – in January 2006 to ensure the creation of animated magic for many years ahead.

> *The acquisition of Pixar was a great strategic move. It will provide the storytelling we need to reach today's and tomorrow's generations, and it will also provide the foundation for building more interactive attractions. In combination with a constant revitalization of classic characters on the Disney channels, we can help ensure that experiences and emotions are shared across the different generations within families.*
>
> **Jeff Archambault, Vice President, Communications & Corporate Alliances**

At Disney resorts, the magic became real and tangible. Walt Disney, visionary founder of the company, pictured the resorts as places where families would go to live the stories – to escape from the real world's worries, highways and "visual pollution" and become immersed in the imaginary world of magic.

> *I love to stand on Main Street, just inside the front gates, and watch guests come through the gates into the park. It's amazing to see their faces light up as they come in! The kids, of course, but even the adults. They lose their self-consciousness, that veneer we put on to be serious in the adult world, and they remember the kid inside. You can see that happening as they walk in!*
>
> **Norbert Stiekema**
> **Vice President, Sales and Distribution**

The animated films provided the link between the real world and the fantasy world: What families watched on screen in the cinemas or their homes was brought to life in the parks, as a multidimensional sharing of *emotions*. Film characters met with guests and signed autographs, many attractions immersed guests in the scenes and plots of the films and other attractions took guests into related fantasy worlds. More than 50 million visitors a year went to Disney resorts around the world to experience this magic.

This powerful experience was created by attention to detail and leaving nothing to chance. The attractions were designed by "Imagineers" – engineers who brought together people and knowledge from hundreds of disciplines to create environments:

> *Guests enter fantasy worlds through portals. Once through a portal, everything in the world – characters, rides, shows, sidewalks, buildings, even the costumes of cleaning staff – plays a part in creating that world's experience for the guests. This is how the magic gets created. Imagineers are the only Cast Members that have a dual reporting relationship in all Disney parks: We report both to the Imagineering head office in Burbank California, and to the local management of the park. We also rotate around parks. I started off here in Paris, creating "It's a Small World" in Fantasyland for the park opening. Then I worked in California and Tokyo before coming back here to head*

Imagineering. We have a strong international community of Imagineers to share ideas and make sure we create this all-encompassing experience everywhere.

Peter McGrath, Director, Creative Development & Show Quality Standards

One afternoon I was called down to the front gates to speak to a family. When I got there, they seemed happy, so I wondered what the problem was. Then the father explained to me that his young daughter was autistic, and she had never responded to anything or communicated anything to the family. That day, at Disneyland, was the first time they had ever seen her smile. He wanted to thank me for creating something that helped them connect as a family for the first time. That's the magic we make.

Roland Kleve
Director
Parks & Resort Operations Support

Disneyland Resort Paris was meticulous about details in service and operations. All resort staff (Cast Members) attended Disney University[2] to learn how to provide the cheerful, friendly and flexible service to create a worry-free fantasy experience for the guests. Disneyland Resort Paris spent more than four times the French minimum legal requirement on training and education and each year they received 70,000 spontaneous job applications as an indication of being an attractive employer in the region. One of the training programs, HAT (hôte d'accueil touristique), was recognized as a professional qualification by the French Ministry of Labor and won an international Worldwide Hospitality Award in 2004.

The more than 12,200 Cast Members came from more than 100 nationalities (73% were French) speaking 19 different languages and were on average 33 years old. Half of the employees had more than 5 years of tenure and 30% had more than 10 years. The total annual staff turnover was 22% which was considered very low for the industry.

Disney's attention to technical innovation, operational excellence and service provided global benchmarks for companies, especially those in the service and creative industries.

Operations is all about making sure the guest has a seamless experience in the park. That goes from helping our shuttle bus drivers to smile and provide good, reliable, on time service taking guests between the park and their hotels, to making sure Cast Members feel comfortable in their costumes so they can focus on providing service, to ensuring that in every part of the resort we have Cast Members who speak different languages so they can help guests in their own language. It's the details that count.

Roland Kleve, Director, Parks & Resort Operations Support

EURO DISNEYLAND TO DISNEYLAND RESORT PARIS: MAGICAL STORIES IN EUROPE

To 1992: It's a Small World

When Tokyo Disneyland opened in 1983, the Disney US theme parks had known nothing but success. The park in Tokyo was deliberately designed to imitate the parks in the US and from the customer perspective little local adaptation was put in place (except covers for rain protection) so the Japanese would have "the real thing." Japanese culture was startlingly different from American, and Disney was aware of the risk. They hedged their investment by working with a Japanese owner who paid royalties on the revenue streams. Tokyo Disneyland soon became the most profitable Disneyland in the world. Everything that worked well in the US was positively received in Tokyo despite the obvious cultural distance.

"When you have a success it's natural that you want to replicate it," Cocquet stated. "We thought: why not Europe? Europeans watched Disney movies, bought Disney products and went to Walt Disney World in Florida. If it worked in Tokyo, it could work in Europe." Because of the enormous success of Tokyo, The Walt Disney Company decided to invest significant equity this time rather than only collect royalties. Many analysts believed that the resort should have been located in Spain, which had vacation-friendly weather and was associated with leisure holidays. But The Walt Disney Company decided to build Euro Disneyland near Paris because Paris was the most visited tourist area in Europe, it offered the greatest number of visitors within driving and short-flight distance, and the French government offered incentives through infrastructure building, labor development and other vehicles.

1992–1994: Culture Shock and the Original Sin

Amidst intense criticism from Europe's cultural elite, Euro Disney S.C.A. opened the Disneyland Park and its hotels on the planned date of April 12, 1992 with much publicity and hype. The initial public offering of 51% of the shares had been sold almost overnight. The future looked very bright, despite the continuously escalating construction costs that had climbed to more than three times the original budget, leaving Euro Disneyland with what seemed to be an eternal debt burden of $3 billion.

Unfortunately, the story did not follow the Tokyo script. The French president, François Mitterrand, did not show up for the opening event, stating that it wasn't his "cup of tea." Fewer guests walked through the gates than expected, especially from France. Labor relations were strained, and some early service controversies became infamous and affected the resort's reputation long after they had been resolved. For example, consistent with other Disney parks, Euro Disneyland did not serve alcohol when it first opened. This decision was ridiculed and scorned by European consumers. Soon after opening, Euro Disneyland started serving wine and beer, but the public did not forget the initial mistake. Also the long queuing for the attractions was something that needed special attention. The original planning was based on "American queue length." As it turned out, the same length of queue in Europe contained twice as many people as an American queue. Guests' expectations regarding line wait times were, therefore, not met.

Another major part of the Euro Disneyland project was the establishment of a number of hotels inside and just outside the Disneyland Park. The original intention was to sell the hotels quickly, then lease them back. However, the real estate value declined dramatically and it was not possible to sell them. Instead, Euro Disneyland was forced to continue payments. The decreased revenues, coupled with an investment burden that was hard to carry, put an end to the optimism and euphoria. Euro Disneyland dove into financially troubled waters in the midst of a European recession.

It was like we bought a house in a promising neighborhood. After we moved in, prices dropped way below the mortgaged value. But we had to make the best of it, ride out the storm and try to forget about what we paid for it in the first place.

Roland Kleve, Director of Parks & Resort Operations Support

Disney Village, located at the resort outside the Disney Parks, opened in 1992 and also struggled to find its balance between on-site resort guests and the Eastern Paris market. Disney Village was a collection of restaurants, night clubs, cinemas and a concert venue, all designed for evening entertainment. Some activities were targeted at families, while others were aimed at young adults. The first years Disney Village was open only for resort guests but it later opened to the broader public. As the Paris subway line went directly to the resort and there was no entry fee to Disney Village, it attracted a large number of local guests.

At the brink of bankruptcy, a financial re-structuring in 1994 gave some breathing space and a new major investor, Prince Alwaleed Bin Talal Abdulaziz Al Saud. Interest charges were cut, principal repayments of loans were deferred and Euro Disneyland was liberated from royalty payments (to The Walt Disney Company) for a period of 5 years.

In the beginning there were mistakes on both sides. From our side perhaps some bloated self-assurance, power and optimism, creating investments as well as expectations that were too large. On the French side, there was some easy and non-rational anti-Americanism.

Dominique Cocquet, Executive VP of Development and External Relations

The financial difficulties of the early years, which Euro Disney managers referred to as "the original sin," occupied much of the media coverage from the opening of Euro Disneyland through the end of the millennium. The high level of debt and increased focus on cost-cuttings, constrained decision-making, and the turnover of senior managers was high.

1995–2001: Becoming a Landmark

From October 1994 Euro Disney began to change the public name of the resort to Disneyland Paris, partly to distance themselves from the controversial Euro currency, and partly to emphasize the Paris location. Euro Disney S.C.A., the operator of Disneyland Resort Paris, became profitable by 1997 with a positive cash flow from operating activities. Things were beginning to look and feel better in every sense. The number of guests climbed, and Disneyland Paris became the most visited tourist destination in Europe; 85% of guests were highly satisfied, and more than 70% intended to return.

The European landscape gradually became clearer. "We had to teach Europeans what a short stay resort destination is," Pieter Boterman, company spokesman, explained. "There is nothing in Europe like Disneyland Paris, so there was no category in customers' minds for what we were offering." Even in 2001, European guests did not stay as long at the resort as American guests did in Florida: In Europe most people stayed only one or two nights. European guests also did not spend as much per capita during their visits. The lower revenue per guest meant that Disneyland Paris managers became experts at providing operational excellence for less money; in fact, the resort provided other Disney theme parks an important benchmark on several important operating measures.

> *Very little in our core product needs adaptation, but the way we position it and sell it is completely different in each of our key markets. This is a result of not only market conditions, competition and distribution legacy, but also the fact that Mickey or Winnie the Pooh mean different things to different people, depending on the national context. For example, Germans want tangible value for money, and it is difficult to position our product in the German market place. Try and describe emotions and a wholesome emotional family experience in a factual datasheet! Those who do come are very satisfied, but it is hard to explain it ahead of time.*
>
> **Norbert Stiekema, VP of Sales and Distribution**

The most difficult challenge was learning to create universal emotional experiences:

> *Picture the jungle cruise, which is a boat going down a river in a jungle. In the US the jungle guide tells you to watch out for the mighty hippopotamus, and then suddenly a hippo rises out of the river and spews water towards the group. Children love the anticipation of watching for the hippo, being just a bit afraid. Now picture the guide in Europe warning passengers about the hippo in six languages. By the time he gets to Spanish, the hippo is already out and the Italians and Dutch – whose languages we haven't got to yet – completely miss the emotion we're trying to create! At Disneyland Paris we had to learn to create emotion without verbal scripts. This was a challenge Disney hadn't ever addressed before, so we've had to start from scratch here.*
>
> **Peter McGrath, Director of Creative Development and Show Quality Standards**

The cultural learning was replicated internally where American and French leadership styles were often confronted.

> *Part of the cultural understanding is in the art of debate here, where people try to understand every angle of an aspect instead of just moving on when 80% is agreed upon*
>
> **Wendy Crudele, VP Human Resources**

In April 2002 a second theme park opened next to the Disneyland Paris. Walt Disney Studios Park was built with an investment of more than $500 million. It was based on the theme of cinema and cartoons, and highlighted movie-making techniques and the history of films. Walking through the front gate was like walking into the studios where animated and live movies are made. Attractions ranged from interactive experiences with the technology to multimedia shows on film-making to animation-based theme rides.

> *We tried to include as many European film-making elements as we could. For example, the stunt show was designed with European stunt expert Rémi Julienne, and in the historical attractions we included European directors and key players. That didn't seem to be important to the guests, but it was important to the European observers.*
>
> **Peter McGrath, Director of Creative Development and Show Quality Standards**

Walt Disney Studios was established to appeal to a broader age range than the Disneyland Paris, including teenagers and young adults. It was also intended to prolong the stay of the average Disney tourist and appeal to a broader spectrum of age categories such as teenagers and young adults.

The least published success was ironically the construction of a "real" city, Val d'Europe. This constantly growing neighboring real estate development project included a shopping center, business center, downtown with cafés and restaurants and a residential area for over 20,000 "real" people, only 10% to 15% of whom worked at Disneyland Paris. The architecture evoked images of classic Paris itself and Val d'Europe was vital to integrating Disney into France and Europe.

> *Val d'Europe is the "yin" to the Disneyland "yang." The imaginary village is not sustainable without the real one, or the other way around. Val d'Europe is a thriving, healthy suburban French community that brings balance to the universal magic of the Disney fantasy. The community belongs to France but has Disney as catalyst. Without the Disney values influence I would not have looked at France, my own country, in the same way. The cultural exchange has made me discover what France is heading for or what has been missing here.*
> **Dominique Cocquet, Executive Vice President, Development & External Relations**

Val d'Europe was a profitable part of the Euro Disney portfolio, and had also been an important public relations success: It created tens of thousands of jobs and – like Disneyland Paris – contributed significantly to the French tax base. The development was done in careful balanced coordination with the public parties. Since the creation of the destination, more than 5 billion have been invested by private investors and €534 million by the public sector, that is €10 of private funds invested for every €1 of public money.

> *It is a very rare and unique opportunity to have a new community built between public and private partners. The backbone of our discussions is always a healthy balance between financial interests, short term interests and long term interests. In a way this also works as an illustration of what it means to do business in a foreign environment and how to integrate and adapt to the culture.*
> **Dominique Cocquet, Executive Vice President, Development & External Relations**

The healthy development of Val d'Europe was perhaps reflected in the fact that it was one of the few Paris suburbs not affected by the French riots in late 2005.

2002–2004: A Test of Character

Starting in 2002, the leaders of Disneyland Resort Paris faced another series of challenges created by events referred to internally as "the plagues of Moses." Although tourism within Europe did not decrease right after the 9/11 tragedy, the consequent war in Iraq did create uncertainty and lower levels of tourism. The German economy shattered, other European economies went into decline and tourists turned to cheaper and more local travel. At the same time, the Euro increased against most other world currencies, and Disneyland Resort Paris became more expensive relative to vacations outside Europe. Tour operators in the US, northern Africa and Asia, were desperate to attract tourists and, therefore, offered vacations at loss-leading prices. As if that were not enough, Euro Disney S.C.A. had to repay €600 million in convertible bonds in late 2001. Financial statements again began to look dim.

Management turnover during this time was very high. Of the nine top management positions, eight were replaced during 2003 and 2004. Four of the eight new executives came from outside Disney. In some cases managers were brought back to Disney after a few years with other companies or at other Disney sites. It was a long-standing practice for managers to rotate between Disney sites across the world and thus act as carriers of cultural and operational practices that should remain consistent across continents.

Local input and innovation was encouraged through both formal and informal methods. For example, in 2003, management led a series of "summer camps" during his first summer at Disneyland Paris. These were brainstorming sessions with cross-sections of Cast Members and created ideas for increasing revenue, guest satisfaction and delight and cost-cutting. Some initiatives from these sessions were grand, such as the new attraction Space Mountain: Mission 2. Others were apparently smaller but had wide impact, such as the "Park Hopper" pass, a new class of ticket which let visitors into both Disneyland Paris and Walt Disney Studios on a single day.

Throughout the turbulent financial times, the operational excellence and spirit among employees and guests stayed high. Attendance rates held stable at Disneyland Resort Paris, while decreasing among European competitors. Satisfaction rates increased, and repeat visit rates shot up. Managers developed sophisticated knowledge about their guests in terms of spending habits, means of transportation, geographical distribution, preferred activities and competing destinations. The revenue also remained stable above €1 billion annually, of which a good half came from the Disneyland and Walt Disney Studios and almost 40% from the Disney Hotels and Disney Village. The seven medium-high standard hotels had a total capacity of 5,800 beds and since 2000 achieved occupancy rates of 80% to 89%.

Financial difficulties had plagued the resort since it opened, crippling its ability to invest and creating urgency for short-term cash flow. Disney managers had focused on survival without compromising quality. After yet another difficult couple of years, Euro Disney S.C.A. leaders sought financial restructuring and investment to allow them to enhance the resort. By the end of 2004, the package was in place. It included restructuring of debt totaling $3 billion, and an infusion of $330 million new capital from existing investors. In March 2005, shares were distributed between the Walt Disney Company (40%), Prince Alwaleed (10%) and other shareholders (50%), with the latter category including a large proportion of French banks.

THE MARKET PLACE – 2005/2006

In its home country, Disneyland Resort Paris was part of a complex vacation and leisure market. France was the world's favorite tourist destination with over 75 million international arrivals each year. Disneyland Resort Paris was the most visited attraction, with twice as many visitors as the Eiffel Tower. France had fourteen attractions that hosted more than one million visitors annually, divided into "cultural" and "non-cultural" categories. The former included well-known Parisian sites such as the Louvre, Notre Dame and the Palace of Versailles, while the latter included Parc Asterix[3] and ParcFuturoscope.[4] Theme parks were the most preferred "paid-for" attractions. "Free" cultural attractions, including all places of historic interest, natural interest and exhibitions, had more visitors than theme parks and zoos. Visitors of theme parks and zoos tended to have average incomes, while cultural attractions often catered to the higher end of the income scale.

The European amusement park industry was much smaller than that of either the United States or East Asia. European theme parks enjoyed an increasing number of visitors, although still only a small fraction of the number in the United States. Nine parks had more than 2.5 million yearly visitors; these parks were distributed through Denmark, Holland, Germany, Spain and the United Kingdom. Unlike the so called "thrill parks," Disneyland Resort Paris also competed with a variety of vacation resorts such as Club Med or hotel/beach resorts.

The evolution of the "resort concept" as a new way of vacationing was gradually establishing itself in the European public's mind. People were increasingly looking for an integrated destination where they could enjoy a wide variety of experiences according to their own choices. This trend was partially driven by socio-economic trends, such as a larger middle class with shorter but more intensive vacations. It was also partially the effect of ongoing marketing by Disneyland Resort Paris and other resorts, and people experiencing and becoming personally familiar with the resort vacation.

2005–2007: DISNEYLAND RESORT PARIS COMES OF AGE

Disneyland Resort Paris had set strategic goals to return to profitability. The strategy targeted long-term traffic and increased average spending per guest through two key measures:

- a multi-year investment plan (€240 million over four years from 2005 to 2009)
- an innovative sales and marketing policy.

Four new or renewed attractions were planned for the four-year period. In 2005 the Disneyland Park star attraction, Space Mountain, was completely reprogrammed and reopened as Space Mountain: Mission 2. This was the first redesign of Space Mountain in any Disney resort. In 2006, Buzz Lightyear's Laser Blast opened, based on the Disney/Pixar movie *Toy Story 2*. This was a sophisticated, interactive ride that pitted guests in a laser shooting competition against the evil Emperor Zurg. In 2007 two new attractions would open in Walt Disney Studios Park, Crush's Coaster and Cars: Quatre Roues Rallye. Finally, in 2008 the Tower of Terror would open in Walt Disney Studios Park. This thrill ride included a long free-fall drop in the elevator of a haunted high-rise building, and was one of the most popular attractions in the other parks.

Innovation was one of Disney's core values, and experience demonstrated that new attractions had the capacity to enhance the quality and impact of the guest experience in the Parks. In addition, new attractions would bolster the Park's attractiveness and capacity. Each new attraction was designed to meet the needs of future guests and round out what was already a one-of-a-kind guest experience. Offering something new and innovative brought guests in and would make them come back.

For many years the company researched key European markets extensively to identify different categories of future guests and to determine the most effective ways to reach them. There was no such thing as "the European consumer." Thanks to continuous research, the company now had detailed knowledge of each of its key European markets and became one of the key experts in understanding European travelers. The challenge was how to use this information to adapt to the different market segments without losing the core of Disney magic.

THE SCRIPT FOR THE FUTURE: JOURNEY TO 2015

The leaders of Disneyland Resorts Paris, including the new CEO Karl Holz, were enthusiastic about the opportunities provided by the 2004 financial restructuring: however, they were also aware that investors would not wait for a financial return forever. Magic could only continue if it earned money.

Disneyland Resorts Paris had learned a lot over the years about how to compete in the European vacation market. But, just as the market signals were mixed about how the park should be positioned when it opened in 1992, the market still sent mixed messages about which road to take to reach financial success in the future. Some research suggested the resort would be more successful if managers did not worry about how true it was to the Disney formula. If Europeans really wanted a Disney experience, they went to Florida or California. Disneyland Resort Paris should, therefore, create its own brand of family experience completely adapted to the local market.

Other research suggested that Disney could never be anything but the American-style Disney, and that Disneyland Resort Paris would be better off to position itself as providing "the real thing" in Europe. This would be a copy of the Tokyo model, which had been highly successful.

> *There is a trade-off between Disney values and cultural sensitivity. In business, as well as in private life, it is all about doing things genuinely. Be true to who you are – work on your delivery.*
> **Jeff Archambault, Vice President, Communications & Corporate Alliances**

The outcome of the analysis had to create a consistent and compelling experience for the guests. Management was debating, however, which principles would best guide the choice of which offerings should stay global and which offerings should be locally adapted – with what levels of adaptation?

Notes

1   Finding Nemo and The Incredibles are produced by Pixar Animation Studios and distributed by The Walt Disney Company.
2   The Disney University is located at Disneyland Resort Paris. The university offers training on-location in over 400 different training programs: from table service to animal care to water quality control to leadership development. In 2006 Disney University was awarded a quality label from the French AFNOR organization, which is highly respected in the continuing education sector.
3   Thrills and shows in a theme park (opened in 1989) 35 km from Paris, based on the Gallic characters of Asterix, Obelix and friends in Brittany who would never surrender to Cesar. Standard admission fee 2005 was €31.
4   Interactive attractions and shows, primarily based on science and technology. This leisure space is situated in Poitiers, between Paris and Bordeaux (1h20 by TGV train from Paris). Standard admission fee in 2005 was €33.

EXHIBIT 1 The Walt Disney Company Timeline

- 1923: The Disney Bros. studio, founded by Walt and his brother Roy Oliver Disney, produces the *Alice in Cartoonland* series
- 1927: The Alice series ends; Walt picks up the contract to animate Oswald the Lucky Rabbit
- 1928: Walt loses of the Oswald series; first Mickey Mouse cartoon: Steamboat Willie
- 1929: First Silly Symphony: The Skeleton Dance
- 1930: First appearance of Pluto
- 1932: First three-strip Technicolor short released: Flowers and Trees; first appearance of Goofy
- 1934: First appearance of Donald Duck
- 1937: Studio produces its first feature, Snow White and the Seven Dwarfs
- 1940: Studio moves to the Burbank, California buildings where it is located to this day
- 1941: A bitter animators' strike occurs; as the USA enters World War II, the studio begins making morale-boosting propaganda films for the government
- 1944: The company is short on cash; a theatrical re-release of Dumbo generates much-needed revenue and begins a reissue pattern for the animated feature films
- 1945: The studio hires its first-ever live actor for a film, James Baskett, to star as Uncle Remus in Song of the South
- 1949: The studio begins production on its first all-live action feature, Treasure Island; the popular True-Life Adventures series begins
- 1954: The studio founds Buena Vista International to distribute its feature films; beginning of the Disneyland TV program
- 1955: Opening of Disneyland in Anaheim, California
- 1961: The studio licenses the film rights to Winnie-the-Pooh, whose characters continue to be highly profitable to this day; international distribution arm Buena Vista International is established
- 1964: The company starts buying land near Orlando, Florida for Walt Disney World – then known as Disneyworld, or 'The Florida Project'
- 1965: The regular production of short subjects ceases, as theatres no longer have any demand for them
- 1966: Walt Disney dies
- 1967: Construction begins on Walt Disney World; the underlying governmental structure (Reedy Creek Improvement District) is signed into law
- 1971: Walt Disney World opens in Orlando, Florida; Roy Oliver Disney dies; Donn Tatum becomes chairman and Card Walker becomes CEO and president
- 1977: Roy Edward Disney, son of Roy and nephew of Walt, resigns from the company citing a decline in overall product quality and issues with management
- 1978: The studio licenses several minor titles to MCA Discovision for laserdisc release; only TV compilations of cartoons ever see the light of day through this deal
- 1979: Don Bluth and a number of his allies leave the animation division; the studio releases its first PG-rated film, The Black Hole
- 1980: Tom Wilhite becomes head of the film division with the intent of modernizing studio product; a home video division is created
- 1981: Plans for a cable network are announced
- 1982: EPCOT Center opens at Walt Disney World; Ron W. Miller succeeds Card Walker as CEO
- 1983: As the anthology series is canceled, The Disney Channel begins operation on US cable systems; Tom Wilhite resigns his post; Tokyo Disneyland opens in Japan
- 1984: Touchstone Pictures is created; after the studio narrowly escapes a buyout attempt by Saul Steinberg, Roy Edward Disney and his business partner, Stanley Gold, remove Ron W. Miller as CEO and president, replacing him with Michael Eisner and Frank Wells
- 1985: The studio begins making cartoons for television; The home video release of Pinocchio is a best-seller
- 1986: The studio's first R-rated release comes from Touchstone Pictures; the anthology series is revived; the company's name is changed from Walt Disney Productions to The Walt Disney Company.
- 1989: Disney offers a deal to buy Jim Henson's Muppets and have the famed puppeteer work with Disney resources; the Disney-MGM Studios open at Walt Disney World
- 1990: Jim Henson's death sours the deal to buy his holdings; the anthology series canceled for second time
- 1992: The controversial Euro Disney opens outside Paris, France

EXHIBIT 1 *(Continued)*

- 1993: Disney acquires independent film distributor Miramax Films; Winnie the Pooh merchandise outsells Mickey Mouse merchandise for the first time; the policy of periodic theatrical re-issues ends with this year's re-issue of Snow White and the Seven Dwarfs but is augmented for video
- 1994: Frank Wells is killed in a helicopter crash; Jeffrey Katzenberg resigns to co-found his own studio, DreamWorks SKG
- 1995: In October, the company hires Hollywood superagent, Michael Ovitz, to be president
- 1996: The company takes on the Disney Enterprises name for non-Walt Disney branded ventures and acquires the Capital Cities/ABC group, renaming it ABC, Inc.; in December, Michael Ovitz, president of the company, leaves "by mutual consent"
- 1997: The anthology series is revived again; the home video division releases its first DVDs
- 1998: Disney's Animal Kingdom opens at Walt Disney World
- 2000: Robert Iger becomes president and COO
- 2001: Disney-owned TV channels are pulled from Time Warner Cable briefly during a dispute over carriage fees; Disney's California Adventure opens to the public; Disney begins releasing Walt Disney Treasures DVD box sets for the collector's market
- 2003: Roy Edward Disney again resigns as head of animation and from the board of directors, citing similar reasons to those that drove him off 26 years earlier; fellow director Stanley Gold resigns with him; they establish "Save Disney" (*http://www.savedisney.com*) to apply public pressure to oust Michael Eisner
- 2003: Pirates of the Caribbean: The Curse of the Black Pearl becomes the first film released under the Disney label with a PG-13 rating
- 2004:
  - The studio breaks off renegotiation talks with Pixar (their current contract expires in 2006); Disney announces it will convert its animation studio to all computer-animated production
  - Announced the closure of their Florida feature-film animation department (*http://www.savedisney.com/news/se/wdfa_closure.asp*);
  - Comcast makes a $66 billion unsolicited bid to buy The Walt Disney Company (Comcast withdraws its bid in April);
  - Disney purchases rights to The Muppets;
  - Company stockholders give Michael Eisner a 43% vote of no confidence; as a result, Eisner is removed from the role as chairman of the board (but maintains his position as CEO) and George J. Mitchell becomes chairman in his place.
  - After investing $6 million into production of the documentary film *Fahrenheit 9/11* by Michael Moore, Walt Disney Pictures announced their previously mentioned intentions of not distributing the film. The director and the heads of Miramax arrange an alternate distribution arrangement and the film becomes the most successful documentary film of all time. At $100 million+, that film earns more than most of Disney's other film releases that year.

- 2005:

  - Disneyland celebrates its 50th birthday on 17 July.
  - Robert A. Iger, currently president of the company, will replace Michael Eisner as CEO on October 1.
  - Disney starts talks with Steve Jobs (Chairman of Pixar) about acquisition of Pixar Animation Studios. The $7.4 billion deal was announced in late January 2006. This made Steve Jobs the single largest Disney shareholder and Jobs also joined Disney's board of directors.

Source: Company information

EXHIBIT 2 Key Figures 2003–2005

BREAKDOWN OF ATTENDANCE BY COUNTRY OF ORIGIN IN 2005

FRANCE 39%
UNITED KINGDOM 20%
SPAIN 9%
NETHERLANDS 8%
BELGIUM/LUX. 7%
GERMANY 5%
ITALY 3%
OTHERS 9%

BREAKDOWN OF REVENUES BY ACTIVITY IN 2005

THEME PARKS 51.1%
HOTELS AND DISNEY VILLAGE 36.7%
OTHERS 9.6%
REAL ESTATE 2.6%

BREAKDOWN OF VISITORS BY TRANSPORTATION IN 2005

CAR 53%
PLANE 17%
TRAIN 14%
COACH 6%
SUBURBAN TRAIN 10%

THEME PARKS ATTENDANCE (IN MILLIONS OF VISITS)

	2005	2004	2003
	12.3	12.4	12.4

HOTEL OCCUPANCY (IN %)

	2005	2004	2003
	80.7%	80.5%	85.1%

THEME PARKS AVERAGE SPENDING PER GUEST (IN EUROS EXCLUDING VAT)

	2005	2004	2003
	44.3	42.7	40.7

AVERAGE SPENDING PER ROOM (IN EUROS EXCLUDING VAT)

	2005	2004	2003
	179.1	186.6	183.5

IN MILLIONS EUROS

	2005	2004	2003 PRO-FORMA*
REVENUES	1076.0	1048.0	1046.8
EBITDA**	117.1	122.9	181.6
INCOME/(LOSS) BEFORE FINANCIAL CHARGES	(26.9)	(23.9)	32.1
NET FINANCIAL CHARGES	(87.9)	(105.7)	(111.2)
LOSS BEFORE EXCEPTIONNAL ITEMS AND MINORITY INTERESTS	(114.8)	(129.6)	(79.1)
NET LOSS	(94.9)	(145.2)	(58.3)
CASH FLOW FROM OPERATING ACTIVITIES	18.4	124.6	124.7
BORROWINGS	1943.4	2052.8	2448.4
SHAREHOLDERS' EQUITY AND QUASI-EQUITY	295.7	(59.9)	85.6
MINORITY INTERESTS	106.3	339.6	(41.3)

*reflects pro forma impact of consolidation of financing companies
**earnings before minority interest, income taxes, exceptional items, interest, depreciation and amortization

Source: Euro Disney S.C. A., 2005 Annual Review

EXHIBIT 3   Stock Information

IDENTIFICATION SHEET OF EURO DISNEY S.C.A. SHARE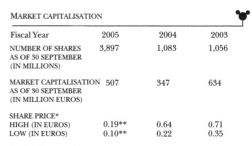

NOMINAL VALUE	0.01 euro per share
NUMBER OF SHARES	3.897.649.046 shares as of 30/09/05
MARKET PLACES	Paris
	London (until 31 October 2005)
	Brussels (until 30 September 2005)
MAIN CODES	Reuters EDL.PA
	Bloomberg EDL.FP
	ISIN FR00001235874

MARKET CAPITALISATION

Fiscal Year	2005	2004	2003
NUMBER OF SHARES AS OF 30 SEPTEMBER (IN MILLIONS)	3,897	1,083	1,056
MARKET CAPITALISATION AS OF 30 SEPTEMBER (IN MILLION EUROS)	507	347	634
SHARE PRICE*			
HIGH (IN EUROS)	0.19**	0.64	0.71
LOW (IN EUROS)	0.10**	0.22	0.35

*based on share price at closing
**share price adjusted for dilution impact of Equity Rights Offering in February 05

SHAREHOLDING STRUCTURE

THE WALT DISNEY COMPANY*
39.8%

PRINCE ALWALEED**
10.0%

OTHER SHAREHOLDERS
50.2%

*Via its wholly-owned subsidiary,
EDL Holding Company

**Via KINGDOM 5-KR-135 Ltd
a company whose shares are held
by trusts for the benefit of Prince
Alwaleed and his family

EVOLUTION OF THE SHARE PRICE (BASE 100 ON OCTOBER 2004)

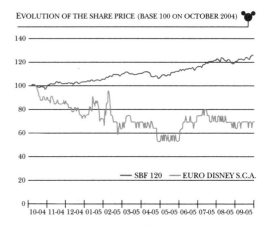

AVERAGE DAILY TRADING VOLUME ON EURONEXT PARIS
(IN MILLIONS)

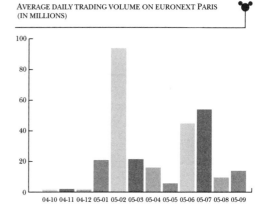

Source: Euro Disney S.C.A., 2005 Annual Review

EXHIBIT 4 World Park Attendance 2004[1]

1.	Magic Kingdom at Walt Disney World, Florida	15.1
2.	Disneyland in Anaheim, California	13.4
3.	Tokyo Disneyland, Japan	13.2
4.	Disneyland Resort Paris, France[2]	12.4
5.	Tokyo Disney Sea, Japan	12.2
6.	Universal Studios Osaka, Japan	9.9
7.	EPCOT at Walt Disney World, Florida	9.4
8.	Disney-MGM Studios, Florida	8.3
9.	Lotte World in Seoul (indoor), South Korea	8.0
10.	Disney's Animal Kingdom, Florida	7.8

[1] The world market for the 50 most visited amusement parks rose to a record level of 252.4 million visitors, an increase of 2.2% from 2003.

[2] Includes visitors to both theme parks, Disneyland Paris and the Walt Disney Studios.

Europe accounted for 11 out of the top 50 parks with a total of 41 million visitors in 2004, an increase of 2.8% from 2003. Tivoli Gardens (Denmark), Europa Park (Germany) and Gardaland (Italy) are the most visited after Disneyland Resort Paris. Tivoli increased its attendance nearly 30% to 4.2 million visitors, thanks in part to a new attraction "the Demon." Europa Park increased its number of attendants to 3.7 million (of which 20% were of French nationality).

Source: Amusement Business Online and le Quotidien Tourisme

EXHIBIT 5 Disneyland Resort Paris: "Magic on Your Doorstep"

Source: Company information

EXHIBIT 6   Early Morning in Val d'Europe

Source: Company information

CASE 4

Charles Foster Sends an Email (A)

Charles Foster was a U.S. national sales manager for a large multinational technology company headquartered in France. He was concerned about the availability of an important new disk drive that was selling better than anticipated. If he could obtain more of these drives, he was sure that they would sell. Since the product had just been launched with the company's various sales forces and distributors, Foster was worried about losing momentum. The sales force and distributors had literally thousands of products to sell and an availability problem could prove fatal to the product line, as the company's sales efforts were redirected to other products or customers chose to purchase from the competition.

The situation was complicated by the fact that the design and manufacturing of the drive had been assigned to a new Franco-Japanese joint venture (JV) located in France. Not only was the joint venture adapting to a new manufacturing system that had been introduced to produce the drive, it was also adapting to the joint venture's new organizational

Professor Henry W. Lane prepared this case solely to provide material for class discussion. The author does not intend to illustrate either effective or ineffective handling of a managerial situation. The author may have disguised certain names and other identifying information to protect confidentiality.

structure. As it tried to adapt, the joint venture encountered numerous complications, particularly those involving logistics.

Over the previous months, several attempts had been made to resolve the availability issue at lower levels but with no success. Foster decided that the problem had become serious enough to warrant the attention of his supervisor, Richard Howe, vice-president of sales for High Technology Products. Because Foster had a good, informal relationship with Howe, he decided to send him an email explaining the situation.

Howe forwarded Foster's email to Maurice LeBlanc, the head of the Strategic Business Unit (SBU) headquartered in France. In turn, LeBlanc, who previously had been head of new product development for the SBU, forwarded the email to Ahmed Hassan, president of the JV. Hassan, raised in the Middle East, had lived most of his adult life in France (see Exhibit 1).

THE PHONE CALL

A couple of days after sending his email, Foster was in his office completing some sales reports when the phone rang. After he answered the phone, he immediately recognized the accented, emotion-laden voice that spilled out into the room.

> This is Ahmed Hassan. Why are you writing such things to my boss in an email? Why are you saying so many negative things about my business? Why didn't you call me?

Foster was stunned. He did not know what Hassan was talking about or what to say. He recalled:

> Ahmed was absolutely livid. And he continued yelling at me for what seemed like an eternity.

EXHIBIT 1   Email String

1. Email to Richard Howe
To: Richard Howe/Techco@USHQ
Subject: Drives Availability - Further info on XD19

Dick,

I wanted to give you some further info on the XD19 stock situation.

I feel strongly that this is a precursor to what we are going to face when all of our manufacturing goes to the JV. I'm including my thoughts on what is going on and I would like your opinion on what we should do in the organization to get a handle on this before it gets too far out of hand. The issues we are facing seem to be driven by two main factors:

- Marketing is asked for forecasts on product use. Manufacturing does not believe them and makes their own forecasts based on run-rates and then ends up shipping even below that. I think that this is being driven by an inappropriately high emphasis on reducing inventory.
- The manufacturing for the XD19 is done in batches. It is often three to five months between batch runs for a specific drive. With such long lead-times, we are unable to respond to sudden swings in the market or new opportunities.

- Our issues right now are magnified by a problem with the firmware[1] on the XD19. This issue is also illustrative of the types of problems that we need to prevent from happening with the JV:
- We have been using Version 07 firmware, but the JV is currently converting all of their stock to Version 08. The Version 08 firmware has a bug that does not provide true three-wire control in a keypad mode, which we consider a major safety issue.[2]
- The JV does not consider this to be a safety issue and has released this firmware for use outside of the U.S. We are going to have to live off of the remaining stock of Version 07 until the release of Version 09 next year.
- This problem is magnified by the use of masked firmware instead of flashable. When there is a mistake, as there is in this case, we are stuck with it until the next set of masks is made. (There is a cost savings in using masked units, but I would be willing to bet that we have never realized it since we are always giving customers new drives and new control boards to cover our bugs.)
- The JV does not fully test functionality like we do, resulting in a huge list of bugs with each firmware release once we test it. We then have to live with these bugs until the next release and the next set of bugs. Since these releases are normally masked before we do our testing, the fixes can't be done on the fly.
- We are currently expediting Version 07 units from France to cover the shortfalls, but there are six catalog numbers that will need to be ordered from Japan. It is also likely that we will completely exhaust the remaining supply of Version 07 masks for all of the other sizes before production of the Version 09 firmware begins. With the batch lead times, I expect this to absolutely kill the XD19 launch and it will be a big hit on us for Core Product.

This is SCARY!   If an opportunity comes along, forget about it, because we are still filling backlog. I already have OEM salespeople giving up on selling the XD19 because it is not in stock.

It is particularly frustrating being told that we are not meeting top-line objectives when we cannot even ship to the current level of sales.

Charles

2.   Email to Maurice LeBlanc

To: Maurice LeBlanc/Techcolnt@HQFrance

Subject: Drives Availability - Further info on XD19

Maurice,

We are having an inventory problem with the XD19 (V07). The issue as I understand it is France does not have the inventory and we have to wait on the JV to build its next batch. In the meantime, we are losing orders due to lack of inventory.

I would like to see if you could talk with JV to expedite its manufacturing process as we need drives now. The list below contains the key part numbers that we need with Version 07.

Please see some other concerns identified by our Drives National Sales Manager — Charles Foster — in the attached email.

Thank you for any help you can provide.

Dick

3.   Email to Ahmed Hassan

To: Ahmed Hassan/Techcolnt@JVFrance

Subject: Attached emails

Ahmed,

Is this correct what the emails from the U.S. say? Why aren't you following our Standard Protocol SPQ that dictates that we safety test products to the safety standards in the U.S.? I am concerned that the JV is not following our normal engineering review practice.

Maurice

Notes

1   Firmware is a software program that is loaded onto a chip and cannot be modified. "Masked" firmware is etched onto the chip. "Flashable" firmware is not etched on a chip, and new versions can be downloaded onto the chip.
2   Three-way wire control was "fail-safe" circuitry required in the United States but not required or used in the rest of the world.

The Leo Burnett Company Ltd.: Virtual Team Management

On July 2, 2001, Janet Carmichael, global account director for The Leo Burnett Company Ltd. (LB), United Kingdom, sat in her office wondering how to structure her global advertising team. The team was responsible for the introduction of a skin care product of one of LB's most important clients, Ontann Beauty Care (OBC). The product had launched in the Canadian and Taiwanese test markets earlier that year. Taiwanese sales and awareness levels for the product had been high but were low for the Canadian market. Typically, at this stage in the launch process, Carmichael would decentralize the communications management in each market, but the poor performance in the Canadian market left her with a difficult decision: should she maintain centralized control over the Canadian side of her team? In three days, she would leave for meetings at LB's Toronto, Canada, office, where the team would expect her decision.

IVEY
Richard Ivey School of Business
The University of Western Ontario

Elizabeth O'Neil prepared this case under the supervision of Professor Joerg Dietz and Fernando Olivera solely to provide material for class discussion. The authors do not intend to illustrate either effective or ineffective handling of a managerial situation. The authors may have disguised certain names and other identifying information to protect confidentiality.

THE LEO BURNETT COMPANY LTD. BACKGROUND

LB, which was founded in Chicago in 1935, was one of North America's premier advertising agencies. It had created numerous well-recognized North American brand icons, including The Marlboro Man, Kellogg's Tony the Tiger, and the Pillsbury Dough Boy.

By 1999, LB had expanded around the globe to include 93 offices in 83 markets. The company employed approximately 9,000 people, and worldwide revenues were approximately US$9 billion. In 2000, LB merged with two other global agencies to form blcom[3] (the actual company name), one of the largest advertising holding companies in the world, but each LB office retained the Leo Burnett company name.

LB Services and Products

As a full-service agency, LB offered the complete range of marketing and communications services and products (see Exhibits 1 and 2). The company's marketing philosophy was to build "brand belief." The idea driving this philosophy was that true loyalty went beyond mere buying behavior. LB defined "believers" as customers who demonstrated both a believing attitude and loyal purchase behavior. The company strove to convert buyers into believers by building lasting customer affinity for the brand.

EXHIBIT 1   LB Agency Services

Traditional core agency services included:

Account Management
Account management worked in close partnership with planning, creative, media, production and the client to craft tightly focused advertising strategies, based on a deep understanding of the client's products, goals and competition, as well as insights into contemporary consumer behavior.

Creative Services
In most LB offices, creative was the largest department. Creative focused its visual art and copywriting talents on turning strategic insights into advertising ideas. This department was a key part of each client's brand team and often interacted with both clients and clients' customers.

Planning
Planners conducted research to gain insights about the consumer and the marketplace. They also provided valuable input to the strategic and creative agency processes in the form of the implications raised by that research, specifically combining that learning with information about a given product, the social context in which it fit and the psychology of the people who used it.

Media
Starcom was the media division for LB's parent holding company. Its role was to identify the most influential and efficient media vehicles to deliver brand communications to the appropriate audience.

Production
Production staff brought creative ideas to life with the highest quality execution in television, cinema, radio, print, outdoor, direct, point of sale, interactive or any other medium.

In addition to these core services, most offices also offered expertise in more specialized services, including:

- B2B Technology Marketing
- Direct and Database Marketing
- Health-care Marketing
- Interactive Marketing
- Multicultural Marketing
- Public Relations
- Sales Promotion and Event Marketing

EXHIBIT 2   LB Agency Products

Traditional Advertising Products

Television Broadcast Advertising — Usually 30-second (:30s) or 60-second (:60s) TV ads that ran during local or national television programming. This also included sponsoring specific programs, which usually consisted of a five-second announcement before or after the show, i.e., "This program is brought to you by . . ." accompanied by the visual of the sponsoring company's logo.

Radio Broadcast Advertising — Usually 15-, 20-, or 30-second (:15s, :20s, :30s) radio ads that were placed throughout local or national radio programming. Radio ads could include sponsoring specific programs, which usually consisted of a five-second announcement before or after the show, i.e. "This program brought to you by . . ."

Print Advertising — Included black and white and color print ads in local, national or trade newspapers, journals and magazines. Magazine ads could be single-page ads or double-page spreads (two pages facing each other.)

Non-Traditional or "Below the Line" Advertising Products

Direct Marketing — Normally a series of mail-out items (letters, post cards, product samples, etc.) sent to a specifically targeted population(s) called "cells", e.g., companies might send promotional mail-outs to current customers, former customers who have not shopped with the company for a period or time, and new prospective customers — each of these groups would be considered a cell.

Digital or Interactive Marketing — Any marketing efforts that were delivered to the consumer online or by wireless networks (e.g., hand-held wireless devices). This could include Web site design and production, banner advertising and promotions on other Web sites, e-mail marketing, and internal corporate marketing tools such as customer relationship marketing or database building tools.

Collateral — Any piece of print material that was not strictly advertising, for instance brochures, annual reports, posters, flyers and in-store materials.

Promotions — Any marketing effort that included a time-limited offer or incentive to either purchase a product or offer personal data. Promotions could involve advertising, direct marketing, interactive marketing, product packaging and/or outdoor marketing.

One of the most important measures of an agency's success was the quality of the creative product that was developed to connect brands to their end consumers. Each local office strove to produce outstanding creative advertising to break through the clutter of marketing messages that the general public was subjected to daily and truly reach the consumer in a memorable way. Award shows were held nationally and internationally to recognize this effort, one of the most prestigious being the annual festival in Cannes, France. With each award, individual employees (usually the art director and copy writer who had worked together to develop the ad) were recognized, as was the local agency office where they worked. These creative accolades were instrumental in helping an office win new client business. Even within the global LB network, awards were given to the local offices that produced the most outstanding creative work.

LB Internal Team Structures

A multidisciplinary team serviced each brand. Each team had representatives from all core areas of the agency as well as members from the specialized services as appropriate for the brand. In most cases, team members had two sets of reporting lines.

First and formally, they directly reported to the supervisor of their home department (for example, account management). It was this formal supervisor who was responsible for conducting performance evaluations and assigning and managing an employee's workload.

Informally, the team members reported to a project team leader, the senior account services person, who usually was an account director or a vice-president of client services director. It was this team leader's responsibility to manage the project in question, ensure that the client was satisfied with project progress, and build and manage the overall relationship between the client and the agency. Employees on the project team would be responsible to this person for meeting project deadlines and managing their individual client relationships. This team leader would often provide input to a team member's performance evaluation, along with other agency colleagues (see Exhibit 3).

At any given time, an agency employee typically worked on two or three different brand teams, virtually all of them face-to-face teams servicing local clients.

LB Typical Office Environment

Most LB employees were young (in their 20s and 30s) and worked about 60 hours per week. Client needs and project deadlines dictated work priorities, and the volume of work often required late nights at the office. Agency office environments were often open-concept and social. Employees spent many hours each day up and about, discussing projects with colleagues and responding to client requests. The pace was fast and the general spirit was one of camaraderie; it was common for LB employees to socialize together after a late night at the office.

EXHIBIT 3   LB Agency Formal And Informal Reporting Lines

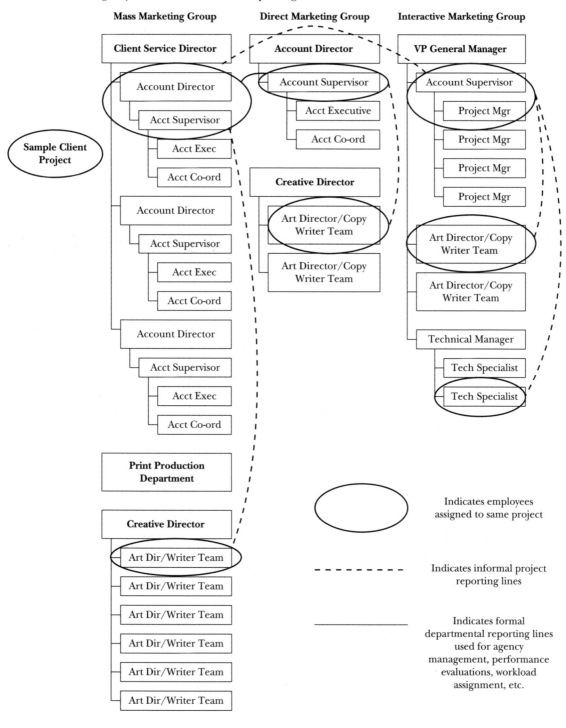

LB Toronto

LB's Toronto office was founded in 1952 to service the Canadian arms of the Chicago-based clients. It was LB's first expansion beyond Chicago. In 2001, it employed a staff of approximately 200 people and billings were approximately $200 million.

LB United Kingdom

LB acquired its London, United Kingdom, office in the mid-1970s as part of an expansion into Europe. By 2001, the office had grown to over 350 employees and billings were approximately $400 million. London was also the regional LB headquarters for all European, Middle Eastern and African offices.

LB'S RELATIONSHIP WITH ONTANN BEAUTY CARE

Ontann Beauty Care (OBC)

OBC was a leading global manufacturer of health and beauty care products. In the late 1990s, OBC made a strategic decision to centralize the global marketing of its brands and products, designating a global team to define the global strategy for a given brand and develop the core communication materials as templates for local markets to follow. Local offices were given the responsibility for adapting the global materials and developing local "below the line" (BTL) materials which would synergize with the global vision and creative templates. Below the line materials included direct marketing, in-store materials, digital marketing, public relations and promotions (that is, everything except strict advertising). In practice, on established brands with well-defined communication templates and strong local knowledge, some local markets (at least key regional markets) were awarded more opportunity to develop their own communication material. The global team, however, retained veto power to ensure all communications were building a consistent personality and look for the brand.

Each OBC global office had as many teams as it had brands. An OBC brand team usually consisted of the global category director, the brand manager and an assistant brand manager, plus a representative from each of the various departments: marketing technology, consumer, trade/distribution, PR, sales, product development, and production.

Relationship Between LB and OBC

OBC, which, like LB, was founded in Chicago, was one of LB's original clients. In 2001, as one of the top three LB clients worldwide, OBC did business with most LB offices. OBC, however, awarded its business to advertising agencies brand-by-brand. As a result, other advertising agencies also had business with OBC. Competition among advertising agencies for OBC business was strong, in particular when they had to work together on joint brand promotions.

OBC had been a client of LB's Toronto office since 1958 and of LB's London office since its acquisition in the mid-1970s. Both the Toronto and London offices initially developed advertising and communications materials for various OBC facial care brands and eventually also worked on OBC's skin care brands.

To better service OBC, LB also centralized its decision-making for this client's brands and appointed expanded and strengthened global teams with the power to make global decisions. For its other clients, LB's global teams were significantly smaller, tending to consist simply of one very senior LB manager who shared learning from across the globe with a given client's senior management.

A NEW OBC BRAND: FOREVER YOUNG

In the fall of 1998, the OBC London office announced a new skin care line called "Forever Young". Product formulas were based on a newly patented process that addressed the needs of aging skin. For OBC, this brand presented an opportunity to address a new market segment: the rapidly growing population of people over the age of 50. The product line was more extensive than other OBC skin care brands. It also represented the company's first foray into premium priced skin care products. Product cost, on average, was double that of most other OBC brands, falling between drug store products and designer products. OBC intended Forever Young to be its next big global launch and awarded the Forever Young advertising and brand communications business to LB.

GLOBAL ADVERTISING AND COMMUNICATIONS TEAM FOR FOREVER YOUNG

Team Formation

For LB, a successful launch of this new product would significantly increase revenues and the likelihood of acquiring additional global OBC brands. An unsuccessful launch would risk the relationship with OBC that LB had built over so many years. LB management in Chicago decided that LB London would be the global team headquarters. This decision reflected the experience that the London office had in leading global business teams and the proximity to the OBC global team for Forever Young. It was also likely that the United Kingdom would be the test market for the new product.

In LB's London office, Janet Carmichael was assigned as brand team leader for the Forever Young product line effective January 1, 1999. Carmichael was the global account director for OBC. The 41-year-old Carmichael, a Canadian, had begun her career at LB Toronto as an account executive in 1985, after completing an MBA degree at the University of Toronto. In 1987, Carmichael moved to Europe, where she continued her career with LB. She became an account supervisor in Italy, an account director in Belgium, and finally a regional and global account director in Germany before taking on a global account director role on OBC brands in the United Kingdom in 1996. She was very familiar with OBC's business and had built excellent relationships with the OBC skin care client group.

LB's initial Forever Young brand team had six members who all were employees of the London office: Carmichael as the team leader, an account director, an account executive (she formally supervised these two employees), the agency's creative director, and two "creatives" (an art director and a copy writer). Carmichael outlined a project timetable (see Exhibit 4). The LB team worked with the OBC team on consumer research, market exploration, brand creative concepts (creative), packaging samples and global copy testing throughout North America and Europe. Carmichael viewed marketing a new product to a new consumer segment in a crowded category as challenging; however, after several months of testing, LB's Forever Young brand team developed a unique creative concept that was well received by OBC.

In the fall of 1999, OBC decided that the United Kingdom would be the lead market for another skin care product. Because North America was a priority for the Forever Young brand and Canada was "clean" (that is, OBC was not testing other products in Canada at that time), Canada became the new primary test market for Forever Young. In addition, Canadians' personal skin care habits and the distribution process for skin care products were more reflective of overall Western practices (i.e., the Western world) than were those in other potential test markets. Taiwan became the secondary test market for Asian consumers. These choices were consistent with OBC's interest in global brand validation.

In keeping with OBC's team structures, LB maintained the global brand team in London and, in January of 2000, formed satellite teams in Toronto, Canada, and Taipei, Taiwan, to manage material execution in their local markets. It was up to the LB Toronto and Taipei offices to determine their members in the Forever Young satellite teams. In Taipei, Cathy Lee, an account director who was particularly interested in the assignment, took the lead on local agency activities. In Toronto, Geoff Davids, an account supervisor from the direct marketing group, was assigned to lead the Toronto team. The global brand team and the two satellite teams now formed the LB side of the global advertising and communications team for Forever Young (see Exhibit 5).

Kick-off Meeting

In February 2000, a face-to-face kick-off meeting took place in Toronto with the intent to bring all senior members of LB's and OBC's London, Toronto, and Taipei teams onto the same page regarding the new brand and the status of the launch process. One or two senior representatives from OBC London, Toronto, and Taipei participated in the meeting. From LB, the complete London team participated, along with Geoff Davids and a senior agency representative from the Toronto office, and Cathy Lee and a senior agency representative from the Taipei office. Carmichael and her U.K. team members shared their initial brand creative concepts, which had already garnered admiration throughout the LB network, and their knowledge about the product and target audience.

EXHIBIT 4   Brand Development Chronology

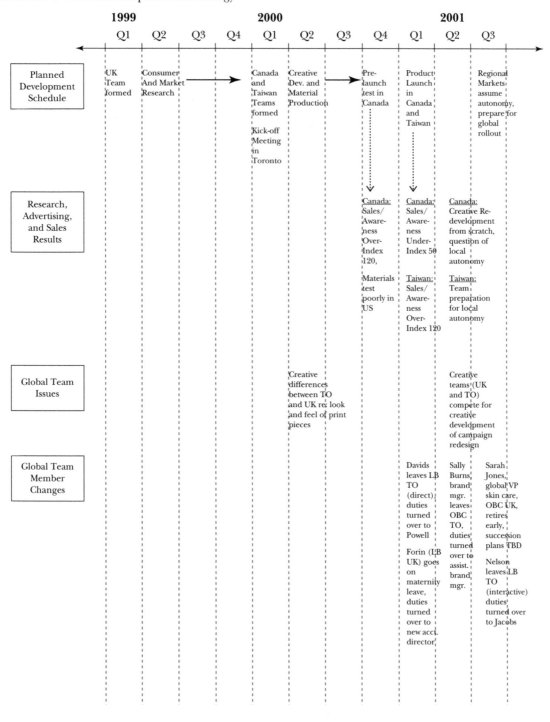

EXHIBIT 5   The Global Forever Young Team

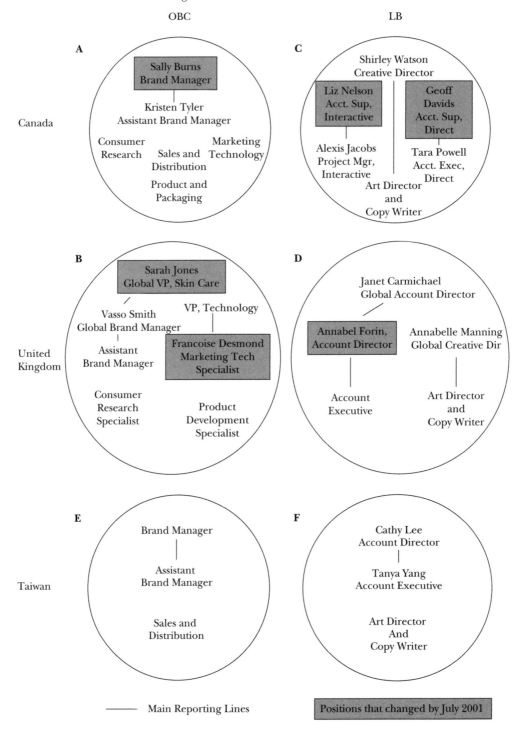

It was decided that Davids and Lee would serve as the main links to LB's London-based global brand team. Specifically, Davids and Lee reported to Annabel Forin, Carmichael's account director in the United Kingdom. Forin then reported to Carmichael and OBC's London team. Besides Forin, Carmichael's primary contacts would be Annabelle Manning, the global creative director at LB United Kingdom and Sarah Jones, OBC's global vice-president of skin care in London. All work produced by LB's satellite teams would require approval from LB's London team.

The Creative Assignments

The creative assignments for the Canadian and Taiwanese teams were slightly different from each other. Normally, the global team would produce a creative template for a brand (meaning the design of the advertising and communications materials), which would then be passed to the satellite teams to be adapted for the local market.

In the Taiwanese market, this would be the case. The Taiwanese LB team would be responsible for adapting the advertising materials, which would include re-filming the television ad to star an Asian actress, as well as retaking photos for the print ads, again, to demonstrate product benefits on Asian skin. The brand message (meaning the text in print ads and the vocal message in television ads) would be adapted to appeal to the Taiwanese audience.

In Toronto, however, the assignment broke from this traditional format. The LB team in London would produce English television and print advertising, which would be used in the Canadian market. The LB team in Toronto would design and produce the direct marketing and Web site materials because the London office did not have strong in-house capabilities in these areas. While the Toronto office would have control of the design of these communication pieces, the U.K. office would require that certain elements be incorporated into the design (for example, specific photos and colors), in order for the pieces to be visually consistent with the print advertising.

EVENTS LEADING UP TO THE LAUNCH

LB's Taipei Office

After returning to Taipei from the kick-off meeting, Lee formed her local team, which consisted of an account executive (Tanya Yang) and a creative team (one art director and one copy writer). In co-operation with OBC's Taipei team, Lee and her team focused first on recreating the television ad. The ad followed the original creative idea developed in the United Kingdom but used a popular Taiwanese actress in the lead. The character differentiation was necessary to demonstrate the product's benefit to Asian skin because the original ad featured a blond, Caucasian actress as the lead. The team moved on to adapt the brand's print advertising and direct marketing pieces and developed a public relations campaign to meet local market needs. These communication elements were visually and strategically consistent with the television ad as they incorporated photos of the same Taiwanese actress.

Throughout this process, the Taipei team regularly updated LB's and OBC's London teams about its progress. Although all work required U.K. approval, the Taiwanese team worked with a significant amount of autonomy because of the cultural differences present in its market. Carmichael and Manning occasionally travelled to Taiwan to meet with the team and approve its creative work, which they generally received well. In addition, the Taipei team communicated with the London offices through videoconference calls and e-mail. The LB Taipei and Toronto teams had contact with each other only during the global team videoconference meetings, held every two months.

LB's Toronto Office

After the kick-off meeting, Davids, with the approval of LB's Toronto management, assigned representatives from the direct marketing group and the interactive marketing group to the brand team. This included account management (Tara Powell, account executive for direct; Liz Nelson, account supervisor; and Alexis Jacobs, project manager for interactive) and creative staff (Shirley Watson, creative director; and one copy writer from each of the direct and interactive groups).

In co-operation with OBC's Toronto team, the LB Toronto team was responsible for developing a full communication plan for its local market. Along with running the television and print ads developed in the United Kingdom, the team would focus on producing the brand's below the line materials (i.e., direct mail, Web site). These communication elements served as the education pieces that supplemented the TV ad. Davids conducted an internal team debrief, outlining the information he had received at the kick-off meeting. From this, the team developed a communications plan that, in Carmichael's opinion, was "on-brief" (i.e., consistent with the original brand strategic direction) and included some very innovative thinking.

Next, the team began determining a creative look and feel for the direct mail pieces. The look and feel could be different from the television creative but had to be consistent across all of the paper-based (print ads, direct mail pieces and in-store materials) and online communication elements. The creatives in LB's Toronto team developed the direct marketing materials, and simultaneously the creatives in LB's U.K. team developed the print advertising. The two sides' creative work evolved in different directions, but each side hoped that the other would adapt their look and feel. Eventually, however, LB's Toronto team told its London counterpart to "figure it out," and they would follow London's lead. Communication between the two sides mostly flowed through Davids and Forin to Carmichael. Carmichael, however, had received a copy of the following e-mail from Watson to Davids:

> Geoff, as you know, it's always a challenge to work with someone else's art direction. I don't think the model that London chose is right for this market, and the photography we have to work with doesn't have as contemporary a feel as I would like.
>
> This would be easier if I could connect directly with Annabelle [Manning] but she's on the road so much of the time it's hard to catch her. We weren't asked for our opinion initially and, given the timing constraints at this point, we don't have much choice but to use what

they've sent us, but could you please convey to Annabel [Forin] that in the future, if possible, we'd like to have the chance to input on the photography before it's taken? It will help us develop good direct mail creative.

For now, though, I think we'll be able to do something with what they've sent us. Thanks.

There had been other challenges for LB's Toronto team. Davids described an incident that had occurred when his direct marketing team tried to present its creative concept to the team in the United Kingdom during a videoconference meeting:

Our direct mail concept was a three-panel, folded piece. We sent two flat files to the United Kingdom via e-mail, which were to be cut out, pasted back-to-back [to form the front and back of the piece] and then folded into thirds. It took us so long to explain how to do that — somehow we just weren't getting through! Our colleagues in London cut and folded and pasted in different places, and what should have been a simple preliminary procedure took up 45 minutes of our one-hour videoconference meeting! By the time we actually got around to discussing the layout of the piece, everyone on the call was frustrated. That's never a good frame of mind to be in when reviewing and critiquing a new layout. It's too bad our clients were on that call as well.

A greater challenge came in September 2000, when the team was behind schedule in the development of the Web site after encountering difficulties with OBC's technology standards. The budgeting for the Web site development came out of the global budget, not the local budget. This meant that the members of LB's Toronto team who were responsible for the Web site development ("interactive marketing") received directions from OBC's London team. The budgeting for direct marketing, however, came out of the local budget, and the members of LB's Toronto team, who were responsible for the development of the direct marketing materials, dealt with OBC's Toronto team. The instructions from these two OBC teams were often inconsistent. Compounding matters, the two OBC client teams repeatedly requested changes of the Web and direct marketing materials, which made these materials even more different from each other and forced the LB Toronto team into extremely tight timeframes.

Carmichael learned about this sort of difficulty mostly through the direct supervisors of the team members. She frequently received calls from LB Toronto's Interactive Marketing Group and Direct Marketing Group senior managers. Carmichael repeatedly had to explain the basic project components to these senior managers and wished that the members of LB's Toronto team would just follow the team communications protocol and forward their concerns to Davids, who would then take up matters as necessary with the U.K. team.

CANADIAN PRE-LAUNCH TEST

Despite these challenges, LB's Toronto team produced the materials in time for the Canadian pre-launch test in October of 2000. The pre-launch test was a launch of the complete communications program (TV ad, newspaper inserts, distribution of trial packs, direct mail, and a Web site launch) in a market whose media could be completely isolated. A small town in the interior of British Columbia, Canada's most westerly province, met these conditions. In terms of product trial and product sales as a percentage of market share, the test indexed 120 against its objectives, which had a base index of 100. Subsequently, OBC and LB decided to move immediately into research to test the advertising in the U.S. market. The global OBC and LB teams worked with their Canadian counterparts to conduct this research, the results of which were very poor. As a result, OBC London required that LB's London and Toronto teams revised the advertising materials even before the Canadian launch.

CANADIAN NATIONAL LAUNCH

The days before the launch were panic-filled, as LB's London and Toronto teams scrambled to revise the advertising. In February 2001, the campaign was launched in Canada with the following elements:

- One 30-second TV ad;
- One direct mail piece;
- The English Web site;
- Product samples available from the Web from direct mail piece, and from an in-store coupon;
- Specially designed in-store displays;
- Trial-sized package bundles (one week's worth);
- A public relations campaign; and
- Five print ads in national magazines.

Research following the national launch showed that the brand did not perform well among Canadian consumers. It indexed 50 against a base index of 100. Because of the success of the Canadian pre-launch test, OBC and LB were surprised. The Forever Young global advertising and communications team attributed the discrepancy between the pre-launch test and national launch, in part, to the fact that the pre-launch test conditions were not replicable on a national scale. The audience penetration in the small B.C. town, the pre-test site, was significantly greater than it was in the national launch. OBC decided that the results of the Canadian launch were below "action standards," meaning that OBC would not even consider a rollout into the U.S. market at the current time.

The tension levels on both LB's side and OBC's side of the Forever Young global advertising and communications team were high. LB's future business on the brand was in jeopardy. The OBC side was under tremendous pressure internally to improve brand trial and market share metrics and already planned to decentralize the local teams for the global product rollout. Despite numerous revisions to the advertising, it never tested well enough to convince OBC that a U.S. or European launch would be successful.

A DIFFERENT STORY IN ASIA

In Taiwan, the product launch was successful. Test results showed that the brand was indexing 120 per cent against brand objectives. Research also showed that Taiwanese consumers, in contrast to Canadian consumers, did not perceive some of the advertising elements as "violent." Moreover, in Taiwan, overall research scores in terms of "likeability" and "whether or not the advertising would inspire you to try the product" were higher, leading to higher sales. By June of 2001, the Taiwanese team was ready to take on more local-market responsibility and move into the post-launch phase of the advertising campaign. This phase would involve creating new ads to build on the initial success and grow sales in the market.

RECOVERY PLAN FOR CANADA

By June of 2001, LB needed to take drastic measures to develop a new Forever Young campaign in order to improve the brand's performance in the Canadian marketplace. Whereas, before the launch, there had been a clear division of responsibilities (with the United Kingdom developing the television and print advertising and Canada developing direct marketing, in-store and Web site communications), now the global LB team in London decided that it would be necessary to have all hands on deck. New creative teams from the mass advertising department in the Toronto office, as well as supplementary creative teams from the London office, were briefed to develop new campaign ideas. Each team had only three weeks to develop their new ideas, less than half of the eight weeks they would normally have, and the teams had to work independent of each other. The London and Toronto creative teams had to present their concepts to the entire global OBC and LB team at the same time. Subsequently, the results of market research would determine the winning creative concept. Squabbling between the offices began over which team would present first, which office received what compensation for the development, and whether or not overall remuneration packages were fair. Moreover, the communication between the account services members of LB's London and Toronto teams, which was the primary communication channel between the two agencies, became less frequent, less candid and more formal. The presentations took place on June 25, 2001, in Toronto. Watson, the creative director in Toronto commented:

> This process has been exciting, but we're near the ends of our collective ropes now. We have a new mass advertising creative team [who specialized in TV ads] on the business in Toronto, and they're being expected to produce world-class creative results for a brand they've only heard about for the past few days. They don't — and couldn't possibly — have the same passion for the brand that the direct marketing creative team members have after working on it for so long. I'm having a hard time motivating them to work under these tight timelines.
>
> We're even more isolated now in Toronto. Our connection to the creative teams and the global creative director in London was distant at best, and now it's non-existent. And our relationship with the local OBC client feels very remote, too. Still, we're moving forward with our work. We're trying to learn from the Taiwanese experience and are considering what success we would have with a nationally recognized actress starring in our television ads.

EVOLUTION OF THE FOREVER YOUNG GLOBAL ADVERTISING AND COMMUNICATIONS TEAM

Personnel Changes

Between January and June of 2001, numerous personnel changes in the Forever Young global advertising and communications team occurred (see Exhibit 5). In LB's London office, Forin, the U.K. account director, had been replaced following her departure for maternity leave. In OBC's London office, Sarah Jones, the global vice-president for skin care, took early retirement without putting a succession plan in place. In LB's Toronto office, Davids, the Toronto brand team leader, had left the agency. Tara Powell, who had reported to Davids, took on his responsibilities, but she had not met most of the global team members. Liz Nelson, the account supervisor for interactive, left LB's Toronto office to return to school. Alexis Jacobs, who had managed the Web site development, took over her responsibilities. Powell and Jacobs did not have close relationships with their international counterparts. At OBC Toronto, Sally Burns, the local brand manager, who had been LB's main contact in the local market and had been with the brand since inception, left OBC. LB's and OBC's Taiwanese teams remained stable over time. Cathy Lee worked with a team that was nearly identical to her initial team.

Communications

Early on (between February and May 2000), Carmichael had orchestrated frequent face-to-face meetings to ensure clarity of communication and sufficient information sharing. In the following months, the team relied on videoconferences and phone calls, with visits back and forth between London and Toronto on occasion. Since early 2001, the team had relied increasingly on e-mails and telephone calls to communicate. In June 2001, Carmichael noted that the communication had become more formal, and she had lost the feeling of being part of a global team. She wondered if giving the LB's Toronto team more autonomy to develop the brand in their market would help the brand progress. Working together as a smaller team might improve the Toronto group's team dynamic as well. Carmichael was concerned that the current discord between LB's London and Toronto offices would negatively affect the relationship to OBC.

Budget Problems

The extra creative teams assigned to the redevelopment of the brand's television advertising and the unexpected changes to the Forever Young communication materials had meant that LB's costs to staff the project had been higher than originally estimated and higher than the revenues that had been negotiated with OBC. Since OBC did not want to pay more for its advertising than had been originally budgeted, LB faced tremendous internal pressure to finish the project as soon as possible. This situation created conflict between LB and OBC in the United Kingdom, who was responsible for negotiating LB's overall fees. Because all fees were paid to the global brand office (in this case, LB's

London office) and then transferred to the local satellite teams, this situation also created conflict between LB's London and Toronto teams, who had both expended additional staff time to revise the advertising materials and wanted "fair" compensation.

WHAT NEXT?

In three days, Carmichael had to leave for Toronto to sit in research sessions to test the recently presented new creative concepts. In the meetings that followed, she would present to the team her recommendation for how to move forward with the brand. Carmichael reviewed the brand events and team interaction of the past two years (see Exhibit 4) to determine the best global team structure for salvaging the Forever Young brand and maintaining the relationship between OBC and LB.

Carmichael felt torn in her loyalties. On the one hand, she was Canadian and knew LB's Toronto office well — she knew that LB's Toronto brand team worked hard, and she wished them every success. On the other hand, she had now worked in LB's London office for several years, and she had always liked the creative that the U.K. team had initially produced. If she maintained the current form of centralized control of the team, either creative concept might be chosen; however, if she decentralized team control, the Toronto team would almost certainly choose their own creative concept for the television ads. Since the creative direction chosen now would become the brand's advertising in most North American and European markets, it needed to be top calibre. Carmichael thought this posed a risk if the creative development was left to the new Toronto-based mass advertising creative team. It would be a shame to lose the U.K. team's original creative concept.

In making her decision on whether to decentralize the team, Carmichael considered the following:

1. Where was the knowledge necessary to create a competitive advantage for the brand in Canada? Would it be in the Canadian marketplace because they understood the market, or would it be in London because they had more in-depth knowledge of the brand?
2. Where was the client responsibility, and where should it be? Now that the London-based global vice-president of skin care was retiring, the client was considering creating a virtual global team to manage the brand, headquartered in the United States but composed of members of the original United Kingdom OBC team, in preparation for a U.S. launch. If the client team had its headquarters in North America, should LB also structure its team this way?
3. If Carmichael decentralized the brand and gave the Toronto team greater autonomy, who would lead the brand in Toronto now that Davids had left the agency? How would the necessary knowledge be imparted to the new leader?
4. If they remained centralized, would the team make it through before it self-destructed? How much would this risk the client relationship? To what extent would it strain the already tight budget?

Carmichael had to make a decision that was best for the brand, LB and OBC.

PART 3

CHAPTER **5**

Executing Global Strategy[a]

Today's global organizations need skilled managers. Cultural understanding and good intercultural skills are important managerial competencies. However, as a manager in the global economy you will need more than intercultural skills. You also have to understand how culture may influence your company's strategy, structure, administrative systems, and operations. The formulation and implementation of a strategy requires understanding market demands, competitors, and external constraints such as government policies. Managers interpret information from their external environment, combine this interpretation with an understanding of the organization's internal strengths and weaknesses, and translate the implications into appropriate organizational action that will lead to desired goals. In addition to choosing markets and manufacturing sites, for example, important organizational actions include choosing structures, work systems, and administrative mechanisms to motivate employees toward the desired goals.

Since a company's knowledge and practices are not always completely documented, or made explicit, there is a great deal of implicit or *tacit* knowledge required to manage a company effectively.[1] Executives need to be aware of the implicit knowledge or assumptions underlying their firm's strategy, structure, systems, and practices. These practices are influenced by both organizational culture and national culture. Culture, the "shoulds" and the "oughts" of life that people usually cannot articulate, is acquired through the socialization process which creates common experiences, shared mental models, and accepted ways of operating – the way things should be done. Using domestic strategy, systems or practices, unmodified, in another country may lead to unforeseen negative

[a]The authors would like to acknowledge Professor Nick Athanassiou for his contribution to this chapter, which is based on his earlier revision of the text, and also to thank Professor Bert Spector for his contribution as well.

consequences. Therefore, global executives need to understand how their assumptions about organizing and managing may differ from those in their company's home country.

If management were a science, we simply would have to learn the laws regarding management. Unfortunately, laws regarding management have not yet been discovered and may never be. If management were an art, we could rely on the intuition and insight of individuals, and there would probably be little that could be done to create managers in the numbers our organizations require. We would rely on a few naturally gifted people.

We prefer to think of management as a craft, an undertaking that requires knowledge of facts and principles and an ability to interpret these in their cultural context. It also requires the development of experience and judgment to aid in the correct interpretation of situations. One can learn about and practice management to improve upon our craft domestically and globally.

As a company spreads beyond its home country and creates a global network, top managers need to recalibrate their cultural "filters" through education and the acquisition of personal experience. Specifically, this should include knowledge about their different market environments, company activities in these countries, and the linkages among this network of activities. The experiences and the understood but unwritten information, as well as the explicit policies and practices shared by a top management group, create the operational and cultural filters used to decode, interpret, and understand context-dependent information flowing from the company's various markets and operations. With properly interpreted information, global executives can make informed strategic decisions and influence the design and implementation of culturally sensitive organization structures and systems to achieve strategic goals.[2] Executives can put into use the global mindset they have developed.

Most companies have a particular organizational heritage that has evolved within the culture of their home countries. This means that a potential cultural bias may exist in their strategy, systems, and practices – "the way things are done in the headquarters' home country." For example, Lincoln Electric, renowned in the United States for its highly skilled and extremely productive employees, used a unique piecework incentive system to pay workers primarily on the number of quality pieces that they produced.[3] Working faster and harder meant a higher salary. This system was instituted around 1907 by James F. Lincoln who strongly believed in the individual human being and in the equality of management and workers. Driven by his philosophy and beliefs about human motivation, he created the system which he believed would generate the best productivity and utilization of the company's human resources. This system was a significant contributor to the company's productivity and profitability. But the question to be answered is "Could it be transferred to another culture without modification?" We will address this question in the following sections.

The Organizational Alignment Model

In this section we will develop the organizational alignment model first in a culture-free mode without considering how culture may affect management practices and systems, and then we will consider the impact of culture. The basic components of this model are shown in Figure 5.1.

FIGURE 5.1 The Organizational Alignment Model

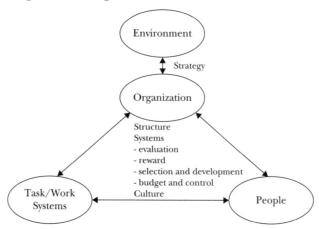

Tasks Global organizations are complex and have many jobs or *tasks* that need to be done. These tasks have different characteristics requiring different skills which mean employing people with different educational backgrounds, knowledge bases, and skills. There are usually patterns of differences, or systematic variances, between people in various functional departments. That idea that segments of a company are organized for specific tasks and that some people by education, experience, and attitude seem more appropriate for some jobs rather than others is the concept of *differentiation* or the "difference in cognitive and emotional orientation among managers in different functional departments."[4] This concept encompasses the specialized knowledge required for the tasks as well as the differences in attitude and behavior of the people in the jobs. As the complexity of an organization increases it is likely that the differentiation increases as well. As this happens, the potential for departments to pursue their own particular goals increases, as does the likelihood for potential conflict. Therefore, it is important to coordinate these functional areas. This is not always easy in large corporations, since people may be separated physically and psychologically by their personal predispositions and orientations.

Once there is a differentiated organization capable of executing the required tasks, then integration is needed. The concept of *integration* includes the coordination of activities and interrelationships and conflict resolution, as well. Integrating mechanisms include task forces, teams, liaison people, product or project managers, product management departments, and matrix organization designs. These are structural responses to the increasing coordination needs of an organization.

To ensure the proper coordination, managers also must be aware of how each area is dependent on the others to achieve its tasks and responsibilities. There are three basic types of internal interdependence in organizations,[5] and most complex organizations exhibit all three types. The simplest is *pooled* interdependence. This means that each part of an organization can pursue the achievement of its goals independently without requiring input from other parts and still contribute to the overall objectives of the organization. For example, in a department store, personnel from the furniture department do not necessarily have to interact with people from sporting goods for each to fulfill its objectives. Each can contribute, independently, to the goals of the store.

Higher up on the complexity scale is *sequential* interdependence. As the name implies, one group must accomplish its task before the next one can begin. There is an ordered progression by which some tasks must proceed. In manufacturing a relatively standard product one can see a progression from the design department to engineering to purchasing to production scheduling and then to manufacturing. On the assembly line of an automobile, for example, the car's frame and axles are assembled before the engine or the body is attached. A specific task must be accomplished before the next is begun.

An even more complex form of interdependence is *reciprocal*, which means "the output of each becomes the input for the others."[6] Rather than having discrete linear relationships between groups, the relationships are continuous and almost circular in nature. For example, in creating sophisticated technology systems, production must understand what the researchers have developed, but the development engineers must also understand the constraints on manufacturing. Similarly, both the researchers and the engineers must understand the customers' needs in order to accurately forecast delivery dates. As can be inferred from this simple example, reciprocal interdependence creates an iterative process and the level of inter-group communication and potential for a conflict can escalate dramatically.

Coordination   As the complexity of organizations increases, the need to coordinate and control the activities of diverse groups of individuals also increases, and formal control mechanisms such as accounting, auditing, and management information systems are important. Most organizations systematically collect, analyze, and disseminate information on production, finances, and personnel. Budgets are developed, refined, and monitored. Like other mechanisms, these give messages about what is required or valued. For example, requiring Manufacturing to concentrate on costs and Sales on customer satisfaction could in some circumstances produce high levels of dysfunctional conflict. Manufacturing would want long productions runs to minimize down time and re-tooling costs, while Sales might want runs stopped to meet a valued customer's urgent need for another product. Both need to understand the other and act in a coordinated fashion if either is to satisfy their needs.

The managerial issue is how to coordinate the various types of interdependence. At the simplest level, standardization by rules and budgets can be used. A department is given a budget, a set of operating procedures, hours of operation, and a set of well defined tasks to do, and measured on its results against set objectives. With sequential interdependence, coordination is usually also accomplished with plans and schedules. However, at the level of reciprocal interdependence, special structural integrating roles such as project or product managers are employed and coordinating mechanisms such as task forces are often used. Direct, face-to-face communication, or coordination through mutual adjustment, usually is required as well.[7]

A problem solving approach to resolving conflict is generally regarded as the most appropriate way to contribute to organizational effectiveness. This means that managers confront problems rather than avoiding them or smoothing them over. As they confront them, they recognize that the conflicts may be rooted in legitimate task differences and different viewpoints held by different specialists. Managers should avoid letting situations develop where functions attempt to prevail and win out over others. Win–lose situations can be very destructive for organizations. Managers should attempt to resolve conflicts so that the organization as a whole wins.

Structure, Systems, and Alignment   We do not intend to deal with particular tools, such as structure, reward systems, or control systems in depth, but to explain how, if used effectively or ineffectively, they can create fits or misfits between people and their jobs, or between people and the organizations in which they work. Each system gives an employee some type of message about what is expected of him or her. These systems send signals and these signals are important. Quite often different systems give people different messages or signals. Ineffectiveness often results when individuals cannot reconcile those different messages. Often they pay attention to one system to the exclusion of messages coming from another.

Organizations should be designed so that the behavior elicited by the administrative systems matches the needs of the organization. All too often, procedures are imposed without due consideration of the job at hand, simply because, *de facto*, they just "have become company policy." In such situations, the administrative heritage of the company may become the controlling factor, with the jobs and the people forced into fitting the existing systems, when it should be the other way around.

These administrative systems are tools, not ends in themselves. Judgment is required in assessing the likely impact of administrative systems on people and in adjusting these systems accordingly to support task achievement and organizational results.

For best performance, there should be a *fit*, or *alignment*, between the people and the jobs that they do. The first, extremely important fit is between the tasks to be performed and the skills of the people who perform them. Then managers can use administrative "tools" to strengthen this alignment between people and tasks. These tools channel the activities of employees; they are relational tools.

The people and tasks they are working at are organized using various divisions of labor and *structures* to achieve coordination, efficiency, and effectiveness. Structure is the set of relationships between people in an organization and is one mechanism that communicates to organization members what behavior is expected of them, what tasks to work on, what not to do, what goals to work towards, with whom to work, whom to obey, and whom to direct. This includes such things as hierarchy, teams, and rules and procedures.

Structure, for example, creates relationships between people at various levels of responsibility, while budgets and performance appraisals direct behavior toward specific tasks and goals. The other alignment "tools" include selection criteria and processes, development programs, allocation of rewards and sanctions, information and control systems, and performance evaluation methods.

The people brought into an organization through its *recruitment* and *selection* systems can have a very dramatic effect on organizational alignment. The most obvious effect is on the pool of knowledge, skills, and attitudes. Selection is the mechanism by which a pool of candidates is narrowed to the number of job vacancies. Several sources of assessment error can enter these decisions. The one most frequently described is the "just like me" error in which the successful candidate is the one who is closest in skills and personality to those making the decision. Although it might augur well for the fit between the person and his or her boss, this type of decision might not provide the required congruence between person and task. Selection, like recruitment, involves a careful analysis of both the job(s) and the organization to determine the right type of person.

Rarely does a selection decision alone provide a perfect person–job (P–J) or person–organization (P–O) fit. P–J fit is the traditional focus of employee selection, the skills and abilities to do the job; while P–O fit is concerned with a person's compatibility with broader characteristics of the organization such as culture, values, and colleagues.[8] If it is only to find out how things are done in the company, most employees need some form of *training* or *development* to make them effective performers. Even if the fit is perfect, it is not likely that condition will last for long. Continual development is needed as conditions change.

Two of the most talked about and studied administrative systems are *performance appraisal* and *rewards*. Appraisal processes are seen in many forms and administered in many ways. However, at the core there are several common purposes:

- to communicate expectations or standards of performance;
- to provide feedback on how well one is doing against expectations or standards;
- to identify areas of developmental need and develop a plan of remedy;
- to provide information and documentation for decisions about salary, promotion, or discipline.

Rewards come in different forms and in different ways for different people. One person's reasons for working are different from another's. Basically, rewards fall into one of two categories: intrinsic, those that come from doing the job itself or being directly part of the work environment, and extrinsic, those more tangible aspects provided by others. More job autonomy is an example of the former, while getting a raise is an example of the latter.

Rewards have different meanings for different people. Some rewards (particularly the financial reward) have instrumental value, helping us get other things of importance such as food and shelter. It often serves as a signal that one's contribution or presence is valued: a form of recognition. It can serve as a signal to others of one's value, thereby enhancing self esteem. Individual needs determine which of these meanings are most important at any one time, and which reward will have the desired effect.

In designing and administering reward systems from the employee's perspective, several issues are important.

1 Are they sufficient? Is the sum of both the intrinsic and extrinsic rewards enough to attract, motivate, and retain employees? Do they get enough of the right things to satisfy their needs?
2 Are they equitable? Are the rewards commensurate with what the employee brings to the job in terms of skill, knowledge, aptitude, attitude, and effort? And is the internal distribution of rewards fair?

And from the organization's perspective, it is important to ask the following questions about rewards,

3 Are they competitive? Can the organization attract the people it wants vis-à-vis its competitors?

4 Do they motivate the right task behavior or do they create a disincentive? Do they motivate for a sustained period of time?

With a range of options, how do you decide which type of system is most appropriate? The answer to these questions should come from the analysis of the organization and the environment in which it operates. Once a strategy is developed, goals have been established, and the key tasks have been laid out, the people required can be identified and the correct systems instituted.

Organizations also have *cultures* that may facilitate or hinder the work of the company and management is responsible for creating the culture of the organization. A set of values and philosophy will develop in every organization, whether it is created explicitly with careful forethought, or whether it happens implicitly without specific guidance and is perhaps less effective. Management's values can encourage a culture of trust, problem solving, and adaptation to another country or one of mistrust, obedience, and domination. Lincoln Electric, based on James Lincoln's philosophy, created a corporate culture of rugged individualism, productivity, and innovation. Workers were responsible for their own success.

If values provide the content of the culture, managers' styles shape the climate and feeling for how other managers and subordinates relate – the day-to-day process of taking action and solving problems. Management style can create an atmosphere of openness and sharing, or one of insecurity and fear. The challenges facing today's organizations would seem to call for flexible, innovative organizations and for managers whose personal styles can create or contribute to those characteristics. The management at Lincoln Electric did not believe in hierarchical distinctions, and sought to erase them.[9] There were no reserved parking spaces for managers and they ate in the same cafeteria as the workers. There also was an Advisory Board of elected employee representatives which met twice a month with Lincoln executives. Management was approachable and had an open door policy. The result was trust between the workers and management.

In summary, people are selected for certain skills and attitudes; trained and educated (developed) to improve these skills; evaluated on how they do their jobs and rewarded. Evaluation and reward systems, development, budgets, and control systems are also used to motivate people. To make sure that the tasks of the organization are coordinated and carried out in the best possible way, companies use various structures. Too often decisions about the administrative systems are made because of unexamined assumptions about motivation, rather than an understanding of the organization in its context.

Organizations are systems and need to be understood as such. In practical terms this means that what happens in one part of the organization has implications for, and probably affects, other parts. Organizations are socio-technical systems, meaning that they have both social and technical components. The "technical" component is the numerous technical and/or functional tasks of the business. These include acquiring inputs such as capital and raw materials, as well as using specific technology and work processes to create finished products or services. Each of the major functional areas of an organization – such as production, marketing, or finance – also is a system within the larger "technical" organizational system. Each has a set of tasks and operations necessary to the functioning of the entire organization.

The "social" component is the human element, the people – the individuals and groups, with their skills, needs, feelings, expectations, experience, and beliefs, that carry out the tasks and operations. Managers have to align the connected and interdependent parts of social and technical elements of a company and solve problems that arise within and between the two in order to achieve the organization's strategic goals.

For example, in an industry like financial printing, companies have long provided *transaction* services such as completing and filing required documents with regulators such as the Security and Exchange Commission when a firm had an Initial Public Offering (IPO) or there was a merger or acquisition. This was a highly customized service based on relationship selling by a sales force, and this service had very high margins. The sales representatives who were hired to sell transaction services were aggressive self-starters who liked the substantial salary, bonuses, and glory that came from being successful in the high margin, relationship-oriented transaction business.

Then, in 2002, the Sarbanes-Oxley Act required firms to file numerous routine, standardized periodic reports that were time consuming to prepare. As a result, financial printing companies, pushed by competitors that were offering a low cost "do-it-yourself" product, introduced a *compliance* service for their customers to meet the requirements of Sarbanes-Oxley. The compliance service was a lower margin offering than the transaction service. However, in terms of company revenue it was growing to become a very important part of a firm's business. One firm which we will call ABC Financial Printing developed a range of products such as computer programs to address this market. However, it had difficulty in motivating its sales representatives to sell these products.

FIGURE 5.2 Organizational Alignment Model[11]

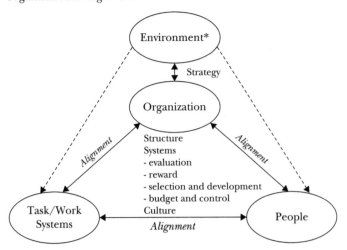

*Social (including cultural), technological, economic (including competition), and political environment

The characteristics of its sales people, its reward and its evaluation systems did not fit with the demands of the new market or its customers for compliance business.

Managers must understand that if they make a change in either the task or the people, their action may have ramifications for the other and implications for overall results – and not always the ones intended. This is one of the properties of a system; a change in one part affects the other parts. This is why a systemic and integrated perspective of organizations is essential in diagnosing problems and considering courses of action.

The organizational alignment model is shown in Figure 5.2.

Context and Alignment

Christopher Alexander, in writing about the process of design of physical things like buildings or transportation systems, commented on the need for fit or alignment:

> Every design problem begins with an effort to achieve fitness between two entities: the form in question and its context. The form is the solution to the problem; the context defines the problem. In other words, when we speak of design, the real object of discussion is not the form alone, but the ensemble comprising the form and its context.[10]

Relating this to global organizations, the form is the result of decisions managers make about how to structure tasks and coordinate them, who to hire, how to reward them, and so forth. The context is the global environment in which it operates. The context [environment] makes demands on the form [organization] and meeting the demands of the environment is "fitness" or alignment. To achieve alignment, managers need to understand their organization and its context.

External complexity affects managers also, as our discussion of globalization earlier in this book pointed out. These organizations are part of an *environment* or context that is comprised of social, political, and economic institutions and technology that affect them. Internationally, the social, political, and economic institutions in the host country may be very different from those in the home country. Also the (national) cultural assumptions about "how things should be done" or the "right way to manage" may differ as well. Firms also have competitors, and they compete in their environment by developing a sustainable, competitive strategy.

Managers are responsible for the functioning of these complex human systems. Obviously, the complexity faced by a manager and his or her responsibility varies by job and by level within the organization. People at the highest levels generally are more concerned with forces outside of the organization, and linking the organization to its external environment while people at lower levels are more concerned with internal operations. However, with globalization and having operations in many countries, people at all levels now are being exposed to the complexities of how other cultures affect both external and internal organizational environments.

Now we will consider the transfer of systems and practices to other cultures. Can structures, systems, and practices developed in one country be transferred to another where cultural assumptions and paradigms about the right way to manage may be different? If so, can they be transferred as is, or do they need to be modified?

Alignment in Different Cultural Contexts

Consider Lincoln Electric again. With its origins in the mid-western United States, it created a set of administrative systems based on a culture of strong individualism. When Lincoln transferred, unchanged, its US manufacturing, labor selection, compensation and incentive systems abroad, it experienced relative success in markets that were culturally "close," or similar, to the USA – Canada, UK, Australia – and problems in others that culturally were "distant," or less similar – Brazil and Germany. A new generation of internationally experienced top managers emerged, who understood the extent to which Lincoln Electric's operations were dependent on its American context and roots. Only at this point were the company's strategy, organization structure, and systems modified to allow for cultural differences. Then, Lincoln's international business began to recover.[12]

An organization's administrative systems and processes have cultural assumptions incorporated into them. Although there is some debate as to whether cultures around the world are converging or diverging and in what areas, there is no doubt that, in the realm of systems and practices preferred in a given country, culture influences preferred behavioral style and the management systems that are acceptable or even desirable. Those of one country (such as hiring of friends and relatives in many Latin countries) are often unacceptable or even ridiculed in another (such as hiring of friends and relatives in the United States and Canada). Earlier chapters provided numerous examples of how culture influenced management systems and processes, so the details will not be repeated here.

Our earlier discussion about alignment and the alignment model could be used by any executive formulating and implementing strategy in his or her home market. Unless they are operating in a very multicultural domestic context, they don't necessarily give much thought to cultural influences in their domestic operations. But they must learn to do so when crossing cultural borders both within and between nation states. When firms start operating in different cultural environments, the ability to create alignment can change – often dramatically.

An additional element of judgment is required of global managers who must work across national boundaries. As described earlier, global business is distinguished from domestic business by home vs. host country cultural differences; differences in policies and operations among national governments; and the degree of integration that must take place among operating units. Administrative systems should be adaptable to changing conditions and work forces and not be ends in themselves. Furthermore, the fit that they create needs to be dynamic. This means that as strategies, competitive environments, or geographic locations change, then structures, systems, and policies also need to be reevaluated and modified as necessary.

Managers have to judge the impact of home country management systems and practices in relation to host country cultural assumptions. For example, in the conduct of domestic business North American companies tend to decide about strategy, structure, and systems with the use of rational, economic cost–benefit analyses. Decisions may be based on discussions that reference and build on implicit sets of shared cultural assumptions; all managers of the domestic companies are assumed to share these (although they don't necessarily). Yet these assumptions of common viewpoints must be challenged and questioned when a manager operates in multiple national markets.

Geert Hofstede has commented that "theories reflect the cultural environment in which they were written" and asked the question, "To what extent do theories developed in one country and reflecting the cultural boundaries of that country apply to other countries?"[13] Management concepts and practices are explained by theories regarding organization, motivation, and leadership. Therefore, theories of management and the derived administrative systems and management practices may work well in the culture that developed them because they are based on local cultural assumptions and paradigms about the right way to manage.

Consider again, for example, Lincoln Electric's experience with its individual-oriented, piece-rate incentive and bonus systems in factories in Europe and Brazil. Lincoln Electric's executives found that in Europe managers were opposed to piecework and preferred more vacation time to extra income from bonuses. In Germany piecework at the time was illegal and in Brazil bonuses paid in two consecutive years became a legal entitlement.[14] These culturally based conflicts went against the very systems that had helped Lincoln Electric become very successful in the United States.

The values underlying managerial systems, in this case reward systems, may not be obvious. It might be easier to conclude that workers were the problem instead of examining the assumptions underlying an incentive scheme. Another question to ask is what would be the effect of a highly individualized compensation system such as Lincoln Electric's in countries such as those in Eastern and Central Europe whose political/cultural systems have reinforced collectivist values under several decades of Communist rule?

Similarly, what are the cultural assumptions underlying practices such as empowerment, self-directed work teams, and 360-degree feedback? How would they work in hierarchical versus individualistic cultures?

However, there are counter-examples. It is important to remember what we said earlier: that cultures are not monolithic and that there is a distribution of values, beliefs, and ways of doing things in each one. Brannen and Salk have described three broad categories of people that can exist simultaneously in each culture and who display mainstream cultural attributes to varying degrees – probably depending on the "issue domain": cultural-normals (the typical or "average" person of that culture); hyper-normals (people who believe and follow very strongly the espoused values of a culture); and marginals (those who believe less strongly or differently).[15]

Recognizing that there is likely a distribution of beliefs and assumptions in any population, one also must be careful about assuming that all practices from the corporate headquarters' home culture cannot be transferred globally. For example, McDonald's transferred its business model and systems to Russia essentially because there was a fit with the Russian culture.[16]

Organizational structures also are not free from the influence of culture. Each structure carries with it identifiable assumptions about the legitimacy of certain practices and relationships and defines the locus of authority, responsibility and bases of power differently. Each legitimizes a different pattern of communication and interaction. In addition to "fitting" better with certain competitive situations or product characteristics, some structures may be more acceptable than others in a given culture.

For example, matrix organization, a structure in which a person has two bosses, has cultural assumptions built into it. It violates the principle of unity of command that some hierarchical cultures may believe is correct, and because of the existence of potentially competing interests, it can force conflict into the open which some cultures may avoid.

André Laurent believed that the national origin of managers affected their views of proper management and also that educational attempts to communicate alternative management processes and structures would fail unless the "implicit management gospels" that they carried in their heads were addressed.[17] Although there are many American managers who do not like the matrix form of organization, the French seemed to have a particular aversion to it. Laurent became convinced of this when he was trying to explain matrix organizations to French managers to whom the idea of reporting to two bosses was "so alien that mere consideration of such organizing principles was an impossible, useless exercise."[18]

A common American attitude toward conflict is that conflict can be positive. It gets issues into the open and differences of opinion help in understanding problems, in providing different solutions, and in increasing creativity. However, not all cultures view conflict the same way. Stella Ting-Toomey's research shows that cultural variability (individualism vs. collectivism, power distance and high vs. low context communication patterns) provides "lenses" through which conflict is viewed; individualists use an outcome-oriented model while collectivists follow a process-oriented model.[19] Where Americans or other individualistic, low context cultures may embrace conflict as potentially beneficial, collectivistic, high context cultures may seek to avoid open conflict. Ting-Toomey states:

> For individualists, effective conflict negotiation means settling the conflict problem openly and working out a set of functional conflict solutions conjointly. Effective conflict resolution behavior (e.g., emphasizing the importance of addressing incompatible goals/outcomes) is *relatively* more important for individualists than is appropriate facework behavior. For collectivists, on the other hand, appropriate conflict management means the subtle negotiation of in-group/out-group face-related issues – pride, honor, dignity, insult, shame, disgrace, humility, trust, mistrust, respect, and prestige – in a given conflict episode.
>
> Appropriate facework moves and countermoves are critical for collectivists before tangible conflict outcomes or goals can be addressed.

In another study comparing French and American managers, Inzerelli and Laurent discovered that US managers held an *instrumental* conception of structure, while the French held a *social* conception.[20] The instrumental viewpoint was that positions in a company were ordered in terms of task requirements and relationships between positions in any way instrumental to achieving organizational objectives. Authority was impersonal and came from a person's role or function implying equality of persons involved. Subordination was the acceptance of the impersonal, rational, and legal order of the organization. The social viewpoint held that positions were defined in terms of social status and authority, and relationships were hierarchical. Authority came from status and it could extend beyond the function. Superior–subordinate relationships were personal, implying superiority of one person over the other, and subordination was loyalty and deference to the superior.

Numerous other examples of the impact of values on systems and management styles were provided earlier in our elaboration of the Map component of the MBI model for improving interpersonal and team effectiveness. You may want to go back and review that discussion.

Executives must decide whether existing practices, systems, and management styles can be transferred from one culture to another or whether they must be changed and adapted in some way when they appear to be in conflict with the norms of another culture. The answer is not always to change a system, even if it is different than in the host country. Sometimes people in another culture simply need to be trained to use a system (remembering, of course, that the best training format may be influenced by the culture). However, neither is the answer always to assume that training is all that is required. Each response has a proper time and place.

The decision regarding transferring, adapting, or possibly even creating a new hybrid practice should be the result of careful, informed judgment based on understanding the cultural biases of the systems and the cultural norms of the country in which the operations are located. Are there rules? Not really, but careful analysis can help sort out the issues and help managers solve the problem. First, one must remember that cultures are not monolithic and in every culture there is a distribution of values. There are variations within cultures and culture is not deterministic. Some people will adhere strongly to the norms of their culture while others will not. It also means that if certain cultural values are a critical part of an organization's model for success, then managers can use the selection system to find employees who display these characteristics.

Questions such as "How important is it that we do it identically to the way it's done at home?" can guide one's decisions. It may not be important that the procedures are exactly the same; rather, results may be more important. Just because it is the way head-quarters does it, or wants it done, does not mean that it is right for a different cultural environment. What are important are the *business imperatives*, tasks that must be done well for the firm to make money.[21]

An example is Carlos Ghosn who turned around Nissan by doing everything he was not supposed to do in Japan. Ghosn said, "[A] lot of advice I received from out-side was, 'You cannot do this, you cannot do that, you cannot do this – because you are in Japan.'"[22] In a culture of lifetime employment, seniority, and interlocking business relationships, he eliminated 21 000 jobs, closed plants, introduced bonuses and stock options, had younger people managing older ones, and reduced the interdependency with suppliers in the *keiretsu*. In this case it is important to recognize that Nissan was in a crisis and in times of crisis traditional norms may not apply. The important point is that managers must understand the situation they face and not rely on stereotypes.

Our answer to the question about whether headquarters should change one or more of its systems or practices to accommodate local employees or whether local employees should adapt to the company's way of doing things is that it all depends on the business imperatives of the company and its industry. Take for example a local American auto parts company that entered into a joint venture in North America with a foreign com-pany to learn about just-in-time manufacturing – a Japanese company that was a leader in this technique. The American company had a short-term orientation to cost control, and as the joint venture progressed, it became uncomfortable with the Japanese part-ner's longer term orientation and wanted to institute a tighter control system, which, however, interfered with its original objective for the joint venture – learning. In this situation whose way should be followed? Clearly the Japanese were the experts in the area and their way should take precedence.[23]

The experience of a Canadian Bank, the Bank of Nova Scotia, in Mexico is another example. When the Mexican banking system was about to collapse after the economic crisis in 1994, the Mexican government put up for sale most of the Mexican banks.

The Bank of Nova Scotia bought Inverlat.[24] In 1982, Mexico's banks had been nationalized and they remained essentially government institutions for many years. It was a period of stagnation despite substantial innovations in technology and practices in the global banking industry. Many Inverlat managers claimed that their bank had generally deteriorated more than the rest of the banking sector in Mexico, and overall had failed to create a new generation of bankers who understood and reflected the changed conditions and times. The bank had been lending primarily to the government, and managers were unfamiliar with the challenges of lending to the private sector and therefore failed to collateralize their loans properly or to ensure that covenants were being maintained. The existing managers did not have the knowledge or the capacity to manage the critical credit assessment function. In this situation whose practices were going to be followed? Banks make money by lending money and the credit function is critical, or what we think of as a business imperative, and the Canadian practices should be followed since they were the experts in this area.

We encourage you to use the Organizational Alignment Model as an analytic tool, but remember not to think of organizations in a static way. Organizations are dynamic. The model simply provides an initial analytic tool of possible solutions and direction for action. Structures and administrative systems should be tools to help organizations and their employees succeed. There is no simple formula for choosing effective structures and systems. Judgment is required in assessing the likely impact of systems on people in jobs and in adjusting the systems to support job achievement and organizational results. Successful implementation means finding the right combination of strategy, structure, and systems that motivates people to strive for high performance. It involves listening to, understanding, and working with people from different cultures in the organization.

STRATEGY IN GLOBAL ORGANIZATIONS

One important component of the alignment model we have not yet discussed is strategy. A strategy defines the way an organization chooses to relate itself to its external environment. It encompasses such things as the firm's chosen niche in its industry and the control of critical factors for competing successfully in that niche.

To be successful in a business or industry there are certain activities that an organization must do well. These key success factors vary from industry to industry and from one industry segment to another. For example, if you are producing a commodity product, it might be critical to have a secure source of supply and efficient production or processing operations so you can be the low cost producer. If you are producing highly differentiated products, advertising, marketing, and product development are likely the critical activities. If you are in the aerospace industry, your R&D capability and the ability to manage contracts to produce on time and within budgets may be key success factors.

The important point is that you have to know what you must do well in a business to succeed and you must recognize that these factors may vary from industry to industry. Although one could say "you have to do everything well," that truism would not reflect the specific competitive situation within an industry. Any firm may need finance, production, marketing, sales, and human resource capabilities, but the relative emphasis or importance of each of these may vary according to the nature of the business.

Once you understand how you have to compete in your business, you can translate this into the tasks that must be performed within the organization. Once you know what tasks need to be done and how they should be done, a structure and set of administrative mechanisms can be implemented to get the jobs done properly.

This is not a chapter about formulating strategy but, rather, executing strategy. However, it is necessary to have a basic understanding of a firm's strategy (or any planned changes to a strategy) to evaluate it in relation to the potential fit with the internal structure, administrative mechanisms, and the skills and abilities of the company's human resources. It is critical that the administrative systems are consistent with an organization's strategy.

Business Strategy   There are multiple levels and types of strategy: corporate, business, international, and functional strategies. *Corporate strategy*, in a diversified company, is about deciding what businesses the company engages in and how these businesses should be managed to create value.[25,26] Both business and corporate strategy tell you what the company does and, just as importantly, what it doesn't do. It also tells executives where to put resources. Peter Drucker said strategic management is "analytical thinking [formulation] and a commitment of resources to action [execution]."[27]

In a single business company or in a business unit of a diversified company, *business strategy*, also called *competitive strategy*, refers to how a company creates competitive advantage by offering better customer value than its competitors.[28] Again, there are multiple frameworks, and our intent is not to explain all of them but to present one or two that we have found particularly useful.

Probably the best known and most widely used framework is Porter's.[29] He identified three generic strategies: cost leadership (low cost), differentiation, and a focus strategy. *Cost leadership* requires keeping costs (and, therefore, prices) low through an emphasis on tight cost control, efficient operations, low overhead, and leveraging the benefits of a well managed supply chain. Industries that produce products such as sugar, chips for calculators, or other commodity-like offerings usually fit in this category. In retailing, for example, companies like WalMart and IKEA come to mind.

Differentiation means creating differences in your products or services that customers are willing to pay a premium for. Differentiation can be created in multiple ways such as through prestige or brand image, proprietary technology or state of the art product features, or outstanding service networks, for example. Examining the first category, prestige or brand image, one can think about automobiles: Mercedes stands for engineering; BMW is the driving experience; and Volvo is safety.

Focus means choosing a narrow niche in an industry and tailoring a strategy to serve clients in this niche.[30] However, even this strategy has to be a cost leadership or differentiated one.

Hax and Wilde argue that Porter's framework does not capture all the ways in which companies compete in a highly changing networked economy and that customers, suppliers, and complementers are important contributors and should be included.[31] Their framework includes Porter's focuses on product characteristics, but they go beyond the product focus to look at customer value.

They propose three strategic options: best product, total customer solutions, and system lock-in. Best product (BP) competition is essentially low cost or differentiation based on *product* economics. Total customer solutions (TCS) competition is based on *customer* economics, and the challenge is to reduce customer costs or increase their profits. Companies may bundle products and services and customize them to the needs of their customers or do joint product development, for example. System lock-in (SLI) competition is based on *system* economics – locking in complementers, locking out competitors, and developing proprietary standards. This means considering all the meaningful players in a system that contribute to the creation of economic value.[32]

The easiest way to think about "complementer" and SLI competition is to think about the software industry. Microsoft, for example, provides an operating system such as XP or Vista for computers. Then there are a number of companies that develop applications for use with that operating system. These companies are complementers and, because of their involvement and products, they contribute to the value of the total system.

Business Models   We said in an earlier section that corporate strategy was the decision about what business a company should engage in and that a business (competitive) strategy referred to a company's competitive advantage by offering better customer value than its competitors. A *business model* is how a firm creates value and earns a profit in a competitive environment.[33] The business model is the link between the internal organization and the business strategy since it encompasses execution and operational effectiveness.[34] Simply stated, it is how a firm delivers its value proposition to customers and how it makes money. An example should help in understanding the business model.

Think about retail book sellers in the late 1990s.[35] Barnes & Noble Booksellers was founded in New York in 1917 and by 1987 had become a national chain in the United States. In the late 1980s and early 1990s, it evolved the concept of the suburban superstore, which generated 96% of its retail sales. The company offered a comprehensive selection of books and music using experienced staff in spacious stores complete with cafes that sell Starbucks coffee. It became a destination for people, a sort of town meeting place, but its business model was to deliver its products and services to its customers in brick and mortar stores that were open certain hours. Although it opened its first online book superstore on America Online in 1997, Amazon.com received the prize for developing the new business model in this industry.

Founded in 1994, Amazon.com went public in 1997 and by 1999 it generated over $1 billion in sales. Amazon.com turned the retail bookselling industry upside down. Its mass marketing business model was to deliver books to customers anytime and anyplace, using the Internet. It created an online community of customers by allowing people to write their own book reviews and share them. Like Barnes & Noble, Amazon.com continued to modify its business model – in this case by morphing from being a specialty book retailer to being an online shopping portal.

Although both companies continued to evolve their business models, this example shows how companies in the same industry, selling the same products, can have vastly different business models to deliver their products and services. And the people, skills, and systems for each model to function are vastly different.

Now we need to link the concept of a business model to the Organizational Alignment Framework and show how changes in an existing business model may necessitate organizational re-alignment. A more complex, international example in which culture played a role was the experience of Global Multi-Products in Chile.[36]

Executing Strategy in Chile   Global Multi-Products had a strategy of continuous introduction of new, innovative products based on proprietary technology that had high margins. Approximately 30 % of its sales came from products introduced in the previous few years. Historically, it used a "best product strategy" in which the value proposition for the customer was: buy our products because they are the best quality based on the latest technology and they are reliable.

To deliver on this strategy, it excelled in R & D where the new products originated and it had a formal program of research and development with 40 technology platforms that were the seedbeds of the company's new products. Historically it distributed its products through separate product-related business units. We now could expand the characterization of the company's business model as: "Buy our products because they are the best quality based on the latest technology, reliable, and we make money by investing in R&D, developing proprietary technology and high margin products and manufacturing them efficiently."

Then the competitive environment in Chile changed. Small sole proprietorships were largely replaced by big American retailers and local retailers developing similar superstore models. Previously local superstores represented approximately 60 % of retail sales. The superstore segment, local and foreign, grew quickly to represent over 90 % of the company's business and power shifted from the manufacturer to the customers. The level of sophistication increased among purchasing managers and they expected more from their suppliers such as more advertising and lower prices. Products that traditionally had margins averaging around 80 % now had margins not very different from those of competitors. Finally, customers wanted to reduce the number of multi-product sales representatives with whom they were dealing. They wanted to see one face representing the manufacturer.

At the time that one of the authors was involved with the company's local organization in Chile, it was in the process of transitioning from a Best Product strategy to a Total Customer Solutions (TCS) strategy forced on it by the shift in power to the new, large retail customers who were interested in increasing their return on investment.

The new value proposition was "buy our [still] high-quality products and save money to be more competitive; and we will make money by selling more products at lower margins [still based on proprietary technology and efficient manufacturing]" (TCS). Internally in Multi-Products this change meant that more integration was required among business units and that employees had to work horizontally across the organization and in teams in order to provide solutions for the customers. It developed a program of strategic relationships with customers to conduct joint R&D to develop new products that could benefit both partners and a program that sought to re-orient the sales and marketing effort around the needs of customers, instead of the company's product groups. The company was now competing on the basis of its technology and organization to provide solutions for its customers.

However, it was not a simple change to institute.

Organizational Re-alignment in Chile   There were a number of barriers getting in the way of the necessary changes. These barriers can be organized using the Organizational Alignment Framework in the following categories:

- *Organizational structure*: product groups and distribution-based selling (products were sold through product groups to distributors), hierarchy, and functional "silos" worked against cooperation. Teams had to work laterally across these groups.

- *Organizational culture:* heads of functions had a great deal of autonomy and it was almost a "feudal" system.
- *Top management team:* executives had no skills with group/team processes and there was no trust among them. They were concerned with their authority and there was resistance to change.
- *Society/national culture:* There was status consciousness on the part of executives reflecting Chile's high power distance culture.
- *Political history:* A legacy of distrust and not speaking out left over from the Pinochet era.
- *People:* The sales representatives' status, lack of required new skills, title, education, age/seniority all worked against their being successful in the new environment. Sales reps were low status jobs in this culture, and the people in them did not have the necessary skills and training to interact with the new, more sophisticated purchasing executives of the "big box" stores. The company had to find new sales reps, provide them with new titles, and improve training.
- *Rewards:* The reward system did not encourage selling someone else's products or working together in teams. The behavior required of Sales Reps was to continually introduce new products and let go of the old ones, which the reward system did not encourage.

It took the Managing Director a number of years to implement the organizational changes necessary to re-align the Chilean organization with its new business model. It is easy to talk about globalization, global strategies, and being customer-centric, but it is not easy to put these ideas into practice.

It has been the authors' experience over the past few years working with a number of companies in various industries such as defense, financial printing, telecommunications, financial services, and even law enforcement that they all were experiencing the need to develop organizations that were customer-centric. This need to behave differently was driven in all cases by changes in the external environment in which the organizations operated. For the companies it usually was the appearance of new competitors with new products and business models that sparked the need to coordinate across functional or business areas. For others, such as financial services firms, both the consolidation of the global players into the Big Four and increased regulation (Sarbanes-Oxley and other changes) impacted their customer orientation. For the law enforcement agency it was the appearance of new organizations posing new threats that drove the change. The other characteristic they all had in common was that they all had difficulty working horizontally across the organization and coordinating information and activities to improve performance in these new environments.

It takes a deep understanding of a company's strategy and management systems and an understanding of the history and culture of the host country to execute a strategy globally. And it takes time.

Culture's Influence on Strategy

What happens when a company takes its strategy "on the road" so to speak – when it begins implementing it in another country? What appears to be obvious and straightforward in a firm's home market or in another international location may not work in a new country. What an executive takes for granted at home may not apply in another country.

Consider the TJX Companies, the world's leading off-price retailer of apparel and home fashions, operating seven businesses – T.J. Maxx, Marshalls, HomeGoods, A.J. Wright and Bob's Stores in the United States, as well as Winners and HomeSense in Canada, and T.K. Maxx in Europe. TJX's value-oriented retailing business model delivers a rapidly changing assortment of fashionable, quality, brand name merchandise at 20–60 % below regular department and specialty store prices. It can do this because it relies on opportunistic buying, disciplined inventory management, and a low expense structure with its stores located in community shopping centers. Its stores are flexible spaces with no permanent, fixed store features. Its core target customer is a middle- to upper-middle-income shopper, who is fashion and value conscious and fits the same profile as a department store shopper.[37]

Customers entering the T. J. Maxx Store in Newport, Rhode Island, for example, would encounter this business model by driving to a shopping mall and taking a shopping cart as they entered the store which they would push to hold all the merchandise they selected. This is a straightforward, common experience in the United States in this type of retail store. However, this business model has a number of built-in culturally influenced assumptions which include:

- Customers can and will drive to the mall where there is plenty of parking.
- Customers will need and use a shopping cart since they will purchase many items.
- Customers can identify the value inherent in their purchases because they can recognize the brand name and its reduced selling price in the store.

When TJX opened its first European stores in the United Kingdom and the Netherlands, it discovered that many of its customers only bought one or two items because the idea of using a shopping cart or "buggie," as they referred to it, was foreign to customers and they initially refused to use them. In the Netherlands, there were more obstacles to overcome than in the UK including language and culture. TJX was not able to replicate the brand/value proposition in the Netherlands as customers did not easily recognize the value offering – the brand versus price trade-off. The business model did not work there as it did in the United States[38]

Monsanto is another example of the potential nontransferability of strategy. It introduced genetically modified soybeans into Europe based on its experience in the United States and the lessons it learned there. It encountered significant resistance and had to realize that the lessons learned in the United States could not necessarily be generalized to other locations.[39] Monsanto's mastery orientation did not fit with a more prevalent harmony orientation in Europe.

One's cultural filters and possible lack of experience with, or knowledge about, a particular country may influence the assumptions used in developing international expansion projects. Very often costs are underestimated at the start of the project and do not become apparent until later, when they outweigh the expected benefits. An experienced entrepreneur observed that "No one ever lost money on a spreadsheet. You can torture the numbers until they confess."[40] This comment attests to an apparent common tendency to make new projects or ventures look attractive by underestimating the time necessary for revenues and profits to materialize or by optimistically forecasting the initial and ongoing costs of operating internationally.

The spreadsheet analysis is only as good as the assumptions that go into it, and one has to remember that it is not reality, only a representation of reality. As the philosopher Alfred Korzybski stated, "The map is not the territory."

Someone in the company has to understand the territory. Someone has to travel to another country to negotiate a contract, arrange a distributorship, or work with people from another culture to make a project or joint venture a reality. Once this person leaves the office to negotiate the contract in Europe or to start up the plant in Southeast Asia, what really takes place? There are a lot of questions to ask and answers to find before the business becomes a reality.

The previous sections have developed the organizational alignment framework and linked it to strategy and business models. We also discussed executing competitive strategy and business models *in global organizations.* Now we turn our attention to global strategy: the strategic decisions about developing a global presence and positioning a company and its value chain *in global markets* to take advantage of location economies while adapting to local differences.

DEVELOPING A GLOBAL PRESENCE

Globalization, in business and economic terms, is often characterized as the erosion of national boundaries that has accelerated due to deregulation and technology. Trade liberalization has opened borders across which capital moves easily since foreign direct investment (FDI) restrictions have been relaxed. Airline travel as well as reliable, inexpensive communications and sophisticated information services and technologies have shrunk the globe so effectively – diminishing physical boundaries – that corporations are able to manage, control, and coordinate activities of far-ranging operations. It is possible to do business almost anywhere through a web site, as the representative of one small, family-owned Japanese company learned. She was able while in Boston to successfully conclude sales to Saudi Arabia and Pakistan without ever going there.

Both responding to and feeding the trend of globalization, companies are "globalizing" in search of growth. Some companies continue to search for growth by expanding into new international markets and some are searching for it from innovations to be achieved by integrating and expanding their current global operations, creating what the UN has called "an international production system."[41] We do not intend to pursue in detail an exposition of the advantages and disadvantages of each strategy or structure that corporations could use in globalizing. There are many books and readings on the topic of international organization that comprehensively cover these issues.[42] However, beyond considering the advantages or disadvantages of the various strategies or structural forms a company can use, one needs to recognize the cultural values and assumptions upon which these structures may be based that has been our focus and has been discussed earlier.

In this section we briefly highlight some decisions that companies face as they respond to globalization pressures: balancing global integration and local responsiveness, organizing for global effectiveness, new market entry modes, international joint ventures and alliances, and global account management.

Balancing Global Integration and Local Responsiveness Two fundamental forces influence companies operating globally: those pushing towards *global integration* and those pulling towards *local responsiveness*.[43] Forces for *global integration,* such as the need to secure commodities or the cost of investment in R&D or new facilities, push companies to minimize duplication of functions, and to increase efficiencies by placing specific value chain activities in the most suitable locations around the world.

The ability to concentrate each value chain activity in the best location has been enhanced by the erosion of national borders. This allows companies to capitalize on their competitive advantage in the particular activity and the host country's comparative advantage vis-à-vis other countries.[44] For example, the USA's Silicon Valley is considered by global technology companies to be a prime location for R&D operations because of the high concentration of professionals, educational institutions, and companies with leading edge knowledge and expertise that nurture each other's learning. Similarly, countries in Southeast Asia have become locations of choice for manufacturing technologically intensive components because of the quality-cost-availability profile of their local labor forces. At the extreme, companies could locate each activity in a region from which the firm could best serve the rest of its global activities. This creates complex interdependencies among the firm's multiple and often culturally diverse geographic locations and poses unique cross-cultural challenges for managers.

The requirement for *local responsiveness* appears when a company has to tailor its business model, systems, and products to meet the needs of a specific national market. Because of different preferences for certain products and services or different government regulations and systems, it is rarely possible, in the long term, to operate in another country exactly the same way as at home. Four elements tend to promote localization of strategy: nontariff barriers, such as requirements to have a local partner or local standards for products; foreign-exchange shortages; cultural differences that influence consumer tastes and preferences even as some products become global; and flexible production technology that reduces the cost advantage of large-scale production while permitting greater local customization.[45] Moreover, cultural preferences that influence how people work and how they relate to each other, as well as government policies regarding human resource practices, may favor localization of structures and systems. To achieve local responsiveness, the value chain activities of the company are tailored to a particular country's needs and a successful company will adapt at least some elements of its operations to the local culture. At the extreme, the value chain activities would be tailored to each locality.

In addition to balancing globalization and localization, a successful global organization engages in *global learning,* that is, the transfer and sharing of new ideas and knowledge among units.[46,47] A new production technology, marketing strategy, or product feature designed for one market often can be transferred to other markets. The challenge is to be able to identify synergistic links among units and to transfer knowledge and skills effectively. The proper organizational structures and systems, as well as the right individuals, play an important role in facilitating global learning.

All companies that operate globally are subject to the pressures of global integration and local responsiveness. The degree to which a company must respond to these forces depends heavily on the characteristics of the industry in which it competes and influences its multinational strategy. One common classification scheme that is based on the

FIGURE 5.3   International Strategy Choices

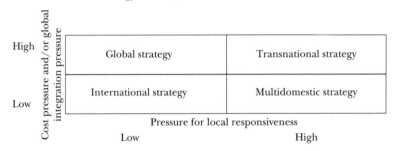

Source: Adapted from Charles Hill, *International Business: Competing in the Global Marketplace;* Irwin McGraw-Hill, 2000.

integration-responsiveness framework identifies four strategies: the *global,* the *multidomestic,* the *international,* and the *transnational.*[48] This is shown in Figure 5.3.

A company that follows a strategy that is highly dependent on global integration for many of its value chain activities and that is locally responsive for few of them is following a *global strategy.* Such a company usually is characterized by a high degree of complex interdependencies among its subsidiaries and has a governance structure that is tightly and centrally controlled. Its managers have to be culturally aware and its senior management is likely to be dominated by a cadre of seasoned career foreign assignment veterans who share similar corporate values. Companies like Ericsson (telecommunications) and Sony (consumer electronics) have been identified as companies with global strategies.

A firm that follows a *multidomestic strategy* is one that is minimally dependent on global integration but highly dependent on local responsiveness for many of its value chain activities. A multidomestic strategy enables a firm to tailor its strategy, product, and operations to specific markets but does not optimize global efficiency. These organizations may operate differently in each country; in an extreme case, each country or region would have its own manufacturing, marketing, and research and development. These firms can be thought of as a confederation of loosely coupled organizations with strong local control and weak central control. The managers of multidomestic subsidiaries often function as independent "feudal lords" who may or may not be expatriate managers depending on the company's administrative heritage. Unilever, Procter & Gamble, and KFC, while not representing the extreme end of the spectrum, tend to use multidomestic strategies.

Third, a multinational that depends minimally on global integration and minimally on local responsiveness follows an *international strategy.* Essentially, it replicates its home market systems in each of its foreign subsidiaries. These companies are very centralized and their subsidiaries are simply outlets for headquarters' decisions. The product categories most suitable to such a strategy would include commodities. For example, grain businesses (AMD, Cargill) are large organizations that deal with commodity products that are traded around the world on the basis of price. Also, the ball bearing industry to a certain extent can be seen as an industry suitable to an international strategy. For this industry there are many consumers (any manufacturer of machinery that has moving parts) and an undifferentiated product that depends on technical specifications that are applicable anywhere in the world.

Finally, a firm that is simultaneously globally integrated and locally responsive is following a *transnational strategy*. This strategy distributes the global responsibility for specific activities to the managers who manage the subsidiary to which the activity has been assigned. Each country manager may report to different persons with different world-wide activity responsibilities. The local responsiveness is achieved by managing each distributed value chain activity with enough flexibility so that the local manager can make the essential compromises necessary to achieve as high a local market fit as possible. The transnational strategy is extremely costly to implement and requires managers who are cross-culturally and interpersonally skilled and flexible. Few – if any – truly transnational corporations exist, but many are aspiring and progressing in that direction, including Nestlé, Shell, and Matsushita.

When formulating a strategy, the ideal balance of global integration and local responsiveness and how best to implement global learning depend on many factors. Rather than present a single ideal solution (since none exists), our orientation is to help you develop insights into issues involved in implementing strategies, structures, and systems to increase the chances of making informed decisions when entering new markets and managing in other countries.

Typical structures for international involvement include *international division, geographical (regional) division, product* or *project division, matrix,* and *transnational*. Each of these structures has its strengths and weaknesses and would be appropriate for different situations. The two main factors that influence strategic choice of structure are the pressures for local responsiveness and the forces pushing toward global integration, as discussed in the previous section. Two additional criteria to be considered in the choice of an appropriate structure are the extent to which a company's sales and profits are derived from foreign operations and the complexity of the company's product line.[49]

In the international division structure, all business conducted outside the firm's home country is organized through one division. This form is often a starting point for firms that are beginning to internationalize and that probably have relatively little international business as a percentage of total revenues. As the overseas involvement of a firm increases, the international division structure may evolve into a geographical division structure in which all products for a particular region are grouped together. This structure is typically more suitable with a multi-domestic or an international strategy. In the product or project division structure, responsibility for all markets around the world is given to a specific product line or project division. This form tends to be adopted by multinationals that are involved in multiple product lines or businesses overseas. The matrix structure form combines regional and product emphases.

The transnational organization tries to simultaneously capture the responsiveness of local organizations and the efficiency and global competitiveness of the more centralized structures by maintaining what could be called a "federal" structure.[50] These organizations often are referred to as network organizations characterized by high degrees of autonomy between headquarters and business units and between business units. Strong multilateral communication which does not necessarily have to pass through a central headquarters unit permits coordination and knowledge sharing.[51] These distributed business units are usually components of a larger corporation.

However, it is useful to keep in mind that the distributed units could also be independent companies functioning as an economic network which permits smaller corporations to compete globally. Regardless of whether the organization is a large global company or an economic colony of smaller ones, the network organization merits special focus because it has become increasingly common and important.

Network Organizations   Faulk has observed that the network has become the most important emergent organizational structure.[52] Network organizations have been defined in terms of their structure as a "collection of autonomous firms or units that behave as a single larger entity using social mechanisms for coordination and control"[53] and in terms of their adaptability as ones that are "fast and flexible in responding to changes in the underlying environment."[54]

Their appearance (or reappearance in the management literature if one thinks about Japanese *keiretsu* or Korean *chaebol*) has been brought about by advanced communication and information technology as well as organizational restructuring.[55] Although Borgatti sees network organizations as a blend between vertical integration and market disaggregation, Faulk suggests that they are qualitatively different from classic market or hierarchy models of traditional economics.

A networked organization (and sometimes what is implied by the term "transnational")[56] is emerging in some global companies. A networked organization combines many or all types of organizational units in relationships of varying degrees of ownership and relationship intensity with the home country's headquarters. Matrix and networked forms are mostly adopted by large diversified companies and tend to be costly to implement and maintain. The network allows a company to have a very high degree of flexibility. Although flexibility and adaptability are admirable characteristics, Vega-Redondo modeled network organizations and found that there was a limit to the environmental volatility that they could handle before they were overwhelmed and required a more rigid structure again.[57]

However, prior to reaching a tipping point networks have some comparative advantages. Conditions that favor networks include:[58]

- Frequent transactions. Infrequent transactions can better be handled by market mechanisms.
- Demand uncertainty for new products or services.
- Customization.
- Task complexity.
- Structural embeddedness. Frequent ties and links and communication flows assist in coordination and control.

Networks can provide the advantages of balancing strategies in a matrix organization and the flexibility inherent in alliances with other organizations. For example, a networked organization might include global research and development in some product areas and local R&D in others, global marketing for some product lines and local marketing for others, and so on. It also could have several different types of alliances for projects having different roles in the firm's overall strategy or for product lines at varying stages of development. However, as might be predicted, a networked structure is complicated and difficult to manage effectively.

New Market Entry Modes Independently of the international strategies or organizational forms selected, companies entering new markets must decide on the appropriate business form, or entry mode, for each overseas market.[59] Entry modes establish the legal form in a foreign market; the extent to which the multinational owns the organization; the degree to which it maintains operating control; and the extent to which this new organization is part of a set of business relationships that extend beyond a one country-market.

There is a large range of entry and ownership forms. Options vary in terms of the amount of capital, other resources invested, and managerial involvement required in the host country. At one extreme, limiting a company's investment and set of activities, is the *exporting* of products or *licensing* of technology to other companies in the foreign market. There also are market entry modes that require capital and human resources investment but permit full control of the *wholly owned businesses or subsidiaries* that can be *acquired* or developed as new, "greenfield" sites. A third set of market entry alternatives includes hybrid modes such as a variety of *equity joint venture* and *strategic alliance* forms. An international equity joint venture involves creating a new entity owned jointly by two or more "parent" organizations to enter a market where at least one of the parent organizations is nonresident. Management responsibilities are contractually delineated. The percent of equity held by each parent generally defines who has formal strategic control. A strategic alliance is an agreement between two or more companies to engage in cooperative activities without equity involvement. For example, a strategic alliance may involve a contractual agreement to cross-sell complementary products or to engage in other activities on a cooperative basis. Passenger airlines have formed global strategic alliances to share reservation systems, complementary routes, aircraft purchasing and technical specifications, maintenance facilities and crews, ground services staff, and even pilots and cabin crews.

Costs and benefits are associated with each of these operating modes and ownership structures. The costs to be considered usually include capital, management time and commitment, impact on strategy, and the cost of enforcing agreements. Some benefits include repatriation of profits, political security, contribution to parent-company knowledge, and local distribution capability.

Although the chapters about culture earlier in the book are applicable when you are working with people from other cultures in exporting or licensing agreements, for example, the primary focus of this chapter is on operating issues in subsidiaries, acquisitions, international joint ventures, and alliances. Specifically, in addition to working with people from other cultures, we focus on a company's ability to execute its strategy and operate in other countries outside its home country.

International Joint Ventures The management of joint ventures is both a particularly important and particularly troublesome element of global strategy. Joint ventures are used for many reasons. Companies may need to share financial risk, respond to government requirements, secure access to natural resources, acquire particular technical skills, gain local management knowledge and experience, or obtain access to markets and distribution systems. From a multinational's perspective, two important reasons for using joint ventures are the needs to understand and have access to local markets and to have local general management knowledge, skills, and experience in the joint venture company.

In establishing joint ventures, managers often make some common mistakes. There can be a tendency to concentrate on the end result and desired outcome and not to think carefully and critically about the *process* through which these results will be obtained. Executives need to invest in the personal relationships that must be built to create a joint venture and commit the time and effort necessary to make the venture successful. They need to think more clearly about *joint venturing*, which is a process orientation.

Another common mistake is to emphasize the "visible" inputs to the decision and the "tangible" aspects of the business. These visible inputs include the legal structure of the venture, the financial considerations of ownership and *pro forma* operating statements, and the market analyses – all the things managers (and specialists like lawyers and accountants) learned in school and deal with daily. These are important considerations that require attention, and they are necessary for success, but they are not sufficient to ensure it.

There are many operational issues beyond the legal and economic ones that may not be given enough careful forethought and may be left to be resolved as problems arise,[60] which often is too late. The "invisible," "intangible," or "nonquantifiable" components of a venture, like trust, commitment, and partners' expectations, often are overlooked or ignored, possibly because they may not be part of a manager's prior training or mind-set. The situation is like an iceberg in that approximately one seventh of it is visible above the water's surface and six-sevenths is below the surface. The result of not knowing what is hidden can be disastrous for companies as well as for ships.

Alliances are not an automatic solution to a lack of experience with or understanding of another culture, as executives sometimes think. An additional cultural interface, besides the one with the external marketplace, is created with the partner in the venture. Perhaps the most critical decision to be made in establishing an international joint venture or alliance is the choice of a partner, as Geringer explains:

> Selecting partners with compatible skills is not necessarily synonymous with selecting compatible partners. . . . Although selecting a compatible partner may not always result in a successful JV, the selection of an incompatible partner virtually guarantees that venture performance will be unsatisfactory.[61]

How does one choose a partner? Where does one look? What characteristics should a partner have? What are one's expectations? What are the potential partner's expectations? There are a number of criteria that should be considered: "complementarity of technical skills and resources, mutual need, financial capability, relative size, complementarity of strategies and operating policies, communication barriers, compatible management teams, and trust and commitment between partners."[62]

The role of relationships in strategy and international joint ventures is worthy of special comment. Often in North America, relationships are viewed as instrumental, as a means to ends, if they are thought of at all in a business context. In contrast, much of the world outside the United States and Canada values relationships in and of themselves. They form a basis of trust and linkage upon which a business activity may be built.

Relationships are a major determinant of strategy, if not part of the strategy themselves. Given such striking differences in outlook on relationships, it is not surprising that partnership problems are one of the most frequently cited reasons for joint-venture failure.[63]

Global Customers and Global Account Management[64]

The foregoing discussion would make it appear that all the decisions to be made about operating globally were at the discretion of a company – which markets to enter, the countries in which to set up operations, and the type of strategy to follow. However, there is another factor driving firms to establish subsidiaries or enter joint ventures in international locations: the emergence of global customers and their requirements.

Jay Galbraith has pointed out that in the last decade the customer dimension has become more important to companies and many are organizing operations around their customers.[65] In the automotive industry, for example, large auto manufacturers are requiring their parts suppliers to be close to production and assembly plants to support just-in-time production systems. As a result, traditional parts suppliers are establishing joint ventures and manufacturing operations in foreign locations for their customers. One company we have worked with was told by their customer, a "Big-Three" auto manufacturer in Detroit, that to continue supplying parts it had to be no more than two hours away from the assembly plant in Mexico.

In addition to the globalization of customers, the factors fueling this trend include a preference for partnerships and fewer suppliers, a desire for solutions to problems not just products, the ease of e-commerce, and the increase in the power of buyers.

The emergence of global customers who have integrated their purchasing on a worldwide basis is driving multinational companies to consider another structural variation, global account management. Although not a new concept, it is appearing more frequently in industrial, high-technology and some consumer goods companies. If a global customer is of sufficient importance, a supplier may decide to implement a global account management structure and to create the necessary reporting relationships on top of already existing structures and reporting lines. Although it sounds good in theory, in practice it is difficult and time consuming to implement since it means new ways of working and a shift in responsibilities and power balances.

The key tension to manage is between the global account managers (GAMs) doing what is best for the customer and the country sales managers doing what is best for the local country organization. Three broad approaches can be identified:

1   *The balance of power lies with country sales managers.* Global account managers act as coordinators across countries, but the account ownership remains at the local level. Global account managers act as information providers, influencers, and coordinators, but they do not have decision-making power over sales to their account.

2   *There is a "matrix organization" in which global account managers report to both their local sales manager and to a corporate executive responsible for global accounts.* This is probably the most common arrangement, seen in such companies as ABB, 3M, HP, and Intel. In cases of conflict, such as the GAM spending time building sales to the global customer in another country, it is up to the local sales manager and the corporate executive responsible for global accounts to agree on a solution. The matrix

is typically not completely balanced, in that the local considerations usually take precedence over the global or vice versa.

3   *The balance of power lies with the global account managers.* This structure is currently fairly rare, but it is starting to emerge in a few companies. The logic of this structure is that global customers are more important than local sales, so the company is organized first and foremost around those customers. Examples include top-tier automotive suppliers such as Magna and Bosch and contract electronic manufacturers such as Solectron and Flextronics, because their activities are structured around a few large customers.

Emerging structural forms such as global account management put high demands on managerial sensitivity and skills. One example of developing capability with this form of organization is Schneider Electric, a recognized world leader in electrical distribution, automation, and control.[66] In June 2007, Schneider Electric's Global Business Development (SGBD) program received the Strategic Account Management Association's (SAMA) award for outstanding corporate performance in strategic customer management. The SGBD program, a dedicated organization for global enterprises interested in developing special relationships with key suppliers, shortens communication and decision-making cycles across Schneider globally to quickly provide solutions and services such as preferred supplier contracts with high-level contacts. SGBD delivers dedicated solutions worldwide to 70 multinational companies. Said Jean-Marc Debeaux, SGBD Senior Vice President,

> Our commitment to making our businesses customer-centric is paying off around the world. The SGBD program has been highly successful in a short period of time. Initially planned to manage 50 large customers, it is now leveraging 70 Global Strategic Accounts. SGBD defines and implements Schneider Electric's strategic account strategy and in every host country, our customers appreciate the personalized support they get from Schneider Electric . . . More than ever, power, automation and safety management are priority issues for our customers. Increasingly, they prefer to sign confidential agreements that enable them to acquire a differentiating competitive advantage in their business.[67]

Schneider Electric's global account managers have to have:

- clear vision and mission statements;
- empowerment, broad acceptability, and cooperation for local implementation;
- an effective communication network with identified regional managers at several levels and a formalized matrix structure;
- "solution-selling" competence;
- cultural adaptability.[68]

France-based Schneider Electric has developed responses to key issues such as the effective development of global account managers, how to plan and budget for customer-specific efforts, and how to measure performance and reward results.

The implementation of a global account management structure and the systems to support it require daily use of all components of the MBI model of interpersonal and team effectiveness. Finally, it stretches the capacity of organizational designers and of more conventional managers who have to share power and be much more flexible than in the past.

Although this form of network is only starting to emerge among global companies, the trends identified suggest that companies like Schneider Electric are at the leading edge of a major development.

Strategic Use of Global Virtual Teams Teams have become a common organizing structure for global companies. The use of global teams has increased dramatically as companies have invested resources in technological infrastructure to connect technical expertise and local knowledge for the purpose of achieving shared global business objectives.[69] We discussed the management of diverse and dispersed teams in detail in Chapter 4. In this section we will discuss briefly the *strategic* use of global virtual teams.

Although the idea of using global virtual teams is an attractive and promising one, similar to the concept of global account management, it is not an easy one to implement successfully as we pointed out earlier. Companies often see global virtual teams as a way to save time and money in designing and developing new products, for example. However, many companies don't appreciate the complexity introduced by the interaction of the task, contexts, members, culture, time, and technology;[70] and many managers, team leaders, and global team members may not have the requisite "cultural acumen"[71] necessary to function in this mode.

Research has shown that teams, on average, outperform individuals on complex, non-routine tasks. The strategic ideal then is to use global teams to take advantage of this *potential* for superior performance to create a competitive edge. The objective is to take advantage of the expertise, experience, perspectives, and local knowledge that exist in the diverse employees and contexts of a global company and by accessing team members' networks as a resource and facilitating cross-project learning and knowledge transfer.

A classic example was the design of the Boeing 777 airplane. Boeing used global virtual design teams. It had members from more than 12 countries linked together by work stations. It was the first jetliner to be 100 % digitally designed using 3-D solid modeling technology.[72,73] The airplane was "pre-assembled" on the computer eliminating the need for a costly, full-scale mock-up. The design goal was to reduce the number of parts that didn't fit by 50 % and the actual reduction was about 80 %. Another benefit was a lower than expected aerodynamic drag which saved about 15–20 minutes on a flight between Seattle and London. Boeing designed and launched an airplane with greater fuel efficiency, at less cost, and faster than teams using a paper-based design approach could have.[74]

The potential strategic benefits from using global virtual teams can be realized – but only if the process is understood and managed appropriately.

Notes

1 Nonaka, I. and Takeuchi, H., *The Knowledge Creating Company*, (New York: Oxford University Press, 1995).

2 Athanassiou, N., *The impact of internationalization on top management team characteristics: A tacit knowledge perspective*, unpublished doctoral dissertation, The University of South Carolina, 1995; and Athanassiou, N. and Nigh, D., 1999. "The impact of company internationalization on top management team advice networks: A tacit knowledge perspective," *Strategic Management Journal*, 19(1) (1999) 83–92.

3   O'Connell, J. and Bartlett, C., "Lincoln Electric: Venturing Abroad," Harvard Business School Case 9-398-095.

4   Lawrence, P. R. and Lorsch, J. W., *Organization and Environment* (Homewood, IL: Richard D. Irwin, 1969).

5   Thompson, J. D., *Organizations in Action* (New York: McGraw Hill, 1967).

6   Ibid.

7   Ibid.

8   For a review of this literature see "Person-Organization Fit and Person-Job Fit in Employee Selection: A Review of the Literature," Sekiguchi, T. and Osaka Keidai Ronshu, Vol. 54, No. 6, March 2004, http://www.osaka-ue.ac.jp/gakkai/pdf/ronshu/2003/5406_ronko_sekiguti.pdf.

9   "Lincoln Electric: Venturing Abroad," n. 3 above.

10   Alexander, C., *Notes on the Synthesis of Form* (Cambridge, MA: Harvard University Press, 1964) 15–16.

11   This organizational design framework and analytic model has been adapted from a number of writers on the contingency theory of organizations: Thompson, J. D., *Organizations in Action* (New York: McGraw-Hill, 1967); Lawrence, P. R. and Lorsch, J. W., *Organization and Environment* (Homewood, IL: Richard D. Irwin, 1969); Galbraith, J. R., *Designing Complex Organizations* (Reading, MA: Addison-Wesley, 1973); Lorsch, J. W. and Morse, J. J., *Organizations and Their Members: A Contingency Approach* (New York: Harper & Row, 1974); Galbraith, J. R., *Organization Design* (Reading, MA: Addison-Wesley, 1977); Lorsch, J. W., American Management Association, "Organization Design: A Situational Perspective," *Organizational Dynamics* 5 (1977); Galbraith, J. R. and Nathanson, D. A., *Strategy Implementation: The Role of Structure and Process* (St. Paul, MN: West, 1978); Kotter, J. P., Schlesinger, L. A., and Sathe, V., "Organization Design Tools," in *Organization: Text, Cases and Readings on the Management of Organizational Design and Change* (Homewood, IL: Richard D. Irwin, 1979). See also Lane, H. W., "Systems, Values and Action: An Analytic Framework for Intercultural Management Research," *Management International Review* 20, No. 3 (1980) 61–70.

12   Hastings, D. F., "Lincoln Electric's harsh lessons from international expansion," *Harvard Business Review* 77(3) (February–March 1999) 162–178.

13   Hofstede, G. H., "Motivation, Leadership, and Organization: Do American Theories Apply Abroad?" *Organizational Dynamics*, Vol. 8, No. 2, Summer (1980) 50.

14   O'Connell, J. and Bartlett, C., "Lincoln Electric: Venturing Abroad," Harvard Business School Case 9-398-095., 7.

15   Brannen, M. Y. and Salk, S., "Partnering across borders: Negotiating organizational culture in a German-Japanese joint venture," *Human Relations* 53(4) (2000) 451.

16   Shea, C. and Lane, H. W., "Moscow Aerostar," Ivey case 9A92C010, Ivey Publishing. See also "Meeting of the Mindsets in a Changing Russia," Puffer, S. M., McCarthy, D., and Zupelev, A., *Business Horizons* (November–December 1996) 52–60; and Vikanski, O. and Puffer, S. M., "Management Education and Employee Training at Moscow McDonald's," *European Management Journal* Vol. 1, No.1, 102–107.

17   Laurent, A., "The Cultural Diversity of Western Conceptualizations of Management," *International Studies of Management and Organization* 13, Nos 1–2 (1983) 75–96.

18   Ibid., at 75.

19   Ting-Toomey, S., "Intercultural Conflict Management: A Mindful Approach," excerpted from the chapter (pp. 194–230) "Constructive Intercultural Conflict Management" in Ting-Toomey, S., *Communicating Across Cultures* (New York: The Guilford Press, 1999) (http://www.guilford.com). Accessed at http://conflict911.com/cgi-bin/links/jump.cgi?ID=11687.

20   Inzerilli, G. and Laurent, A., "Managerial Views of Organization Structure in France and the USA," *International Studies of Management and Organization* 13, Nos 1–2 (1983) 97–188.

21   This statement is a good example of the North American instrumental orientation.

22   Brooke, J., "Speaking the Language of Success," *New York Times*, October 23, 2001.

23   Geringer, J. M. and Miller, J., "Japanese-American Seating Inc. (A)," Ivey case no. 9A92G004, Ivey Publishing, London, Canada.

24   Slaughter, K., Lane, H. W., and Campbell, D., "Grupo Financiero Inverlat," Ivey case no. 9A97L001, Ivey Publishing, London, Canada.

25   Afuah, A., *Business Models: A Strategic Management Approach* (McGraw-Hill Irwin, 2004) 12–13.

26   Thompson, A. A. and Strickland, A. J., *Crafting and Executing Strategy* (McGraw-Hill Irwin, 2001) 53.

27   Drucker, P. F., *Management: Tasks, Responsibilities, Practices* (New York: Harper, 1974) 123.

28   Ibid.

29   Porter, M. E., *Competitive Strategy* (New York: McGraw-Hill, 1980).

30   Dess, G. G., Lumpkin, G. T., and Taylor, M. L. *Strategic Management* (McGraw-Hill Irwin, 2005) 169.

31   Hax, A. and Wilde, D., *The Delta Project* (New York and United Kingdom: Palgrave, 2001). See also a summary article, "The Delta Model: Adaptive Management for a Changing World," *Sloan Management Review* (Winter 1999) 11–28.

32   Hax and Wilde, *Sloan Management Review* (Winter 1999) 13.

33   Dess, G. G., Lumpkin, G. T., and Taylor M. L., *Strategic Management* (McGraw-Hill Irwin, 2005) 277.

34   Afuah, n. 25 above, at 12.

35   This example relies on information from the following sources (accessed November 26, 2008): Barnes & Noble company web site, http://www.barnesandnobleinc.com/our_company/history/bn_history.html and Frey, C. and Cook, J., "How Amazon.com survived, thrived and turned a profit: E-tailer defied predictions it would do none of those," *Seattle Post-Intelligencer*, Wednesday, January 28, 2004, http://seattlepi.nwsource.com/business/158315_amazon28.html.

36   Lane, H. W. and Campbell, D., "Global Multi-Products Chile," Ivey case no. 9A98C007, Ivey Publishing, London, Canada. Although this is a disguised case, the company is real and is a Fortune 100 company.

37   TJX web site, http://www.tjx.com/ceo/ceomessage.html (accessed November 26, 2008).

38   Personal communication from Ted English, previously CEO of TJX Companies at the time the company entered Europe.

39   Wesley, D., Spital, F. and Lane, H. W., "Monsanto Europe (A) and (B)," Ivey Publishing, Case nos 9B02A007 and 9B02A008, 2002.

40   Jesus Sotomayor, Mexico City, 2003, personal communication.

41   *World Investment Report 2000: Cross-border Mergers and Acquisitions and Development*, United Nations, New York and Geneva, 2000; xx.

42   See, for example, Bartlett, C. A. and Ghoshal, S., *Managing Across Borders: The Transnational Solution*, 2nd edn (Boston: Harvard Business School Press, 1998); and Prahalad, C. K. and Doz, Y. L., *The Multinational Mission: Balancing Local Demands and Global Vision* (New York: The Free Press, 1987).

43   Bartlett and Ghoshal; Prahalad and Doz, n. 42 above.

44   Kogut, B., "Designing Global Strategies: Comparative and Competitive Value-Added Chains," *Sloan Management Review* 26(4) (Summer 1985) 15–28.

45   Ibid.

46   Bartlett and Ghoshal, n. 42 above.

47   For an interesting case example of mutually beneficial learning between newly acquired local companies and the headquarters of the global new owner, see "Merging Two Acquisitions: How Minetti Built a High Performance, Cohesive Organization (A) and (B)" cases, IMD-3-1484 and 3-1485.

48   Hill, C., *International Business: Competing in the Global Marketplace* (Irwin McGraw-Hill, 2000).

49　Bartlett and Ghoshal, n. 42 above; and Stopford, J. M., and Wells Jr,, L. T., *Managing the Multinational Enterprise: Organization of the firm and ownership of the subsidiaries* (New York: Basic Books, 1972).

50　Beaman, K. V. and Guy, G. R., "Sourcing Strategies for the Transnational Organization," *IHRIM Journal* (July/August 2004) 30.

51　Ibid., at 31.

52　Faulk, J., "Global network organizations," *Human Relations*, Vol. 54(1) (2001) 91.

53　Borgatti, S., "Virtual/Network Organizations," http://www.analytictech.com/mb021/virtual. htm, February 5, 2001.

54　Vega-Redondo, F., "Network organizations," EUI Working Paper, ECO 2008/09. January 21, 2008.

55　Faulk, n. 52 above.

56　C. A. Bartlett and S. Ghoshal, n. 42 above. See also C. K. Prahalad and Y. L. Doz, n. 42 above.

57　Vega-Redondo, n. 54 above, at 1.

58　Borgatti, n. 53 above.

59　Beamish, P. W., Killing, J. P., Lecraw, D. J., and Morrison, A. J., *International Management: Text and Cases*, 2nd edn (Burr Ridge, IL: Richard D. Irwin, 1994).

60　Beamish, P. W., *Multinational Joint Ventures in Developing Countries* (London: Routledge, 1988).

61　Geringer, J. M., "Partner Selection Criteria for Developed Country Joint Ventures," *Business Quarterly* 53, No. 1 (1988) 55.

62　Ibid.

63　Beamish, *et al*, n. 59 above.

64　This section is adapted from Birkinshaw, J. and DiStefano, J. J., "Global Account Management: New Structures, New Tasks," Chapter 14 in Lane, H.W. Maznevski, M. L., Mendenhall, M., and McNett, J., *The Blackwell Handbook of Global Management: A Guide to Managing Complexity* (Blackwell Publishers, 2004). Used with permission.

65　Galbraith, J., "Building Organizations Around the Global Customer," Ivey Business Journal, September/October 2001, 66(1).

66　The information about Schneider came from the company's web site.

67　http://schneiderelectric.net/wps/portal/corp/kcxml/04_Sj9SPykssy0xPLMnMz0vM0Y_Qj zKL94w39PcESZnFW8ZbuupHogu5oAkBmaFeEDEjIwOEmCdUzMASIRYE1RvmARfzMUO Y5-uRn5uqH6TvrR-gX5AbCgIR5Y6OigCf5Ji4/delta/base64xml/L3dJdyEvd0ZNQUFzQUMv NElVRS82X0lfMjJV?toservice=WIBNW_5008_CORP&Language=en&fromservice=WIBNW_ 0005_CORP&&idContent=CD30F96C657C4701852572FF002FE256.

68　This list is a partial set of requirements as described by the first global account manager for the vendor. (Personal communication, September 1994.)

69　Lane, H. W., Maznevski, M. L., Mendenhall, M., and McNett, J., "Introduction to Leading and Teaming," in *The Blackwell Handbook of Global Management: A Guide to Managing Complexity* (Blackwell Publishers, 2004) 171–173.

70　Cohen, S.G. and Bailey, D. E., "What makes teams work: Group effectiveness research from the shop floor to the executive suite," *Journal of Management* 23 (1997) 239–290. These authors among many others have identified that team effectiveness is a function of factors related to task, group, and organizational design factors, environmental factors, internal processes, external processes, and group psychosocial traits.

71　Javidan, M. and House, R. J., "Cultural acumen for the global manager: Lessons from Project Globe," *Organizational Dynamics* 29(4) (2001) 289–305.

72　http://www.boeing.com/commercial/777family/background.html (accessed January 9, 2009).

73　Shokralla, S. H., "21st Century Jet, The Boeing 777," http://bits.me.berkeley.edu/mmcs/ b777/main.shtml (accessed January 9, 2009).

74　Benson-Armer, R. and Hsieh, T.-Y., "Teamwork Across Time and Space," *The McKinsey Quarterly*, No. 4 (1997) 19–27.

Selecting and Developing Global Managers

GLOBALIZATION AND GLOBAL COMPANIES

Before examining issues regarding the selection and development of global managers, we need to say more about globalization and what it means for managers.

What is globalization? The *Stanford Encyclopedia of Philosophy* states that "the term 'globalization' has quickly become one of the most fashionable buzzwords of contemporary political and academic debate" and most often is nothing more than a synonym for the spread of classical liberal, "free market" economic policies; the spread and dominance of "Westernization," or even "Americanization" of political, economic, and cultural life; and the rise of new information technologies such as the Internet – all of which are bringing the world closer together. And there is often an unarticulated assumption that globalization is good. We should remember, however, that globalization is a process and not a destination.

In *The Lexus and the Olive Tree*, Thomas Friedman points out that in addition to politics, economics, technology, and culture we need to include the environment and national security. Terrorism and pollution also have "gone global." This highlights the fact that there can be negative aspects of globalization as well as positive or what Peter Temu calls "good and bad globalization" and that globalization can spread evil as well as good.[1] On the negative side, Temu adds criminal activities such as drugs and money laundering. On the positive side he adds development. So, there is a need to be specific when we discuss globalization – the "globalization of what?"[2]

There is also an implicit assumption that globalization and global organizations are new phenomena. By some accounts globalization is as old as mankind and began when people started migrating out of Africa.

Globalization is an historical process that began with the first movement of people out of Africa into other parts of the world. Traveling short, then longer distances, migrants, merchants, and others have always taken their ideas, customs, and products into new lands. The melding, borrowing, and adaptation of outside influences can be found in many areas of human life.[3]

A more modern example, but still one that predates the founding of the United States, is the British Empire. Another example of a global organization that has been around for a long time is the Catholic Church. So the process of globalization and the existence of global organizations are not new. However, the basic feature of globalization is that people, countries, and organizations all around the world have become more interdependent. And it is true that more activities affecting more peoples' lives have become more interdependent than ever before. In this book we focus primarily on the economic dimension of globalization and on companies that operate in many countries around the world and that attempt to integrate their global activities.

Modern globalization can be thought of as the erosion of national as well as company boundaries and the increase of economic interdependence. Trade liberalization has opened borders across which capital and products move easily. Airline travel and reliable, inexpensive communication have reduced distances and minimized the impact of physical boundaries so that corporations are able to manage far-flung operations. Alliances and networks blur the lines of organizational boundaries. The forces of deregulation, industry consolidation, and technology reshaped corporate and social landscapes. Both responding to and feeding the trend of boundary erosion, companies are rapidly seeking to globalize.

In the early 1980s, Levitt, a pioneering observer of globalization, defined globalization as a "shift toward a more integrated and interdependent world economy . . . having two main components: the globalization of markets and the globalization of production."[4] Many academics and executives over-simplified the meaning of globalization and extrapolated it as simply "the production and distribution of products and services of a homogeneous type and quality on a worldwide basis."[5]

Not everyone agrees with the standard globalization picture described above. Rugman and Moore, for example, argue that "globalization is a myth." They show that large firms' business activities and their trade in goods and services take place not globally but in clusters (for example, Silicon Valley, Hollywood, Grenoble), regional blocks (for example, European Union, NAFTA, Japan), and within nations. Their advice is to "think regional, act local and forget global."[6] If globalization is defined by standard terms, then in reality there are few, if any, truly global companies operating in all markets.

Most of the globalization descriptions refer to an increasing global reach but from narrow perspectives. These include the number of markets served; the global reach of the supply chain and sources of supplies; the locations in which parts of the company's value chain are located; and alliances or mergers and acquisitions to source intellectual capital (knowledge). However, such perspectives suggest that companies and executives simply are doing more of what they have always done, just in more places and with more technological sophistication. These perspectives are economic, market-oriented, and technology-oriented ones that, although not incorrect, describe only a part of the reality of globalization.

The measures of globalization employed also tend to focus on measurable external factors such as a percentage of international sales to total sales, for example. However, when we examine the processes of companies that globalize, the sterile statistics disappear and the people who create and manage the processes appear. The picture at the operational or "execution/make it happen" level often is much less rosy than the one provided by macro-level descriptions. The road to globalization has been littered with the debris of ill-considered mergers, acquisitions, and new market entry attempts. Globalization is easy to talk about but difficult to do.

What exactly is a global company that operates in this new world of increased interdependence? Is it a company that has plants and subsidiaries in many countries? Or is it a company that sells its products and services around the world and derives more of its revenue from international sales than domestic sales, for example? There is no doubt that these are some of the characteristics.

However, just because a company operates in multiple locations around the world does not make it a global company. It simply means that it functions in a lot of countries. Global strategy is executed by, and global operations are managed by, people from one culture interacting with people from another country and culture. These are the managers who interface with the suppliers, alliance partners, and government officials. These also are the people who manage the plants and workforces around the world. It is our perspective that *you don't globalize companies unless you globalize people.* Think of a German company, for example, operating in many countries but whose top managers all have German passports. In our opinion this is a German company operating in many countries – but not necessarily a company that has been truly globalized. Yes, a global company operates in many locations but it also has developed a cadre of managers who have global mindsets and understand how to operate in this world of economic, political, and cultural interdependence.

Sam Palmisano, the CEO of IBM, characterized the modern global company as a globally integrated enterprise [GIE] that "fashions its strategy, its management, and its operations in pursuit of a new goal: the integration of production and value delivery worldwide. State borders define less and less the boundaries of corporate thinking or practice."[7] These GIEs use new technology and business models which allow them to combine functions and operations in multiple ways in "increasingly complex intercompany production networks" requiring new forms of collaboration and "high-value skills" that he said would allow managers to handle the "fluid and collaborative nature of work today."

Over a decade ago, C. K. Prahalad characterized the world of global business:[8]

> A world where variety, complex interaction patterns among various subunits, host governments, and customers, pressures for change and stability, and the need to re-assert individual identity in a complex web of organizational relationships are the norm. This world is one beset with ambiguity and stress. Facts, emotions, anxieties, power and dependence, competition and collaboration, individual and team efforts are all present . . . Managers have to deal with these often conflicting demands simultaneously.

Prahalad saw the outline of globalization and described it accurately. Although he did not use the term "complexity," he described this characteristic of globalization well. Rather than think about globalization as the proportion of trade conducted across national borders, or by some other economic or social measure, we argue that, as we talk about it in business, globalization is a manifestation of complexity and requires new ways of thinking and managing. Executives today have to be able to manage internal and external networks in a very complex environment.

Global Managers Manage Complexity[9]

The current environment facing companies is a *mélange* of global competitors, multiple countries, and governments with differing social, legal, regulatory, and political constraints and physical infrastructures; numerous cultures and languages; all facilitated by technology and more tightly linked than ever in the past. Lane, Mendenall, and Maznevski identified several characteristics which together function as a foundation for the increasing complexity of globalization: multiplicity, interdependence, and ambiguity. Each of these characteristics is difficult to manage by itself but they also are interrelated which presents an even greater challenge. And as if that were not enough, they are continually in flux.

- **Multiplicity** With globalization, executives deal with more organizations, governments, and people. Importantly, though, many of these entities are also different from the executive's own organization, government, and people, and from each other as well. Globalization is not just about "more;" it's about "more *and* different."[10] There are more competitors, partners, different types of organizations such as networks, and customers with different needs in different markets. Companies have more operations in more locations to manage and, of course, have more governments in these locations to contend with as well.
- **Interdependence** With fast and easy movement of capital, information, and people, geographically distributed units are no longer isolated. Globalization has created a world of complex political and economic interdependence. The global financial system crisis in 2008 that started in the United States with the sub-prime mortgage defaults is a perfect illustration of this increased interdependence. However, companies are finding that they *must* enter into interdependent arrangements through out-sourcing, alliances, and network arrangements related to their value chains in order to stay price-competitive or continue to create value. Interdependence is not only a feature of the external environment; it also is something companies create themselves though alliances, for example, to cope with the challenges of the competitive environment.
- **Ambiguity** Although there may be plenty of information, the meaning or implications of the information may not be clear. It is a condition of multiple meanings, incorrect attributions, erroneous interpretations, and conflicting interests. Situations, intentions, corporate actions, and individual behaviors can be interpreted in many different ways, and implications for action can be confusing. The problem here is not the need to obtain more information and apply probabilities to the outcomes; that is uncertainty. Ambiguity involves not being able to understand and interpret the data in a way that guides action effectively. Ambiguity goes beyond uncertainty. Three aspects of ambiguity contribute to the complexity of globalization:
  - lack of information clarity. Information itself can be simply unclear – sometimes we cannot even know "the facts." For example, reports or statistics from different

sources may use different indicators to analyze the same subject, coming to different conclusions. Or data may simply not be available.

- cause–effect relationships. This is confusion about the relationship between means and ends, inputs and outputs, actions and outcomes.
- equivocality. This is a condition in which multiple interpretations of the same facts are possible. Given a set of facts, there can be two or more things they could possibly mean, but to identify the "right" interpretation is difficult.

There also is the multiplier effect: *Multiplicity* × *Interdependence* × *Ambiguity* = *Dynamic Complexity*.[11] Tightly linked, complex global organizations operating in a tightly coupled global environment potentially become more vulnerable as interdependence increases.[12] For example, a single email sent simultaneously to several locations in the world can not only be interpreted differently, but also forwarded to several other destinations, each generating varied interpretations and, possibly, actions. The increase in complexity leads to a decrease in buffers, slack resources, and autonomy of units. There also is less time to contemplate corrective action. Ambiguity makes problem diagnosis and action planning difficult. Problems appear and must be resolved. "Now" has become the primary unit of time in the world of global managers.

If customers, governments, interest groups, and competitors were passive then a corporation could manage the complexity by simply adding more managers and computers. That would be an increase in detail complexity.[13] The increase in interdependence and multiplicity leads to more ambiguity. Ambiguity makes understanding multiplicity difficult. And so on. Such a scenario can create messy situations for executives but this is the reality of global managers.

- **Flux** As if multiplicity, interdependence, and ambiguity were not enough on their own, the whole system is always in motion, always changing. And it seems to be changing at a faster rate all the time.

There are alternative ways for dealing with increased complexity: *amplification* or the *elimination* of input variety. Elimination of variety is the reduction of environmental input achieved by not being able to, or willing to, see and understand the nuances in the environment or by creating situations of certainty that delude executives into thinking they can be controlled.[14] Such ostrich-like behavior does not usually bring success.

Amplification[15] means increasing the number of decision-makers. Generally speaking, more decision-makers or team members provide greater "variety decoding" potential. Yet simple amplification will not necessarily work. If, for example, executives operating out of a corporate headquarters in Norwich, Connecticut cannot generate the requisite variety in their decisions to match the variety existing in a global marketplace, simply increasing the size of the team may not work. If multiple decision-makers are highly homogeneous, with similar outlooks, a similar vested interest in the outcome, and reliance on the same selected sources for their information, they may be fooled. That is, they may think they are facing less variety than they actually are.[16]

Organizational structures have become more and more complex, with more managers and more multi-dimensional matrices. The more complex structures become, the more unwieldy they are. Moreover, they cannot always adapt quickly to new circumstances, since they are designed to fit a particular set of contingencies. More complex sets of policies may not work either. In a continually changing, dynamically complex environment, the policies have to be changed continually and thus lose their effectiveness.

The appropriate response to complexity is through the deliberate development of human *requisite variety*.[17] In human information processing terms, development of requisite variety means that when there are complex, ambiguous inputs coming from the environment, organizational decision-makers must have the cognitive complexity, and firms need the organizational capacity, to notice these inputs, decode them, and process them. Simply, this means that global organizations need to employ managers capable of recognizing, understanding, and interpreting correctly events and information from the global marketplace. Ashby said: "Only variety can destroy variety."[18] To respond to today's global complexity, organizations must find the right people to decipher the informational content in the environment and create the appropriate organizational processes for managing the complexity and executing action plans. Weick and Van Orden stated: "Globalization requires people to make sense of turbulence in order to create processes that keep resources moving to locations of competitive advantage."[19]

Effective Global Managers Are the Key to Responding to Complexity

A global mindset enables executives to manage the complexity of globalization. In an earlier chapter we defined the global mindset as

> The capacity to analyze situations and develop criteria for performance that are not dependent on the assumptions of a single country, culture or context; and to make decisions and plan action appropriately in different countries, cultures and contexts.

When managers have the capacity to think across cultures and contexts and make decisions based on that analysis, they can use the variety and resources within the firm to respond to threats and opportunities in the environment. Jack Welch called this the globalization of intellect: "The real challenge is to globalize the mind of the organization. . . . I think until you globalize intellect, you haven't really globalized the company."[20] As managers globalize their companies, they face an increasing complexity whose challenges require a more complex view of the world, put into action through the mechanism of a global mindset. If they don't, they may be prone to deciding on the wrong, simple solutions to their problems. As the American journalist H. L. Menken observed "for every complex problem there is a simple solution. And it is always wrong."

The global mindset is not an additional managerial capability; it is a different capability. What does it really mean for executives to think globally or, as Begley and Boyd suggested, to think "glocally," which means to be able to think globally and able to think locally and able to think globally and locally simultaneously? At the heart of the global mindset is the ability to see and understand the world differently than one has been conditioned to see and understand it. We particularly like a quote from Marcel Proust (whose life spanned the nineteenth and twentieth centuries) as expressing the essence of the global mindset. Proust said, "The real voyage of discovery consists not in seeking new landscapes, but in having new eyes." It is a meta-capability that permits an individual to function successfully in new and unfamiliar situations and to integrate them with other existing skill and knowledge bases.

This definition does not include, for example, specific business knowledge or skills. It is helpful to see a global mindset as separate from business knowledge, which tends to be developed in a more traditional way through formal education and business experiences. Business knowledge helps a manager understand the *business*; a global mindset helps the manager understand the *context* in which the business operates. It is also helpful to differentiate a global mindset from skills. Skills put into *action* the knowledge and perspectives from the business understanding and the global mindset. Business knowledge, a global mindset, and a global skill set all are critical for effective performance in global companies; but they are not the same thing.

There is little doubt that dealing with the complexity of global operations requires having managers with the orientations, competencies discussed earlier, and skill sets beyond those required in domestic organizations. The challenge is to find or develop managers with business knowledge and experience, a global mindset, and a global skill set. Acquiring and retaining people who can function effectively in this new context becomes a critical human resource management undertaking.

The process of finding and developing globally-minded managers with the requisite skills is more difficult than it might appear. High-potential individuals must be carefully selected and prepared for their international assignments to achieve the necessary professional development and responsively repatriated so that they remain with the organization and use their new skills to help it attain its strategic objectives.

Global Talent Management[21]

A McKinsey & Company study, *The War for Talent*, published in 1998, identified talent management and, specifically, "the war for senior executive talent [as] a defining characteristic of the competitive landscape for decades to come;" and probably ushered the term "talent management" into the management lexicon.

In late 2005, Worldwide ERC conducted human resource benchmarking conferences in Amsterdam, Chicago, and Hong Kong with human resource professionals from a varied range of industries.[22] One conclusion was that competition for qualified managers had become global and companies did not necessarily only look at a domestic pool of candidates. A McKinsey Global Survey in 2007 also found that executives believed that the most significant trend for the following five years (or through 2012) was that the "competition for talent will intensify [and] become more global."[23] Talent management has become a global activity. Finding the high-potential global managers needed to run global companies no longer takes place solely in a company's home country.

From its human resource benchmarking conferences in the USA, Europe, and Asia, Worldwide ERC also learned that international assignments were generally considered essential for career development and that international assignments had increased in importance to career development over the previous five years.[24] However, international assignments for home country managers where they become an expatriate for two to three years are less frequent than previously.

Historically used in a management control role, expatriates for decades went abroad for a duration of usually two to three years, very often accompanied by a trailing spouse who did not have a career or expect to work. It was viewed as an interesting or exciting opportunity and a possible chance to make some additional money or save money because of tax treatment. Surviving the assignment often was a measure of success.

That scenario has changed. Today managers are transferred (to and from the parent company) to learn about affiliated operations in other countries, to fill a skills gap, to transfer knowledge and technology, to launch projects, to facilitate integration of the global value chain, to transfer corporate culture, and for management development.[25] Expatriates now are more likely to have a dual-career partner and, in fact, GMAC in its 2008 Survey Report found that 54 % of the spouses/partners were employed before, but not during, the assignment and the second most common reason for refusing an assignment (62 %) was spouse/partner career concerns.

Another change has been an increase in measuring the performance of international assignees in order to gauge the effectiveness of the managers and the return on investment (ROI) of international assignments. Although still not widely practiced, companies are attempting to understand and measure the cost–benefit tradeoff of international assignments. Some companies use specific assignments or projects which can be assessed as completed or not, while others attempt to measure more formally the successful completion at the expected cost.[26]

International assignments are important tools in the coordination and integration of organizational resources which are essential activities for successful strategy implementation in geographically dispersed companies embedded in differing cultural environments. Although it is true that numerous electronic communication and data processing system options allow the creation of sophisticated enterprise information systems to coordinate dispersed operations and the activities of suppliers and customers, cultural nuances of information that provide the deepest comprehension of market-specific knowledge may not be transferable electronically.

Tacit knowledge, which is deep-rooted and usually not codified, explains the most important nuances of operations in a particular cultural context. This knowledge is acquired experientially and must be shared through face-to-face interactions.[27] Firms gain sustainable competitive advantage from executives acquiring experiences and lessons that are held as tacit knowledge and then shared across the organization.

Given the dispersed nature of multinational organizations, knowledge-sharing is particularly difficult. Some solutions to this challenge include the use of short-term assignments as well as cadres of expatriates and inpatriates (an employee transferred from a foreign country to a corporation's home country operation or headquarters) to acquire and share this tacit knowledge. Used strategically, short-term assignments, inpatriation, and expatriation can be used to implement projects, fill positions and, as a management development experience, to provide high-potential employees with a global orientation – or all three.[28] These employees create global relationships, inside and outside the company, in addition to explicit and implicit operating knowledge. The relationships and knowledge then become essential to the value creation process in global operations.[29]

We have dealt with some companies that were increasing the number of inpatriates to headquarters. These inpatriate assignments were usually short-term, two to three months at headquarters for a special project. This had a double advantage of exposing the inpatriate to headquarters processes, concerns, and perspective, while allowing headquarters personnel to become acquainted with cultural orientations and views of divisions from around the world. At the same time, some of these firms were establishing formal policies that required international experience as a prerequisite for consideration for promotion to senior ranks, thereby "localizing" management and eliminating many of the perks that were formerly needed as incentives for executives to accept international assignments.

One of the criticisms of the North American international human resource management literature has been its heavy, some would say almost exclusive, focus on expatriates. However, expatriates still represent the majority of international assignees. GMAC reported that in 2002 75%, on average, of expatriate assignments were to or from the headquarters' country. Since 2002, that number has dropped to 59% on average and 41% involved transfers between nonheadquarters' countries.[30]

Although companies remain optimistic about the continued use of expatriates, numerous surveys of multinationals also have shown an increasing trend of using "non-standard international assignments" which include commuting, rotations, virtual, and short-term (up to 12 months) assignments, the latter being the most common.[31],[32]

A major reason for the rise in nonstandard assignments is the expense associated with relocating expatriates and their families. Expatriates' salaries are usually higher than those of local managers, and they usually receive benefits to make an overseas move attractive. Benefits often include items like housing or a housing allowance, moving expenses, tax equalization, and schooling for children. Many of these benefits are not usually provided to local employees. In addition to lowering costs, having fewer expatriates has reduced conflict between employees and groups in the local environment and increased the development of host country managerial and technical capabilities.

The use of local managers to reduce costs has increased. In many developing countries, larger pools of better educated management talent are appearing. In developed countries, where sufficient management talent exists, there are employment and immigration laws with which a firm must comply. Companies also are now using third country nationals (TCNs) more frequently to reduce labor costs and are converting the status of expatriates to local employees, thereby reducing costs.

Selection Finding appropriate candidates is a challenge, as is preparing them and their families for successful assignments.

In 1973, published research showed that managers were selected for international assignments based on their proven performance in a similar job, usually domestically.[33] The ability to work with foreign employees was at or near the bottom of the list of important qualifications. Unfortunately, over 35 years later the situation has not changed dramatically for the better. Very often technical expertise and knowledge are used as the most important selection criteria. Mercer Human Resource Consulting, in its Expatriate Risk Management Survey, found that in 2002 companies still continued to "mainly look for technical expertise followed by leadership qualities. Good organizational skills and adaptability are also sought-after qualities."[34]

Although technical skills, leadership, and organizational skills are important, they should not be given undue weighting relative to a person's ability to adapt to and function in another culture. It does no good to send the most technically qualified engineers or finance managers, for example, to a foreign subsidiary, if they cannot function there and have to be brought home prematurely.

Kealey developed a useful model for thinking about overseas effectiveness that focuses on adaptation, expertise, and interaction.[35] He states that for a person to be effective, he or she "must adapt – both personally and with his/her family – to the overseas environment, have the expertise to carry out the assignment, and interact with the new culture and its people."[36]

Success in an international assignment, managerial effectiveness, is the ability to live and work effectively in the cross-cultural setting of an assignment. Effectiveness is a function of professional expertise; plus the ability to adapt to one's host country; plus intercultural communication skill to interact with the locals; and situational readiness, such as having a family that is willing, able, and probably excited to take the assignment or not having old or sick parents to care for.[37] Our shorthand notation for this is $E = f(PAIS)$ or *Effectiveness = f (Professional expertise + Adaptation + Intercultural interaction + Situational readiness)*.

Effectiveness on the job is the important outcome for an international assignment. Many studies have used outcome variables such as expatriate satisfaction with an assignment as a surrogate for performance. Kealey, however, explained variables such as satisfaction and previous experience in relation to effectiveness. An international assignee who is satisfied with his or her assignment is not necessarily an effective manager nor is a manager with previous experience necessarily effective, although they are likely to be more satisfied in their assignment. Previous experience is related to increased satisfaction, ease of adjustment, and less stress, all of which are good. However, global companies need effective managers and an ineffective one can damage relationships in the host country. Poor performance in an international assignment also can result in high professional and personal costs to the individual and his or her family. Therefore, all the variables in $E = f(PAIS)$ are important.

Women as Global Managers A more commonly occurring decision in corporations is about the international assignments of female executives. This has become an issue as more women have graduated from business schools and are in line for senior management and international careers. It is also a relevant concern both under employment equity guidelines and legislation in some countries like the United States and Canada, which encourage or require companies to promote women into positions of higher responsibility in organizations, and in the interest of ensuring that talented resources are used effectively throughout the organization.

In its survey of 154 companies (50% headquartered in the Americas; 48% in Europe, the Middle East, and Africa; and 2% in the Asia Pacific), GMAC Global Relocation Services found that the percentage of female expatriates in 2007 was 19%. In 2002 it had predicted that the female expatriate population would exceed 20% by 2005. It actually reached an all time high of 23% in 2005. In its first survey in 1993, the percentage of female expatriates was 10%.

Nancy Adler conducted some of the early, pioneering research on female expatriates.[38] Her research showed that, contrary to conventional wisdom at the time, women did want careers as international managers. In a recent class of MBAs one of the authors asked the women in the class how many wanted to be international managers. In a class of 90 students that was approximately 30 % female, the response showed 100 % interest in international careers.

One lesson learned about women expatriates included that a common problem was more a perceptual one with men in the home country than the behavior of men in the foreign country. Men in the company's home country tended not to select women for international assignments in order to protect them from imaginary difficulties in foreign countries. However, Adler learned that a foreign woman is not expected to act like a local woman and being foreign was more noticeable than being female.

Our advice is to send the best *person* for the job. If a woman is the best person to be sent on an international assignment, then she should be sent. However, she should be at a senior level and have significant decision-making responsibility so that executives in the foreign company will understand that she is a senior executive and the person that they must deal with.

Finally, being a woman expatriate in some countries is undoubtedly more difficult than in others and companies have a responsibility to prepare women well for the challenging assignments in difficult countries.

Training and Preparation for the International Assignment   The training that a person undergoes before expatriation should be a function of the degree of cultural interaction which they will experience.[39] Two dimensions of cultural exposure are the degree of integration and the duration of stay. The integration dimension represents the intensity of the exposure. A person could be sent to a foreign country on a short-term, technical, trouble-shooting matter and experience little significant contact with the local culture. The same person could be in another country only for a brief visit to negotiate a contract, but the cultural interaction could be very intense and might require a great deal of cultural fluency to be successful. An expatriate assigned abroad for a period of years is likely to experience a high degree of interaction with the local culture simply from living there.

The training framework shown in Figure 6.1 suggests that, for short stays and a low level of integration, an "information-giving approach" will suffice.[40] This includes, for example, area and cultural briefings and survival level language training. For longer stays and a moderate level of integration, language training, role plays, critical incidents, case studies, and stress reduction training are suggested. For people who will be living abroad for one to three years and/or will have to experience a high level of integration into the culture, extensive language training, sensitivity training, field experiences, and simulations are the recommended training techniques. Effective preparation would also stress the realities and difficulties of working in another culture and the importance of establishing good working relationships with the local people.

The Canadian International Development Agency (CIDA) developed a useful approach to training for situations in the top right-hand corner of the figure. After extensive pre-departure training, expatriates are sent abroad. Shortly after they begin in their new posting, more training is provided them along with their new co-workers, thus facilitating a productive integration. During the expatriates' stay abroad, periodic "refreshers" or debriefing sessions are held. Finally, the expatriates are actively involved in repatriation

FIGURE 6.1 Relationship between Degree of Integration into the Host Culture and Rigor of Cross-Cultural Training and between Length of Overseas Stay and Length of Training and Training Approach

Length of Training	Level of Rigor	Cross-Cultural Training Approach		
1 – 2 months +	High			**Immersion Approach** Assessment center Field experiences Simulations Extentive language training
			Affective Approach Culture assimilator training Moderate language training Role-playing Cases, critical incidents Stress reduction training	
1 – 4 weeks				
Less than a week	Low	**Information-giving Approach** Area briefings Cultural briefings Films/books Use of interpreters "Survival-level" language training		

DEGREE OF INTEGRATION		Low	Moderate	High
	Length of Stay	1 month or less	2 – 12 months	1 – 3 years

(Reprinted with permission of John Wiley & Sons Inc., Mendenhall, M.E., Dunbar, E. and Oddou, G., "Expatriate Selection, Training, and Career Pathing: A Review and Critique." *Human Resource Management*, 26, No.3 (1987) 340, Copyright © 1993.)

training both prior to and after their return home. The expatriate's spouse and family are also provided with similar training and resources.[41]

Another example is Royal-Dutch Shell's OUTPOST Global Network Program.[42] Shell provides assistance to its expatriates and their families in 35 countries through the Internet.[43] The network provides information and professional services on most aspects of life abroad, particularly in the expatriates' specific locations. It provides various guides, newsletters, and information exchange services with other expatriates and facilitates social networking. It also organizes networks of volunteers of many nationalities to welcome new arrivals in a location.

Historically companies have provided little, if any, cross-cultural training. This is another area where not much has changed. More companies are offering cross-cultural training to include family members, but such training is not required and participation rates continue to be low. GMAC found the "low rate of participation in these programs ironic for two reasons: 1) the high effectiveness of these programs reported by respondents; 2) the nature of family challenges faced by expatriates."[44]

Adaptation and the Reality of Culture Shock   Despite a strong desire to understand and to adapt to a new environment in order to be effective as a manager, nearly everyone experiences disorientation when entering another culture. This phenomenon, called culture shock[45] or, more appropriately, acculturative stress, is rooted in our psychological processes.[46] The normal assumptions used by managers in their home cultures to interpret perceptions and to communicate intentions no longer work in the new cultural environment. Culture shock is not a shock experienced, for example, from exposure to conditions of poverty. Culture shock is more the stress and behavioral patterns associated with a loss of control and a loss of sense of mastery in a situation. Culture shock, in normal attempts to socialize or in a business context, can result in confusion and frustration. Managers are used to being competent in such situations and now find that they are unable to operate effectively.

An inability to interpret surroundings and behave competently can lead to anxiety, frustration, and sometimes to more severe depression. Most experts agree that some form of culture shock is unavoidable, even by experienced internationalists.[47] People who repeatedly move to new cultures likely dampen the emotional swings they experience and probably shorten the period of adjustment, but they do not escape it entirely. In fact, research on intercultural effectiveness has found that those who eventually become the most effective expatriates tend to report experiencing greater difficulty in their initial adjustment. This is because those who are more sensitive to different patterns of human interaction are likely to be both disrupted by changes in these patterns and likely to become adept at new patterns.[48]

There are four modes of responding to a new environment:[49]

- Going Native (assimilation): "acceptance of the new culture while rejecting one's own culture;"
- Being a Participator (integration): "adaptation to the new culture while retaining one's own culture;"
- Being a Tourist (separation): "maintenance of one's own culture by avoiding contact with the new culture;" and
- Being an Outcast (marginalization): "the inability to either adapt to the new culture or remain comfortable with one's own culture."

The pattern experienced by people who move into a new culture usually comes in three phases as shown in Figure 6.2: (1) the elation of anticipating a new environment and the early period of moving into it; (2) the distress of dealing with one's own ineffectiveness and, as the novelty erodes and reality sets in, the realization that one has to live and function in a strange setting; and (3) the adjustment and effective coping in the new environment.

During the first and second periods, performance is usually below one's normal level. The time of adjustment to normal or above average performance takes from three to nine months, depending on previous experience, the degree of cultural difference being experienced, and the individual personality. Frequently observed symptoms of culture shock are similar to most defensive reactions. People reject their new environment as well as the people who live there, often with angry or negative evaluations of "strangeness." Other symptoms include: fatigue; tension; anxiety; excessive concern about hygiene; hostility; an obsession about being cheated; withdrawal into work, family, or the expatriate community; and, in extreme cases, excessive use of drugs or alcohol.

The vast majority of people eventually begin to accept their new environment and adjust. Most emerge from the adjustment period performing adequately and some

FIGURE 6.2 Acculturative Stress[50]

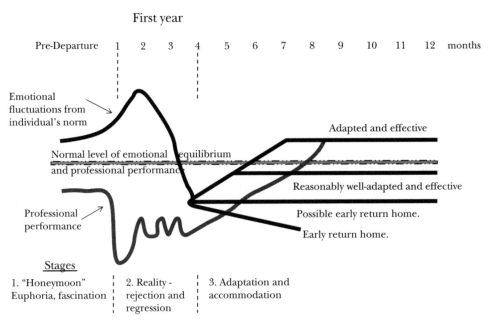

people perform more effectively than before. A smaller percentage either "go native," which is usually not an effective strategy, or experience very severe symptoms of inability to adjust (alcoholism, nervous breakdown, and so on). These types of reactions seem to occur independently of the direction of a move. For example, North Americans going to Russia will probably exhibit patterns similar to Russians coming to North America.

Different people have different ways of coping with culture shock. Normal stress management techniques, regular exercise, rest, and balanced diet are helpful. As noted earlier, some use work as a bridge until they adjust. Usually, the work environment does have some similarities to that of one's home culture. But for the nonworking partner who is often left to cope with the new environment on his or her own, the effects can be more severe. Language training is one very effective way of coping and provides an entry into the host culture. Education about the local history, geography, and traditions of the new culture and then exploration of the new environment also help adjustment. Whatever methods are employed, it is wise to remember that everyone experiences culture shock. Diligent preparation can only moderate the effect, not eliminate it.

Support systems are especially important during the adjustment period. One obvious source of support is the family. Doing more things together as a family, more often, is a way to cope with the pressures. Another is to realize that it is acceptable to withdraw from the new culture, temporarily, for a respite. Reading newspapers from home or enjoying familiar food is a good cultural insulator – if not carried too far. After eight months in Switzerland, an eight-year-old asked her American grandfather to bring her cheddar cheese and a Hershey bar on a visit, even though she had grown to enjoy Swiss fondue and Swiss chocolate! It is important that the use of such temporary interruptions to one's reality be restricted to bridges to the new culture, not as permanent anchors to an old environment.

In company situations, it must be understood that the international manager in a new culture goes through these stresses. Local colleagues should not be surprised at less than perfect performance or strange behavior and can provide crucial support for the managers and their families. When one goes overseas, there are two jobs to accomplish. There is the functional or technical job – for example, the engineering, finance, marketing, or plant management responsibilities. This is obvious. However, too often it is only this job that people identify, focus on, and prepare for. The other job is cultural adaptation. If you cannot adapt successfully, you may be requested to go (or may be sent) home early – often in a matter of months. Such a manager may never get a chance to use his or her technical or functional skills.

You do not have to leave your own country to experience culture shock, as the following demonstrates. A Canadian volunteer on a project in Ghana experienced the symptoms of culture shock, even after participating in an orientation program organized by the sponsoring agency. This same person reported severe symptoms of culture shock on returning to an urban-based MBA program. However, the ultimate culture shock came upon graduating and starting work for a manufacturer located in a small, rural community in one of Canada's Maritime Provinces. In all three experiences, the patterns were the same, and the sharpest disorientation occurred within this person's native country, perhaps because it was least expected. It is important to note that this individual experienced a "reverse culture shock" on the return home.

Return Shock

"Return shock" or "reentry shock" to one's home culture also is an adjustment phenomenon that people experience and for which they need to be prepared.[51] There can be a significant readjustment to one's home country, especially if a manager has been away for a long period of time.

Osland[52] points out that there can be a high degree of uncertainty surrounding one's career upon repatriation that, combined with a loss of prestige and autonomy of being abroad, possibly at the forefront of a company's global strategy, may give an executive pause to think about his or her future career with the company. Both at work and in one's personal life, a returned international assignee may find others lack interest in their experience. They have grown personally and changed during their assignment, but people at home only want to hear the 30-second sound-bite about the experience. Their idealized image of how perfect the home country was and how everything worked there is often shattered upon return. A person who worked for one of the authors in Nairobi, Kenya often commented about how she could not wait to get back to North America where the copy machines worked. When she returned she discovered that the copiers often broke down there as well. And personally, returned assignees often find that they miss life abroad. All of these factors probably play a role in the high attrition rate of returnees discussed in the next section.

Repatriation

Selecting the right people, training them properly, and sending them and their families to their foreign posting is not the end of the story. Reintegrating these people into the company after the foreign assignment so that the company can continue to benefit from their experience and expertise is important, and it also has proven to be a problem.

There is also the problem of failure rates, defined as early return. There are estimates of failure rates anywhere from 20–50 % for American expatriates. Some of the higher numbers have been called into question, but the number is still high especially given the investment a firm makes in sending an employee and her or his family abroad.[53] There are many reasons for failure or early return. One survey found that the two major causes were the inability to demonstrate a global mindset and poor leadership skills. An aversion to change and lack of networking skills also were problems.[54] Another survey found that the key factors of expatriate failure were partner dissatisfaction, family concerns, inability to adapt, poor candidate selection, and the job not meeting the expatriate's expectations. The number one reason prompting early return is usually family-related issues.

Expatriate attrition, leaving the company, is also a problem. GMAC in its 2008 Survey found that the turnover rate for expatriates during an assignment was 25 %, or twice the attrition rate of the general employee population, and it was 27 % within the first year after returning. To minimize attrition companies need to think more coherently about career-pathing for their expatriates, so their returnees can use their newly acquired international experience and skills, and provide them with adequate repatriation support and a wider choice of positions after repatriation.

Regardless of the exact numbers on failure rate or attrition, it pays to get the expatriate cycle right – the right people, the right preparation, and the right repatriation. A failed assignment can cost a company anywhere from $250000–$1000000 and that does not consider the personal costs to employees and their families.

Research suggests that the average repatriation attrition rate – those people who return from an overseas assignment and then leave their companies within one year – is about 25 %.[55] GMAC Global Relocation Services found a 22 % rate in its survey. If companies want to retain their internationally experienced managers, they will have to do a better job managing the repatriation process, to include using that international experience, offering job choices upon return, recognition, repatriation career support, and family repatriation support, and improving evaluations during an assignment. There are indications that some companies such as FedEx, Honeywell, and Medtronic recognize this problem and have developed programs to address attrition issues.[56]

An international assignment is an important vehicle for developing global managers; achieving strategic management control; coordinating and integrating the global organization; and learning about international markets and competitors, as well as about foreign social, political, and economic situations. However, the idealized goal of becoming a global, learning organization will only be reached if the right people are selected for foreign assignments, trained properly, repatriated with care, valued for their experience, and then offered assignments that draw on their unique backgrounds.

Challenging Destinations

There are at least three dimensions on which to categorize countries as challenging destinations: administrative problems for expatriate program managers, cultural difficulty in adapting to a new country, and personal risk such as security and health issues.

GMAC's 2008 Survey Report identified China, India, Russia, and, most likely surprisingly for Americans reading this book, the United States as challenging destinations. In China the administrative issues were suitable housing, immigration issues, bureaucracy, and remote locations. In India and Russia the issues were similar but also included security concerns. Cultural problems were common in these three countries and language was also a challenge in China and Russia. In the United States respondents noted that immigration and work permits were issues as well as security. Outside its borders, the United States has a reputation for high crime rates in its cities and for there being too many guns.

Today a successful assignment also means a safe assignment. GMAC Global Relocation Services found that many companies had formalized programs to ensure the safety and security of their expatriates and families.[57] 44% of the respondents reported that they received inquiries from employees about security issues and it appears that companies are responding to these concerns to improve security and minimize international assignment turndowns, attrition, early returns, and failures. Many companies had instituted security briefings for selected countries and some provided security briefings for all international assignments. Security systems were upgraded, evacuation procedures were put in place, and companies were updating their employee contact information.

In addition to executing strategy globally under relatively "normal" conditions, executives also may find themselves in difficult environments and threatening situations. These usually reflect historical or economic events and cultural factors of a given country or region, and could pose a threat to corporate assets or to employees. Some of these situations include expropriation, currency collapse, civil war, and global terrorism.

The first half of this decade, marked by the events of September 11, 2001, saw continued economic and political volatility as well as the rise of global terrorism. Kidnapping also has become an all too common phenomenon in countries like Mexico and Colombia. Executives could be tempted to say: "The world has become a dangerous place and maybe we should concentrate on places like the United States and Western Europe."

We believe that global business is a long-term proposition. Companies cannot succeed by jumping in and out of countries when the going gets a little tough. Not only is it expensive, but customers and suppliers often remember when they were "deserted." Nestlé had some of its operations in South America nationalized and later resumed ownership. It then went through a second full cycle of nationalization and renewed ownership. Although the company contested and fought the actions as best it could, the attitude of senior executives was one of patience, knowing that these things happen and that, eventually, the regime would change and the assets would be returned. This company has had a real commitment to its global business and a long-term perspective, both of which have contributed to its unusual success.

Many countries could be considered difficult places in which to do business. It is important to have a realistic attitude toward these situations and to learn to live and work in a world of uncertainty and risk. The more you learn about other countries, the better you understand the risks involved. This enables better decisions to be made about entering a certain country and the steps necessary to manage the risks in that country.

The following story illustrates this well. One of the authors was having dinner with the president of a British bank's Canadian subsidiary and was describing some of his activities in East Africa to the bank president. The bank president commented about how risky it was to operate in Africa. This comment surprised the author, who understood the difficulties involved but had thought it possible to manage them. The bank president then described all the countries in South America in which the bank was operating and making money. To the author, South America had to be one of the riskiest places to operate at that time, and he said so. The bank president replied, "Not really; the bank has been there for a long time, and we understand the situation." Therein lies the moral: Familiarity with and understanding of a country provide the necessary perspective for accurately assessing risks, determining acceptable levels of risk, and managing those risks.

Companies need to have strategic and tactical plans for managing risks. Large companies can develop specialists in assessing risks to contribute to informed decision-making, and smaller ones can access specialist firms or consultants for information relevant to specific decisions. All companies are advised to listen to expatriates and locals working in the field when they provide systematic assessments of their environments required periodically as part of the normal business plan by the home office. Individual managers can add to the quality of their own decision-making by reading broadly, by understanding the history of regions in which they operate, and by seeking (and paying attention to) information from international field personnel. As globalization increases, more international representation in the senior ranks of corporate headquarters personnel will also increase the ability to assess risks in specific countries. A global viewpoint, an understanding of the culture, political and social situations, and a long-term commitment to global operations are essential.

Operating globally is different from operating at home, and those differences must be, and can be, understood. The costs of entering the global game can be high. But the experience can be rewarding financially for the corporation, as well as personally and professionally for the manager.

Notes

1   Temu, P. E., *The Unspoken Truth About Globalization: Eight Essays* (Lincoln, NE: iUniverse, 2007) 5, 7.
2   Ibid., at 5.
3   http://yaleglobal.yale.edu/about/history.jsp (accessed October 21, 2008).
4   Hill, C. *International Business: Competing in the Global Marketplace*, 3rd edn (Irwin McGraw-Hill, 2000) 5.
5   Rugman, A. M. and Hodgetts, R. M., *International Business: A Strategic Management Approach*, 2nd edn (Financial Times Prentice Hall, 2000) 438.
6   Alan Rugman and Karl Moore.
7   Palmisano, S., "The Globally Integrated Enterprise," *Foreign Affairs*, Vol. 85, Issue 3, May/June 2006, 127–136. See also "A Bigger World: A special report on globalization," *The Economist*, September 20, 2008, 12.
8   Prahalad, C. K. (1991) 51.

9   This section has been adapted from "Globalization: Hercules Meets Buddha," Lane, H. W., Maznevski, M. L., and Mendenhall, M., *The Blackwell Handbook of Global Management: A Guide to Managing Complexity* (Blackwell Publishers, 2004) 3–25.

10 Wilson, M., Center for Creative Leadership, personal communication.

11 Senge, P., *The Fifth Discipline* (Doubleday, 1990).

12 Weick, K. E. and Van Orden, P., "Organizing on a Global Scale: A Research and Teaching Agenda," *Human Resource Management*, Spring 1990, Vol. 29, No. 1, 49–61.

13 Senge, P. (1990) n. 11 above.

14 Harnden and Allenna (1994) 135.

15 Harnden and Allenna (1994) 16.

16 Beer (1981) 356.

17 Ashby, W. R., *Design for a Brain* (London: Chapman Hall Ltd. and Science Paperbacks, 1972) and *Introduction to Cybernetics* (London: Chapman Hall Ltd. and University Paperbacks, 1973).

18 Ashby, 207, n. 17 above.

19 Weick and Van Orden, 49, n. 12 above.

20 Rohwer, J. and Windham, L., "GE Digs into Asia," *Fortune*, October 2, 2000.

21 To understand and keep up to date on what is happening in the corporate world regarding international assignments of executives, we recommend obtaining a copy of the latest *Global Relocation Trends* published by GMAC Relocation Services and available at http://www.gmacglobalrelocation.com/.

22 *Worldwide ERC Global Benchmarking*, Volume 1, 2006. www.erc.org.

23 Chambers, E. G., Foulon, M., Handfield-Jones, H., Hankin, S. M., and Michaels, E. G., "The War For Talent," *The McKinsey Quarterly*, August 1998.

24 *Worldwide ERC Global Benchmarking*, Volume 1, 2006. www.erc.org.

25 GMAC 2005 *Global Relocation Trends*.

26 For a more in-depth discussion of the issue of the ROI of international assignments see McNulty, Y. and Tharenou, P., "Expatriate Return on Investment," Academy of Management Best Conference Paper, 2004, IM:F1; http://webusers.anetchi.com/~smcnulty/docs/AoM%20Best%20Conference%20Paper%202004%20IM%20-%20Expat%20ROI%20(Refs)%20(Copyright).pdf.

27 Athanassiou, N. (1995).

28 Harzing, A.-W., "Of Bears, Bumble-Bees, and Spiders: The Role of Expatriates in Controlling Foreign Subsidiaries," *Journal of World Business*, 36(4) (2001) 366–379.

29 Nahapiet, J. and Ghoshal, S.. "Social capital, intellectual capital, and the organizational advantage," *Academy of Management Review*, 23(2) (1998) 267–284. Nonaka, I., "A dynamic theory of organizational knowledge creation," *Organization Science*, 5(1) (1994) 14–37.

30 GMAC, *Global Relocation Trends*. 2008 Survey Report.

31 Tahvanainen, M., Welch, D., and Worm, V., "Implications of Short-term International Assignments," *European Management Journal*, Vol. 23, Issue 6, December 2005, 663–673.

32 GMAC, *Global Relocation Trends*. 2008 Survey Report.

33 Miller, E. L., "The International Selection Decision: A Study of Some Dimensions of Managerial Behavior in the Selection Decision Process," *Academy of Management Journal*, 16, No. 2 (1973) 239–252.

34 Loraine, L., *2002 Expatriate Risk Management Survey*, op. cit.

35 Kealey, D. J., *Cross-Cultural Effectiveness: A Study of Canadian Technical Advisors Overseas* (Ottawa: Canadian International Development Agency, 1990). This study was based on a sample of over 1300 people including technical advisors, their spouses, and host-country counterparts.

36 Ibid., at 8.

37 Franke, J. and Nicholson, N., "Who Shall We Send? Cultural and Other Influences on the Rating or Selection Criteria for Expatriate Assignments," *International Journal of Cross Cultural Management*, Vol. 2, No. 1, April 2002.

38 Adler, N. J., "Pacific Basin Managers: A *Gaijin*, not a Woman," *Human Resource Management*, Vol. 26(2), 1987. See also Adler, N. J. and Izraeli, D. N. (eds), *Women in Management Worldwide*, (M. E. Sharpe Inc, 1988). For a more recent article see Caligiuri, P. and Cascio, W. F., "Can We Send Her There? Maximizing the Success of Western Women on Global Assignments," *Journal of World Business*, 33(4), Winter 1998.

39 Mendenhall, M., Dunbar, E., and Oddou, G., "Expatriate selection, training and career-pathing: A review and critique," *Human Resource Management Journal*. In Lane H. and DiStefano, J. *International Management Behavior*, 2nd edn,

40 Ibid.

41 Matteau, M., *Towards Meaningful and Effective Intercultural Encounters* (Hull, Canada: Intercultural Training and Briefing Centre, Canadian International Development Agency, 1993).

42 Martin, D. C., and Anthony, J. J., "The Repatriation and Retention of Employees: Factors Leading to Successful Programs," *International Journal of Management*, September 2006.

43 Company web site http://www.outpostexpat.nl/default.asp?path=izaodwvo (accessed December 2, 2008).

44 GMAC, *Global Relocation Trends*. 2008 Survey Report.

45 Some suggested readings on the topic of culture shock include: Torbiorn, I., *Living Abroad: Personal Adjustment and Personnel Policy in the Overseas Setting* (Sussex, England: John Wiley & Sons Ltd, 1982); Adler, N., *International Dimensions of Organizational Behavior*, 3rd edn, (Cincinnati, OH: South-Western College Publishing, 1997) Chapters 8, 9; Oberg, K., "Culture Shock: Adjustment to New Cultural Environments," *Practical Anthropology* 7 (1960) 177–182; Grove, C. L. and Torbiorn, I., "A New Conceptualization of Intercultural Adjustment and the Goals of Training," *International Journal of Intercultural Relations* 9, No. 2 (1979).

46 Research on stress and adapting to stressful situations also suggests that there are physiological contributions as well. One reference that links physiology and culture shock is Wederspahn, G., "Culture Shock: It's All in Your Head . . . and Body," *The Bridge* (1981) 10.

47 For these generalizations we are drawing on Torbiorn, *Living Abroad*; the research literature described by Adler, *International Dimensions*; an excellent, but unpublished paper by C. B. Sargent, "Psychological Aspects of Environmental Adjustment," Oberg, K., "Culture Shock," *Practical Anthropologist* 7 (1960) 177–182; and our own experience with numerous executives and students around the world.

48 Kealey, D. J., *Cross-Cultural Effectiveness*, n. 35 above.

49 Ibid., 39. This framework was developed by Berry, J. W., "Acculturation as Varieties of Adaptation," in Padilla, A., (ed.), *Acculturation: Theory, Model, and Some New Findings* (Washington, D.C.: AAAS, 1980).

50 This figure was adapted from "Psychological Aspects of Environmental Adjustment," Sargent, C., source and date unknown.

51 See Adler, *International Dimensions*, Ch. 8.

52 Osland, J. S., *The Adventure of Working Abroad: Hero Tales from the Global Frontier* (Jossey-Bass Publishers, 1995) 165–192.

53 Harzing, A.-W., "Are our referencing errors undermining our scholarship and credibility? The case of expatriate failure rates," *Journal of Organizational Behavior* 23 (2002) 127–148.

54 *2002 Expatriate Risk Management Survey*, Mercer Human Resource Consulting, August 12, 2002. http://www.mercerhr.com/pressrelease/details.jhtml?idContent=1065135.

55 Stewart Black, J. and Gregersen, H. R., "When Yankee Comes Home: Factors Related to Expatriate and Spouse Repatriation Adjustment," *Journal of International Business Studies* 22, No. 4 (1991) 671–694; Stewart Black, J., Gregersen, H. R., and Mendenhall, M. E.,

"Toward a Theoretical Framework of Repatriation Adjustment," *Journal of International Business Studies* 23, No. 4 (1992) 737–760.

56   Gross Klaff, L., "The Right Way to Bring Expats Home," *Workforce,* July 2002, 40–44. See also the following articles for further discussions of repatriation: Bossard, A. B. and Peterson, R., "The Repatriate Experience as Seen by American Expatriates," *Journal of World Business* 40 (2005) 9–27; MacDonald, S. and Arthur, N., "Connecting Career Management to Repatriation Adjustment," *Career Development Journal,* Vol. 10, No. 2, 2005, 145–159.

57   GMAC 2002 Survey Report.

CHAPTER **7**

Managing Change in Global Organizations[a]

This chapter deals with the implementation of strategic organizational changes. As discussed in Chapter 5, managers have to be able to build global organizations that balance global integration against local responsiveness to effectively serve global customers. As the competitive environment changes, as it seems to do ever faster all the time, they also may have to reformulate their organization's strategy, which, in turn, may necessitate a realignment of how employees do their work and revised organizational structures and/or systems to support the new behaviors and the new strategy.

Global organizational change has been defined as "strategically aligned alterations in patterns of employee behavior within organizations operating across national borders."[1] For example, responding to market forces, the manager of a large Swiss-headquartered global chemical company decided that it would switch its European marketing strategy for its resins from selling on volume to increasing profit margins.[2] This strategic change necessitated adjustments in the organizational systems and in employee behaviors across its European subsidiaries. To increase profit margins, the organization had to offer more service to its customers in the form of advanced product know-how. The Swiss-located research and development division of the company possessed such knowledge, but systems had to be developed to share this knowledge across the European subsidiaries. The employee behavior also had to change. The engineers in the research and development division at headquarters now had to provide service to the sales managers of the European subsidiaries. Furthermore, the sales managers in each country location had to attract new customers who valued service over price and were willing to pay a premium for service, and the employees had to provide the service to these customers.

[a]We dedicate this chapter to the memory of Al Mikalachki who taught us about organizational change over two decades at the Ivey Business School in London, Canada and on whose work a large part of this chapter is based.

In the above case, being convinced of the ultimate success of his new strategy, the marketing manager neglected to prepare the organization and the employees for the change and instead merely announced it, which might have worked in the company's hierarchy-dominated headquarters in Basel, Switzerland. The employees in the other European subsidiaries overwhelmingly resisted. There were calls for the resignation of the manager, and the early results of the new strategy were poor. Only after the manager started to engage in meetings with the employees, offered employee training on the new service and customer behaviors, and slightly modified the strategy, did the employees adopt the necessary new behaviors. Some time later the new strategy became a huge success, substantially increasing the profit that the company made in the resin business.

The manager could have avoided, or at least ameliorated, the pains of executing the new strategy if he had paid attention to two issues. First, to be successful, a new strategy had to be the right response to the market and, second, it had to be implemented carefully. Even the "right" strategy will fail if it is not executed properly. Implementing global organizational change is neither a science nor an art, but it is a craft that takes discipline and attention to details. This chapter outlines a three-stage model that managers can use as a checklist for managing change. We will first explain the model and then we will address challenges that managers face in implementing change in global organizations.

THE CHANGE MODEL[3]

There are at least three types, and perhaps phases, of change: anticipatory, reactive, and crisis, as shown in Figure 7.1.

Ideally companies would like to be able to anticipate environmental shifts and make changes through a process of continuous learning and follow the path of renewal. This

FIGURE 7.1 Types of Change[b]

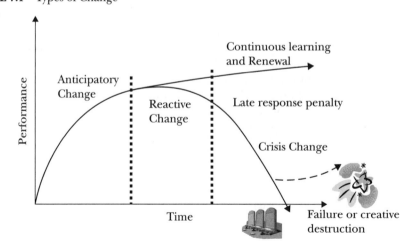

[b]This diagram was adapted (liberally) from our colleagues Peter Killing, Nick Fry, Rod White and Mary Crossan at the Ivey Business School and at IMD.

is not always easy to do when performance is still good and there are no real indicators that there is trouble ahead. And usually not everyone in the company will be looking out into the future far enough or be sensitive to important environmental shifts. The management challenge at this stage is educating people about the potential dangers and convincing them that they pose a threat. Anticipatory change generally proceeds at a pretty slow pace.

In the reactive stage, as performance begins to suffer after an environmental shift, more managers see the warning signs but they very likely may interpret them differently depending on their roles or functional perspectives. Change initiatives, although still not guaranteed, may move faster now, as more people acknowledge potential threats.

In the crisis stage, the problems are clear for everyone to see and crises generally encourage and permit rapid change. Indeed, they require it to survive. History is littered with examples of companies that resisted change or that did not respond fast enough to major changes in their industries. Polaroid missed the shift to digital photography. About the same time the Boston area was the center of the mini-computer industry that included companies like Digital Equipment, Wang, Prime, and Data General; none of these survived the personal computer revolution. Prior to December 2008, we often used the American automobile industry and General Motors in particular, as examples of the late response penalty. As we write this chapter, Chrysler has just filed for bankruptcy and many industry changes are underway, but the outcome won't be known for a while.

The change model (Figures 7.2–7.4) serves as a guide for change implementation. The model evolved from many case studies of discontinuous strategic change that altered how an organization conducted its business.[c] The model is applicable for anticipatory and reactive changes that permit executives time for environmental scanning, problem definition, and preparing the organization. It describes the steps in the management of one discontinuous strategic change, recognizing that the completion of one change effort becomes the foundation for future changes. Hence, it is a cyclical model. It is not a crisis management model. Crises, such as the problem of faulty Firestone tires on Ford sport utility vehicles, require immediate responses that typically may not allow for an extended analysis and the involvement of employees and other stakeholders.

The model illustrates the change process from the beginning to the end of the change cycle. Each step of the process identifies (1) the factors to which managers must attend and (2) the stakeholders that managers must involve. It takes into consideration the change phases when employees' old behaviors transition into new behaviors. A period of discomfort and resistance during the transition period occurs in most cases. People have to get used to breaking with the old behaviors while simultaneously learning the new behaviors. Operations during this period are not the most efficient, as the old system is not working as well as it used to and the new system is not yet working as well as it should be. During this period there is a risk of abandoning the change as people question the logic of working harder while performance declines. Understanding and preparing for these difficulties helps managers to guide the organization through the change process. The model encourages managers and other key players to take a planned and organized approach during each step, and keeps everyone aligned throughout the entire change process.

[c] Several of these case studies are listed in various footnotes in this chapter.

The model also recognizes that change occurs in a larger organizational context. If organizations can build a culture for change that becomes part of the organizational mindset, change processes will become more efficient (and the need for crisis management will decrease). Hence, the model can be a tool for creating a perpetual state of change readiness, the first step to the path of continuous renewal.

Finally, the model invites revisions to the change process depending on the organizational and cultural context. Although, for example, trust and respect are central to successful change processes, the ways of establishing trust and respect differ among cultures. In Canadian and American cultures, managers typically gain the trust of their employees by involving them as well as inviting and responding to their feedback. In other cultures this approach is less appropriate. When the Canadian manager of a Guyanese children's home applied participatory and team-based practices while leading a change effort, the Guyanese employees did not buy into her ideas.[4] They found her practices dubious and indicative of weakness ("Why would she ask us? Doesn't she know herself?"). They only started to trust and respect her when she finally employed authoritarian means of introducing changes in employee behaviors including punishment. The employees expected to be treated authoritatively and took it as a sign of competent leadership.

Determining the Required Changes

Presumably, having used the organizational alignment model in Chapter 5 as a diagnostic tool, executives have a good idea of the necessary changes needed in support of a new or modified strategic initiative. Clearly defining and articulating the strategic objective (e.g., increase the market share to 20 % in the Chinese market) is important in designing the change process and in communicating the change. Additionally it motivates employees with a goal. Managers determine the new tasks that the organization will now need to do well (e.g., generate more contacts with buyers) and specify the new employee behaviors (e.g., call buyers during the morning when they are most likely to be available, limit conversations to five minutes per buyer). Behaviors that are specific, concrete, observable, and easy to visualize are a powerful tool for communicating change initiatives to employees. They help employees to focus on what they will do in the future, thereby reducing their uncertainty about the implications of the strategic change. It is important that managers be able to describe strategic objectives, new employee behaviors, and the new systems and structures clearly, in easily understood language. More importantly, employees benefit from understanding how they can contribute towards achieving this goal.

To facilitate the performance of the new behaviors, managers also must consider adjustments in the alignment model. Too often these efforts focus only on changes in the reward system (e.g., a bonus for generating more than 100 new contacts per month). However, most often strategic change and the resulting alterations in employee behavior require much more than changes in the reward system. As discussed in Chapter 5, if employees do not have relevant experience for enacting the new behaviors, managers may need to offer training. Furthermore, new behaviors may necessitate new technology (e.g., advanced phone systems) and a new organizational structure (e.g., change from a structure by product to a structure by client).

Having done the analysis and having determined what needs to be done, the managers are now in a position to design the change. This is often a neglected step as managers tend to go right from the "answer" to implementation, often with unintended consequences. One example of this "rush to implementation" was the Swiss chemical example described earlier in this chapter.

Another example that avoided this mistake was the American company Black & Decker.[5] The president of the Asia region wanted to revamp the HR strategy by putting more emphasis on internal feedback. The intent was to help his managers and employees improve their job performance. The president decided to introduce a 360-degree feedback system that had been designed and already implemented successfully in the US. This new system required more assertive feedback behaviors from employees. He even provided specific examples of these new behaviors, such as giving and receiving constructive feedback not only from superiors but also peers and subordinates.

However, he immediately met resistance from local Asian managers, who raised concerns that local employees would not accept and use the system because of culturally engrained attitudes towards staffing, leadership, feedback, and confidentiality. Therefore, the president made adjustments to the system such as using the 360-degree feedback for management level employees only and rolling out the new system in phases. Had he not taken the time to assess the readiness for change in the organization with his managers, he likely would not have been successful.

Phase 1: Appraising the Readiness for Change

An organization's readiness for change is determined by analyzing several factors that affect the support of or resistance to the change initiative, such as the visibility of the need for change, the organization's management style, the past history of change processes, and the timing of the change.

Visibilty of the Need for Change

- How visible is the need for change? When an organization is doing well and engages in anticipatory change (preparing for future changes in the environment), managers and employees will not necessarily see the need for change. "If it ain't broke, don't fix it," or "Why should we change something that works well?" are common comments in organizations. If, however, changes in the environment have already occurred and the organization engages in reactive change, managers and employees will more easily recognize why the organization's strategy and employees' behaviors have to change.
- Diagnosing the visibility of the need for change is important because (1) employees will not partake in the change unless they see the need for change forcing managers to establish it; (2) the more the need for change is visible to employees, the more managers can accelerate the change process.
- What is the organization's management style and what is the management style required for the change? Employees may be used to a management style that differs from the management style needed to lead the change effort. Many change practitioners in

the West advise a participatory style for managing change that involves the employees (change targets). In many cultures, however, employees are used to authoritarian management styles and might be confused if they had a voice in the change process. The earlier mentioned example of the employees in the Red Cross Children's Home in Guyana was such a situation. Conversely, in reactive change efforts (and even more so in crisis change efforts), the change agent (leader of the change process) may decide on a less participatory style in order to speed up the process.

- What is the history of change processes? If change processes went awry in the past, employees may mistrust new change efforts. In the foreign subsidiaries of global organizations, often expatriates come in for limited term assignments, unleash a major change effort, and then leave after a couple of years, independent of the completion of the change process. This leaves local employees distinctly uncomfortable with the next expatriate's change initiative.
- What is the timing? Managers have to assess the timing of the change effort. If the resources of the organization are already stretched to the limit, it does not make sense to launch an anticipatory change effort that will further stretch resources. Such situations can arise during recessions, peak seasons, or when changes occur concurrently with other change efforts (e.g., a product launch).

Top Management Support and Commitment   Employees evaluate the sincerity of a change effort in large part on the basis of top management support and commitment. Hence, the visibility of top management support is critical for implementing change successfully, especially in the early stages of the change process. Top managers, in conjunction with the change agent, should be the initial communicators of the change effort. Employees will be more likely to engage the change effort enthusiastically if top managers make the effort to explain the goals of the change (e.g., new employee behaviors) and the change process. In addition, top management signals the importance of an organizational change through the allocation of resources. Top management support alone will not elicit a change in employee behaviors. However, the absence of top management support might result in resistance or indifference among employees.

Change Agent Appraisal   In selecting a change agent, managers need to ask three questions:

- Does the change agent have power to implement the change? Power can be positional, expert, or personal, all relating to the credibility of the change agent. But note that different cultures emphasize different aspects of the bases of power. If employees do not have confidence or trust in the change agent, it will be difficult to motivate them to change. What are the change agent's personal motivations? The change agent must support the change and act as a positive example for change targets.
- What are the change management knowledge, skills, and abilities of the change agent? The change agent should have communication, management, and conflict resolution skills to carry out the change effort. And the more cultural boundaries that the change crosses, the greater the need for cross-cultural skills in these areas.

Target group identification   The key players in a change process include the immediate change targets (employees who will have to engage in new behaviors) and other stakeholders, such as unions, suppliers, or customers whose business, systems, or behavior may be affected. Managers need to think about this group in the broadest possible terms by considering links between the immediate target group and others with whom they may be interdependent.

If a global organization embarks on an organization-wide change effort, both headquarters and foreign subsidiaries are affected. Subsidiaries may differ with regard to effective change processes, depending on local cultural differences, proximity to headquarters, and the relationship between headquarters and subsidiaries. Hence, managers of global change must understand local differences to determine the processes needed to motivate the expected change in employee behaviors. Furthermore, implementing a strategic change throughout locations in many countries will require a team of change agents. The Swiss-headquartered global chemical company described at the start of this chapter illustrated the different reaction to a strategic change of headquarters and subsidiaries. In assessing change targets, two questions are critical.

- First is the ability question. Can they do it? What are the knowledge, skills, abilities, and resources the change targets need to perform the new behaviors? Even if they support the change, they may not be able to behave appropriately. The fear of inability often leads to anxiety and can undermine support for a change. If employees cannot perform the new behaviors, the change process will have to include employee training and the provision of other resources (e.g., tools and machinery) needed to perform new behaviors. A lack of resources will lead to frustration.
- Second is the motivation question. Will they do it? What is the predisposition of employees toward the change? Will they support or resist it? In our opinion, this is the single most important question to assess the organization's readiness for change because high motivation leads people to acquire the needed skills and to exert the extra effort that contributes to success. Managers need to identify opponents as well as supporters and analyze the reasons for the resistance or support.[d] This analysis provides information about how opposition may be turned into support. If change targets resist because, for example, they do not see the need for change, managers, could explain the links between the new strategy, the new behaviors, and the improvements for the organization and the employees.

Are there preemptive problems like previous failed change efforts and a lack of trust that will discourage employees from engaging the change effort? If so, then these issues need to be addressed before moving forward.

Here also is where cultural differences potentially play an important role and managers need to understand cultural differences, especially with respect to expectations of employees about the way managers should go about making changes and the employees' expected role in any change process. Good knowledge of local ways of expressing agreement and disagreement and about dealing with conflict are also very important.

---

[d]For a good, succinct discussion of this topic see Paul Strebel, "The Politics of Change", IMD Perspectives for Managers, No. 2, February 1997

FIGURE 7.2   Assessing the Readiness for Change

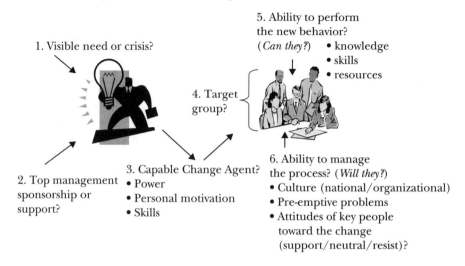

Figure 7.2 is a summary of Phase 1. Assessing the readiness for change can be viewed as a gap analysis that assesses an organization's and its employees' current capabilities against the capabilities and behaviors needed to enact the new strategy. Our advice is that if any of the answers to the questions asked in Figure 7.2 are "no," then it is important to stop and work to turn those answers into "yes." On the basis of this gap analysis, managers create an initial action plan and select a change agent.

Phase 2: Initiating Change and Adopting the New Behavior

Leading a strategic change is a full-time effort and requires intimate knowledge of the organization, which is why in most cases the change agent is a capable and respected insider. A capable change agent is one who has the requisite power, motivation, and change management skills. These skills include analysis, communication, conflict resolution and, in global organizations, cultural intelligence. Once chosen, he or she needs to initiate the change by making sure the right people are in place for the new tasks and by building support for the change effort.

Selection and Training   To perform new behaviors, employees must be able to do so. If the change calls for behaviors that current employees do not have the potential to perform, managers must select new employees. If current employees have the potential to perform the new behavior, but do not yet possess the ability to do so, the change agent has to find a way to get them the necessary training. Selection and training should occur early because inability to perform the new behaviors causes employees to be frustrated, leading to lowered efforts or resistance.[6]

We want to be clear about our use of the terms "selection" or its opposite, "de-selection." By "de-selection" we do not necessarily mean firing a person. They may be transferred to another job or department, for example. The important point to remember is that if new tasks are part of the strategic change, then it is important to have in place people who can perform these new behaviors.

Building Support for the Change   The change agent needs to build commitment and a winning coalition to support the change, establish the need for change, and devise and communicate a roadmap to all stakeholders.

Devise and communicate a road map   The first priority is to devise a roadmap that shows change participants how to achieve the strategic objectives, new behaviors, and new organizational systems that were determined in step one. The roadmap includes a description of the goals of the change process (strategic objectives, new behavior) and the path towards these goals (e.g., skill training to learn the new behaviors) with specific timelines. The road map serves as a starting point, and the change agent updates it throughout the change process.

Establish the need for change   The change agent needs to ensure top management support or build support for it as necessary. Top management can provide both direction and resources (e.g., funds) and has the power to remove obstacles. More importantly, top management support signals the importance of the change effort. If top management is not on board, neither the change agent nor the target group will be either. The best way for top management to support the change is to be visibly involved by attending and leading meetings and contributing in task forces. The change agent facilitates the involvement of top management and also makes sure that top management has reasonable expectations. Because of its symbolic value, visible top management support is particularly critical in the early phases of the change process. It is preferable that top management announce the launch of the change process.

Demonstrate that past behavior has been costly and cannot be continued   Put more positively, it means it is essential to convince the target group that learning the new behaviors will lead to benefits such as improved performance for their organization, recognition for them or, possibly, monetary rewards. Learning new behaviors can be stressful and at first glance seems more costly than sticking with old habits. It is imperative that managers convincingly show that, after a suitable adjustment period, survival and success will follow.

Since change is a complex undertaking that involves many different people and possibly different cultures and many different interpretations of the situation, it is usually difficult to convince people of the need to change with just our words or a memo. We encourage you to use as many different media and types of data as possible. In the case of the Swiss-headquartered chemical company we have been using as an example in this chapter, the manager had to demonstrate that the switch from a volume-oriented to a profit-margin-oriented strategy would improve the bottom line of the subsidiaries. The manager showed that the market was saturated and, hence, increasing sales volumes would be difficult if not impossible. Understanding this relationship between the new marketing strategy and the bottom line, the subsidiary managers were more willing to learn the new customer service behaviors. In other words, the manager spoke to the subsidiary managers' self-interest and addressed the question of "What's in it for us?" Customer service behaviors were instrumental in moving prices up, which in turn improved profit margins and ultimately the compensation of the subsidiary managers.

Other types of first-hand data could be generated by visiting customers or suppliers, for example.

Obtain commitment

Obtain commitment   Next, the change agent needs to obtain commitment from the target group and build a winning coalition. A clearly communicated and a data-driven new strategy will build commitment as will a diligent assessment of the readiness for change. However, it is most important that the target group is involved in the change process. Involvement breeds ownership of and commitment to the change process and to the solutions.

Involvement requires skillful leadership, as people may initially resist a change effort. It also takes time and, hence, is hardly feasible in crisis-driven change management. As soon as top management has announced the change effort, you can invite and react to the feedback. Input by the change agent and employees who will be involved, in particular with regard to the new behaviors, increases the likelihood of learning and enacting the behaviors.

Maintain participation in the change effort

Maintain participation in the change effort   The change agent also must ensure that the target group stays involved throughout the change process. This involvement has to give the employees a voice through, for example, meetings, suggestion boxes, and one-on-one conversations. An effective change process typically includes joint discussions between the target group, the change agent, and top management. If the change yields negative outcomes for employees, such as job loss, outside facilitators may join the discussions to assist handling potential hostility.

The benefits of involving the target group are obvious. Employees will know more about the change process and their task-related knowledge is relevant in particular for determining new behaviors. As mentioned before, the most important benefit is a sense of ownership. It also becomes easier for this group to convince their peers to join in the change effort.

In obtaining commitment and gaining participation of employees in the change effort, the *mode* of involvement needs to be appropriate to the cultural norms of the situation. But it is equally important that the assessment of the appropriate mode not be based on stereotypes or assumptions based on partial or inaccurate information. A good example of this occurred in Argentina when Holcim, one of the top global cement companies with headquarters in Switzerland, bought two competing family companies outside of Buenos Aires.[e] Early in the period after the takeover, the training and development head from Switzerland suggested that one way of helping the managers and supervisors in the acquired firms to understand the business model was to run a tailor-made simulation of Holcim operations (called Ecoman). But when the Argentine-born Swiss CEO and his technical director (also Swiss) offered the opportunity, the local company managers and supervisors declined to attend, citing how busy they were. The CEO then decided to invite the union members and senior workers to attend the training. At first glance

---

[e] See *"Merging Two Acquisitions: How Minetti Built a High-Performance, Cohesive Organization"* (A & B), IMD cases 3-1484 and 3-1485), Joseph DiStefano and Mope Ogunsulire.

this would seem to clash with the hierarchical sensitivities of Latin managers, and both this technical director and other locals warned the CEO against this move "brought in from outside."

But he understood that the union employees were highly motivated to improve operations (there had already been some lay-offs and the very severe Argentine financial crisis had just devastated the economy), and he knew they were well-educated and thoughtful. It turned out that they not only benefited from better understanding the complexities and imperatives of the business operations, but, stimulated by their new knowledge, started offering suggestions to significantly improve performance. Soon the CEO and his technical director realized that this was a new way of using the simulation, and they attended the closing sessions of all the programs. And it wasn't long afterwards that the managers, who were "too busy" earlier, eagerly joined in the development program themselves. Conventional wisdom in international settings isn't always right.

Adopting New Behaviors   The previous process of selection and training should have put in place employees who are able to engage in the new behaviors. Furthermore, the processes of establishing the need for change and obtaining commitment should have built motivation to engage in the new behaviors. The adoption of new behaviors, in most cases, however, is not a one-day event. It is a process with ups and downs that can be smoothed by using such tools as (1) continuous management of resistance, (2) transition devices to remove obstacles and improve employee performance, and (3) ongoing, open, and honest communication of progress.

1   **Continuous management of resistance** In the adoption phase, managers continue to manage resistance by eliminating reasons for resisting change. Even within a single change effort, these reasons likely vary among change targets. Five common reasons for resistance are poor communication, lack of trust, failure to establish the need for change, ignoring change targets' self-interest, and low tolerance for change.

    a.   *Poor communication*: In anticipatory change and even reactive change, resistance is most likely a result of different interpretations of the company's situation. The challenge is to establish the most accurate interpretation and to educate the employees.

    In the case of Minetti, the Argentine cement company, the CEO constantly visited the factories in various locations, talking to the workers as well as the managers about the threats from the financial upheaval as well as the opportunities by becoming the industry leader during the turmoil. This constant communication at all levels and in all locations was a critical element in the success of the changes.

    •   Top management must state the problem that the change is designed to solve (e.g., task duplication or customer complaints), the change goal (expected outcome), the relevance of the problem (e.g., solving the problem will improve market share by 10 %), and communicate a first draft of the change process, with a timetable. This draft should include concrete opportunities for target group involvement (e.g., feedback tools and time-lines) and a timeline for updates by top management or the change agent.

- Often, the initiators of a change forget that the target group is not yet on the same page with regard to the problem, change goal, and change process. In addition, the initiators of the change and the change targets may have different cultural backgrounds. Thus, the change agent has to take into consideration the perspectives of various groups of employees with regard to their knowledge of the change and their preferred mode of communication. Remember, this is the *Bridging* (B) part of the MBI model. If managers are not highly skilled or knowledgeable about the local culture, they may benefit from the use of facilitators and cultural mentors.

- The communication strategy should include feedback opportunities such as meetings (town hall and small group), surveys, and suggestion boxes. The purpose is to develop a dialogue. Depending on the cultural background, employees will react differently to feedback devices. In the case of the Red Cross Children's Home in Guyana, employees did not take advantage of the Canadian change agent's open door policy. When, however, she actively sought feedback and offered alternate solutions, employees did not hesitate to offer their opinion.

Despite a communication strategy, employees may misinterpret the messages because they do not listen openly. In that case, managers have likely failed to identify the true reason for employee resistance. In other cases, it may be the managers themselves who have missed or misinterpreted the employees' messages because the manner of delivering the feedback was unfamiliar. For example, indirect feedback through a trusted third party may be the local way of disagreeing upwards, while simultaneously *seeming* to agree when talking directly to a superior. This can be very confusing to a manager from a culture where disagreement is openly and directly expressed, regardless of different status levels of those involved.

b. *Lack of trust.* Employees may not trust managers. There are three primary reasons for lack of trust:
- Employees harbor doubts about the ability of the managers and change agent to lead the change successfully. Managers and change agents can overcome these doubts only through their actions. This point illustrates the importance of selecting a capable change agent.
- Employees are concerned whether top management, managers, and the change agent will "walk the talk." Be careful not to make and then break promises. Instead, act predictably. Change is a time of uncertainty and it is important that those who lead the change help people regain a sense of control which results from knowing what to expect.
- Employees suspect that top management, managers, and the change agent are not entirely forthcoming and complete in their communication. Overcoming this suspicion is handled by interacting frequently with employees. Frequent interactions in most cases result in more open communication and allow for involvement.

c. *Failure to establish the need for change.* As we said earlier, in anticipatory and reactive change efforts, it may be difficult to establish the need for change. The target group may view a change effort through the lens of current or past successes and ask why something should be fixed that is not broken. Success breeds comfort and inertia. It takes considerable dedication to overcome the negative side effects of success. The key tool for doing this is open dialogue:

- Managers and change agents share and explain all the data that convinced them to launch a change initiative.
- Although top management may initially announce the change, subsequently they, the change agents, and the target group listen and provide input.
- Effective dialogue means that the quality of the ideas, not the status of the sender, determines the contribution to the change effort.

An open dialogue fulfills several purposes. First, it clears the air. Open dialogue initially often leads to the release of built-up emotions. Secondly, it creates involvement. Thirdly, it builds understanding of the problem, the change goal, and the change process. Fourthly, it results in shared and hence credible interpretations of the data and the change process.

Open dialogue takes time, something that managers do not have in crisis change. Instead, they must act quickly. It may be tempting to push through with a change process by creating crises. We do not recommend the use of such a tactic, as employees will either call the manager's bluff or the organization is exposed to unnecessary risks.

d. *Self-interest.* Whether a change serves the self-interest of the target group is a function of the cost and benefits of the new behaviors in which they will have to engage. Different combinations of costs and benefits suggest different courses of action for managers and change agents:

- If it is anticipated that benefits will outweigh costs, change agents may accelerate the change process by fully involving the target group.
- If the target group anticipates only costs and no benefits, they likely will resist the change. Involvement is counterproductive. In the case of downsizing, for example, managers should downsize first and then work with the remaining employees. The morale of the remaining employees will still suffer from the downsizing. And remember, the process of downsizing is important. How it was done and how the employees who were let go were treated will be important to those who remain. It is also important for the remaining employees to have as clear an idea as possible of the extent of downsizing.

The CEO of Minetti and his team treated the people initially laid off generously and were certain that they had gained the trust of those who remained. But as the economic crisis deepened and continued long past their earlier estimates, the benefits to those who had stayed, only to be laid off later, were much diminished by the devaluation of the currency. The emotional distress caused to them, and to the CEO and his team who initially had actively persuaded some key people to stay, was severe. This lesson may be especially appropriate in the circumstances that we write this chapter, as each day seems to bring more bad news without the expected "bottoming out" of the recession.

- If the target group expects a balance of benefits and costs, change agents have to allow for negotiations. Change targets will seek to improve the benefits or reduce the costs of the change. It is imperative that managers and change agents do not abuse their power in negotiations. The abuse of power leads to perceptions of unfairness. It alienates the other party in the negotiation and observers.

  e. *Low tolerance for change.* Three common scenarios are:
     - A general fear of changes. Bad experiences in the past or a predisposition against changes can lead to resistance.
     - A fear of the specific change. There may be fear because of potential negative consequences. Address general and specific fears by being empathetic and demonstrating with a person-centered perspective (*de-centering*) that the change will have benefits.
     - Stress because of too many changes. If too many changes take place in the organization, it makes sense to prioritize change initiatives to avoid organization-wide stress. If the stress stems from other changes outside the organization, managers and change agents are limited in their actions.

When employees show a low tolerance for change, managers and change agents have to be sensitive not to step outside their abilities. It can be helpful to seek outside help. As mentioned earlier, in addition to the continuous management of resistance, managers and change agents use transition devices to improve employee performance on new behaviors.

2 **Transition devices** Other tools to smooth the ups and downs of the adoption of new behaviors are facilitators, task forces, and allocation of additional resources.

   a. Facilitators can play the role of mediators in negotiations among managers, change agents, and the target group. They can also assist in dealing with individual employees. Finally, facilitators also may be trainers who improve the target group's knowledge, skills, and abilities.

   b. Task forces are effective in dealing with unforeseen obstacles in the change process. Strategic change is a complex endeavor, and more often than not, additional problems are uncovered as the process unfolds. Alternately, task forces can be a forum for negotiations, for example, between management and unions. Task forces typically bring together a small group of managers and employees to solve a specific problem. A clear mandate and timeline help task-forces succeed.

   c. To adopt the new behaviors, employees must not only be motivated and capable. In addition, they need the resources to enact the behaviors. In the Swiss-headquartered global chemical company, for example, subsidiary managers needed access to detailed product information to improve their customer service. The research and development division at headquarters had to make this information available.

3 **Ongoing, open, and honest communication about progress** Change agents need to "showcase" short-term wins but not declare victory too soon.

a. *Showcasing short-term wins:* The sharing of short-term wins, even if they are small, will reduce uncertainty. In the Swiss-headquartered global chemical company, while the early overall results of the new strategy were poor, in some subsidiaries local managers quickly enacted the new customer service behaviors and soon observed that many customers willingly paid a higher price for a commodity product (resins). The sharing of this information indicated that the change goal of moving from a volume-based to a profit-margin-based strategy might work. Moreover, sharing this information showed that management had rewarded employees who engaged in the new behaviors. Managers and change agents can plan for small wins by providing interim performance goals.[f]

It is not sufficient to only benchmark behaviors against strategic goals. The results of the benchmarking have to be made public. They will either represent a new need for change (in the case of negative results) or become a reason for a celebration of success. Showcasing successes is critical because employees appreciate being part of a winning team, which in turn increases commitment and breeds self-confidence.

b. *Not declaring victory too soon:*[7] As important as it is to showcase small wins, it is equally important not to confuse achieving interim goals with final success. George W. Bush's premature declaration of the end of major combat operations in Iraq signaled by the huge banner behind him stating "Mission Accomplished" during a televised speech from a US Navy aircraft carrier on May 1, 2003 may be the best modern example of the dangers of this point.

Many writers on the subject of change would argue in favor of the "theory of the small win." It is the small, incremental changes that stand the best chances of success.[8] Unless forced by a crisis into making major, system-wide changes, you may be wise to start small and let the change mature and grow. The diffusion of change beyond its initiation depends in large measure on perceived success – continuation of change is fueled by such success and, unless early success is apparent, the chances of realizing your goals are slim.

FIGURE 7.3 Initiating the Change

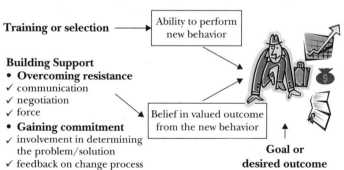

[f]"Leading Change", John Kotter, *Harvard Business Review,* March-April 1995

"Small" wins are not necessarily small but rather they are intermediate changes on the road to a larger strategic change. Keep in mind that they are real and visible success stories that validate your decisions and actions. They build credibility, commitment, and allies and reduce the power of critics. Our recommendation in planning a change effort is to make sure you have designed in some small wins.

Figure 7.3 is a summary of Phase 2.

Phase 3: Reinforcing the Change

New behaviors are sustainable only if the organization supports and rewards them.

Reward new behaviors The first rule is that what you told the target group would happen actually does happen. Recognizing that it is not feasible to control all variables in a change process, this is where the theory of the small win plays an important part. If you design your change plan to incorporate small wins, then you have some control over positive reinforcement that supports the change. Employees will continue to engage in the new behaviors if the rewards (both tangible and intangible) match their expectations. They must see that their behaviors advance the organization's goals and serve their self-interests.

Realignment of the organizational alignment model If the present alignment model is not consistent with the new behaviors, managers must adjust it. Typically, a new alignment model is already part of the change goal, but additional modifications may be necessary. For example, as mentioned earlier, in the Swiss-headquartered global company, information systems were put into place to allow the sharing of product information between headquarters and subsidiaries.

This step is critical. Employees respond to signals that systems such as reward and evaluation systems send. It does no good to train employees in new behaviors and attitudes and then put them back in an organizational system that inhibits these new behaviors.

Benchmark new behaviors The new behaviors must contribute to the new strategic goals; otherwise they represent a new need for change. Hence, managers and change agents benchmark the new behaviors against the new strategic goals. In the Swiss-headquartered global company, the manager could benchmark customer service behaviors against profit margin goals. He also could benchmark these behaviors by comparing them to the profit margins of competitors that did not require employees to engage in these behaviors. Figure 7.4 is a summary of Phase 3.

Organizational change efforts are not one-time events. They are processes that require discipline and communication. Skipping a part of the change process can result in failure of the change initiative.[9] The change mode focuses on issues that managers have to consider in change efforts. It also suggests actions that they can take. The model, in particular, centers on enabling and motivating employees to engage in the new behaviors.

Although the change model suggests a process for completing one change, it should not be interpreted to suggest that change is a one-time effort. It is more meaningful to think about change as a continuous process that can be broken into meaningful phases.

FIGURE 7.4 Reinforcing the Change

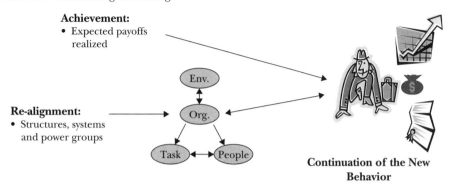

The Change-Ready Organization In Chapter 5, we noted that the role of senior managers was to interpret information from their external environment, combine this with an understanding of the organization's internal strengths and weaknesses, and create alignment to achieve strategic objectives. Organizational scholars traditionally have viewed organizational alignment models as a means of reducing the variability and increasing the stability of human behavior,[10] and models like total quality management or Six Sigma programs, for example, do that. Global corporations, however, do not operate in stable and predictable environments. The 2008 Global CEO study by IBM characterized it as a frenetic environment – and the pace of change is increasing.[11] This study of 1130 CEOs from 40 different countries in 32 industries found that:

> Organizations are bombarded by change, and many are struggling to keep up. Eight out of ten CEO's see significant change ahead, and yet the gap between expected change and the ability to manage it has almost tripled since our last Global CEO Study in 2006.[12]

The 2006 study found that 61 % of the CEOs expected substantial change in the following three years, but only 57 % said that their organizations had changed successfully in the past. Those numbers in 2008 were 83 % and 61 % respectively.

In Chapter 6, we pointed out that trying to manage a global company with models and processes designed to reduce variation in an environment that is characterized by dynamic complexity will probably be ineffective or possibly work only in the short term; and in responding to dynamic complexity, organizations had to find the right people and to create the appropriate organizational processes for managing the complexity and executing action plans.

Global managers have to develop organizational cultures and alignment models that facilitate change, on the one hand, to fulfill the traditional task of creating stability and predictability and, on the other hand, to allow for agility, flexibility, and adaptation to changing environmental conditions.[13] As one of the CEOs in the IBM study stated:

> *The key to successful transformation is changing our mind-set. For large companies, it is easy to be complacent – we have to change this. Our company culture must have a built-in change mechanism.[14]*
> **Masao Yamazaki, President and CEO, West Japan Railway Company**

Below we describe elements of an organizational alignment model for the change-ready organization:

People   Change-ready organizations require change-ready people, and not just at top management levels – people who are motivated to change and who have the knowledge, skills, and abilities to change. With a cadre of change-ready people it is easier to develop a culture of embracing change.

Motivation   The motivation to embrace change may be hard to train. Hence, change-ready organizations assess the change attitudes of job applicants. WestJet Airlines, a Canadian airline, for example, looks for people who seek involvement, are generally positive, have a high tolerance for change, and want to learn.

Knowledge, skills, and abilities   Organizations that are change-ready either have change agents who can assume numerous roles throughout the change process or have the ability to involve a set of people who can assume at least one of the roles. Lawrence and his colleagues found that change-ready organizations had evangelists, autocrats, architects, and educators.[15]

Evangelists share ideas and create conditions for employee involvement in change efforts. They are skillful communicators, use diverse influence strategies, and can present messages from different perspectives. Carlos Ghosn, the CEO of Renault/Nissan, emphasized the role of communication in managing the French-Japanese merger of Renault and Nissan. When asked about communication, he stated that he communicated 24 hours a day adhering to the notion that "(1) you say what you think, (2) you do what you think, (3) you make sure that it is understood, and (4) you accept that you are going to be measured on what you communicated."

Autocrats are critical for the translation of good ideas into action. Top management support is a critical ingredient for successful change efforts. Although employee involvement is the key to lasting change, the prudent use of authority is needed to move along change processes. Autocrats endorse change ideas and accept accountability. Their key skill lies in understanding when change efforts need a push toward action. At McDonald's Mexico, the Mexican managers and employees were uncertain about the prospects of offering a breakfast menu. The Canadian CEO took a risk and obtained the funds for rebuilding the kitchens. The Mexican managers and employees then moved forward with the breakfast project, which became a solid contributor to revenues.

Architects embed the change into systems and structures by realigning the organization and creating a new organizational alignment model. They make sure that the systems support the new employee behaviors through, for example, information systems or through a redesign of work spaces. Their key skill is a deep understanding of how the organization functions.

Finally, educators strive to implant the organizational change into the fabric of the organization. They present data that the new employee behaviors help the organization achieve its strategic objectives. In doing so, they show employees the meaning of their contribution to organizational success and seek to reenergize them for future change efforts.

Tasks   In traditional stable organizations, employees have clearly specified tasks. In change-ready organizations, core tasks are more fluid. Employees engage in the following behaviors to support the change readiness of their organization.

Stay in touch with the environment   Organizations that embrace change continuously scan their environment. The early detection of environmental shifts facilitates anticipatory change and possibly results in first mover advantages. The tasks of most if not all employees include contact with the environment, particularly customers. Other contact points include suppliers, members of the surrounding community, and law-makers. IBM, for example, has largely abandoned the separation of the customer contact and design of information technology solutions. Instead, most members of a customer-focused team are in contact with the customer.

Share and acquire information   Employees actively search for and share information. Information about environmental shifts is quickly spread throughout the organization. Information acquisition and sharing is particularly important in global organizations because different subsidiaries might have experience in dealing with similar environmental shifts. When the Canadian CEO of McDonald's Mexico led the subsidiary through the 1994 Peso devaluation crisis, he contacted his Brazilian colleague. The Brazilian subsidiary had already experienced a currency devaluation and his colleague recommended that McDonald's Mexico should immediately increase its prices because the government would likely move to freeze prices. The CEO of McDonald's Mexico followed that advice, and indeed shortly thereafter the Mexican government froze the prices.

Seek involvement   The Change Model suggests that employee involvement is the most powerful means of obtaining commitment to change because it breeds a sense of ownership. In change-ready organizations employees seek out change opportunities. They involve themselves and do not have to be asked to be involved. In these organizations, job descriptions that narrowly define tasks are antithetical. Instead employees look to increase task scope as necessary. Hence, compared to traditional, stable organizations, the responsibility for determining tasks and task scope lies more with the employees than simply with the organizational model.

Continuously develop knowledge and skills   In organizations that are ready to change, learning and training are not occasional events but ongoing activities. Training can help build change management skills and a future-directed orientation. It occurs both systematically and on an ad hoc basis.

Organization   The organization enables people to accomplish their tasks. Without getting into too much detail, we provide examples of the structures and systems in change-ready organizations.

Structures   The larger organizations become, the more difficult it is to react to environmental changes. Change-ready organizations break their structures into smaller units and push accountability down the line. The result is dispersed leadership that needs to be reconnected through integration mechanisms. Common examples of accountable units are cross-functional teams that address the demands of internal and external customers. Change-ready organizations also do not only tolerate but encourage informal structures. Informal structures and networks accelerate the dissemination of information, and they can make up for deficiencies in formal structures. For example, in customer-centric structures, informal networks among product engineers serve as an integration mechanism across products.

Systems Change-ready organizations use systems that connect their employees with each other and the organization. For example, Procter and Gamble's intranet includes a feature that allows employees to share their ideas for product improvement and new products. The globally operating consulting firm Accenture uses social networking technologies to connect its 180 000 employees.

Reward Systems Traditionally organizations have paid employees (and most organizations still do so) on the basis of their jobs. Instead of job-based pay, change-ready organizations use person-based pay. Person-based pay recognizes that in change-ready organizations, job descriptions are largely mute, as employees' core tasks may continuously change.[16] Instead, periodic goal-setting meetings and subsequent goal achievement determine person-based pay.

Conclusion

When the IBM study compared the financial performance of the companies in its sample, it found that the change gap, the difference between expected change and the history of successful change in higher performers, was smaller not because they faced fewer challenges but because they anticipated more changes. The study concluded that "outperformers are simply more successful at managing change."

Changing an organization is easier said than done. Strategic changes of the type we have discussed involve people and the tasks they perform. In our opinion there probably is no such thing as "immaculate" strategic change in which the organization transforms itself without requiring some employees to change their behavior in some way. Organizations do not change, people do, but we can be lulled into thinking about organizational change too remotely and impersonally. Therefore, it is important to remember that *change means behavioral change*. People in key roles have to change their behavior, which is a function of their beliefs, assumptions, perceptions, tasks, and roles. And the tasks and roles are reinforced by evaluation, measurement, and reward systems. These do not change easily or quickly. To accomplish strategic change, managers have to work with individuals and groups of people as well as structures, systems, and practices.

Change can be a challenge in any culture, but when trying to make changes in a global company in multiple countries, the challenge can be compounded by different cultural understandings. The MBI (Chapter 3), organizational alignment (Chapter 5), and change models are tools that will give you greater confidence to negotiate the challenges.

Notes

1   Spector, B., Henry W. Lane, H. W., and Shaughnessy, D., "Managing Strategic Change in a Global Firm," *Journal of Applied Behavioral Science* (forthcoming 2009).
2   Kashani, K., "Alto Chemicals Europe (AR1)," IMD case IMD-5-0484, 2008.

3   Most three-stage models of organizational change like the one we present in this chapter trace their conceptual lineage back to Kurt Lewin. His article "Frontiers in Group Dynamics: Concept, Method and Reality in Social Science; Social Equilibria and Social Change" was published in *Human Relations* Vol. 1, No. 1, in 1947. This article presented a three-stage model (unfreeze, move, refreeze) as well as the concepts of constancy and resistance to change, social fields, force fields, and group decisions as a change procedure.

Al Mikalachki built on and modified Lewin's work in his development of a model for thinking about and managing organizational change. Mikalachki's complete model was first outlined in Mikalachki, A. M., *Managing organizational change,* unpublished manuscript, Richard Ivey School of Business. University of Western Ontario, 1997. It also appeared in Mikalachki, A. and Gandz, J., *Managing Absenteeism* (London: University of Western Ontario, School of Business Administration, 1980). We are appreciative to Al for his work and support in our teaching at the Western Business School (now Ivey) and want to recognize clearly the intellectual lineage of these ideas about change and the model.

4   Dietz, J., Goffin, M., and Marr, A., "Red Cross Children's Home: Building Capabilities in Guyana (A)," Ivey case 9B02C042, 2002.

5   Morrison, Allen J. and Black, J. Stewart "Black & Decker-Eastern Hemisphere and the ADP Initiative (A)," Ivey case 98G005, 1998.

6   Mikalachki, n. 3 above.

7   Kotter, J., "Leading Change," *Harvard Business Review,* March–April 1995.

8   Quinn, J. B., "Managing Strategic Change," *MIT Sloan Management Review* (Summer 1980).

9   "Leading Change," n. 7 above.

10   Katz, D. and Kahn, R. L., *The Social Psychology of Organizations* (1978).

11   *The Enterprise of the Future* (IBM, 2008).

12   Ibid., at 14.

13   Worley, C. G. and Lawler, E. E., "Designing organizations that are built to change," *MIT Sloan Management Review* 48(1) (2006) 19–23.

14   *The Enterprise of the Future,* n. 11 above, at 17.

15   Lawrence, T. B., Dyck, B., Maitlis, S., and Mauws, M. K., "The underlying structure of continuous change," *MIT Sloan Management Review,* 47(4) (2006) 59–66.

16   Worley and Lawler (2006), n. 13 above.

CASE 6

Blue Ridge Spain

Yannis Costas, European managing director of Blue Ridge Restaurants, found it difficult to control the anger welling up inside him as he left the meeting with the company's regional vice-president (VP) earlier in the day. That evening, he began to reflect on the day's events in the relative peace of his London flat. "Ten years work gone down the drain," he thought to himself, shaking his head. "What a waste!"

Costas recalled the many years he had spent fostering a successful joint venture between his company, Blue Ridge Restaurants Corporation, and Terralumen S.A., a mid-sized family-owned company in Spain. Not only had the joint venture been profitable, but it had grown at a reasonably brisk pace in recent years. Without a doubt, partnering with Terralumen was a key reason for Blue Ridge's success in Spain. Therefore, Costas

Jeanne M. McNett prepared this case under the supervision of David Wesley and Professors Nicholas Athanassiou and Henry W. Lane solely to provide material for class discussion. The authors do not intend to illustrate either effective or ineffective handling of a managerial situation. The authors may have disguised certain names and other identifying information to protect confidentiality.

was somewhat dismayed to find out that Delta Foods Corporation, Blue Ridge's new owner, wanted out. Yes, there had been recent tension between Terralumen and Delta over future rates of growth (see Exhibits 2 and 3), but the most recent round of talks had ended in an amicable compromise — he thought. Besides, Delta's senior managers should have realized that their growth targets were unrealistic.

They had gone over the arguments several times, and Costas tried every angle to convince his superiors to stick with the joint venture, but to no avail. To make matters worse, Costas had just been assigned the unpleasant task of developing a dissolution strategy for the company he had worked so hard to build.

BLUE RIDGE RESTAURANTS CORPORATION

Blue Ridge was founded in Virginia in 1959, and quickly established a reputation for quality fast food. In 1974, after establishing more than 500 food outlets in the United States and Canada, Blue Ridge was sold to an investment group for US$4 million.

Over the next five years, the company experienced sales growth of 96 per cent annually. However, international sales were haphazard and there was no visible international strategy. Instead, whenever a foreign restauranteur wanted to begin a Blue Ridge franchise, the foreign company would simply approach Blue Ridge headquarters with the request. As long as the franchise delivered royalties, there was little concern for maintaining product consistency or quality control in foreign markets.

In 1981, Blue Ridge was acquired by an international beverages company for US$420 million. Under new ownership, the company made its first major foray into international markets, and international operations were merged with the parent company's existing international beverage products under a new international division.

The strategy at the time was to enter into joint ventures with local partners, thereby allowing Blue Ridge to enter restricted markets and draw on local expertise, capital and labor. Partnering also significantly reduced the capital costs of opening new stores. The strategy of local partnering, combined with Blue Ridge's marketing know-how and operations expertise, quickly paid off in Australia, Southeast Asia and the United Kingdom, where booming sales led to rapid international expansion.

On the other hand, there were some glaring failures. By 1987, Blue Ridge decided to pull out of France, Italy, Brazil and Hong Kong where infrastructure problems and slow consumer acceptance resulted in poor performance. Some managers, who had been accustomed to high margins and short lead times in their alcoholic beverages division, did not have the patience for the long and difficult road to develop these markets and would tolerate only those ventures that showed quick results.

These early years of international expansion provided important learning opportunities as more managers gained a personal understanding of the key strategic factors behind successful foreign entry. The success of the company's international expansion efforts helped Blue Ridge become the company's fastest growing division. When Blue Ridge was sold to Delta Foods in 1996 for US$2 billion, it was one of the largest fast-food chains in the world and generated sales of US$6.8 billion.

Delta was a leading soft drink and snack food company in the United States, but at the time of the Blue Ridge acquisition, it had not achieved significant success internationally.

It had managed to establish a dominant market share in a small number of countries with protected markets in which its main competitors were shut out. For example, one competitor was shut out of many Arabic countries after deciding to set up operations in Israel.

The company's senior managers disliked joint ventures, in part because they were time-consuming, but also because they were viewed as a poor way to develop new markets. Delta was an aggressive growth company with brands that many believed were strong enough to support entry into new overseas markets without the assistance of local partners. When needed, the company either hired local managers directly or transferred seasoned managers from the soft drink and snack food divisions.

Delta also achieved international growth by directly acquiring local companies. For example, in the late 1990s, Delta acquired the largest snack food companies in Spain and the United Kingdom. However, given that joint ventures had been the predominant strategy for Blue Ridge, and that some countries, such as China, required local partnering, Delta had no choice but to work with joint venture partners.

YANNIS COSTAS

Yannis Costas was an American-educated Greek who held degrees in engineering and business (MBA) from leading U.S. colleges. Although college life in a foreign country had its challenges, it afforded him an opportunity to develop an appreciation and understanding of American culture and business practices. Therefore, upon completing his MBA, Costas turned-down several offers of employment from leading multinational corporations that wanted him to take management positions in his native country. Such positions, however appealing they may have been at the time, would have doomed him to a career as a local manager, he thought. He chose instead to accept a position in international auditing at Blue Ridge headquarters in Virginia, mainly because of the opportunity for extended foreign travel.

The transition from university to corporate life was a difficult one. Social life seemed to revolve around couples and families, both at Blue Ridge and in the larger community. Although Costas met some single women from the local Greek community, his heavy travel schedule prevented him from establishing any meaningful relationships. Instead, he immersed himself in his work as a way to reduce the general feeling of isolation.

Costas was fortunate to have an office next to Gene Bennett, the company's director of business development. Bennett had served as a lieutenant in the U.S. Navy before working in the pharmaceutical industry setting up joint ventures in Latin America and Europe. He was hired by Blue Ridge specifically to develop international joint ventures. As Costas' informal mentor, Bennett passed on many of the lessons Costas would come to draw on later in his career.

It was at the urging of Bennett that Costas applied for a transfer to the international division in 1985. Three years later, Costas was asked to relocate to London, England, in order to take on the role of European regional director for Blue Ridge. In this position, he became responsible for joint ventures and franchises in Germany, the Netherlands, Spain, Northern Ireland, Denmark, Sweden and Iceland.

In 1993, Costas was transferred to Singapore where, under the direction of the president of Blue Ridge Asia,[1] he advanced in his understanding of joint ventures, market entry and teamwork. Over the next five years, Costas built a highly productive management team and successfully developed several Asian markets. He was eager to apply these new skills when he returned to London in 1998 to once again take up the role of European director (see Exhibit 1 for a summary of Costas' career).

EXHIBIT 1   TIMELINE

Year	Blue Ridge Restaurants	Yannis Costas
1959	Company founded in Virginia	
1974	Blue Ridge sold for $4 million	
1975–1980	96 per cent annual growth	Leaves Greece to study in United States
1981	Blue Ridge sold for $420 million	
1982	International expansion	Completes his BS in United States
1983	Begin negotiations for JV in Spain	
1984		Completes MBA and is hired by Blue Ridge; moves to Virginia
1985	JV agreement with Terralumen S.A.	Applies for transfer to International Div.
1986	Rodrigo appointed managing director of Blue Ridge Spain	
1987	Company pulls out of France, Brazil, Hong Kong and Italy	
1988		Promoted to European regional director; moves to London
1988–1993	Spanish JV grows slower than expected	
1993	U.S. manager sent to oversee Spanish JV	Transfer to Singapore
1995	Rodrigo replaced by Carlos Martin	
1996	Blue Ridge sold to Delta for $2 billion	
1995–1998	Spanish JV grows more rapidly	
1998	5-year plan for 50 restaurants in Spain, Blue Ridge has 600 stores in Europe/ME	Costas asked to return to London
Jan. 1999		Rescues JV in Kuwait
May 1999	Södergran hired as Delta VP for Europe	
June 1999	Directors meeting for Spanish JV	
December 1999	Dryden withholds Delta payment to JV; Alvarez sells prime Barcelona property	
January 2000		Asked to develop dissolution strategy for Spain

THE SPANISH DECISION

When the decision was first made to enter the Spanish market, Bennett was sent overseas to meet with real estate developers, construction companies, retail distributors, agribusiness companies, lawyers, accountants and consumer product manufacturers in order to gather the preliminary knowledge needed for such an undertaking. Bennett soon realized that Blue Ridge would need a credible Spanish partner to navigate that country's complex real estate and labor markets.

Few Spaniards among Bennett's peer generation spoke English. However, Bennett had a basic knowledge of Spanish, a language that he had studied in college, and this helped open some doors that were otherwise shut for many of his American colleagues. Still, Bennett knew that finding a suitable partner would be difficult, since Spaniards frequently appeared to distrust foreigners. The attitude of one investment banker from Madrid was typical:

> Many Spaniards do not want to eat strange-tasting, comparatively expensive American food out of paper bags in an impersonal environment. We have plenty of restaurants with good inexpensive food, a cozy atmosphere and personal service, and our restaurants give you time to enjoy your food in pleasant company. Besides, we don't even really know you. You come here for a few days, we have enjoyable dinners, I learn to like you, and then you leave. What kind of relationship is that?

Luckily, Bennett had a banker friend in Barcelona who recommended that he consider partnering with Terralumen.

TERRALUMEN S. A.

Terralumen was a family-owned agricultural company that had later expanded into consumer products. In doing so, Terralumen entered into several joint ventures with leading American companies. In recent years, Terralumen had also begun to experiment with the concept of establishing full-service restaurants.

Bennett was introduced to Francisco Alvarez, Terralumen's group vice-president in charge of restaurant operations and the most senior non-family member in the company. In time, Bennett had many opportunities to become well acquainted with Terralumen and its managers. On weekends he stayed at Alvarez's country home, attended family gatherings in Barcelona and had family members visit him in Virginia. Over the span of their negotiations, Bennett and Alvarez developed a solid friendship, and Bennett began to believe that Terralumen had the type of vision needed to be a successful joint venture partner.

After two years of negotiations, Blue Ridge entered into a joint venture with Terralumen to establish a Blue Ridge restaurant chain in Spain. Upon returning to Virginia, Bennett could not hold back his euphoria as he related to Costas the details of what he considered to be the most difficult joint venture he had ever negotiated.

BLUE RIDGE SPAIN

Alvarez hired Eduardo Rodrigo to head up the joint venture as its managing director. An accountant by trade, Rodrigo was a refined and personable man who valued his late afternoon tennis with his wife and was a professor at a university in Barcelona. He also spoke fluent English.

Before assuming his new role, Rodrigo and another manager went to Virginia to attend a five-week basic training course. Upon his return, Rodrigo's eye for detail became quickly apparent as he mastered Blue Ridge's administrative and operating policies and procedures. He knew every detail of the first few stores' operating processes and had an equally detailed grasp of each store's trading profile. As a result, Blue Ridge Spain began to show an early profit.

Profitability was one thing; growth was another. Although the Blue Ridge concept seemed to be well received by Spanish consumers, Rodrigo was cautious and avoided rapid expansion. Moreover, one of the most important markets in Spain was Madrid. Rodrigo, who was Catalan,[2] was not fond of that city and avoided travelling to Madrid whenever possible. As personal contact with real estate agents, suppliers and others was necessary to develop new stores, Blue Ridge's expansion efforts remained confined to the Barcelona area. Terralumen, becoming impatient with Blue Ridge's sluggish growth, decided to focus more resources on its consumer product divisions and less on the restaurant business.

For Costas, one of the challenges during his first assignment as European director was to convince Terralumen to focus more on the joint venture and support faster growth. Rodrigo positively opposed more rapid growth, even though Alvarez, his direct superior, voiced support for the idea. Although he had been very cordial in his interactions with his American counterparts, Rodrigo believed himself to be in a much better position to judge whether or not the Spanish market would support faster growth.

In 1993, shortly after Costas was transferred to Singapore, Blue Ridge decided to send one of its own managers to oversee the Spanish joint venture. Under pressure, Rodrigo began to ignore criticism about the company's lack of growth. On one occasion, Rodrigo decided to close the Blue Ridge offices for an entire month just as Blue Ridge's international director of finance arrived in Barcelona to develop a five-year strategic plan.[3]

Terralumen finally replaced Rodrigo with a more proactive manager who had just returned from a successful assignment in Venezuela. Under the new leadership of Carlos Martin, Blue Ridge Spain began to prosper. Soon everyone was occupied with the difficult task of acquiring new sites, as well as recruiting and training employees.

COSTAS RETURNS TO EUROPE

In late 1998, Costas was transferred from Singapore to London to resume the role of European managing director. The previous director had performed poorly and it was felt that Costas had the experience needed to repair damaged relations with some of Blue Ridge's Middle Eastern joint venture partners. By this time, Blue Ridge had more than 600 stores in Europe and the Middle East.

One of Blue Ridge's more lucrative joint ventures was in Kuwait. However, the partners were threatening to dissolve the enterprise after the previous managing director became upset that the Kuwaitis were not meeting growth targets. The partners were especially concerned when they discovered that he had begun to seek other potential partners.

Costas decided to schedule a visit to Kuwait in early January. The partners counselled against the visit since Costas would be arriving during Ramadan,[4] and therefore would not be able to get much work done. Nevertheless Costas went to Kuwait, but spent nearly all of his time having dinners with the partners. He recalled:

> Most American managers would have considered my trip to be a waste of time, since I didn't get much "work" done. But it was a great opportunity to get to know the partners and to re-establish lost trust, and the partners felt good about having an opportunity to vent their concerns.

Costas returned to London confident that he had reassured the Kuwaiti partners that Blue Ridge was still committed to the joint venture.

Costas was also happy to be working with his old friend Alvarez again, as the two began working on an ambitious plan to develop a total of 50 stores by 2002 (see Exhibit 2).[5] As Blue Ridge Spain continued to grow, stores were opened in prime locations such as the

EXHIBIT 2 Development Plan Agreed Between Blue Ridge Restaurants and Terralumen (as of December 1998) (in 000s U.S. dollars)

	1998	2000	2001	2002	2003	2004
No. of Stores	12	24	37	50	65	80
Avg. Annual Sales	700	770	847	932	1,025	1,127
Gross Sales	$8,400	18,480	31,339	46,600	66,625	90,160
Cost of Goods Food	1,680	3,322	5,474	8,141	11,639	15,770
Cost of Goods Direct Labor	1,680	3,323	5,641	8,374	11,646	15,766
Advertising/Promotion	504	1,109	1,880	2,796	3,998	5,410
Occupancy Costs	1,260	1,848	3,129	4,660	6,663	9,016
Fixed Labor	840	1,478	2,507	3,728	5,330	7,213
Miscellaneous	168	277	470	699	999	1,352
Royalties to Blue Ridge U.S.	420	924	1,560	2,330	3,331	4,508
Total Costs	6,552	12,281	20,662	30,728	43,606	59,035
Contribution to G&A	1,848	6,199	10,677	15,872	23,019	31,125
Salaries and Benefits	875	1,531	2,641	3,493	4,580	5,899
Travel Expenses	120	240	300	375	469	586
Other	240	312	406	527	685	891
Occupancy Costs	240	720	828	952	1,095	1,259
Total G&A	1,475	2,803	4,175	5,347	6,829	8,635
Earnings Before Interest/Tax	$373	3,396	6,502	10,525	16,190	22,490
% of Gross Sales	4.44	18.38	20.75	22.59	24.30	24.94
Office Employees (Spain)	10	20	30	35	40	45

Notes to Exhibit:

- This plan was agreed before Yannis Costas' appointment to Blue Ridge Europe in late 1998.
- End 2004 plan: 20 stores in Barcelona, 30 in Madrid, 30 in other cities
- Capital Investment per store $700,000 to $1 million
- Site identification, lease or purchase negotiation, permits, construction: 18 to 24 months. Key Money is a part of occupancy costs. It is a sum paid to property owner at signing; varies by site $100,000 plus. Up to 1999, many owners wanted Key Money paid off the books, often in another country.
- Store Staffing (at the average sales level):
  - One manager, two assistants full time (larger stores three to four assistants)
  - 10 to 12 employees per eight-hour shift (40 hours per week); 980 employee hours per week
- Store employees needed by end of 1999: 300; by the end of 2004: 2,250 (approx.)
- Store employee attrition: approximately 25 per cent per year
- Dividends from earnings were declared periodically and then were shared equally between partners.

Source: Company files.

prestigious Gran Via in Madrid and Barcelona's famous Las Ramblas shopping district. Costas and Alvarez, both of whom had been involved from the beginning of the joint venture, were delighted to see how far the company had come.

EUROPEAN REORGANIZATION

Delta began to take a more direct and active role in the management of Blue Ridge. In Europe, for example, Delta created a new regional VP position with responsibility for Europe, the Middle East and South Africa. When Costas became aware of the new position, he asked whether or not he was being considered, given his extensive experience in managing international operations. The human resources department in the United States explained that they wanted to put a seasoned Delta manager in place in order to facilitate the integration of the two companies.

Although disappointed, Costas understood the logic behind the decision. He also considered that by working under a seasoned Delta manager, he could develop contacts in the new parent company that might prove favorable to his career at some future date.

In May 1999, Costas received a phone call from Bill Sawyer, Blue Ridge's director of human resources, whom Costas had known for many years.

> *Sawyer:* We hired someone from Procter and Gamble. He's 35 years old and has a lot of marketing experience, and he worked in Greece for three years. You'll like him.
>
> *Costas:* That's great. Have your people found anyone for the VP job yet?

The line was silent, then Sawyer replied in an apologetic tone, "He is the new VP." Costas was dumbfounded.

> *Costas:* I thought you said you were planning to transfer a Delta veteran to promote co-operation.
>
> *Sawyer:* Nobody from Delta wanted the job, so we looked outside the company. Kinsley (president, international division) wanted a "branded" executive, so we stole this guy from P&G.

Sawyer went on to explain that Mikael Södergran, who was originally from Finland, had no background in restaurant management, but had achieved a reputation for results in his previous role as a P&G marketing manager for the Middle East and Africa. He had recently been transferred from Geneva, Switzerland to P&G European headquarters in Newcastle upon Tyne.[6] Södergran was not happy in Newcastle and saw the Delta position both as an opportunity to take on greater responsibility and to move back to the civilization of London.

"You couldn't find anyone better than that?," Costas exclaimed. He was furious, not only for having been deceived about the need to have a Delta manager as VP, but also that he, with 10 years' experience managing international operations, had been passed over in favor of someone with no experience managing operations, joint ventures or a large managerial staff. Nevertheless, the decision had been made, and Södergran was scheduled to start in two weeks.

THE DIRECTORS' MEETING

It was Södergran's first day on the job when he met with Blue Ridge Spain's board of directors to discuss a recently drafted consultants' report and negotiate new five-year growth targets (see Exhibit 3). The study, which was conducted by a leading U.S.-based management consulting firm, projected significant expansion potential for Blue Ridge in Spain, as well as in France and Germany, where Blue ridge had no visible presence.[7] Delta also wanted to increase the royalties and fees payable from the joint venture partner in order to cover the cost of implementing new technologies, systems and services (see Exhibit 4).

Other Blue Ridge managers at the meeting included Yannis Costas and Donald Kinsley, Blue Ridge's new international president. Although Kinsley had formerly been president of a well-known family restaurant chain in the United States, this was his first

EXHIBIT 3 Consultants' Recommendations Blue Ridge European Expansion (Selected Markets)

	1998	*2000*	*2001*	*2002*	*2003*	*2004*
Stores						
Spain	12	30	65	100	135	170
France	0	10	20	55	90	130
Germany	3	15	30	65	100	150
Total	15	55	115	220	325	450
Regional Managers (London)	1	15	20	22	24	26
Country Staff/Managers	12	40	90	180	220	250
Store Employees	215	1,650	3,450	6,600	9,750	13,500

Source: Company files.

EXHIBIT 4   Blue Ridge Spain Exceptional Term Highlights

	Blue Ridge U.S. Desired Objective	Blue Ridge Spain – Variance
Joint Venture Outlets		
Royalty	At least 4 per cent	No royalty
Fees	$20,000	$5,000
Term	10 years	5 years
Exclusivity	Avoid exclusivity	Spain, Canary Islands, Spanish Sahara, Balearic Islands
Advertising	5 per cent, right of approval	No obligations
Outlet Renewal Requirements	Renewal fee at least $2,000; Upgrading or relocation	No fee or other specific requirements
Delta Products	Required	No requirement
Development Program	Schedule for required development of territory	No requirement
Non-Competition	Restrictions on similar business	No provision
Assignment	First refusal right; approval of assignee	No provision
Sub-Franchising		
Contract privity	Blue Ridge U.S. should be a party and successor to franchisor	Blue Ridge cited; Blue Ridge succeeds on JV dissolution
Royalty	At least 4 per cent	None
Fees	$20,000	None
Joint Venture Operation		
Equity Participation	More than 50 per cent	50 per cent
Profit Distribution	At least 50 per cent	Additional 20 per cent when profits are greater than 20 per cent
Actual Management	Blue Ridge U.S. should appoint General Manager	General Manager is from JV partner
Board Control	Blue Ridge U.S. should have majority	Equal number of board members

Source: Company files.

international experience. Terralumen was represented by company president Andres Balaguer, Francisco Alvarez and Carlos Martin, Blue Ridge Spain's managing director.

Even before the meeting began, Delta's management team assumed that Terralumen was content to keep growth rates at their current levels and would have to be pressed to accept more aggressive targets. As expected, Martin protested that his team of 10 managers could not handle the introduction of 30 new stores a year, as suggested by the study. The meeting's cordial tone quickly dissolved when Södergran unexpectedly began to press the issue. His aggressive stance was not well received by Terralumen, who in turn questioned the ability of the consulting firm's young freshly minted American MBAs to understand the intricacy of the Spanish fast-food market. Balaguer simply brushed off the study as "a piece of American business school cleverness."

Södergran became visibly annoyed at Balaguer's refusal to consider Delta's targets. "The contract says that you are required to grow the markets," Södergran demanded. Balaguer, a tall, elegant man, slowly stood up, lifted a sheaf of papers and replied, "If this is your contract, and if we rely on a contract to resolve a partnership problem, well, here is what I think of it and of you." He walked across the room and dropped the papers into a garbage can. Then upon returning to his seat, he remarked in Spanish, "If this meeting had been conducted in my language, you would have known what I really think of you," in reference to Södergran.

After a long pause, Costas tried to mend the situation by pointing out that Terralumen had already committed to considerable growth, and had therefore already come some way toward Delta's expansions goals. He suggested that the two companies break to consider alternatives.

A few weeks later, Costas sent an e-mail to Södergran outlining his recommendations (see Exhibit 5).

EXHIBIT 5   Costas' Recommendations

From: Yannis Costas [Costas@deltafoods.co.uk]
Sent: Wednesday, July 7, 1999 10:16 AM
To: 'Sodergran@deltafoods.co.uk'
Subject: Key Issues - Here is what I believe we should be going for in Spain.

Mikael:
Here are my recommendations for Spain.

A   PRESERVE PARTNERSHIP
  • Need a "real" market success while developing markets elsewhere in Europe.
    —Fuel interest of potential partners elsewhere.
    —Keep Blue Ridge and Delta believing in European potential.
    —Market for real testing of concepts and ideas.
    —No complete reliance on UK for "successes."
B   REVERSAL NOT EASY TO OVERCOME
  • May have to pay a high premium to buy out joint venture.
  • Will lose all key managers (no substitutes on hand)
  • If we inherit "green field"
    — Down time close to 2 years.
    —Why? From decision to opening will take approximately nine months to one year.
    —In a new market this will be longer as we have no human resource experience to draw on.
    —Potential new partners need to be convinced about why we broke up with a "good" partner.
    —Real estate market does not want to deal with foreigners or raises the price.
  • If the divorce is messy, we may be bound by the current contract for another year.
C   WORK TOWARDS ACHIEVING ACCEPTABLE INTEGRATION WITH OUR DESIRABLE CONTRACT FRAMEWORK OVER CURRENT DELTA PLANNING HORIZON (5 YEARS)
  • Strong development schedule for joint venture.
  • Royalty integration over mutually acceptable period.
  • Designated "agency" for franchisees immediately, but fee flow indirectly to Blue Ridge only the amount over current terms with existing franchisees. Phase-in higher flow on schedule similar to royalties.
  • Accept the notion of phasing in royalties as we phase in systems and services (If we don't phase them in there won't be much of a business anyhow!)
D   KEY RATIONALE
  • We may have the perfect contract, but no stores to apply it to for three years - hence no income to cover overheads. SO . . .
  • Accept half the current growth targets with the full expectation that by year 3 or 5, there will be a decent system for the contract's objectives to be meaningful.

EMERGING CONFLICTS

Costas tried his best to keep an open mind with regard to Södergran and to support him as best he could. However, as time went on, Costas began to seriously question Södergran's ability. He never seemed to interact with anyone except to conduct business. On one occasion Costas suggested that they have dinner with the joint venture partners. Södergran replied, "Oh, another dinner! Why don't we get some work done instead?"

Costas became more concerned after Södergran rented a suite two floors below the company offices "in order to have some peace and quiet." Some of the regional headquarters staff began to wonder if Södergran had taken on too much responsibility and whether he was avoiding them because of the pressure he was under. Costas also believed that Södergran was uncomfortable with him, knowing that he resented not being offered the VP position.

In October 1999, Delta sent a finance manager from the snack foods division to become the company's new VP of finance for Europe. Geoff Dryden had no overseas experience, but when he was in the United States, he had been involved in several large international acquisitions. Dryden, who was originally from North Carolina, was pleasant, well polished in his manners and dress, and very proud of his accomplishments at Delta. For him, the European assignment was an opportunity to move out of finance and, if all went well, to assume greater managerial responsibilities.

Costas, who had specialized in finance when doing his MBA, had always done his own financial projections and was not very fond of the idea of surrendering this responsibility to someone else. Still, he helped Dryden as much as needed to make accurate projections, taking into account the unique aspects of each market.

A NEW STRATEGY

Over the next six months, the joint venture board of directors met four times. In the end, Terralumen committed to half the growth rate originally proposed by Delta and agreed to make upward revisions if market conditions proved favorable. Delta's managers were clearly becoming frustrated by what they perceived to be their partner's entrenched position.

After the final meeting, Södergran and Costas met with their European staff to discuss the results. Dryden asked why they put up with it. "Why don't we just buy them out?" he asked, calling to mind Delta's successful acquisition of a Spanish snack food company. Costas reminded Dryden that not only were snack foods and restaurants two very different enterprises, but all the joint venture managers had come from Terralumen, and most would leave Blue Ridge if Delta proceeded to buy out the partners.

After the meeting, Dryden discussed the situation privately with Södergran. Noting that a major loan payment would soon be due to one of their creditors (a major Spanish bank), Dryden suggested holding back Delta's contribution, thereby forcing the joint venture company to default on the loan. If all went according to plan, the joint venture would have to be dissolved and the assets divided between the partners. This, he noted, would be much less expensive than trying to buy out their partner.

As expected, Terralumen requested matching funds from Delta, but Dryden simply ignored the request. However, unbeknownst to Dryden or anyone else at Delta, Alvarez proceeded to sell one of the company's prime real estate properties and lease back the store as a means of paying the loan.

Costas happened to be in Barcelona working on Blue Ridge Spain's marketing plan with Carlos Martin. One evening, Costas was dining with his counterparts from Terralumen when Alvarez mentioned the sale of the company's Barcelona property. Costas, who at the time was unaware of Dryden's strategy, was dismayed. Real estate values in Barcelona were expected to appreciate significantly over the short term. Selling now seemed illogical. Furthermore, Costas was surprised to discover that Alvarez had been given power of attorney to make real estate transactions on behalf of the joint venture. Alvarez explained:

> Quite a few years ago, when you were in Singapore, Blue Ridge decided to give Terralumen this authority in order to reduce the amount of travel required by your managers in the United States. Besides, as you know, it is not often that good properties become available, and when they do, we must act quickly.

On his return to London, Costas discussed the real estate transaction with Dryden, who, upon hearing the news, furiously accused Costas of "siding with the enemy." Costas was quick to remind Dryden that he had not been privy to the dissolution strategy and, besides, the whole thing was unethical. Dryden retorted, "Ethics? Come on, this is strategy, not ethics!"

Dryden was clearly surprised by the news, especially given the fact that Delta would never have given such powers of attorney to a joint venture partner. The company's lawyers could have warned Dryden, but he had not been very fond of the "old hands" at Blue Ridge's legal affairs department, and therefore had chosen to not disclose his plan. Now that his strategy had failed, an alternative plan would have to be devised.

Costas felt torn between his responsibility to his employer and his distaste for the company's new approach. This whole thing was a mistake, he believed. Costas discussed his views with Södergran:

> We cannot hope to take over the stores in Spain while simultaneously developing new markets in Germany and France. Where are we going to find suitable managerial talent to support this expansion? People in Europe don't exactly see the fast-food industry as a desirable place to grow their careers. And besides, Delta hasn't given us sufficient financial resources for such an undertaking.
>
> Why don't we focus on France and Germany instead, and continue to allow Terralumen to run the Spanish operation? Revenue from Spain will help appease Delta headquarters while France and Germany suffer their inevitable growing pains. In the meantime, we can continue to press Terralumen for additional growth.

Södergran dismissed these concerns and instead gave Costas two weeks to develop a new dissolution strategy. Costas was furious that all his suggestions were so easily brushed off by someone who, he believed, had a limited understanding of the business.

On his way home that evening Costas recalled all the effort his former mentor, Gene Bennett, had put into the joint venture 16 years earlier, and all the good people he had

had the privilege to work with in the intervening years. Just as all that work was about to pay off, the whole business was about to fall apart. Why hadn't he seen this coming? Where did the joint venture go wrong? Costas wondered what to do. Surely he had missed something. There had to be another way out.

This case was made possible through the generous support of Darla and Frederick Brodsky through their endowment of the Darla and Frederick Brodsky Trustee Professorship in International Business.

APPENDIX 1   Management Styles For Selected Nationalities[a]

Spain

In Spain, a strong differentiation of social classes and professional occupations exists. Business communication is often based on subjective feelings about the topic being discussed. Personal relationships are very important as a means to establish trust, and are usually considered more important than one's expertise. Established business contacts are essential to success in Spain. Therefore, it is important to get to know someone prior to conducting business transactions. Only intimate friends are invited to the home of a Spaniard, but being invited to dinner is usual.

Spaniards are not strictly punctual for either business or social events, and once a business meeting is started, it is improper to begin with a discussion of business. National pride is pervasive, as is a sense of personal honor. To call someone "clever" is a veiled insult. Only about 30 per cent of local managers speak English, while French is often the second language of choice for many older Spaniards.

Greece

Greek society employs a social hierarchy with some bias against classes, ethnic groups and religions. For Greeks, interpersonal relationships are very important when conducting business, and decisions are often based on subjective feelings. Much importance is placed on the inherent trust that exists between friends and extended families. Authority lies with senior members of any group, and they are shown great respect. They are always addressed formally.

While punctuality is important, it is not stressed. Greeks have a strong work ethic and often strive for consensus.

a   Based on Kiss. Bow. or Shake Hands: How to do Business in Sixty Countries. Adams Media, 1994. The descriptions do not account for individual differences within each nationality or culture.

United States

Americans are very individualistic, with more stress placed on self than on others. Friendships are few and usually based on a specific need. Personal contacts are considered less important than bottom line results. Americans have a very strong work ethic, but a person is often considered to be a replaceable part of an organization. Great importance is placed on specialized expertise. Punctuality is important.

Business is done at lightning speed. In large firms, contracts under $100,000 can often be approved by a middle manager after only one meeting. Often companies and individuals have a very short-term orientation and expect immediate rewards. Small talk is very brief before getting down to business, even during dinner meetings and social gatherings.

Finland

Finns have a strong self orientation. More importance is placed on individual skills and abilities than on a person's station in life. Decisions are based more on objective facts than personal feelings. Privacy and personal opinions are considered very important. Finns often begin business immediately without any small talk. They are very quiet and accustomed to long silences, but eye contact is important when conversing. Authority usually rests with the managing director. Punctuality is stressed in both business and social events.

Notes

1   At the time, Blue Ridge Asia was one of the company's most successful operations with nearly 800 restaurants in Singapore, Malaysia, Taiwan and Thailand.
2   Catalonia, a state in northeast Spain, had a distinct culture and language (Catalan).
3   In Spain, the month of August was traditionally set aside for vacations.
4   Ramadan is the holy month of fasting ordained by the Koran for all adult Muslims. The fast begins each day at dawn and ends immediately at sunset. During the fast, Muslims are forbidden to eat, drink or smoke.
5   The plan to develop 50 stores was agreed to in 1998, prior to Costas' arrival.
6   Newcastle upon Tyne, United Kingdom, was an important industrial and transportation center located in northeast England (approximately 3 hours from London). It had a population of 263,000 (1991 census).
7   Large restaurant chains served only four per cent of fast food meals in Spain, compared with 15 per cent for the rest of Western Europe, and 50 per cent for the United States.

CASE 7

Global Multi-Products Chile

INTRODUCTION

As he drove to his office in Providencia, a modern commercial and residential area in Santiago, Bob Thompson, Managing Director of Multi-Products Chile, was eagerly anticipating the upcoming week. He had spent a pleasant weekend with his family that had started well on the previous Friday afternoon with what he saw as real progress at work.

He had received an e-mail from one of the sales representatives in the North branch office reporting the minutes of the first branch sales meeting ever held in the company. Among other items, the minutes stated that the team had identified six accounts on which they were going to work together under the Integrated Solutions program and that they had chosen a team leader.

Dan Campbell wrote this case under the supervision of Professor Harry Lane solely to provide material for class discussion. The authors do not intend to illustrate either effective or ineffective handling of a managerial situation. The authors may have disguised certain names and other identifying information to protect confidentiality.

Copyright © 2007, Ivey Management Services   Version: (A) 2007-10-03

Thompson was surprised but delighted. The sales reps never knew what this type of meeting could accomplish or what they could do as a group. He had not expected these teams to function so well from the beginning. Maybe making changes in the organization would not be as difficult as he first had thought.

Upon entering his office, Thompson learned that two of his Business Unit managers were anxious to see him. The first, to whom the formally designated Integrated Solutions Manager reported, commented that he was just checking about the e-mail with Thompson and politely asked, "Have you seen the e-mail from the North? What's your opinion about the comments about Integrated Solutions? Isn't this our responsibility?"

The second Business Unit manager was more concerned and was disturbed with the tone of the e-mail: "What do you think about the note? These comments go way beyond the responsibilities of the branch people."

His earlier mood of satisfaction had turned to consternation. It appeared to him that his top executives, members of his Management Operating Committee, were suggesting a stop to his changes before they got out of hand. He found himself starting to have doubts about what he was doing. Maybe this wasn't going to be so easy after all. Should he keep pushing ahead with change when his senior management team did not appear to support it? He began to reflect on events that had led to this point.

BACKGROUND

Multi-Products Inc. was founded in the early 1900s to manufacture abrasives. The company's creation of the world's first waterproof sandpaper in the early 1920s, followed by numerous other new products, established the company's identity as an innovative, multi-product, manufacturing company. The company manufactured and distributed over 55,000 products for a diverse range of applications. Some products were brands found in households and offices all over the world. Others became components of customer products such as computers, automobiles and pharmaceuticals. Many became the standards in their industry. All these products were the result of combining the company's core technologies in ways that solved their customers' problems.

International sales totaled US$14.1 billion and net income was US$3.85 billion. International sales represented almost 62 per cent of total sales. Multi-Product subsidiaries operated in over 60 countries and were the channels to sell products into almost 200 countries.

THE COMPANY VISION

According to Bob Thompson, the global growth drivers for the company were technology and innovation; the supply chain; and a customer focus. He explained that the company's vision was to be the most innovative enterprise and the preferred supplier by developing technologies and products that created a new basis of competition and by helping customers grow their businesses.

The Annual Report stated that the company succeeded by being able to:
— see customer needs and then meet them by drawing on [a] deep pool of technologies
— a pool supported by R&D-related investment averaging more than 6 percent of sales and [by creating] entirely new product categories

This ability was rooted in the company's "very mindful method of driving discovery and innovation."

TECHNOLOGY AND INNOVATION

A leading business magazine ranked Global Multi-Products as one of the five most innovative companies globally and in each of the three "triad" regions.[1] Nearly 30 per cent of sales came from products introduced within the previous four years. Those new products were derived from 40 "technology platforms" where Multi-Products believed it possessed a competitive advantage. These technologies ranged from adhesives and fluorochemistry, to even newer technologies like micro-replication with potential in abrasives, reflective sheeting, and electronic displays. These technology platforms were considered the path to the goal of developing products that would create a new basis of competition.

INNOVATION IN CUSTOMER SERVICE

Historically, sales efforts were by product group. Often, sales representatives from one product group built strong relationships with customers that could benefit from products from other divisions as well. Eventually the company implemented a program referred to as "Related Sales." Later it was replaced by "Customer Focused Marketing" that sought to re-orient the sales and marketing effort around the needs of customers, instead of the company's product groups.

A program known as "Integrated Solutions" carried the process a step further. Company documents explained the program:

> Customers rely on Multi-Products not only for innovative, high quality products, but also for solutions to other important needs. We help them develop, manufacture and merchandise their products; meet occupational health and safety standards; expand globally; and strengthen their businesses in other ways. We aim to be the first choice of customers. We strive for 100 per cent customer satisfaction.
>
> Multi-Products has an innovative way of doing business through which the client can easily access the [company's] products. The system has been labelled "Integrated Solutions" and voices the ideal of "one voice, one face, one company," which means that a single employee can provide you access to all products and solutions.

MULTI-PRODUCTS CHILE[2]

The company had a long history in Latin America and operated in 18 Spanish speaking countries.

Multi-Products began operating in Chile in January 1976 in a large shed that served as the warehouse, production, and administration areas. In adherence to Chile's foreign investment legislation at the time, the company was required to establish a manufacturing operation as part of its investment.

Since its beginnings, Multi-Products Chile strove to project a presence throughout the country. The first company branch was created in Concepción in the south of the country; the second in Valparaíso near Santiago, two years later; and three years later, a third branch was established in Antofagasta north of Santiago.

Multi-Products Chile served multiple markets with multiple technologies and products, each of them with solid positions in their category. It supplied numerous manufacturing and service sectors, such as the health and first aid area (hospitals, drugstores, dentists); the industrial sector (safety products, abrasives, reflectors, packing systems, electrical and mining products, graphic communication products); the mass consumption area (cleaning, hardware and bookstore products); office, audio-visual and automobile sectors, and the large productions areas, such as forestry and construction.

Multi-Products' reputation for innovation also was recognized in Chile. A newspaper survey of 117 directors and general managers of medium and large-sized companies headquartered in Chile ranked Multi-Products Chile sixth in response to the question: "Which are the top companies in Chile in innovative capacity and incorporation of technology?"

The company had a staff of 270 that included 80 sales representatives, nine technical support staff, 45 people in manufacturing, and the remainder in management, administrative, and maintenance positions.

CHILE: A BRIEF OVERVIEW[3]

Politics

In 1970, Salvador Allende became the first elected Marxist president in a non-Communist country. He quickly established relations with Cuba and the People's Republic of China, introduced economic and social "reforms," and nationalized many private companies, including U.S.-owned ones. The banking, communications, textiles, insurance and copper mining industries were nationalized. Problems were soon apparent: Chile's currency reserves were gone; business groups were dissatisfied; the U.S. led a boycott against international credit for Chile; and strikes paralyzed the country. In 1973 inflation reached 300 per cent.

In September 1973, Allende was overthrown and killed in a military coup headed by General Augusto Pinochet, who eventually assumed the office of president. Committed to "exterminat[ing] Marxism," the junta suspended parliament, banned political activity, and severely curbed civil liberties. During Pinochet's regime, thousands of Chileans were imprisoned, tortured, disappeared, executed and expelled.

The economy gradually improved after Chile's return to privatization under Pinochet. After losing a plebiscite on whether he should remain in power, he stepped down in January 1990. In October 1998, he was arrested and detained in England on an extradition request issued by a Spanish judge in connection with the disappearances of Spanish citizens during his rule. British courts denied his extradition and he returned to Chile in March 2000. He died in December 2006 at age 91.

Economy

The north of Chile had great mineral wealth, principally copper. The relatively small central area dominated the country in terms of population and agricultural resources and was the cultural and political center from which Chile expanded in the late 19th century. Southern Chile was rich in forests and grazing lands.

After a decade of impressive growth rates, Chile began to experience a moderate economic downturn in 1999. The economy remained sluggish until 2003, when it began to show signs of recovery, achieving 3.3 per cent real GDP growth. Real GDP growth reached 6.3 per cent in 2005. For the first time in many years, Chilean economic growth in 2006 was among the weakest in Latin America.

The Pinochet government sold many state-owned companies and the three democratic governments since 1990 continued privatization, though at a slower pace. The government's role in the economy was mostly limited to regulation. Chile had free trade agreements with the United States, the European Union, South Korea, New Zealand, Singapore, Brunei, China and Japan.

High domestic savings and investment rates helped Chile's economy to average growth rates of eight per cent during the 1990s. A privatized national pension system encouraged domestic investment and contributed to an estimated total domestic savings rate of approximately 21 per cent of GDP.

Chile's 16 million inhabitants shared a per capita GDP of approximately US$12,700, one of the highest in Latin America. About 85 per cent of Chile's population lived in urban areas, with 40 per cent living in greater Santiago. Most have Spanish ancestry.

Chilean Culture

Numerous Chilean managers at Multi-Products Chile shared their opinions about Chilean culture.

> Compared with the rest of Latin America, we are formal, closer to Argentina. We are the most serious people in Latin America. We often describe other Latin American cultures as less formal and see them as paying less attention to details. We are very professional at all levels and some people think Chileans are boring.
>
> We are also polite and indirect. For example, an e-mail or Lotus Notes that might be five lines from the United States, might be two pages long, on the same subject, if written by a Chilean.
>
> Many Chileans are workaholics. We work from 8 a.m. to 8 p.m. and we often take work home with us on weekends. However, we still have scheduling problems. Time is flexible. A meeting scheduled for 10:00 may not start until 10:20.

Another manager observed:

> Why are we, as a country, not as developed as the United States over the same period of time? Chileans are more isolated from one another. I have been living in the same place for

three or four years, and I don't know my neighbors. Nothing, names, number of children, nothing. In Chile, we tend to care about ourselves, our families, and maybe our friends, but that's it.

We haven't paid enough attention to implement programs that make people work together. We haven't paid enough attention to organization development or to developing a sense of community. We don't have a tradition of taking responsibility for a wider group.

Another commented on the "silo effect" stating that, in addition to age and educational background differences, recent political history had polarized society and had not encouraged trust. He commented:

Things are starting to change slowly, but the wounds haven't healed over the years. This is the biggest barrier to working in teams. People didn't trust each other, don't trust each other.

Bob Thompson

Prior to going to Chile, Bob Thompson had been an executive with Multi-Products Canada. Multi-Products Canada was a mature company with a well-trained sales force backed by good technical support that Thompson felt was the company's classic model and was essential to long-term success.

However, in the late 1990's, facing a flat economy and stagnating organization, Multi-Products Canada began a change process that sought to empower managers within the organization. Thompson commented:

The message was that we just couldn't continue with that style of management. We needed to get the best out of people. We needed to be more creative. I think the change process was successful. People felt part of the company in a much deeper way. I, personally, felt very positive about it.

In Chile, his predecessors had always come from the United States; in fact, most had spent considerable time in the head office. Thompson, on the other hand, had spent his career outside of the head office and, in keeping with the Canadian subsidiary's model of management, was more comfortable with broadly shared authority. He believed in encouraging positive risk-taking and empowerment.

Multi-Products Chile had been successful, growing at about 17 per cent per year which was acceptable for a subsidiary in an emerging market. Multi-Products liked to grow at between two and four times the growth-rate of the local gross domestic product and it maintained a strong focus on incrementally improving profitability.

Although there was no crisis in Multi-Products Chile when Thompson arrived, profitability had declined and the message to him was that it could be improved. As Thompson sized up the organization, he believed it could achieve those profitability objectives. On the other hand, he could make more substantial changes to achieve the potential that headquarters felt existed in Chile.

CUSTOMER AND DISTRIBUTION CHANNEL CHANGES

The group of retailers and distributors that Multi-Products Chile had traditionally served was changing quickly. Bob Thompson commented:

> The last five years have been dramatic. Big American retailers are here or are coming. That has meant that our organization needed to change.

U.S. superstores were rapidly changing the retail market in the country. One manager commented that in the past, local superstores might have represented 60 per cent of retail sales, with small sole-proprietorships making up the rest. This superstore segment had been growing at eight to 10 per cent per year and Thompson believed superstores, local and foreign, represented over 90 per cent of the business.

As the level of sophistication increased among retailers, expectations of their suppliers increased as well. Purchasing managers, due to the volume of products they were purchasing, were reluctant to deal with distributors, preferring instead to deal directly with suppliers. They also expected lower prices. Multi-Product managers commented:

> Customers are asking for direct service at lower prices. With the big U.S. retailers, negotiation requirements have changed. We have lost power. Our products have traditionally had solid margins and I feel they were higher in the past. Before we might have averaged 80 per cent margins. Now, it is difficult to have a different price from everyone else because communication systems like the Internet let people know the world price.

One manager recounted the entry of a new office products retailer into the Chilean market:

> They have been putting a lot of pressure on margins. We are assisting them to enter the market with special programs but it is costly. We have competitors, but Multi-Products has the most complete line of products. We try to add more value to the product. For example, our competitor may sell one kind of tape, where we will sell six.

Retailers were demanding more than just price discounts. They demanded a commitment to advertising support before they would place a product on their shelves. In the case of the office supplies retailer, Multi-Products paid CLP$5 million[4] for a photograph of its office products to be included in a supplementary catalogue. The catalogue would be followed up by a telemarketing campaign that was also a new concept for Chile.

Retailers also wanted more timely delivery to reduce inventories and better communication with their suppliers around ordering, billing and logistics. One manager commented:

> We had to learn to make the delivery and leave the invoice at the same time. As an industrial products company we were used to loading a big truck and sending it to the customer. In consumer products, we use smaller trucks and make more stops. We had to wait at the new, large retailers because the big, traditional consumer goods suppliers had more clout and were unloaded first.

Retailers wanted to reduce the number of Multi-Product sales representatives they were dealing with from four or five down to one. As a result, that sales person had to have access to information about all of the company's products being delivered to that retailer, even though they might originate from multiple product divisions.

The company also wanted to consolidate and had re-organized product responsibilities to achieve this. For example, although the Marketing Manager for Consumer Goods had been responsible for tape sales within his or her channel, responsibility for all tape sales, industrial and consumer, now resided with another manager in the Home and Office Division. This meant that the Marketing Coordinators of the Home and Office and Consumer Products Division now had to work together more closely than in the past. Cross-divisional selling had become an established fact. One manager commented:

> We have to learn to work together. They have the products and product knowledge. We have the relationship with the superstores and the skill in negotiating with them. Last year 44 per cent of our division's sales were from non-consumer products to supermarkets, home centers and hardware stores.

In many instances, the company continued to use distributors, in part, because nearly 80 per cent of their product sales went to industrial users. In some industries, the number of distributors had decreased after consolidation and the sophistication of the remaining distributors was increasing. Managing the relationship with distributors had become increasingly difficult as sales representatives began selling directly to end users previously serviced by a distributor.

It was not just the retail sector that had changed, but industrial products companies as well. The mining industry used to be government-controlled but large mining multinationals were commonplace and they operated differently. One executive commented, "Everything has been challenged. We need new skills."

NEW ROLE FOR SALES REPRESENTATIVES

Changes in the company's customer base were resulting in new responsibilities and requirements for Multi-Products' sales representatives. Generally, Chile was a fairly structured society. In business, titles conferring status in the organization were very important. The selling role was not held in the same regard as other positions, and levels of education tended to be lower. Indeed, it was often difficult for sales reps to access more senior managers in the selling process. Thompson commented that "the idea of a sales executive meeting with a client's executive does not exist commonly here."

A business unit manager described a typical sales call in the past:

> When sales representatives visited a business, they would usually sit down and have a coffee with their contact. A significant portion of their conversation would revolve around non-business-related topics such as the client's family or maybe football. The relationship was very important. Eventually, the sales representative would inspect the client's inventories and make suggestions for orders of our products.

Because of increased client sophistication and more advanced products from Multi-Products, more was required from a sales representative. Another Business Unit manager commented:

> A sales rep now needs to teach as well as to sell. In the past, they were specialists. They may have only sold simple office products. Now they need to know how to sell a multimedia projector, connect it to a notebook computer and train clients on how to use it, too! People need to be more professional in their commercial relationships and make an effort to learn. We don't sell products anymore, we sell solutions.

Instead of casual sales visits, it was not uncommon now to have a team of five or six sales people, coordinated by one single client contact, making presentations that could last two or three days. Consumer products sales reps also were now focused on visiting a given number of stores in a day and handling smaller orders faster and more frequently since there were no warehouses — just the shelves in the customers' stores. Not all the sales reps were happy with this conversion from maintaining a relationship with a store owner to being, in their view, an "ant" running all over the place.

Multi-Products Chile had started placing more emphasis on recruiting high caliber people including those for sales positions. However, most university graduates showed much greater interest in positions that appeared to offer faster mobility to executive positions such as in marketing.

INTEGRATED SOLUTIONS AND KEY ACCOUNTS IN MULTI-PRODUCTS CHILE

When Thompson arrived in Santiago, he learned that, although there was an awareness of the "Integrated Solutions" approach, little real progress appeared to have been made. He commented:

> This was our most important commercial activity globally, but it was not present in Chile. Our product line is so broad and deep, that customers were confused. "Why can't we see just one sales representative?" they would ask.
>
> The company had been organized for distribution-based selling, taking product lines to distributors. We needed to start understanding client and business applications of products . . . acting like a consultant. This approach proved new and challenging for the organization.

Sales representatives were responsible for sales of a specific product or line of products. Performance was measured on the ability of a representative to sell certain products, and there was no incentive to sell products from other areas of the company. As a result, customers who purchased a range of products from Multi-Products were forced to deal with several different sales representatives. If the customer was a multinational, it would often have to deal with a separate sales organization in each country in which it did business.

Structural Changes

When Bob Thompson arrived at Multi-Products Chile, he found an organization that had been very successful with traditional distribution-based selling. The deeper Multi-Products

EXHIBIT 1 Multi-Products Chile Organization Chart

"footprint" that he was used to, especially technical support groups, was limited. He added technical support positions along with a technical council to foster its development. As well, marketing, sales and manufacturing councils were added in time.

He also created the new position of Integrated Solutions Manager, reporting to the manufacturing products business unit manager. This person would be responsible for the implementation of Integrated Solutions in Chile and would coordinate the sales teams that would service large clients where the program was being implemented.

A short time later, a position of National Accounts Leader for Key Accounts was also created, reporting directly to Thompson. A new manufacturing manager was hired from Multi-Products Argentina where a more established manufacturing organization existed. See Exhibit 1 for a diagram of the revised organizational structure.

Accounts of special significance to Multi-Products Chile would now be viewed in one of two ways: Key Accounts and Integrated Solutions Targets.

Key Accounts

The Key Account concept was not new to Multi-Products Chile. However, in the past, a key account was identified as a customer with the potential to purchase large quantities of the company's products. Multi-Products Chile sold directly to these customers using programs different from distributors especially in pricing structure and logistics support, but the sales effort remained similar. Multiple sales representatives from each of the product areas selling to the client would service the account. Little, or no, coordination existed between the product groups.

Now, Key Accounts were those customers whose relationship with Multi-Products took on a strategic significance beyond a buyer/supplier relationship in that Multi-Products' technology could augment the customer's business and possibly change the basis of competition. Multi-Products Chile wanted to identify strategic partnerships with its customers where activities such as research and product development could be coordinated between the organizations, creating long-term competitive advantages for both organizations.

This process had only recently been initiated, and partners, as well as the specific nature of the desired relationships with these partners, were in the process of being determined. However, the criteria for selecting Key Accounts were: a) a strong relationship with Multi-Products Chile, b) purchase potential, c) potential importance as an Integrated Solutions account, and d) an important company in Chile concerned about the environment and society and having the same values as Global Multi-Products Inc.

Multi-Products Chile was one of the first of the company's Latin American subsidiaries to create this formal Key Accounts position. The National Accounts Leader felt that his challenge was going to be to convince the other Multi-Products' companies to be consistent in their business model and prices with the Chilean company so that multinational customers could benefit from the relationship. He commented;

> This is a strategic program and will take a big change in mentality. We can't think short term, anymore. Free trade is helping to stabilize the country but we could still have big changes. This is the reason that business executives in Chile think short term.

Integrated Solution Targets

The Integrated Solutions program began with the collection of data about which customers would make the best targets for an initial effort. The idea was to discover those product divisions that had good relationships with clients and use the relationship to sell other products. Where the National Account Program, Key Accounts, was a strategic approach to link with a few very large accounts to create new products, Integrated Solutions was a broadly based tactical approach involving many more accounts.

Integrated Solutions represented an opportunity to sell products from multiple product groups to a client in a concerted effort. Within a year, more than 30 customers had been identified as targets. Exhibit 2 shows this concept for the mining industry.

The next stage involved taking an "x-ray" of these companies to determine which products the company was already using. A group of specialists would map a customer's business process to find opportunities for other products that might reduce a customer's costs. This process was complicated because a single company could purchase its products directly from Multi-Products Chile, although from different product groups, as well as from a range of distributors. Once managers knew what the company was purchasing, they could measure any increase in sales to those accounts and measure that against the general market to determine if the Integrated Solutions effort was succeeding.

An individual sales representative was then selected as the leader for a specific client and would act as the single point of contact for all sales to that client, including sales outside of the sales representative's own product area. These sales representatives would then request support from other representatives as required. This leader was determined by selecting the person having the best relationship with the client, who usually was obvious.

EXHIBIT 2 Integrated Solutions

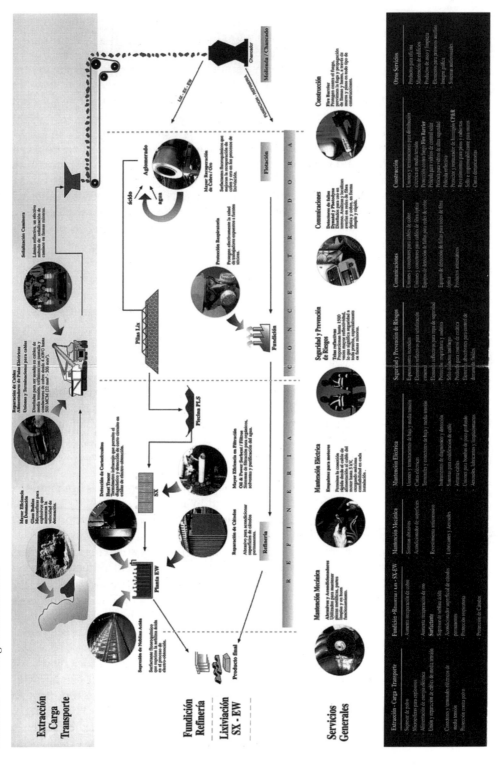

Sales Representatives and Integrated Solutions

Managers often described the Multi-Products Chile organization as silos, with individual product groups functioning independently of one another. One manager commented:

> We used to describe the situation as feudal. There were some sales reps that supported other divisions, but there was no program to formalize the activity.
>
> Sales people feel they have ownership over their product areas. They would ask: "Why would I use my time opening doors for another sales rep when I can use that time to visit my own customers?"

With the implementation of Integrated Solutions, it was recognized that sales staff needed to work as a team, helping one another to sell products. Everyone had not adjusted well to working with other product divisions. Some managers demanded: "Give me the products and I will sell them and earn the commission!" One manager commented:

> Not all the sales people are with the program; 15 per cent are with the program, another 60 per cent are with the program but are not leading it. The others are saying: "I will look after my own business and nothing else."
>
> Sales people need a change in terms of mentality. They also need to develop new sales techniques and knowledge about the products. The younger people are generally more adaptable to the change.

The increased sophistication in the buying process of some of the company's clients had also caused problems. Some sales representatives felt they had less influence in the process. They had grown accustomed to pushing new products that had been created in the US. Now marketing people were often involved in the initial process of approaching retailers with new products and negotiating the terms of sale.

Compensation also became an issue, because sales representatives usually were measured against sales targets in their product areas.

Sales Representative Compensation

When sales representatives joined Multi-Products Chile, they were given a six-month grace period during which time their compensation was 100 per cent fixed. After that time, 40 per cent of their compensation was fixed while the remaining 60 per cent was variable or "at risk", and tied to the achievement of various targets. As a sales representative became more senior, the variable portion was reduced to 20 per cent which reduced uncertainty about pay. As one manager commented, "We Latins don't like uncertainty."

The variable compensation targets were set by the sales manager, and were designed to encourage desired activity for that period. For example, 20 per cent of the variable pay could be for the sale of new products.

Other percentages could be used for sales calls on new clients, or sales of certain high-margin items. To accommodate Integrated Solutions, a sales manager could include sales of other product areas as a target within a sales representative's variable compensation. These targets were usually adjusted annually to meet the needs of the sales division.

Sales representatives could also receive additional pay in extra-compensation for exceeding their targets. For example, sales reps with 30 per cent variable compensation could earn up to 130 per cent of their salary and a senior sales rep with 20 per cent variable compensation could earn up to 120 per cent.

The Sales Contest

Until two years earlier, the sales contest was designed and administered by the Human Resources Department when it was transferred to Corporate Marketing. The Corporate Marketing Manager invited the Sales Council,[5] of which he was the head, to design a new program.

The new program eliminated the prizes that had been given in the past such as trips and microwave ovens which, as was clearly evident, the winners usually sold. Instead, it provided monetary rewards. If sales reps made 123 per cent of their target they would get, in effect, a bonus payment of x per cent. If the sales team of which they were a part met its objectives, they would get an additional y per cent. And, if the Business Unit met its objectives, they could receive another z per cent.

This new sales contest presented difficulties for Bob Thompson. The Manager of Human Resources and other managers were not pleased with it. They felt that a) it was too expensive, potentially costing as much as the whole training and education budget; b) it should not have been monetarized; c) it permitted everyone to get a prize; and d) it had become part of the compensation system which was senior management's responsibility.

Thompson knew there was dissatisfaction among his managers with the new sales contest. His Human Resources Manager preferred to see changes in the plan but Thompson liked some elements of the design and since it came into effect when sales growth exceeded 23 per cent it was to a degree self-funding.

INITIATING THE CHANGE PROCESS

Soon after Thompson's arrival, a retreat was held in Iquique, a resort area north of Santiago, for senior managers from Multi-Products Chile as well as from Multi-Products Bolivia and Peru. Prior to the managers of the three countries meeting as one group, they met individually to confirm their primary mission and goals. The Chile group appeared to struggle at working together.

One of the purposes of the retreat was to establish a general mission statement for the region created by the three countries. The discussion went poorly. Managers seemed to have trouble defining a clear mission and did not touch on broader objectives for the region. As the discussion, originally scheduled for two or three hours, entered its second day, Thompson became increasingly disappointed, not only with the group's inability to reach a conclusion, but with what appeared to him to be the quality of the discussions. Frustrated, Thompson stopped the discussion and asked the group why things were going so poorly. To his surprise, one of the Chilean managers stood up and said: "We don't trust each other."

Thompson had hired a consultant to act as a professional facilitator for the retreat. As part of his services, he later provided a report outlining his conclusions about the meeting and the group. His executive summary included the following points about the executive team:

> Generally, this appears to be a strong task- and results-oriented group. They are autonomous in doing what they do and are well adjusted to standard requirements. Because of this they are able to focus on task structure and output evaluation but are less aware of group process and its importance to productivity and teamwork. At times they seem isolated and defensive. There are also some unresolved personal conflicts with no methodology about resolving those conflicts.

This information gave Thompson some idea about the nature of the Multi-Products Chile organization, and pointed out some challenges to be met as he worked to make it more responsive to the customers and markets they served.

Additionally, the company conducted company-wide employee surveys every three years. They included information from various levels of the organization, about employees' opinions on various aspects of the company such as salaries, empowerment, and safety. As a part of the data analysis, a comparison was made of the opinions of senior managers in contrast with the opinions of lower level employees on each dimension. While opinions differed on many issues, certain areas showed senior managers having a much more positive opinion than their employees (a difference of ≥ 20 per cent). These included: work conditions, training, job progress, pay, safety and empowerment. About the change process, one executive observed:

> There has been resistance and conflict generated because of the changes. Maybe it has been too aggressive or too quick. People need to understand why we are changing and we are addressing this. We are in the process of changing even though not much has really changed yet.
>
> These programs promote involvement beyond your scope of responsibility. They are long-term programs, sophisticated techniques. They won't create sales tomorrow. We are measured by our results and there is no need to change. The company is doing well. There are no rewards for thinking strategically. You can be comfortable and do well not doing these things. Thompson is doing it because he thinks it is right. It takes courage. Others do only what they are rewarded for.

CONCLUSION

Thompson's secretary interrupted his reflections to remind him that he had a meeting shortly with his human resources manager. Thompson thought to himself that, maybe, he had introduced enough change to Multi-Products Chile and that it was not necessary to go further. After all, business was good and things were going well.

Notes

1   The triad regions are Asia, Europe and North America.
2   Much of this information was taken from company documents.
3   This section is adapted primarily from http://www.infoplease.com/country/profiles/chile.html and the US Department of State Background Note on Chile, accessed September 28, 2007.
4   In October 2006, US$1 purchased 510 Chilean pesos (CLP$).
5   The composition of this council included the corporate marketing manager, and senior sales representatives from the business units.

CASE **8**

Managing Performance at Haier (A)

FROM BANKRUPT COLLECTIVE ENTERPRISE TO THE COVER OF FORBES

One spring day in early 1985, anyone visiting the production facilities of Qingdao Refrigerator General Factory, a home appliance manufacturer in the northeastern Chinese city of Qingdao, would have been forgiven for thinking that company CEO Zhang Ruimin had taken leave of his senses. Just a few months after taking the helm of the company, at the age of 35, this former Qingdao city official in charge of the home appliance sector gathered all factory personnel outside the factory. There, they watched a group of co-workers implement an order from their young CEO: Destroy 76 refrigerators just off the production line.

The refrigerators being pounded to bits had been found to be defective in some way, even though some defects, such as chips in the paintwork, may have seemed minor. The workers who had assembled them were now handed the tools to destroy them. Wielding

Research Associate Donna Everatt prepared this case under the supervision of Professors Vladimir Pucik and Katherine Xin as a basis for class discussion rather than to illustrate either effective or ineffective handling of a business situation.

sledgehammers, the workers, plus Zhang himself, began the noisy demolition of the glistening new refrigerators – products that would have retailed for RMB 1,560[1] each, or four times their annual salary. Some swung their hammers with tears in their eyes. Though his employees may have doubted it that day, Zhang had a very clear message: The company would no longer produce substandard products.

Since that day in 1985, Haier, with its unique performance management system, has often been heralded as a model for the transformation of an ailing socialist enterprise to a thriving multinational. The company was seen as capable not only of succeeding in China but also of competing on the world stage.

Qingdao Haier Refrigerator

In 2006 Haier was ranked as the world's sixth largest maker of large kitchen appliances with a 4% global market share[2] (refer to Exhibit 1) and a particularly strong position in washing machines (#2) and refrigerators (#3). Starting from an almost hopeless position, in just over two decades Haier had managed to achieve what its peers had taken on average 95 years to accomplish.[3] Haier's story was one of a remarkable turnaround.

In 1985 what was then the Qingdao Refrigerator General Factory had run up a debt of RMB 1.47 million – equivalent to the combined annual salaries of its nearly 3,000 employees – and was virtually bankrupt. At that time, Haier's performance was similar to that of many other local Chinese enterprises, characterized by bureaucracy and inefficiency, with little regard for cost or quality control or for customer needs.[4]

A shift in the company's fortunes came when Zhang was appointed CEO in 1985. Since then, he has turned the small loss-making refrigerator factory into a group of more than 240 plants and companies, employing over 50,000 workers. Between 1984 and 2006 Haier's revenues jumped from RMB 3.48 million to RMB 104 billion (refer to Exhibits 2a and 2b for selected financials for its publicly listed main business – refrigerators).

Since 2002 Haier has been recognized annually as China's most valuable brand, based on its success in "introducing market competition in the whole electric home appliance industry."[5] The company has become a source of national pride, both for its performance in the domestic markets and its increasing successes around the world. Overall exports increased to $1.7 billion in 2006 and the company's products were sold in 160 countries, in 12 of the 15 top European retailers and in all of the top 10 retail chains in North America.

Since it began exporting in the early 1990s, Haier had pursued a strategy of creating, then dominating, market niches. For example, it manufactured compact refrigerators of the kind typically found in college dorms or hotel rooms – and for which it had captured almost half that market in the US. Another niche in the US for Haier was electric wine cellars (refrigerators specially designed to store wine). With this niche marketing strategy, by 2008 the Haier brand held over 5% of the North American market in refrigeration appliances.[6]

EXHIBIT 1   Global Ranking: Large Kitchen Appliances

Company Shares (by Global Brand Owner) Retail Volume – % breakdown							
	2001	**2002**	**2003**	**2004**	**2005**	**2006**	**2007**
Whirlpool Corp	8.6	8.8	8.6	8.6	10.2	12.0	11.6
Electrolux AB	9.8	9.7	9.8	9.3	9.1	9.0	8.9
Bosch-Siemens Hausgeräte GmbH	5.7	5.6	5.5	5.6	5.7	5.9	6.3
LG Group	3.1	3.4	3.7	4.0	4.5	4.8	5.1
General Electric Co (GE)	5.0	5.1	5.0	5.0	4.8	4.5	4.3
Haier Group	2.5	2.8	3.1	3.3	3.5	3.7	4.0
Indesit Co SpA	–	–	–	–	3.2	3.2	3.2
Matsushita Electric Industrial Co Ltd	2.7	2.8	2.8	2.9	3.0	3.1	3.2
Samsung Corp	2.2	2.4	2.5	2.5	2.6	2.7	2.9
Sharp Electronics Corp	2.5	2.4	2.4	2.4	2.3	2.2	2.2
Maytag Corp	2.8	2.7	2.6	2.6	2.5	–	–
Merloni Elettrodomestici SpA	3.0	3.0	3.1	3.1	–	–	–

Source: Domestic Electrical Appliances: Euromonitor from trade sources/national statistics

©2008 Euromonitor International

EXHIBIT 2A   Selected Financials Qingdao Haier: Refrigerators (RMB million)

	1999	**2000**	**2001**
Turnover	3,974	4,828	11,442
Gross profit	819	870	1,903
Operating profit	346	358	955
Net profit	311	424	618
Net profit growth	(70)%	37%	46%
Gross margin	21%	18%	17%
Net margin	8%	9%	5%
Dividend yield	1.2	1.8	2.6

Source: Company information

EXHIBIT 2B   Selected Financials Qingdao Haier (RMB million)

	2006	2007
Turnover	23,214	29,469
Gross profit	3,690	5,535
Operating profit	831	899
Net profit	638	754
Net profit growth	N/A	19%
Gross margin	16%	19%
Net margin	2.7%	2.6%
Dividend yield	1.1%	0.7%

Note: 2005 data is not comparable to that of 2006 and 2007 as China adopted new accounting standards in 2007, retrospective to 2006.

N/A = not applicable

Source: Company information

Key Success Factors

A summary of Haier's key success factors included:

- *Product diversification*
  Haier evolved from one refrigerator model in 1984 to 86 different product categories with over 13,000 specifications, including microwave ovens, air conditioners, small home appliances, TVs, washing machines and MP3 players.
- *Product innovation to create niche markets*
  For example, in China's major cities, living space was limited, families were small[7] and energy was relatively more expensive. Haier invented a miniature washing machine as a secondary household machine to wash small loads of laundry daily in summer.
- *Marketing initiatives that emphasized product quality and market research*
  In contrast to many Chinese manufacturers which competed on price, Haier sought to differentiate its products. In a recent price war in both the domestic and international appliance market, Haier actually increased its price to send a message to the market of Haier's quality and service.
- *Globalization*
  By 2007 Haier had set up many overseas production bases, service and sales facilities, procurement networks and international technology alliances and joint ventures with foreign players to better penetrate international markets.
- *Innovative human resource management practices*
  Haier was one of the first Chinese companies to tie salaries, and even job security, to performance. Its organizational strategies included transparency, fairness and justice.

Haier Group's Management Philosophies

Zhang's management principles integrated Japanese management philosophy, American innovation and aspects of traditional Chinese culture, as well as Haier's own learning. These policies were introduced into an environment framed at the beginning by the Chinese cultural values of harmony, face, relationships and hierarchy, as well as by the management practices inherited from state-owned enterprises (SOEs). (Refer to Exhibit 3 for a summary of characteristics of SOE managers.)

Zhang remarked on the importance of effective human resource management policies:

> An enterprise is like a ball being pushed up a hill (F1). Under pressure of market competition and internal stress (F2), the ball needs a strong braking force (F) to prevent it from rolling back down. This braking force is the internal management infrastructure.

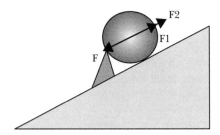

A Sense of Urgency   Zhang explained that Haier was prepared for "moving forward in times of danger." He continued:

> We are not safe in that Haier has not achieved its goal so far – a goal that is limitless. Haier has been developing for 18 years, but so far we haven't seen a day of peace and safety. The outside world is always forcing or pushing us to move forward without stopping.

This sense of urgency was heightened by internal competition as well as external. Xiwen Zhou, president of Haier University, explained:

> Each Haier employee is a customer of his fellow workers. For example, Haier's Environmental Testing Laboratory must satisfy the needs of its "customers" in the Design

EXHIBIT 3   Characteristics of SOE Managers
Characteristics of managers in Chinese SOEs frequently mentioned in current books and articles on Chinese economy:
- Information conduits, not decision makers
- Comfortable working only in functional silos
- Risk averse/compliant
- Preference for ambiguity in oversight roles
- Averse to transparency
- Paternalistic[10] and coalitional (*guanxi* networks)
- Reliance on informal contacts
- Not fully appreciative of the market (incomplete buy-in)
- Professionally undereducated
- Inflexible (or constrained by unwieldy economic system).

Department by meeting deadlines and producing excellent data and useful test results. The Design Department, in turn, serves customers in the Production Department by innovative and successful designs for the manufacture of goods.

Zhou used another example from a particular division:

> For example, we have 22 vacuuming technicians engaged in different divisions. They used to care only about their own job and their division. There was no communication among business divisions, and creative ideas were not shared. Now we rank them across the Group according to several indexes such as quality, cost and output. Thus everybody knows he is No. 1, No. 2 or No. 3 among the vacuuming technicians, etc., and the sense of competition instantly increases. All the workers are motivated to do better and better.

In this way, Zhang noted that "employees can begin to feel market pressures even though they are inside the organization." Further, he felt that this philosophy had helped Haier avoid two problems that had traditionally characterized Chinese organizations: hierarchy and interpersonal networks (referred to as guanxi),[8] or what Zhang called "speed-absorbers."

Another fundamental element of Zhang's performance management system was accountability, at all levels, at all times.

OEC: Overall, Every, Control and Clearance   A guiding principle of Haier's management system was OEC: Overall, Every, and Control and Clearance. The term "overall" meant that all performance dimensions had to be considered. "Every" referred to everyone, every day and everything. "Control and clearance" referred to Haier's end-of-work procedure each day, which stated that each employee must finish all tasks planned for that day before leaving work. Clearance was conducted through self-assessment and meeting with one's supervisors. The concept of OEC laid the groundwork for a management system that had both breadth and depth: It applied to every aspect of work, every employee, every day.

According to Mianmian Yang, the president of Haier Group:

> It is really hard to keep track of all employees every day. Since Haier started the OEC practice (i.e., a self-management system) in 1989, we have been training our employees and managers to learn how to set up, achieve and be accountable for the targets that they set for themselves every day. The targets set have to be continuously improved and stretched. We raise the bar all the time. Human beings tend to get used to the status quo. A worker must finish the task he and his supervisors set to be accomplished every day. As a manager, if you can tell the employee – with his agreement and participation – his targets, then he knows what is expected of him. Each employee should set his own challenging targets.

Once the worker knew what was expected of him, his performance was closely monitored, evaluated and rewarded.

80:20 Principle   Under Haier's "80:20 Principle," the 20% of employees who were managers were held responsible for 80% of company results (good or bad). For example, if a worker was fined for equipment damage, he would be held responsible for 20% of the problem and his supervisor would be held responsible for 80%. This did not directly translate to a 20:80 ratio of fines, bonuses, etc. It was a slogan in Haier that communicated a clear and loud message: Managers have to have the courage and conscientiousness to assume responsibility at Haier.

Racetrack Model   A key aspect of Haier's management principles was the system used for performance evaluations and promotions – and demotions – based on the concept of a racetrack. All employees were welcome to compete in work-related "races" such as job openings and promotions. But winners had to keep racing – and keep winning – to defend a title. There was no such thing as a permanent promotion. In keeping with this philosophy, every employee in the Haier Group (except the top eight senior executives) underwent frequent and transparent performance appraisals – going against the traditional Chinese culture in which "face" was extremely important.

Tracking Individual Profit and Loss

Monthly measures were used to track performance, according to the revenue and profit the managers had earned for the company. A senior manager gave an example:

> Let's take the relationship between a refrigerator division director and a refrigerator production unit manager for example. If the production unit has the capacity to produce 50,000 refrigerators, the division director must provide orders for 50,000 refrigerators to the production unit, enough orders to meet its entire capacity. If you only provide orders for 45,000 refrigerators, then you, the division director, rather than the production unit manager, must be responsible for the lack of orders for 5,000 refrigerators. That is your expense. Similarly, the division director can earn his income by achieving his target (of 50,000 refrigerators) [and if] the production unit does not meet the quality standards, or delays delivery, the division director can claim for compensation. This would be extra income for his account, as one of his normal income items would be. The claim is a cost to the production unit, but an income to the division director.

Another example was provided:

> We have seven refrigerator production units altogether in our refrigerator division. They must share their best experiences to improve the lowest performer. When the average performance level is raised, the unit managers can achieve their incomes.

However, although the unit's income was attributed to the unit manager, that manager also had his own income and expenditure, accounted for in a "bankbook."

Deposit Book[9]   Although each manager was accountable for only a small portion of the overall profits, Zhang believed each one could function as a miniature company (MMC), each with his own profit and loss statement, mimicking a company's accounting records. As each MMC profited, so did the Group. Increasing revenues was similar to depositing money in a bank – the more a division profited, the more the manager accumulated in his resource bankbook. As long as a manager stayed with the company, his account existed, regardless of department or division.

Zhou explained the system:

> We set basic goals for managers. Only when they meet or exceed those goals will they have money (i.e., savings) in their account, otherwise they have to pay. This is an incentive to do a better job. But this is effective for those who reach their goals first, for the goals we have set for them are merely basic ones. We give them three or five more months, and whoever reaches his goal earlier will receive more income, and the later ones do not receive any income and have to pay.
>
> Let me give you an example. Yongshao Zhang used to be one of our purchasing agents for the logistics department. All he needed to do was buy what you wanted according to your requirements, without taking any responsibility for when these materials were used. Now we have changed the practice, and Zhang has become a purchasing manager. As a manager, he has to ensure that the steel plates he buys are the least expensive in the world and are of the best quality. Moreover, he has to provide the steel plates in time according to the demands of the business divisions, while trying not to store them in the warehouse for long, because he is charged for warehouse space. Zhang's office expenses – including water and electricity, machines, customs declarations, employees' salaries – are all "paid" by him. If the steel plates have quality problems according to the feedback from the market, Zhang Yongshao is entirely responsible. Passive job performance has turned into a practice that actively drives all the units. Passive management has turned into active procedures.

Managing Performance

Haier used several performance management and motivational tools. One involved a set of colored footprints on the factory floor (refer to Exhibit 4). Before 1998 a pair of yellow footprints was used as a kind of warning. Every day, a poor performer would stand on the yellow footprints to "reflect." The worker was expected to share how he could improve performance the next day. Subsequently, the color was changed to green to represent encouragement. Now, a top performer – either worker or manager – would stand on the footprints and explain why he had done a good job or how he accomplished his job by being innovative and what others might learn from this. According to Zida Yu, vice president in charge of research and development promotion, "Our main purpose is to motivate our people effectively."

Another tool used to motivate workers was a board placed in the factory workshop that recorded workers' performance on a daily basis. Under a system of self-management, employees set clear goals for themselves in a brief meeting with their supervisor at the beginning of their shift. At the end of the day, the employee and supervisor met again to assess how well these goals had been fulfilled. Each employee received a colored face, representing an informal grade for the day: red meant "excellent," green denoted "average" and yellow was "below average or below expectations" (refer to Exhibit 5).

Haier had a formal policy for managing those employees who did not meet set expectations. The lowest-performing 10% of employees were dismissed, based on

EXHIBIT 4   Footprints on Factory Floor

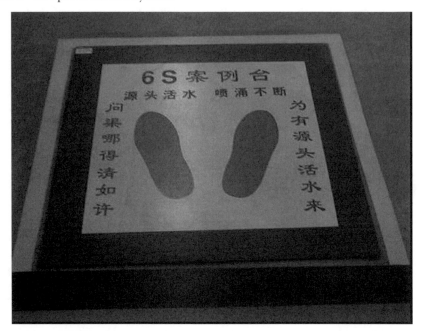

Source: Company information

EXHIBIT 5   Chart Rating Workers' Performance

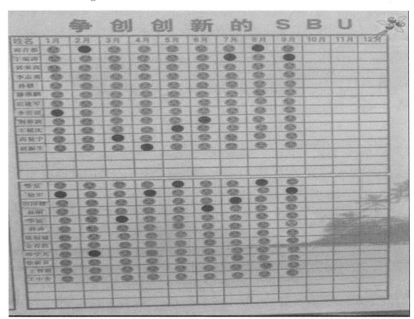

Source: Company information

a three-phase system. In the first review (either annual or quarterly), an employee who ranked in the bottom 10% was "asked to be on leave" and sent for job training at Haier's expense. If he remained in the bottom 10% during the second review, he was sent for more training – again on leave, but at his own expense. Continued performance in the bottom 10% in the third review resulted in the employee's dismissal.

The flip side of this approach was the emphasis on recognizing and rewarding successes and creativity. If an employee developed or improved a product, or suggested an efficient new procedure, the innovation carried the employee's name, and notice of it was prominently displayed.

Appraising Managers

Although it was more challenging to evaluate the performance of managers than of workers, Haier had developed a system of review based partly on quantifiable results. For a manger responsible for domestic or overseas business development, indicators such as volume of sales and selling speed, share of local market and share of global market were used. For a division head, the number of product orders, quality, cost, time for delivery, etc. were used. And for a senior manager, strategic business unit results and profit and loss were used.

Each manager's performance was reviewed weekly. The criteria for weekly evaluation involved both achieving quantifiable goals and the degree of innovation and process improvement, for example. At the end of the month, managers received a performance grade of A, B or C. The results of this evaluation were announced at a monthly meeting for middle and upper level managers on the eighth day of the month.

The results of managers' performance ranking were openly displayed at the entrance to the company cafeteria, with a green or red arrow indicating whether their score had gone up or down that month (refer to Exhibit 6). Haier had been doing this for over 15 years. Promotions or demotions were also published in the *Haier Ren Bao*.

Haier devoted significant resources to training and development. An important part of the appraisal process also included identifying more than 80 of the mid to upper level managers in the Group. They were sent on courses at "Haier University" every Saturday morning. The classes, called Interactive Learning sessions, focused on developing an action plan and implementing improvements in operations. The grades received in these courses accounted for about 40% of each manager's performance evaluation.

Developing Talent   When new positions opened up, Haier ensured that a wide pool of candidates competed for the position rather than promoting only from among employees of a certain position or tenure. Job rotation was critical to promote employee development and to avoid territorialism. New recruits tried out two or three different jobs before being finally assigned to a position. Later on, even when an employee performed well in a particular post, he was rotated into a new job. The average length of stay in a management position was three years (the maximum term was six years), ensuring that managers understood many different areas of the company.

EXHIBIT 6 Managers' Performance Ranking

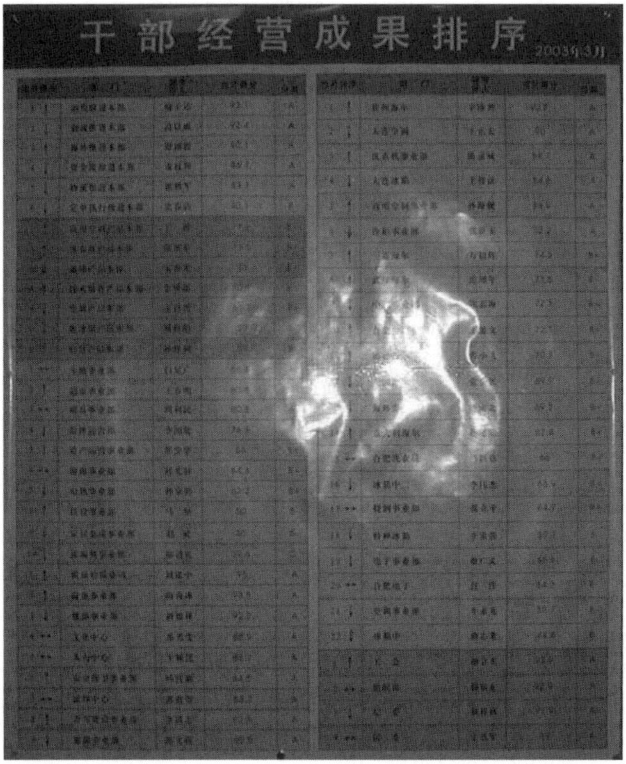

Source: Company information

At the monthly management evaluation meetings, top performers were identified, and those with the most potential were transferred into the Haier talent pool. The competitive threshold was high and selections for the talent pool were drawn from scratch every quarter, then evaluated separately for every new position. There was no philosophy of "once you're in, you're in" at Haier. However, unlike the general employee pool, the company did not have a fixed percentage of people in the talent pool that had to be eliminated.

A points system was used to assess whether a manager was achieving the performance standards to remain in the talent pool. Five points were allocated for monthly performance, five for accumulative performance, and five for current project reviews. A score of less than 10 for several months in a row would result in a transfer out of the talent pool.

Dealing with Low Performance of Managers   The pressure to perform and improve was relentless. In 2000, 13 of 58 senior managers in the headquarters in Qingdao were identified and penalized at different levels because they were not performing to ever-increasing Haier standards.

The low-performing managers were classified in three categories. If minor improvements in management performance were necessary, managers were "put on medication," which indicated that they needed to change and received training on those specific issues. More serious underperformers were referred to as "IV users" and demoted. Managers with serious performance issues were "hospitalized," and would be removed from their position.

Going Global   Haier was among the first Chinese manufacturers to have established manufacturing bases overseas. An interesting question was whether the performance management practices that had earned Haier such success in China were transferable to other cultures as it continued with its aggressive pushes toward international expansion.

Many of Haier's performance management philosophies were considered groundbreaking not only for a Chinese company but also for any firm anywhere. How, then, could Haier's performance management systems be applied in other regions of the world?

Notes

1   Chinese Yuan Renminbi (RMB) = US$0.12
2   Euromonitor, February 2008.
3   The average age of the world's top five global players in the household electrical market was 95 years (Euromonitor, 2001)
4   One of the first rules Zhang set was, "Do not urinate on the factory floor."
5   Annual report of the Beijing Famous-Brand Evaluation Co. Ltd., 2002
6   Euromonitor, February 2008.
7   Due to China's one-child policy.
8   *Guanxi* refers to the Chinese cultural system of forming social – and business – relationships based on mutual obligation. In other words, "I'll help you now; you help me later."
9   Haier referred to the credits employees earned with their contribution to productivity and/ or innovation as income [points], recorded in a book that functioned like a bankbook, which accompanied the employee until the end of his/her career with Haier. At the same time, the employee would pay for resources used. When income was greater than expenses, it was recorded as profit (or value added). When expenses were greater than income, the employee was in debt. Thus, every employee functioned with profit/loss, as a strategic business unit. Each employee earned a salary if he/she made a "profit" (a positive contribution to the company and the unit). An employee's salary was determined by his/her bankbook.
10 Chinese society was hierarchically structured based on Confucian principles of emperor over general, father over son (highly paternalistic), husband over wife, older brothers over younger brothers, for example.

CASE **9**

Ellen Moore (A): Living and Working in Korea

Ellen Moore, a Systems Consulting Group (SCG) consultant, was increasingly concerned as she heard Andrew's voice grow louder through the paper-thin walls of the office next to her. Andrew Kilpatrick, the senior consultant on a joint North American and Korean consulting project for a government agency in Seoul, South Korea, was meeting with Mr. Song, the senior Korean project director, to discuss several issues including the abilities of the Korean consultants. After four months on this Korean project, Ellen's evaluation of the assigned consultants suggested that they did not have the experience, background, or knowledge to complete the project within the allocated time. Additional resources would be required:

> I remember thinking, "I can't believe they are shouting at each other." I was trying to understand how their meeting had reached such a state. Andrew raised his voice and I could hear him saying, "I don't think you understand at all." Then, he shouted, "Ellen is not the problem!"

 Richard Ivey School of Business

The University of Western Ontario

Chantell Nicholls and Gail Ellement prepared this case under the supervision of Professor Harry Lane solely to provide material for class discussion. The authors do not intend to illustrate either effective or ineffective handling of a managerial situation. The authors may have disguised certain names and other identifying information to protect confidentiality.

WSI IN KOREA

Joint Venture Inc. (JVI) was formed as a joint venture between a Korean company, Korean Conglomerate Inc. (KCI), and a North American company, Western Systems Inc. (WSI) (Exhibit 1). WSI, a significant information technology company with offices world wide employing over 50,000 employees, included the Systems Consulting Group (SCG). KCI, one of the largest Korean "chaebols" (industrial groups), consisted of over 40 companies, with sales in excess of US$3.5 billion. The joint venture, in its eighth year, was managed by two Regional Directors—Mr. Cho, a Korean from KCI, and Robert Brown, an American from WSI.

The team working on Ellen's project was led by Mr. Park and consisted of approximately 40 Korean consultants further divided into teams working on different areas of the project. The Systems Implementation (SI) team consisted of five Korean consultants, one translator, and three North American SCG consultants: Andrew Kilpatrick, Ellen Moore, and Scott Adams, (see Exhibit 2).

This consulting project was estimated to be one of the largest undertaken in South Korea to date. Implementation of the recommended systems into over 100 local offices was expected to take seven to ten years. The SCG consultants would be involved for the first seven months, to assist the Korean consultants with the system design and in creating recommendations for system implementation, an area in which the Korean consultants admitted they had limited expertise.

Andrew Kilpatrick became involved because of his experience with a similar systems implementation project in North America. Andrew had been a management consultant for nearly 13 years. He had a broad and successful background in organizational development, information technology, and productivity improvement, and he was an early and successful practitioner of business process reengineering. Although Andrew had little international consulting experience, he was adept at change management and was viewed by both peers and clients as a flexible and effective consultant.

The degree of SCG's involvement had not been anticipated. Initially, Andrew had been asked by SCG's parent company, WSI, to assist JVI with the proposal development. Andrew and his SCG managers viewed his assistance as a favor to WSI since SCG did not have plans to develop business in Korea. Andrew's work on the proposal in North America led to a request for his involvement in Korea to gather additional information for the proposal:

> When I arrived in Korea, I requested interviews with members of the prospective client's management team to obtain more information about their business environment. The Korean team at JVI was very reluctant to set up these meetings. However, I generally meet with client management prior to preparing a proposal. I also knew it would be difficult to obtain a good understanding of their business environment from a translated document. The material provided to me had been translated into English and was difficult to understand. The Korean and English languages are so different that conveying abstract concepts is very difficult.
>
> I convinced the Koreans at JVI that these meetings would help demonstrate our expertise. The meetings did not turn out exactly as planned. We met with the same management team at three different locations where we asked the same set of questions three times and got the same answers three times. We did not obtain the information normally provided at these

EXHIBIT 1   Organizational Structure — Functional View

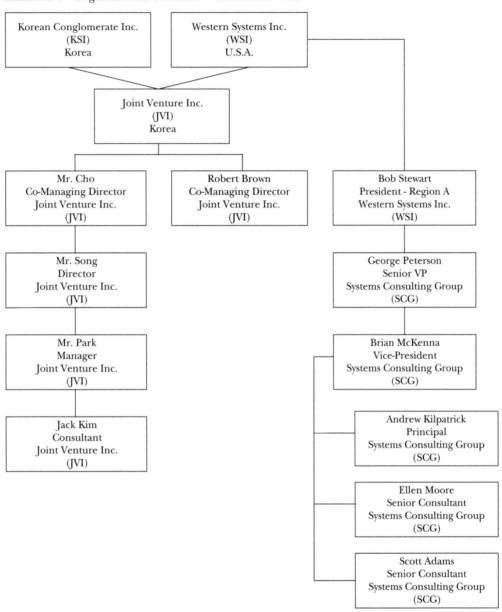

fact-gathering meetings. However, they were tremendously impressed by our line of questioning because it reflected a deep interest and understanding of their business. They also were very impressed with my background. As a result, we were successful in convincing the government agency that we had a deep understanding of the nature and complexity of the agency's work and strong capabilities in systems development and implementation—key cornerstones of their project. The client wanted us to handle the project and wanted me to lead it.

EXHIBIT 2 Organizational Structure — SI Project Team

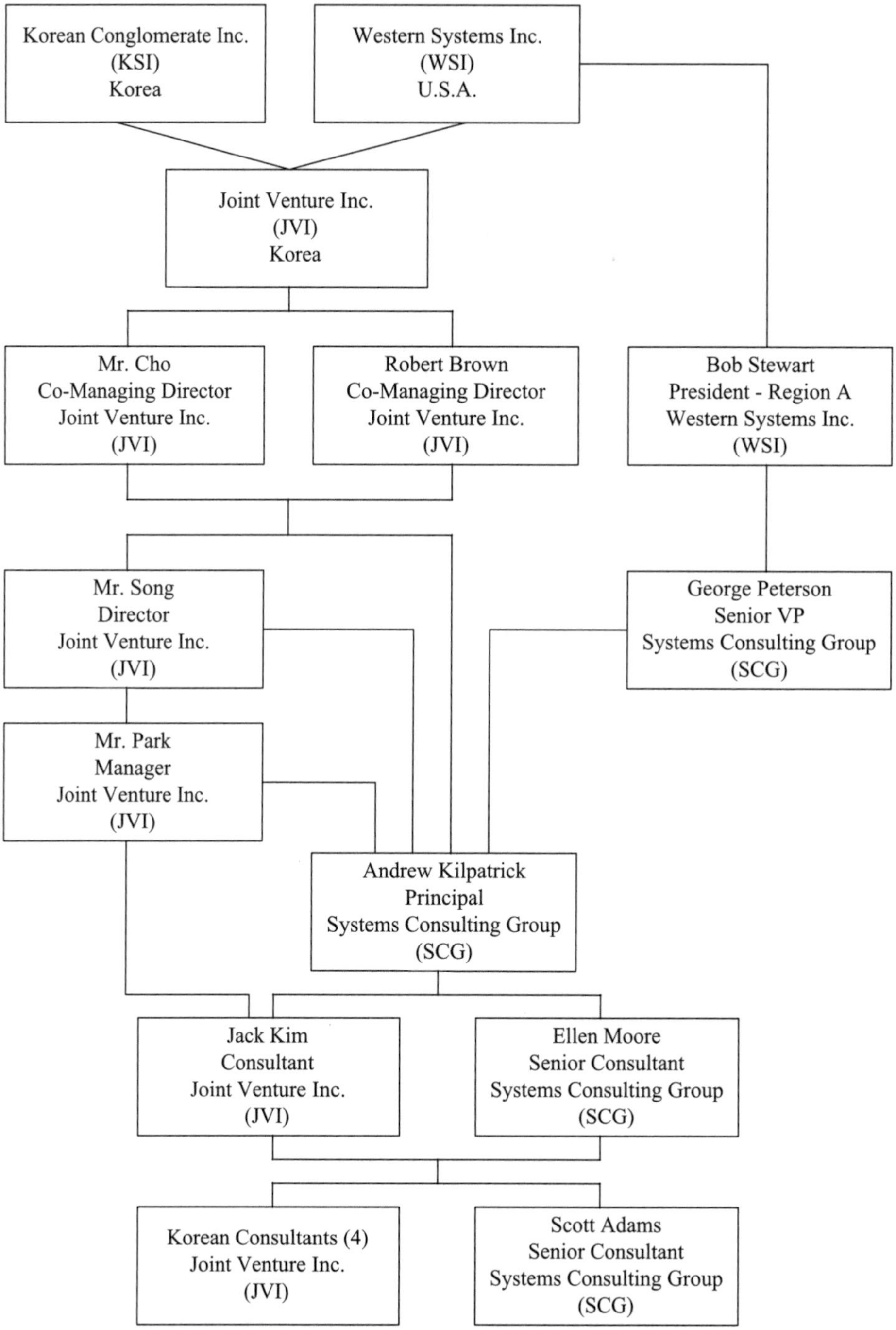

JVI had not expected to get the contract, because its competitor for this work was a long-time supplier to the client. As a result, winning the government contract had important competitive and strategic implications for JVI. Essentially, JVI had dislodged an incumbent supplier to the client, one who had lobbied very heavily for this prominent contract. By winning the bid, JVI became the largest system implementer in Korea and received tremendous coverage in the public press.

The project was to begin in June. However, the Korean project team convened in early May in order to prepare the team members. Although JVI requested Andrew to join the project on a full-time basis, he already had significant commitments to projects in North America. There was a great deal of discussion back and forth between WSI in North America, and JVI and the client in Korea. Eventually it was agreed that Andrew would manage the SI work on a part-time basis from North America, and he would send a qualified project management representative on a full-time basis. That person was Ellen Moore.

At that time, Andrew received immediate feedback from the American consultants with WSI in Korea that it would be impossible to send a woman to work in Korea. Andrew insisted that the Korean consultants be asked if they would accept a woman in the position. They responded that a woman would be acceptable if she were qualified. Andrew also requested that the client be consulted on this issue. He was again told that a woman would be acceptable if she were qualified. Andrew knew that Ellen had the skills required to manage the project:

> I chose Ellen because I was very impressed with her capability, creativity, and project management skills, and I knew she had worked successfully in Bahrain, a culture where one would have to be attuned to very different cultural rules from those prevalent in North America. Ellen lacked experience with government agencies, but I felt that I could provide the required expertise in this area.

ELLEN MOORE

After graduating as the top female student from her high school, Ellen worked in the banking industry, achieving the position of corporate accounts officer responsible for over 20 major accounts and earning a Fellowship in the Institute of Bankers. Ellen went on to work for a former corporate client in banking and insurance, where she became the first female and youngest person to manage their financial reporting department. During this time, Ellen took university courses towards a Bachelor Degree at night. She decided to stop working for two years, and completed her degree on a full-time basis. She graduated with a major in accounting and minors in marketing and management and decided to continue her studies for an MBA.

Two years later, armed with an MBA from a leading business school, Ellen Moore joined her husband in Manama, Bahrain, where she accepted a position as an expatriate manager for a large American financial institution.[1] Starting as a Special Projects Coordinator, within one year Ellen was promoted to Manager of Business Planning and Development, a challenging position that she was able to design herself. In this role, she managed the Quality Assurance department, coordinated a product launch, developed a senior management information system, and participated actively in all senior management decisions. Ellen's position required her to interact daily with managers and staff from a wide range of cultures, including Arab nationals.

In March, Ellen joined WSI working for SCG. After the highly successful completion of two projects with SCG in North America, Ellen was approached for the Korea project:

> I had never worked in Korea or East Asia before. My only experience in Asia had been a one-week trip to Hong Kong for job interviews. I had limited knowledge of Korea and received no formal training from my company. I was provided a 20-page document on Korea. However, the information was quite basic and not entirely accurate.

After arriving in Korea, Ellen immediately began to familiarize herself with the language and proper business etiquette. She found that English was rarely spoken other than in some hotels and restaurants which catered to Western clientele. As a result, Ellen took advantage of every opportunity to teach herself the language basics:

> When Andrew and I were in the car on the way back to our hotel in the evening, we would be stuck in traffic for hours. I would use the time to learn how to read the Korean store signs. I had copied the Hangul symbols which form the Korean language onto a small piece of paper, and I kept this with me at all times. So, while sitting back in the car, exhausted at the end of each day, I would go over the symbols and read the signs.

SCOTT ADAMS

The third SCG consultant on the project, Scott Adams, arrived as planned three months after Ellen's start date. Upon graduation, Scott had begun his consulting career working on several international engagements (including Mexico, Puerto Rico, and Venezuela), and he enjoyed the challenges of working with different cultures. He felt that with international consulting projects the technical aspects of consulting came easy. What he really enjoyed was the challenge of communicating in a different language and determining how to modify Western management techniques to fit into the local business culture. Scott first met Ellen at a systems consulting seminar, unaware at the time that their paths would cross again. A few months later, he was asked to consider the Korea assignment. Scott had never travelled or worked in Asia, but he believed that the assignment would present a challenging opportunity which would advance his career.

Prior to arriving in Seoul, Scott prepared himself by frequently discussing the work being conducted with Ellen. Ellen also provided him with information on the culture and business etiquette aspects of the work:

> It was very fortunate for me that Ellen had arrived first in Korea. Ellen tried to learn as much as she could about the Korean language, the culture, mannerisms, and the business etiquette. She was able to interpret many of the subtleties and to prepare me for both business and social situations, right down to how to exchange a business card appropriately with a Korean, how to read behavior, and what to wear.

ABOUT KOREA[2]

Korea is a 612-mile-long peninsula stretching southward from North Korea and the Asia mainland into the waters of the western Pacific and is bounded by the Yellow Sea, the Sea of Japan and the Korea Strait. The Republic of Korea, or South Korea, consists of approximately 38,000 square miles, slightly larger than Indiana or Portugal, for example. The South Korean population is about 49 million, with more than 10 million residing in the capital city, Seoul.

Korea has an ancient heritage spanning 5,000 years. The last great traditional dynasty, the Yi Dynasty or Choson Dynasty, brought about changes in which progress in science, technology, and the arts were achieved. Hangul, the Korean script, also was developed in this period. Although Confucianism had been influential for centuries in Korea, it was during this time that Confucian principles permeated the culture as a code of morals and as a guide for ethical behavior. Confucian thought came to underpin education, civil administration, and daily conduct. Lasting over 500 years, the Yi Dynasty came to a close in 1910. Today, in Korea's modern era, traditional Confucian values mix with Western lifestyle habits and business methods.

Many Korean people, particularly in Seoul, have become quite Westernized, but they often follow traditional customs. Although the major religions are Christianity and Buddhism, Korean society is strongly influenced by Confucian values and beliefs. Confucianism dictates strict rules of social behavior and etiquette. The basic values of the Confucian culture are: (1) loyalty to a hierarchical structure of authority, whether based in the family, the company, or the nation; (2) duty to parents, expressed through loyalty, love, and gratitude; and (3) strict rules of conduct, involving complete obedience and respectful behavior within superiors-subordinate relationships, such as parents-children, old-young, male-female, and teacher-student. These values affect both social and work environments substantially.

MANAGING IN KOREA

Business etiquette in Korea was extremely important. Ellen found that everyday activities, such as exchanging business cards or replenishing a colleague's drink at dinner, involved formal rituals. For example, Ellen learned it was important to provide and to receive business cards in an appropriate manner, which included carefully examining a business card when received and commenting on it. If one just accepted the card without reading it, this behavior would be considered very rude. In addition, Ellen also found it important to know how to address a Korean by name. If a Korean's name was Y.H. Kim, non-Koreans would generally address him as either Y.H. or as Mr. Kim. Koreans would likely call him by his full name or by his title and name, such as Manager Kim. A limited number of Koreans, generally those who had lived overseas, took on Western names, such as Jack Kim.

WORK TEAMS

Teams were an integral part of the work environment in Korea. Ellen noted that the Korean consultants organized some special team building activities to bring together the Korean and North American team members:

On one occasion, the Korean consulting team invited the Western consultants to a baseball game on a Saturday afternoon followed by a trip to the Olympic Park for a tour after the game, and dinner at a Korean restaurant that evening. An event of this nature is unusual and was very special. On another occasion, the Korean consultants gave up a day off with their families and spent it with the Western consultants. We toured a Korean palace and the palace grounds, and we were then invited to Park's home for dinner. It was very unusual that we, as Western folks, were invited to his home, and it was a very gracious event.

Ellen also found team-building activities took place on a regular basis, and that these events were normally conducted outside of the work environment. For example, lunch with the team was an important daily team event which everyone was expected to attend:

You just couldn't work at your desk every day for lunch. It was important for everyone to attend lunch together in order to share in this social activity, as one of the means for team bonding.

Additionally, the male team members would go out together for food, drink, and song after work. Scott found these drinking activities to be an important part of his interaction with both the team and the client:

Unless you had a medical reason, you would be expected to drink with the team members, sometimes to excess. A popular drink, soju, which is similar to vodka, would be poured into a small glass. Our glasses were never empty, as someone would always ensure that an empty glass was quickly filled. For example, if my glass was empty, I learned that I should pass it to the person on my right and fill it for him as a gesture of friendship. He would quickly drink the contents of the glass, pass the glass back to me, and fill it for me to quickly drink. You simply had to do it. I recall one night when I really did not want to drink as I had a headache. We were sitting at dinner, and Mr. Song handed me his glass and filled it. I said to him "I really can't drink tonight. I have a terrible headache." He looked at me and said "Mr. Scott, I have Aspirin in my briefcase." I had about three or four small drinks that night.

Ellen found she was included in many of the team-building dinners, and soon after she arrived in Seoul, she was invited to a team dinner, which included client team members. Ellen was informed that although women were not normally invited to these social events, an exception was made since she was a senior team member.

During the dinner, there were many toasts and drinking challenges. During one such challenge, the senior client representative prepared a drink that consisted of one highball glass filled with beer and one shot glass filled to the top with whiskey. He dropped the whiskey glass into the beer glass and passed the drink to the man on his left. This team member quickly drank the cocktail in one swoop, and held the glass over his head, clicking the glasses to show both were empty. Everyone cheered and applauded. This man then mixed the same drink, and passed the glass to the man on his left, who also drank the cocktail in one swallow. It was clear this challenge was going around the table and would eventually get to me.

I don't generally drink beer and never drink whiskey. But it was clear, even without my translator present to assist my understanding, that this activity was an integral part of the team building for the project. As the man on my right mixed the drink for me, he whispered that he would help me. He poured the beer to the halfway point in the highball glass, filled the shot glass to the top with whiskey, and dropped the shotglass in the beer. Unfortunately, I could see that the beer didn't cover the top of the shot glass, which would likely move too quickly if not covered. I announced "One moment, please, we are having technical difficulties." And to the amazement of all in attendance, I asked the man on my right to pour more beer in the glass. When I drank the concoction in one swallow, everyone cheered, and the senior client representative stood up and shouted, "You are now Korean. You are now Korean."

The norms for team management were also considerably different from the North American style of management. Ellen was quite surprised to find that the concept of saving face did not mean avoiding negative feedback or sharing failures:

It is important in Korea to ensure that team members do not lose face. However, when leading a team, it appeared just as important for a manager to demonstrate leadership. If a team member provided work that did not meet the stated requirements, a leader was expected to express disappointment in the individual's efforts in front of all team members. A strong leader was considered to be someone who engaged in this type of public demonstration when required.

In North America, a team leader often compliments and rewards team members for work done well. In Korea, leaders expressed disappointment in substandard work, or said nothing for work completed in a satisfactory manner. A leader was considered weak if he or she continuously provided compliments for work completed as required.

Hierarchy

The Koreans' respect for position and status was another element of the Korean culture that both Ellen and Scott found to have a significant influence over how the project was structured and how people behaved. The emphasis placed on hierarchy had an important impact upon the relationship between consultant and client that was quite different from their experience in North America. As a result, the North Americans' understanding of the role of a consultant differed vastly from their Korean counterparts.

Specifically, the North American consultants were familiar with 'managing client expectations.' This activity involved informing the client of the best means to achieve their goals and included frequent communication with the client. Generally, the client's customer was also interviewed in order to understand how the client's system could better integrate with their customer's requirements. Ellen recalled, however, that the procedures were necessarily different in Korea:

The client team members did not permit our team members to go to their offices unannounced. We had to book appointments ahead of time to obtain permission to see them. In part, this situation was a result of the formalities we needed to observe due to their rank in society, but I believe it was also because they wanted to be prepared for the topics we wanted to discuss.

The Korean consultants refused to interview the customers, because they did not want to disturb them. Furthermore, the client team members frequently came into the project office and asked the Korean consultants to work on activities not scheduled for that week or which were beyond the project scope. The Korean consultants accepted the work without question. Ellen and Scott found themselves powerless to stop this activity.

Shortly after arriving, Scott had a very confrontational meeting with one of the Korean consultants concerning this issue:

> I had been in Korea for about a week, and I was still suffering from jet lag. I was alone with one of the Korean consultants, and we were talking about how organizational processes should be flow-charted. He was saying the client understands the process in a particular manner, so we should show it in that way. I responded that, from a technical standpoint, it was not correct. I explained that as a consultant, we couldn't simply do what the client requests if it is incorrect. We must provide value by showing why a different method may be taken by educating the client of the options and the reasons for selecting a specific method. There are times when you have to tell the client something different than he believes. That's what we're paid for. He said, "No, no, you don't understand. They're paying our fee." At that point I raised my voice: "You don't know what you are talking about. I have much more experience than you." Afterwards, I realized that it was wrong to shout at him. I pulled him aside and apologized. He said, "Well, I know you were tired." I replied that it was no excuse, and I should not have shouted. After that, we managed to get along just fine.

The behavior of subordinates and superiors also reflected the Korean's respect for status and position. Scott observed that it was very unusual for a subordinate to leave the office for the day unless his superior had already left:

> I remember one day, a Saturday, when one of the young Korean consultants who had been ill for some time, was still at his desk. I made a comment: "Why don't you go home, Mr. Choi?" Although he was not working for me, I knew his work on the other team was done. He said, "I can't go home because several other team members have taken the day off. I have to stay." I repeated my observation that his work was done. He replied: "If I do not stay, I will be fired. My boss is still here, I have to stay." He would stay and work until his boss left, until late in the evening if necessary.

Furthermore, Scott found that the Korean consultants tended not to ask questions. Even when Scott asked the Korean consultants if they understood his instructions or explanation, they generally responded affirmatively which made it difficult to confirm their understanding. He was advised that responding in a positive manner demonstrated respect for teachers or superiors. Asking a question would be viewed as inferring that the teacher or superior had not done a good job of explaining the material. As a result, achieving a coaching role was difficult for the North American consultants even though passing on their knowledge of SI to the Korean consultants was considered an important part of their function on this project.

WOMEN IN KOREA

Historically, Confucian values have dictated a strict code of behavior between men and women and husband and wife in Korea. Traditionally, there has been a clear delineation in the respective responsibilities of men and women. The male preserve can be defined as that which is public, whereas women are expected to cater to the private, personal world of the home. Although change has taken place, these old values have lingered and the attitude of male superiority has not entirely disappeared. Korean public and business life still tend to be dominated by men.[3]

Nevertheless, compared to the Yi dynasty era, the position of women in society has changed considerably. There is now virtual equality in access to education for men and women, and a few women have embarked on political careers. As in many other areas of the world, the business world has until recently been accessible only to men. However, this is changing as Korean women are beginning to seek equality in the workplace. Young Korean men and women now often participate together in social activities such as evenings out and hikes, something that was extremely rare even 10 years ago.

Dual income families are becoming more common in South Korea, particularly in Seoul, although women generally hold lower-paid positions. Furthermore, working women often retain their traditional household responsibilities, while men are expected to join their male colleagues for late night drinking and eating events which usually exclude women.

Although the younger generation are breaking from such traditions, Scott felt that the gender differences were quite apparent in the work place. He commented:

> The business population was primarily male. Generally, the only women we saw were young women who were clerks, wearing uniforms. I suspected that these women were in the work-force for only a few years, until they were married and left to have a family. We did have a few professional Korean women working with us. However, because we are a professional services firm, I believe it may have been more progressive than the typical Korean company.

THE SYSTEMS IMPLEMENTATION TEAM

Upon her arrival in Korea, Ellen dove into her work confident that the Korean consultants she would be working with had the skills necessary to complete the job in the time frame allocated. The project work was divided up among several work groups, each having distinct deliverables and due dates. The deliverables for the SI team were required as a major input to the other work groups on the project (see Exhibit 3). As a result, delays with deliverables would impact the effectiveness of the entire project:

> JVI told us they had assigned experienced management consultants to work on the project. Given their stated skill level, Andrew's resource plan had him making periodic visits to Korea; I would be on the project on a full time basis starting in May, and Scott would join the team about three to four months after the project start. We were informed that five Korean consultants were assigned. We believed that we had the resources needed to complete the project by December.

JACK KIM

J.T. Kim, whose Western name was Jack, was the lead Korean consultant reporting to Mr. Park. Jack had recently achieved a Ph.D. in computer systems from a reputable American university and he spoke English fluently. When Andrew initially discussed the

EXHIBIT 3 Project Time Frame

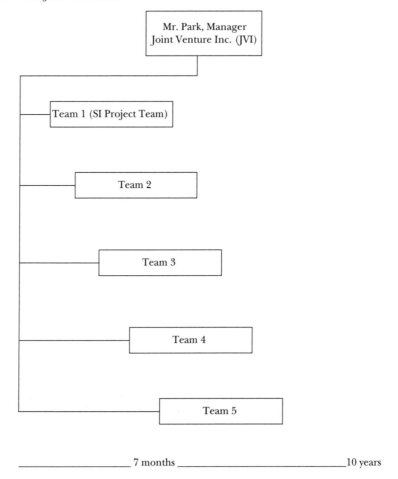

————————————— 7 months ——————————————————————10 years

organizational structure of the SI team with Mr. Park and Jack, it was agreed that Jack and Ellen would be co-managers of the SI project.

Three weeks after her arrival, Jack informed Ellen, much to her surprise, that he had never worked on a systems implementation project. Additionally, Ellen soon learned that Jack had never worked on a consulting project:

> Apparently, Jack had been made the lead consultant of SI upon completing his Ph.D. in the United States. I believe Jack was told he was going to be the sole project manager for SI on a daily basis. However, I was informed I was going to be the co-project manager with Jack. It was confusing, particularly for Jack, when I took on coaching and leading the team. We had a lot of controversy—not in the form of fights or heated discussions, but we had definite issues during the first few weeks because we were clearly stepping upon each other's territory.

Given Jack's position as the lead Korean consultant, it was quite difficult for Ellen to redirect team members' activities. The Korean team members always followed Jack's instructions. Scott recalled:

There were frequent meetings with the team to discuss the work to be completed. Often, following these meetings the Korean consultants would meet alone with Jack, and it appeared that he would instruct them to carry out different work. On one occasion, when both Andrew and Ellen were travelling away from the office, Andrew prepared specific instructions for the team to follow outlined in a memo.

Andrew sent the memo to me so I could hand the memo to Jack directly, thereby ensuring he did receive these instructions. Upon his return, Andrew found the team had not followed his instructions. We were provided with the following line of reasoning: you told us to do A, B and C, but you did not mention D. And, we did D. They had followed Jack's instructions. We had a very difficult time convincing them to carry out work as we requested, even though we had been brought onto the project to provide our expertise.

In July, a trip was planned for the Korean client team and some of the Korean consulting team to visit other project sites in North America. The trip would permit the Koreans to find out more about the capabilities of WSI and to discuss issues with other clients involved with similar projects. Jack was sent on the trip, leaving Ellen in charge of the SI project team in Korea. While Jack was away on the North American trip, Ellen had her first opportunity to work with and to lead the Korean consultants on a daily basis. She was very pleased that she was able to coach them directly, without interference, and advise them on how to best carry out the required work. Ellen felt that everyone worked together in a very positive manner, in complete alignment. When Jack returned, he saw that Ellen was leading the team and that they were accepting Ellen's directions. Ellen recalled the tensions that arose as a result:

On the first day he returned, Jack instructed someone to do some work for him, and the person responded, "I cannot because I am doing something for Ellen." Jack did not say anything, but he looked very angry. He could not understand why anyone on the team would refuse his orders.

THE MARKETING RESEARCH PROJECT

A few days after Jack returned from the North American trip, the project team realized they did not have sufficient information about their client's customer. Jack decided a market research study should be conducted to determine the market requirements. However, this type of study, which is generally a large undertaking on a project, was not within the scope of the contracted work. Ellen found out about the proposed market research project at a meeting held on a Saturday, which involved everyone from the entire project—about 40 people. The only person not at the meeting was Mr. Park. Jack was presenting the current work plans for SI, and he continued to describe a market research study:

I thought to myself, "What market research study is he talking about?" I asked him to put aside his presentation of the proposed study until he and I had an opportunity to discuss the plans. I did not want to interrupt his presentation or disagree with him publicly, but I felt I had no choice.

DINNER WITH JACK

Two hours following the presentation, Ellen's translator, Susan Lim, informed her that there was a dinner planned for that evening and Jack wanted everyone on the SI team to attend. Ellen was surprised that Jack would want her present at the dinner. However, Susan insisted that Jack specifically said Ellen must be there. They went to a small Korean restaurant, where everyone talked about a variety of subjects in English and Korean, with Susan translating for Ellen as needed. After about one hour, Jack began a speech to the team, speaking solely in Korean. Ellen thought it was unusual for him to speak Korean when she was present, as everyone at the dinner also spoke English:

> Through the limited translations I received, I understood he was humbling himself to the team, saying, "I am very disappointed in my performance. I have clearly not been the project leader needed for this team." The team members were responding "No, no, don't say that." While Jack was talking to the team, he was consuming large quantities of beer. The pitchers were coming and coming. He was quite clearly becoming intoxicated. All at once, Susan stopped translating. I asked her what was wrong. She whispered that she would tell me later. Five minutes went by and I turned to her and spoke emphatically, "Susan, what is going on? I want to know now." She realized I was getting angry. She told me, "Jack asked me to stop translating. Please don't say anything, I will lose my job."
>
> I waited a couple of minutes before speaking, then I interrupted Jack's speech. I said, "Susan is having difficulty hearing you and isn't able to translate for me. I guess it is too noisy in this restaurant. Would it be possible for you to speak in English?" Jack did not say anything for about 30 seconds and then he started speaking in English. His first words were, "Ellen, I would like to apologize. I didn't realize you couldn't understand what I was saying."

Another thirty minutes of his speech and drinking continued. The Korean team members appeared to be consoling Jack, by saying: "Jack, we do respect you and the work you have done for our team. You have done your best." While they were talking, Jack leaned back, and appeared to pass out. Ellen turned to Susan and asked if they should help him to a taxi. Susan insisted it would not be appropriate. During the next hour, Jack appeared to be passed out or sleeping. Finally, one of the team members left to go home. Ellen asked Susan, "Is it important for me to stay, or is it important for me to go?" She said Ellen should go.

When Ellen returned to her hotel, it was approximately 11 p.m. on Saturday night. She felt the situation had reached a point where it was necessary to request assistance from senior management in North America. Andrew was on a wilderness camping vacation in the United States with his family, and could not be reached. Ellen decided to call the North American project sponsor, the Senior Vice President, George Peterson:

> I called George that Saturday night at his house and said: "We have a problem. They're trying to change the scope of the project. We don't have the available time, and we don't have the resources. It is impossible to do a market research study in conjunction with all the contracted work to be completed with the same limited resources. The proposed plan is to use our project team to handle this additional work. Our team is already falling behind the schedule, but due to their inexperience they don't realize it yet." George said he would find Andrew and send him to Korea to further assess the situation.

THE MEETING WITH THE DIRECTOR

When Andrew arrived in August, he conducted a very quick assessment of the situation. The project was a month behind schedule. It appeared to Andrew that the SI team had made limited progress since his previous visit:

> It was clear to me that the Korean team members weren't taking direction from Ellen. Ellen was a seasoned consultant and knew what to do. However, Jack was giving direction to the team which was leading them down different paths. Jack was requesting that the team work on tasks which were not required for the project deliverables, and he was not appropriately managing the client's expectations.

Andrew held several discussions with Mr. Park concerning these issues. Mr. Park insisted the problem was Ellen. He argued that Ellen was not effective, she did not assign work properly, and she did not give credible instructions to the team. However, Andrew believed the Korean consultants' lack of experience was the main problem.

> Initially, we were told the Korean team consisted of experienced consultants, although they had not completed any SI projects. I felt we could work around it. I had previously taught consultants to do SI. We were also told that one of the Korean consultants had taught SI. This consultant was actually the most junior person on the team. She had researched SI by reading some texts and had given a presentation on her understanding of SI to a group of consultants.

Meanwhile, Andrew solicited advice from the WSI Co-Managing Director, Robert Brown, who had over ten years' experience working in Korea. Robert suggested that Andrew approach Mr. Park's superior, Mr. Song, directly. He further directed Andrew to present his case to the Joint Venture committee if an agreement was not reached with Mr. Song. Andrew had discussed the issues with George Peterson and Robert Brown, and they agreed that there was no reason for Ellen to leave the project:

> However, Robert's message to me was that I had been too compliant with the Koreans. It was very important for the project to be completed on time, and that I would be the one held accountable for any delays. Addressing issues before the Joint Venture committee was the accepted dispute resolution process at JVI when an internal conflict could not be resolved. However, in most cases, the last thing a manager wants is to be defending his position before the Joint Venture committee. Mr. Song was in line to move into senior executive management. Taking the problem to the Joint Venture committee would be a way to force the issue with him.

Andrew attempted to come to a resolution with Mr. Park once again, but he refused to compromise. Andrew then tried to contact Mr. Song and was told he was out of the office. Coincidentally, Mr. Song visited the project site to see Mr. Park just as Ellen and Andrew were completing a meeting. Ellen recalls Mr. Song's arrival:

> Mr. Song walked into the project office expecting to find Mr. Park. However, Mr. Park was out visiting another project that morning. Mr. Song looked around the project office for a

senior manager, and he saw Andrew. Mr. Song approached Andrew and asked if Mr. Park was in the office. Andrew responded that he was not. Mr. Song proceeded to comment that he understood there were some concerns about the project work, and suggested that perhaps, sometime, they could talk about it. Andrew replied that they needed to talk about it immediately.

Andrew met with Mr. Song in Mr. Park's office, a makeshift set of thin walls that enclosed a small office area in one corner of the large open project office. Ellen was working in an area just outside the office when she heard Andrew's voice rise. She heard him shout, "Well, I don't think you're listening to what I am saying." Ellen was surprised to hear Andrew shouting. She knew Andrew was very sensitive to what should and should not be done in the Korean environment:

> Andrew's behavior seemed so confrontational. I believed this behavior was unacceptable in Korea. For a while, I heard a lot of murmuring, after which I heard Andrew speak adamantly, "No, I'm very serious. It doesn't matter what has been agreed and what has not been agreed because most of our agreements were based on inaccurate information. We can start from scratch." Mr. Song insisted that I was the problem.

The Richard Ivey School of Business gratefully acknowledges the generous support of The Richard and Jean Ivey Fund in the development of this case as part of the RICHARD AND JEAN IVEY FUND ASIAN CASE SERIES.

Notes

1   For an account of Ellen's experience in Bahrain, see Ellen Moore (A): Living and Working in Bahrain, 9A90C019, and Ellen Moore (B), 9A90C020; Ivey Publishing, Ivey Management Services, c/o Richard Ivey School of Business, University of Western Ontario, London, Ontario, Canada, N6A 3K7.

2   Information for this section was taken from Official website of Korea tourism, http://english.visitkorea.or.kr/enu/index.kto; Korean Confucianism, http://www.asia-pacific-connections.com/confucianism.html; and the U.S. Department of State website, http://www.state.gov/r/pa/ei/bgn/2800.htm#people; accessed January 22, 2009.

3   See for example "Women's Role in Contemporary Korea", http://www.askasia.org/teachers/essays/essay.php?no=21, and "Women's Development and Information on Women in Korea", Young-Joo Paik, Korean Women's Development Institute, Seoul, Korea. Paper presented at the 64th IFLA General Conference, August 16 – August 21, 1998; *http://www.ifla.org/IV/ifla64/112-122e.htm,* accessed January 22, 2009. See also Korea: The Essential Guide to Customs & Culture, Culture Smart, 2008.

PART 4

CHAPTER **8**

Competing with Integrity in Global Business: Personal Integrity

OVERVIEW

In earlier chapters we discussed how culture affects behavior as well as its potential impact on strategy and operations. Now, we will examine the issues of personal ethical behavior that you, as managers, may face in your careers. We highlight personal integrity in this chapter because we believe that issues of individual responsibility and ethics do not always receive the attention that they deserve in business courses.

The objective is to challenge you to consider your responsibilities as a business leader more broadly than simply from a financial perspective. There can be social consequences resulting from your decisions as well as financial ones. The human and social impacts of decisions should be considered at the time these decisions are being made. And it is not just the consequences to some faceless group of people in some faraway land that you need to consider. There can be personal consequences to you as well from your decisions.

Following the global mindset framework presented in the beginning of this book (See Figure 8.1), we will now consider these issues at the individual level (ethical behavior) in this chapter and at the organizational level (corporate citizenship or more commonly referred to as corporate social responsibility or "CSR") in Chapter 9. What is the difference between ethical behavior and corporate citizenship? We think of the distinction as being between the decisions and behavior of an individual or a small group of people and a formal initiative of an organization.

In this chapter we will explore the distinction between ethical and legal behavior as well as the differences in major ethical frameworks or theories of moral philosophy such

FIGURE 8.1 Global Mindset Framework Applied to Ethics and Corporate Citizenship

	Individual	Organizational
Self	Clarify and understand my beliefs about ethical behavior.	Clarify and understand my organization's approach to corporate citizenship.
Other	Clarify and understand other beliefs about ethical behavior in the context of other cultures and principal theories of moral philosophy.	Clarify and understand other approaches to corporate citizenship in the context of other companies, other cultures and principal codes of conduct.
Choice	Belief in and commitment to a set of ethical principles.	Belief in and commitment to an approach to corporate citizenship.

as consequential (results focused), rules-based (universal), and cultural relativism. We hope that these discussions of competing with integrity, personal and corporate, help you develop your own way of thinking about competing with integrity.

De George suggests that executives should act and compete with integrity in international business.[1] Acting with integrity is the same as acting ethically, but the word integrity does not have the negative connotation, the moralizing tone, or the sense of naïveté that the word "ethics" carries for many people. What is integrity and how does one compete with integrity? According to De George: "Acting with integrity means both acting in accordance with one's highest self-accepted norms of behavior and imposing on oneself the norms demanded by ethics and morality."[2]

Competing with integrity means that executives of multinational corporations should compete in a way that is consistent with their own highest values and norms of behavior. Although these values and norms are self-imposed and self-accepted, they cannot be simply arbitrary and self-serving; but neither is there a requirement to be perfect. "The imperative to act with integrity cannot insist on moral perfection. It can and does demand taking ethical considerations seriously."[3]

ETHICAL ISSUES

The least clear aspect of managerial responsibility may be in the domain of ethics, which is the "moral thinking and analysis by corporate decision makers regarding the motives and consequences of their decisions and actions."[4] Ethics is the study of morals and systems of morality, or principles of conduct. The study of ethics is concerned with the right or wrong and the "should" or "should not" of human decisions and actions. This does not mean that all questions of right and wrong are ethical issues, however. There is right and wrong associated with rules of etiquette – for example, in which hand to hold your knife and fork, in the use of language and rules of grammar, and in making a computer work. Holding a fork in the wrong hand or speaking ungrammatically does not constitute unethical behavior.

The ethical or moral frame of reference is concerned with human behavior in society and with the relationships, duties, and obligations between people, groups, and organizations. It is concerned with the human consequences associated with decisions and actions, consequences not fully addressed by profits, more sophisticated technology, and larger market share. In this concern for human outcomes, it differs from other perspectives such as financial, marketing, accounting, or legal. An ethical perspective requires that you extend consideration beyond your own self-interest (or that of your company) to consider the interests of a wider community of stakeholders, including employees, customers, suppliers, the general public, and even foreign governments. It also advocates behaving according to what would be considered better or higher standards of conduct, not necessarily the minimum acceptable by law.

Not all problems come with neat labels on them. Ethical decisions do not arise separately from strategy, marketing, or operating decisions, for example, because problems in the real world do not come with neat labels attached: here is a finance problem; here is a marketing problem; and now, an ethical problem. Managers may categorize the issues by functional area or break up a complex problem into components such as those mentioned. Usually policy issues and decisions are multifaceted and simultaneously may have financial, marketing, and production components. They also may have ethical dimensions that managers should consider. However, in considering a typical complex problem with more than one dimension, the ethical dimension may be overlooked.

If situations did come with labels on them, a person could apply the techniques and concepts he or she had learned, such as net present value to a financial problem or market segmentation to a marketing problem. What would happen if a problem labeled "ethical dilemma" arrived? A manager probably would be in a quandary because he or she most likely would not have a way of analyzing, let alone resolving, this type of problem. The decision-making tools for this type of situation probably would be lacking. Business schools, traditionally, have not emphasized the teaching of ethics as rigorously as they have the teaching of finance or marketing, for example. Business students and managers generally have not been trained to think about ethical issues as they have been trained in the frameworks and techniques for functional areas of specialization. However, after numerous scandals in the United States (e.g. Enron, Tyco, WorldCom) and in Europe (e.g. Parmalat), this is changing as business schools move to address the issue of managerial ethics.

Some Examples

There have been many examples of ethical lapses by executives from many companies and many nations. European defense contractors allegedly were involved with corruption and bribery related to arms deals in South Africa;[5] Xerox admitted making improper payments to government officials in India over a period of years;[6] and the Norwegian state-run oil group, Statoil, was involved in a bribery scandal with Iran in 2003. WalMart, Kathie Lee Gifford, and Payless Shoes, among others, have been implicated in using sweatshops to produce shoes and apparel.[7] Nike received significant criticism for employing child labor in countries such as Cambodia and Pakistan and, as a result, suffered boycotts of its products.

Ethical questions can arise in many areas of operations: the type of products produced, marketing and advertising practices, business conduct in countries where physical security is a problem, requests for payments to secure contracts or sales, and payments to prevent damage to plants and equipment or injury to employees. Some products are controversial in themselves, such as tobacco or the abortion pill since they facilitate behavior that some people would consider unethical. Other products such as jeans or rugs may not create dilemmas for the end user, but their production may raise questions. Some examples follow.

Product Safety

Cigarettes   According to the World Health Organization (WHO):[8]

> Tobacco is the leading preventable cause of death in the world. It causes 1 in 10 deaths among adults worldwide. In 2005, tobacco caused 5.4 million deaths, or an average of one death every 6 seconds. At the current rate, the death toll is projected to reach more than 8 million annually by 2030 and a total of up to one billion deaths in the 21st century.

One half of the smokers today will eventually be killed by tobacco. And it is not just the smokers who will die. Second-hand smoke kills also. The WHO Fact File states that the International Labor Organization estimates that at least 200 000 workers die every year due to exposure to smoke at work and that the United States Environmental Protection Agency estimates that second-hand smoke is responsible for about 3000 lung cancer deaths annually among nonsmokers in the USA.[9] WHO also notes that "a cigarette is the only legally available consumer product that kills through normal use."

The problems associated with smoking are well known now, including disease, deaths, and economic costs. On May 21, 2003, the 192 Member States of WHO adopted the world's first public health treaty, the WHO Framework Convention on Tobacco Control (FCTC). This treaty was designed to reduce tobacco-related deaths and disease around the world. Before it goes into effect, however, countries have to sign and ratify it. Among its measures, the FCTC requires that countries impose restrictions on tobacco advertising, sponsorship, and promotion; and establish new packaging and labeling of tobacco products. Achieving agreement on the FCTC was not easy, and the eventual treaty was significantly "watered down" in large measure due to the actions of the Bush (George W.) Administration.[10]

In a letter to President George W. Bush on April 29, 2003,[11] Democratic Representative Henry Waxman, the ranking minority member of the House Committee on Government Reform, said:

> At the most recent, and final, negotiating session, held from February 17 to February 28, 2003, the United States again attempted to weaken the tobacco control treaty on key issues. Indeed, your negotiators even opposed international efforts to restrict the distribution of free samples and to prohibit the sale of tobacco products to children.

The US, Canada, and Germany all opposed a total advertising ban claiming that their constitutions protect freedom of speech and do not permit them to implement a comprehensive ban. NGOs proposed the adoption of a "constitutional carve out" that allowed the FCTC to have a full ban on tobacco advertising, except for countries whose constitutions would not allow for a full ban. The US and Germany opposed it.[12]

Does freedom of speech cover cigarette advertising? Is trade more important than public health? Even if there are US Constitutional issues involving tobacco advertising bans, should the United States try to prevent other nations from banning tobacco advertising if it is permitted by their own legal systems?

In 2003, the Government Accounting Office (GAO) found that the Foreign Agricultural Service may have violated Congress' prohibition on the US Department of Agriculture from spending any funds to promote the sale or export of tobacco products.[13] Should one part of the US government spend money to combat smoking in the United States while other parts are spending it to promote cigarette exports to other countries? One side could argue that countries like the United States, Britain, and Japan, where the majority of big tobacco companies are located, are exporting death and disease to the developing world. The other side could counter that cigarettes are not illegal, are manufactured and sold in many countries, and, therefore, manufacturers would not be introducing these items for the first time. They would argue that since manufacturing and selling cigarettes is not illegal, international tobacco companies should have access to the developing world's markets.

At a company level, what obligations should a corporation have regarding advertising in other countries? Should the company follow the local laws, even if they are less restrictive than at home, or would there be a responsibility to advertise that cigarette smoking is hazardous to your health and include all warnings required in the United States or even elsewhere, if they are stricter? Should they oppose large warning sizes because they may "infringe" on their trademarks on the packages?

All the issues regarding exporting and advertising cigarettes could be treated simply as considerations in international trade, marketing, or advertising, if one chose. Advertising cigarettes in other countries could also be treated as primarily a legal question, as the US and German governments apparently saw it. Is treating complex situations and decisions that involve harmful consequences to humans primarily as trade, marketing, or legal issues without addressing the ethical implications, a mistake and unethical?

Toys   In August 2007, Mattel recalled almost 20 million toys made in China. On August 2, the company recalled 1.5 million toys because of a fear that hazardous levels of lead paint had been used on them. This recall came shortly after recalls involving toothpaste, tires, and pet food ingredients imported from China. Consumers in the United States and the US government were extremely concerned and there was a popular sentiment developing against dangerous products "made in China." On August 13, Zhang Shuhong, owner of the Lida Toy Company, hanged himself in his factory.

On August 14, Mattel recalled 18 million more toys made in China because they contained small, powerful magnets that could come loose and potentially be swallowed by small children, possibly causing them serious harm – in fact at least three children needed surgery after swallowing them.[14] This was obviously another "made in China" problem. Or was it?

China pushed back and it came to light that all the problems were not Chinese ones. On August 21, Thomas A. Debrowski, executive vice president for Mattel's worldwide operations, apologized to China's product safety chief, Li Changjang. Mattel had said that many of the toys were recalled because of design problems. It also had blamed some vendors in China for violating Mattel's rules by failing to use safe paint or to run tests on paint. Mattel, in Debrowski's apology, accepted blame for its part in the problem which was that the "vast majority of those products that were recalled were the result of a design flaw in Mattel's design, not through a manufacturing flaw in China's manufacturers."[15]

In a study of the toy recall issue, *Toy Recalls – Is China Really the Problem?* authors Bapuji and Beamish state:

> . . . an examination of the reasons for the increase [in toy recalls] shows that the number of defects related to design issues attributable to the company ordering the toys is far higher than those caused by manufacturing problems in China.[16]

In its recall of the defectively designed toys and its associated press releases, was Mattel trying to blame China for a known company failure and to shift the locus of responsibility? Was the company acting ethically? And was the company adequately supervising its foreign vendors?

Labor and Employment Practices

Jeans and Rugs   The previous examples had public health considerations and, in the case of Mattel, supervision of foreign contractors. There are potential ethical issues with products that don't involve public health such as jeans and rugs when they are manufactured by or purchased from contractors that abuse human rights.

- **Clothing** Levi Strauss stopped purchasing from subcontractors in Myanmar and China because of practices such as using child and prison labor to manufacture products.[17] In 1991, the company developed a set of standards called the "Global Sourcing Guidelines," which address workplace issues for its partners and subcontractors, and the selection of countries for sourcing products.[18] It was the first apparel company to establish a comprehensive ethical code of conduct for manufacturing and finishing contractors.[19] The company's "terms of engagement" are based on standards set by the United Nations (particularly the Universal Declaration of Human Rights) and include ethical standards, legal requirements, environmental requirements, and community involvement; and specifically address issues of child labor, forced labor, disciplinary practices, working hours, wages and benefits, freedom of association, discrimination, and health and safety.
- **Rugs** In the 1980s, attention was drawn to the illegal use of child labor in the handwoven rug industry by the International Labor Organization (ILO), the US Department of Labor, and human rights groups. In 1994, the RugMark Foundation was established by a coalition of nongovernmental organizations, businesses, government entities, and multilateral groups like UNICEF to combat child labor.[20] The

first carpets bearing the RugMark label were exported from India at the beginning of 1995, mainly to Germany. Later countries promoting the RugMark label grew to include England and the United States. To date, more than four million carpets bearing the RugMark label have been sold in Europe and North America.[21]

What is a company's responsibility toward ensuring that its suppliers are not using child labor? Some people would argue that children are better suited to making rugs because of their greater dexterity than adults and that their families, who need the money, would be worse off if the children were not working. Opponents, however, point out that many of the children were found to be victims of debt bondage or forced labor, practices banned by the United Nations and condemned as modern forms of slavery.[22]

Nina Smith, RugMark USA's Executive Director has stated, "We need to get some major retailers – like Macy's Inc, IKEA, Pier One, Ethan Allen – on board. If they don't do it they're perpetuating [the child labor] problem."[23] Is joining RugMark the only way to counter child labor?

Ethical issues, by definition, are never simple. Is it ever acceptable to use child labor? The issue about manufacturing rugs is not a simple as "do not use child labor." We spoke at length with a small business owner who exports rugs from Pakistan and Afghanistan. She visits her manufacturers regularly and encourages community development around the making of rugs. There were many girls as young as eight years who were working in her craft shops:

> If I did not hire these girls, they would not be in school. They would be in the fields. Their life expectancy would be shorter; they would be working alone. In the workshop, they sit together with women of three or more generations, they learn a skill, and they learn about their culture. Because they are in my workshop, I can provide good meals and people and materials to provide at least some education and social support for them. Am I doing the right thing? According to the press and many consumers, definitely not! But I do believe that, in this case, hiring these girls and trying to provide a better environment for them is the right thing.

IKEA also recognizes that child labor abuses exist in countries where its products are manufactured, but it has created its own program to prevent child labor based on the United Nations Convention on the Rights of the Child (1989). It also has a Children's Ombudsman and a code of conduct called "The IKEA Way on Preventing Child Labour" including unannounced visits by an auditor at suppliers and subcontractors. In addition, it supports a project to eliminate child labor by addressing its root causes such as lack of education, debt, and poverty.[24] Is IKEA perpetuating child labor by not being a part of RugMark, or is it acting ethically and responsibly in its own way?

Human Rights and Security

Nigeria Human rights and fundamental freedoms were issues in Nigeria in November 1995 when Ken Saro-Wiwa was executed by the military government. In 1994, General Sani Abacha had declared the death penalty for "anyone who interferes with the government's efforts to 'revitalize' the oil industry."[25] The declaration was his response to striking oil workers and demands for increased revenue sharing by local communities. Saro-Wiwa was a political activist who was campaigning on behalf of his people, the Ogoni, and against the degradation of the environment by oil spills and pollution caused by Royal Dutch/Shell.[26] In 1995, Saro-Wiwa's activities were construed as "interference" and he was executed by the Nigerian government.

Initially, Shell responded defensively with full-page advertisements in major newspapers around the world explaining its position.[27] Later, under pressure from shareholders who filed a resolution at its annual meeting in 1997, it changed the tone of its response dramatically. It named Cor Herkstroter, at the time Chairman of Royal Dutch (the Dutch half of the company), to be responsible for human rights and environmental issues. Mr Herkstroter accepted the criticism that Nigeria Shell should have been more proactive in improving its environmental performance.[28] He also conducted a review of the company's business principles and added commitments to support human rights and sustainable development.

Since 2000, Shell has been actively translating this commitment into practice.[29] The company has conducted intensive training in countries where it operates that have poor human rights records. For example, with the Danish Institute for Human Rights, Shell has trained more than 1500 staff in Nigeria since 2005 in managing difficult situations, like responding to conflict in local communities.

It also created a human rights management primer that provides staff with practical help to develop competence in managing human rights issues and a series of human rights dilemmas to help managers to understand their responsibilities regarding human rights. It also developed a risk assessment tool to analyze the human rights risks associated with entering or operating in politically sensitive areas. And it became a participant in a new initiative to support human rights, the Voluntary Principles on Security and Human Rights.

The Voluntary Principles on Security and Human Rights were developed through a dialogue among the governments of the United States, the United Kingdom, the Netherlands, and Norway, companies in the extractive and energy sectors, and non-governmental organizations (NGOs). All had an interest in human rights and drafted a set of voluntary principles to "guide companies in maintaining the safety and security of their operations within an operating framework that ensures respect for human rights and fundamental freedoms."[30]

Executive Security   Situations in which physical security of managers could be a problem may present ethical issues for managers and employees. Consider a situation in which British expatriate women working in the Middle East training center of a North American-based bank found themselves. They were en route to conduct a training program in Lagos, Nigeria, and were supposed to be met by one of the bank's local staff who would assist them through difficulties in customs at the airport. When the local staff member failed to appear, the women felt forced to pay bribes to bring legitimate training materials and equipment into the country. Soon after paying the money, their taxi was stopped at the darkened perimeter of the airport and machine guns were jabbed at them through the windows by uniformed men. The women were "shaken down" again and felt very vulnerable, particularly with no foreign currency left. After repeatedly showing their documents and denying that they were violating any laws, they were finally permitted to pass. The women were deeply shaken by the experience and vowed never to travel into that country alone again.

What responsibility did the local management bear for abandoning them? And what was the ethical responsibility of the experienced managers for whom the women worked who sent them into such a situation so ill-prepared? What is a manager's responsibility regarding the implementation of his or her decisions, particularly when the specific action has to be taken by another person?

Unfortunately, in recent years the world has become a more dangerous place and situations in which physical security has become a managerial concern are becoming more common in global companies. As this chapter is being written, a sophisticated, well-planned and coordinated, large-scale terrorist attack has just ended in Mumbai, India that left more than 170 people dead. The perpetrators were not immediately known and may have been a group with a primarily regional agenda such as the Kashmir conflict. However, news reports suggested that they were apparently searching for and targeting foreigners, although many more Indians died in the attack than did foreigners. *Business Week* reported that the CEO of Unilever "narrowly escaped death in the massacre at the Taj Mahal hotel where he was dining with colleagues."[31]

Many companies currently are operating in countries where personal security concerns are considerations and/or where political violence and terrorism are issues.[32] On March 11, 2004, terrorists bombed a train in Madrid, killing 191 people and injuring 2000 others. In late May 2004, terrorists killed 22 people in oil company office compounds and in an expatriate housing compound in Saudi Arabia and took over 40 hostages, including Americans and Europeans, while earlier in the month terrorists killed six Westerners and a Saudi in another attack.[33] In India, executives of the Korean company Posco were kidnapped.[34]

What is a company's ethical responsibility associated with assigning an employee to one of these countries? What should it do regarding training and protecting employees who work in these areas? What is the responsibility of individuals who agree to work there?

Bribery and Corruption

Other dilemmas that executives may encounter are requests for bribes or even extortion. For example, mobsters threatened Otis Elevator that they would firebomb its operation in Russia if it did not pay protection money.[35] How should this situation be handled? Otis has a code delineating its view of right and wrong behavior that all executives sign each year. Its response was not to give in to the extortion, but to pay more for security.[36] Situations involving extortion and bribery have many facets and usually are not resolved simply.

Another example was Statoil (now StatoilHydro) which was founded in 1972 with a mandate to explore and develop Norway's offshore oil and gas reserves.[37] Operating in Norway's harsh waters demanded a high level of innovation, which helped Statoil to become one of the world's foremost authorities in offshore production. By the end of the century, Statoil faced declining reserves at home and sought to expand through international investment.

In the years following the death of the Ayatollah Khomeini, the Iranian government decided to reopen the country to international investment. In 2001, the National Iranian Oil Company (NIOC) sought tenders to develop South Pars, an offshore oil field that held approximately 8 % of known world gas reserves, and 40 % of Iran's known reserves. In October 2002, NIOC awarded Statoil a 40 % stake in the South Pars project. Under the terms of the agreement, Statoil was to invest $300 million over four years as part of its $2.6 billion investment in the Persian Gulf.[38]

Less than one year after being awarded the contract, Statoil's future in Iran appeared to be in jeopardy. The controversy centered on alleged bribes paid by Horton Investments, on Statoil's behalf, in order to secure lucrative petroleum development contracts.

In early 2003, Statoil's internal auditors had uncovered secret payments of $5 million to Horton Investments,[39] a Turks and Caicos Islands registered consultancy thought to be run by the son of a former Iranian president. According to Statoil, Horton Investments was hired to provide "insight into financial, industrial, legal, and social issues associated with business development in Iran."[40] But according to the Iranian government, the secret $15 million contract between Horton and Statoil was used to channel bribes to unnamed government officials..

According to the company's web site, Statoil settled with the United States, accepted a fine of US$10.5 million for violating the US Foreign Corrupt Practices Act, and accepted responsibility for the bribery, as well as for accounting for those payments improperly and for having insufficient internal controls to prevent the payments. The company also paid a fine of US$3 million to Norway for violation of Norway's law.[41]

The Foreign Corrupt Practices Act[42]   In 1977, the United States Congress passed into law the Foreign Corrupt Practices Act (FCPA) in response to investigations that discovered that over 400 US companies had made questionable or illegal payments to foreign government officials, politicians, and political parties for a range of reasons, from facilitating payments to get low level government officials to just do their jobs to high officials to secure favorable decisions. Twenty years later, the United States and 33 other countries signed the OECD Convention on Combating Bribery of Foreign Public Officials in International Business Transactions.

Under the FCPA it is illegal for a US citizen as well as foreign companies with securities listed in the United States to make a payment to a foreign official to obtain business for or with, or directing business to, any person or company. Since 1998, the rules also apply to foreign firms and persons while in the United States. The Act does contain an exception for "facilitating payments" for "routine governmental actions."

The law also requires companies whose securities are listed in the United States to make and keep records that accurately reflect the transactions of the corporation and to maintain an adequate system of internal accounting controls.

Bribery and corruption are global problems that are not limited to public officials in a few developing countries. Executives of global corporations headquartered in developed countries are affected and some, even, have been implicated in scandals. Global executives should not be smug about the locus of the problem or their responsibilities. There is an old saying, "It takes two to tango."

An organization that has been established to combat the problem of bribery and corruption is Transparency International.

Transparency International[43]   Since 1993 when it was founded, Transparency International (TI) has become the leading NGO combating national and international corruption. TI has developed chapters in approximately 90 countries and has worked with organizations like the OECD, the Organization of American States (OAS), the European Union, and the African Union to develop and monitor anti-corruption legislation and treaties. It analyzes corruption by measuring its occurrence through surveys, and it has created resources and tools used by people around the world in the fight against corruption. These tools include the Corruption Perceptions Index, Global Corruption Barometer, Global Corruption Report, Bribe Payers Index, and the latest anti-corruption information on TI's web site (http://www.transparency.org/).

TI's Bribe Payers Index (BPI) evaluates the likelihood of firms from the world's 30 leading exporting countries to bribe. Transparency International says:

> Companies from the wealthiest countries generally rank in the top half of the Index, but still routinely pay bribes, particularly in developing economies. Companies from emerging export powers India, China and Russia rank among the worst. In the case of China and other emerging export powers, efforts to strengthen domestic anti-corruption activities have failed to extend abroad.[44]

The Corruption Perception Index ranks 180 countries by their perceived levels of corruption, as determined by expert assessments and opinion surveys. The score ranges between 10 (highly clean) and 0 (highly corrupt) for 133 countries. The 10 countries that scored the highest (highly clean) on the 2008 Index were Denmark, New Zealand, Sweden, Finland, Singapore, Iceland, the Netherlands, Australia, and Canada. The United Kingdom was 16th and the United States was tied for 18th with Japan and Belgium. The countries that scored the lowest (highly corrupt) were Sudan, Afghanistan, Haiti, Iraq, Myanmar, and Somalia.

Responding to Ethical Problems

How might managers respond when they encounter ethical problems such as the examples that we have just seen or work in countries where corruption is rampant and where they may encounter requests for bribes? One of the first things they may do is avoid the ethical dilemma through the process of rationalization. They may focus on some other aspect of the problem. They may transform the ethical problem into a legal or accounting problem, for instance. The reasoning seems to be that, so long as one is behaving legally or in accordance with accepted accounting practices, for example, nothing else is required. As will be discussed later, compliance with laws and professional regulations is a minimum requirement for responsible managers.

Another kind of avoidance behavior is to see the problem as only one small piece of a larger puzzle and to assume that someone higher up in the organization must be looking after any unusual aspects, such as ethical considerations. Alternatively, the decision-maker might turn it into someone else's problem – perhaps a customer, supplier, or person in higher authority – with the comment: "I am following my boss's orders" or "my customer's instructions." When a customer asks for a falsified invoice on imported goods for his or her records, with the difference deposited in a foreign bank, and you provide this "service," is it only the customer's behavior that is questionable?

Rationalizing one's behavior by transforming an ethical problem into another type of problem, or assuming responsibility for only one specific, technical component of the issue, or claiming that it is someone else's problem gives one the feeling of being absolved from culpability by putting the burden of responsibility elsewhere.

Who is responsible for ensuring that managers act ethically? We believe that corporations have a responsibility to make clear to their employees what sort of behavior is expected of them. This means that executives in headquarters have a responsibility, not just for their own behavior, but also for providing guidance to subordinates. A number of companies have corporate codes to do just this. For example, General Electric (GE) has an integrity policy entitled, *The Spirit & Letter* that covers, among other issues, ethical business practices, health, safety, and environmental protection, and equal employment opportunity. Employees sign a pledge that they will adhere to the policy. Jeffrey Immelt, CEO of GE, in his introduction to this policy, explained:

> For more than 125 years, GE has demonstrated an unwavering commitment to performance with integrity . . . This reputation has never been stronger. In several surveys of CEOs, GE has been named the world's most respected and admired company. We have been ranked first for integrity and governance.
>
> But none of that matters if each of us does not make the right decisions and take the right actions. At a time when many people are more cynical than ever about business, GE must seek to earn this high level of trust every day, employee by employee.
>
> This is why I ask each person in the GE community to make a personal commitment to follow our Code of Conduct. This set of GE policies on key integrity issues guides us in upholding our ethical commitment. All GE employees must comply not only with the letter of these policies, but also their spirit.
>
> If you have a question or concern about what is proper conduct for you or anyone else, promptly raise the issue with your manager, a GE ombudsperson or through one of the many other channels the Company makes available to you. Do not allow anything – not "making the numbers," competitive instincts or even a direct order from a superior – to compromise your commitment to integrity.
>
> GE leaders are also responsible not only for their own actions but for fostering a culture in which compliance with GE policy and applicable law is at the core of business-specific activities. Leaders must address employees' concerns about appropriate conduct promptly and with care and respect.
>
> There is no conflict between excellent financial performance and high standards of governance and compliance – in fact, the two are mutually reinforcing. As we focus on becoming the preeminent growth company of the 21st century, we must recognize that only one kind of performance will maintain our reputation, increase our customers' confidence in us and our products and services, and enable us to continue to grow, and that is performance with integrity.[45]

Although a company has a responsibility to outline what behavior it expects from an employee, the person on the spot facing the decision is ultimately responsible for his or her own behavior, with or without guidance from headquarters.

Codes of conduct requiring ethical behavior are common in many companies. Links to companies in the United Kingdom, for example, and their codes of conduct can be found on the web site of the Institute of Business Ethics in London.[1]

However, an issue that global executives need to consider carefully is whether or not codes of conduct are effective. Donaldson[46] found that effective codes of conduct meet three criteria:

1 Senior management has to be committed to ethical behavior and the codes of conduct; and the codes have to affect "everyday decisions and actions."
2 External or "imposed" codes are not generally effective. Companies have to develop their own and take "ownership" of their codes.
3 Various important stakeholders (employees, customers, suppliers, nongovernmental organizations) have to be involved in shaping the development and implementation of the codes.

In the cases that you study in this course, you will be asked to develop your own stance on the issues. We encourage you to think carefully about the problems to develop reasoned positions. You may find yourself in a similar situation some day, and you will have to make a critical decision. We hope that, by working through the decisions in these cases now, you will be better able to deal with similar decisions later.

As we personally encountered ethical dilemmas or heard about others who had experienced them, we wrote cases and developed a managerial framework for thinking about and analyzing the problems. We make no claim that the framework to be presented is a complete or definitive treatment of the topic of ethics. We think it does provide a practical and useful way to start addressing the topic.

Ethical versus Legal Behavior

A question always arises as to the distinction between legal and ethical behavior. If one acts legally, in accordance with laws, is that not sufficient? Not all of society's norms regarding moral behavior have been codified or made into law. There can, therefore, be many instances of questionable behavior that are not illegal.[47] It would seem that acting legally is the minimum required behavior for executives. However, society relies on more than laws to function effectively in many spheres of endeavor. In business, trust is essential also. Finally, it also should be recognized that not all laws are moral; an example would be apartheid in South Africa, which was legal but clearly not moral.

Henderson has provided a useful way to think about the relationship between ethical and legal behavior.[48] He created a matrix based on whether an action was legal or illegal and ethical or unethical, similar to that shown in Figure 8.2. Assuming that executives want to act legally and ethically (quadrant 4) and avoid making decisions (or acting in ways) that are illegal and unethical (quadrant 2), the decisions that create dilemmas are the ones that fall into quadrants 1 and 3.

[1] http://www.ibe.org.uk/whoweare.html, accessed December 6, 2008.

FIGURE 8.2   Framework for Classifying Behavior

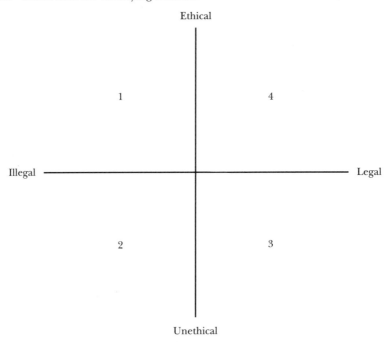

For example, consider the decision of a chemical company manager who refuses to promote a pregnant woman to an area of the company where she would be exposed to toxic chemicals that could damage her child. In the United States or Canada the manager probably would be acting ethically, but illegally (quadrant 1). Maybe he could solve the problem by delaying the promotion, if that was possible. This simple example illustrates that a decision can be ethical but not legal; there also may be solutions that allow a win–win outcome in which the decision is legal and ethical because of the way it is made.

In quadrant 3, there will be situations like the marketing of infant formula in developing countries. Infant formula, which was misused in many countries with poor sanitation and polluted water and where people were illiterate and could not read directions, was blamed for the deaths of hundreds of thousands of babies each year. This activity was not illegal, but a vote of the United Nations regarding infant formula declared it unethical.[49] In an interesting twist to this story, studies now have shown that the AIDS virus can be transmitted through breastfeeding and the UN has estimated that one third of all infants with HIV got it through their mother's milk.[50] Infant formula may now be a way to combat the transmission of HIV. This example also points out that society's notions of ethical behavior may change with the times, and with new conditions and knowledge. Another example in quadrant 3 would be apartheid in South Africa.

The last example raises the question about whose laws and values should be followed when there are conflicts. Although it might seem that we are avoiding answers, we believe that these are questions each person and company need to answer for themselves. The challenge is to find ways of operating that are consistent with local laws and high standards of conduct. We believe that this goal is attainable with thorough analysis and carefully considered action. In those situations where such a win–win outcome is not possible, there is always the option of choosing not to operate in that environment.

The decision to walk away and lose the business may seem naïve, but we have met and interviewed a number of executives of very successful companies that have done just that. One described how his company turned down a $50 million contract in a Latin American country because there was no way to avoid paying a bribe to a government official. Another explained that, in his experience, if a company developed a reputation for acting ethically, it was not usually subjected to unethical demands. Each person has to make his or her own decision and live with the consequences of his or her actions. The information in the following sections is designed to help you in the decision-making process.

ETHICAL FRAMEWORKS[51]

Moral philosophers have developed frameworks for thinking about moral issues and for analyzing ethical problems, but these frameworks generally have not been included in international business curricula. There are various frameworks for analyzing ethical problems and there are conflicting positions and prescriptions among them. In classes we have observed that people advocate actions representing some of the major frameworks, but without understanding the foundations or the strengths and weaknesses of their positions. Consider the following discussion.

Person X: "If we don't pay what he is asking we will lose the contract and people back home will lose jobs. Is that ethical when people can't feed their families?"

Person Y: "I don't care. What you are suggesting is absolutely wrong."

Person Z: "Now hold on, it doesn't seem to be against the rules there. It is different in that culture. Everyone is doing it. They need the extra money to support their families. Besides, we should not impose our system of morality on other cultures."

You may have heard or have taken part in similar exchanges. The people in the conversation above may not realize it, but they are engaged in a discussion of moral philosophy. However, it is the type of discussion that tends to excite emotions and generate heat and argument, rather than provide insight and a thoughtful course of action.

Since you may likely take part in similar discussions (or arguments) at some time in your career, we think that knowledge of these three frameworks will be useful. The intent is to help you link some everyday reasoning and the positions you might espouse to the ethical frameworks underlying them. In the brief exchange above, one sees elements of Kant's categorical imperative, utilitarianism, and cultural relativism. These are commonly invoked frameworks, which is why they were chosen. Each represents a different moral calculus, a different ethical map.

The main categories of ethical theories can be divided into: consequential (or teleological) theories, which focus on the consequences, outcomes, or results of decisions and behavior; rule-based (or deontological) theories, which focus on moral obligations, duties, and rights; and cultural theories, which emphasize cultural differences in standards of behavior. These are discussed briefly here.

Consequential Theories

Consequential theories focus on the goals, end results, and/or consequences of decisions and actions. They are concerned with doing the maximum amount of "good" and the minimum amount of "harm." Utilitarianism is the most widely used example of this type of moral framework. It suggests doing the best for the greatest number of people. Another example is acting in a way that provides more net utility than an alternative act. It is essentially an economic, cost–benefit approach to ethical decision-making. If the benefits outweigh the costs, then that course of action is indicated.

The limitations of this approach are that it is difficult or impossible to identify and account for all the costs and benefits, and, since people have different utility curves, it is difficult to decide whose curve should be used. In real life, how do you compute this utility curve? Finally, in an effort to weigh the costs and benefits, one relies on quantitative data, usually economic data, and many important variables that should be considered are not quantifiable and, therefore, are often ignored.

Rule-based Theories

Rule-based theories include both absolute (or universal) theories and conditional theories. The emphasis of these theories is on duty, obligations, and rights. For example, if an employee follows orders or performs a certain task, management has an obligation to ensure that the task is not illegal or harmful to that person's health. People in power have a responsibility to protect the rights of the less powerful. These theories are concerned with the universal shoulds and oughts of human existence – the rules that should guide all people's decision-making and behavior wherever they are.

One of the best-known absolute theories is the categorical imperative of Immanuel Kant. Whereas utilitarianism takes a group or societal perspective, the categorical imperative has a more individualistic focus: individuals should be treated with respect and dignity as an end in itself; they should not be used simply as a means to an end. A person should not be done harm, even if the ultimate end is good. The criteria should be applied consistently to everyone. One of the questions to ask is: "If I were in the other person's (or group's or organization's) position, would I be willing for them to make the same decision that I am going to make, for the same reasons?"

A variation on absolute theories is fundamentalism. In this case, the rules may come from a book like the Bible, Koran, or Torah. In these systems, one is dealing with an authoritative, divine wisdom that has been revealed through prophets. Difficult questions arise when considering which book or prophet to follow and whose interpretation of the chosen book to use. Priests, mullahs, or rabbis who may reflect the views of an elite segment of society, or possibly an isolated group, usually interpret the books. There can be conflicting interpretations within the same religion as well. Also, the interpretations may be inconsistent with current social and environmental circumstances, as well as with the beliefs of large segments of a society. The rules that people follow can also be secular as well as religious, as was the case in Nazi Germany.

One shortcoming of these types of prescriptions is that they allow you to claim that you are not responsible for your own behavior: "I was just following orders" is a common excuse. The end result may be the same – you do not have to think for yourself or make a moral judgment, but rather you can avoid it by claiming to be following a higher authority. However, the war crimes trials after World War II established that following orders is not an acceptable legal defense for committing atrocities.

Cultural Theories

With cultural theories, local standards prevail. Cultural relativism is interpreted to mean that there is no single right way; in other words, people should not impose their values and standards on others. The reasoning behind the argument usually is that we should behave as the locals behave. The familiar expression tells us: "When in Rome, do as the Romans do." One problem, however, comes from the fact that the local people we are encouraged to emulate may not necessarily be the most exemplary. In your own culture, you know that people exhibit different standards of behavior. Does that mean we should advocate that business people coming to the United States act like the people convicted in the accounting scandal at Enron, for example, just because those people were Americans? Or should expatriate managers working in Italy follow the example set by Parmalat executives, because they were Italians? Adopting this philosophy also can encourage denial of accountability and the avoidance of moral choice. Using arguments based on this philosophy, the morality of bribes or actions of repressive regimes, for example, do not have to be examined very closely. These theories are summarized in Figure 8.3.

Perry has described a perspective that provides more insight into relativism arguments that managers may find useful – a process of intellectual and ethical development.[52] Although we should recognize that Perry's ideas reflect a cultural bias towards individualism and were derived from a narrow part of the US population, his ideas can help managers think about their positions on these issues.[53] The first category is *dualism*, in which a bipolar structure of the world is assumed or taken for granted. According to this perspective there is a clear right and wrong, good and bad, we and they. These positions are defined from one's own perspective based on membership in a group and belief in or adherence to a common set of traditional beliefs.

The next category, posited by Perry as a "more developed" perspective, is *relativism*, in which the dualistic world view is moderated by an understanding of the importance of context, which helps a person to see that knowledge and values are relative. As we have seen through earlier parts of this book, different people in different parts of the world think and believe differently, and a relativistic mode of making ethical judgments recognizes this fact. As originally observed by Blaise Pascal, Hofstede notes in the preface to his book, *Culture's Consequences*: "There are truths on this side of the Pyrénées which are falsehoods on the other."[54]

In Perry's scheme, the third "level" of development is *commitment in relativism*, in which a person understands the relativistic nature of the world but makes a commitment to a

FIGURE 8.3   Analytical Frameworks

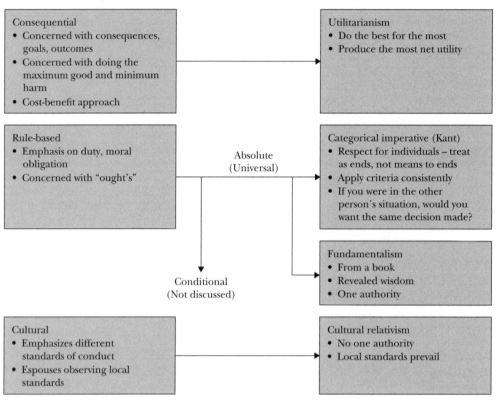

set of values, beliefs, and a way of behaving within this expanded world view. The goal is to arrive at the point where you assume responsibility for your own actions and decisions based upon careful consideration and the application of the "essential tools of moral reasoning – deliberation and justification."[55]

Perry suggests that progression to this stage is not automatic or guaranteed and that people may become "delayed" in their development or even "stuck" in the earlier stages. People who adhere to a set of absolute rules, however, may reject this notion of a hierarchy of development.

Our inclusion of Perry's ideas is not meant to judge others' choices in this regard, but rather to encourage self-awareness and recognition that simple, cultural relativism is not the highest end point of moral development. Underlying our perspective throughout this book are (1) the assumption that you are interested in developing a relativistic understanding of the world, and (2) the encouragement for you to decide about your own commitments within this relativistic framework. We understand that voicing this position is a reflection of our own values.

Universalism, Relativism, and the "Asian values" Debate

The previous brief discussion of different theories in moral philosophy provides a context for understanding the underlying ethical positions of what has been termed the "Asian values" debate. At one level it is the age-old debate in moral philosophy about universalism versus relativism. Is there a universal set of rules that should be followed or are morals and ethics all relative depending on the culture? Are one culture's beliefs, values, and practices superior and preferable to those of another? Whose laws, values, or ethics should be followed if and when a disagreement develops, a different course of action is proposed, or a conflict arises? This theoretical debate became more tangible when it turned into an international debate about human rights and economic growth.

Asian Values in Recent History   In 1948, the United Nations' Universal Declaration of Human Rights was signed.[56] Since that time, there have been discussions and disagreements over which of the human rights specified in its 30 Articles are universal and which are culturally influenced. China, long criticized by the West for human rights violations, issued a *White Paper on Human Rights in China* in November 1991. Although it "endorsed the language of human rights and praised the development of the international human rights regime . . . [it] argue[d] that the specific contents of human rights vary with 'differences in historical background, social system, cultural tradition, and economic development.'"[57] This proclamation of cultural sovereignty was followed by other pronouncements made by quasi-political bodies and prominent Asian leaders.

In 1993, the Bangkok Declaration was signed by more than 30 Asian and Middle Eastern countries. It presented the view that universal human rights represented statements of Western values and that they were at odds with "Asian values" and not applicable to Asia. This theme was later reiterated by notable Asian leaders.

The imposition of Western values as a form of "cultural imperialism" was alleged by Singapore's Lee Kuan Yew in 1994, when he stated: "It is not my business to tell people what's wrong with their system. It is my business to tell people not to foist their system indiscriminately on societies in which it will not work."[58] In this interview he described some of the differentiators that he saw between East and West:

> The fundamental difference between Western concepts of society and government and East Asian concepts – when I say East Asians, I mean Korea, Japan, China, Vietnam, as distinct from Southeast Asia, which is a mix between the Sinic and the Indian, though Indian culture also emphasizes similar values – is that Eastern societies believe that the individual exists in the context of his family. He is not pristine and separate. The family is part of the extended family, and then friends and the wider society.[59]

Lee also commented on American society from his viewpoint as an East Asian. While admiring parts of the American system he was critical of other parts.

> As an East Asian looking at America, I find attractive and unattractive features.
>   I like, for example, the free, easy and open relations between people regardless of social status, ethnicity or religion. And the things that I have always admired about America,

as against the communist system, I still do: a certain openness in argument about what is good or bad for society; the accountability of public officials; none of the secrecy and terror that's part and parcel of communist government.

But as a total system, I find parts of it totally unacceptable: guns, drugs, violent crime, vagrancy, unbecoming behavior in public – in sum the breakdown of civil society. The expansion of the right of the individual to behave or misbehave as he pleases has come at the expense of orderly society. In the East the main object is to have a well-ordered society so that everybody can have maximum enjoyment of his freedoms. This freedom can only exist in an ordered state and not in a natural state of contention and anarchy.[60]

In 1996 at the 29th International General Meeting of the Pacific Basin Economic Council, Dr Mahathir Mohamad, Prime Minister of Malaysia, continued to defend cultural relativism when he said that there was a belief among many in the West that their values and beliefs were universal.[61] Later in 2000, echoing Lee, he said that too much democracy could lead to violence, instability, and anarchy; and that the West was using ideals such as democracy and human rights as tools to re-colonize parts of Asia.[62]

In the remarks of Lee and Mahathir one can see the primary values that are in conflict in this debate.

- The East values community and family (collectivism) while the West values the individual. In the East, responsibility towards family and community takes precedence over individual interests and privileges. In the East, people have *duties* while in the West they have *rights*.
- The East values order and harmony while the West values personal freedom, individual initiative, and competition. In the East this is reflected in respect for age, leaders, persons of authority, hierarchy, and institutions. In the West it is reflected in democracy, the rights of individuals, and capitalism.
- The West believes in universalism, while the East practices particularism. Universalism emphasizes rules, laws, and generalizations, while particularism emphasizes exceptions, circumstances, and relations.[63] Particularism often is expressed in the East in practices like *guanxi* (the use of interpersonal relationships) in China, which also can be interpreted from a Western perspective as corruption or bribery.

The debate was later extended from human rights to economic development. In addition to using "Asian values" as the justification for sacrificing political and civil freedoms to maintain social stability, some Asian governments have argued that since not all Asian countries are as economically developed as the West, they cannot be expected to uphold all of the rights in the Universal Declaration. Some have claimed that "Asian values" are supportive of "paternalistic authoritarianism" (such as practiced in Singapore and Malaysia), which has fostered economic development and provided economic security for their people. However, these same values were also cited by Western observers who said they supported "crony capitalism" and contributed to the Asian financial crisis in 1997–1998,[64] while still other observers say these values contributed to the region's quick recovery.[65]

In light of the global financial crisis occurring as we write these pages in December 2008, there is sufficient reason for it to remind us to be careful about pointing the finger of "crony capitalism" in the direction of the East. It was more than simple greed that led to the unraveling of subprime mortgages and the worldwide consequences that followed.

Encouragement of and cooperation in unwise and perhaps illegal actions could easily be described by the same label of "crony capitalism" that was used to blame the Asian countries for the crisis of 10 years ago. We need to be reminded that a most critical part of the MBI model described in Chapter 3 is "*decentering without blame.*"

Not Everyone in Asia Agrees   Although some Asian political leaders and academics see "Asian values" as different from, and as an alternative to, Western cultural beliefs, others are critical of the way that the idea of special "Asian values" is often invoked.

Asia is not a monolithic, homogeneous area. Critics dismiss the idea that a common set of distinctively Asian principles exists, given Asia's immense cultural, religious, and political diversity. There are regional differences between East, Southeast, and South Asia, and these nations have highly varying historical and religious backgrounds, such as Hindu, Muslim, Confucian, Shinto, and Buddhist.

Critics argue the debate is not so much about cultural values but about maintaining political power and an excuse for autocratic governments that suppress individual rights and dissidents. Human Rights Watch and Amnesty International called China's *White Paper* a "whitewash."[66]

Not all Asians believe that human rights are an artifact of solely the Western culture. Some of those who disagree with the proponents of the "Asian values" thesis include Nobel Laureate Amartya Sen who has said:

> What about the specialness of "Asian values," about which so much is now being said by the authorities in a number of East Asian countries? These arguments . . . dispute the importance of human rights and press freedoms in Asian countries. The resistance to Western hegemony – a perfectly respectable cause in itself – takes the form, under this interpretation, of justifying the suppression of journalistic freedoms and the violations of elementary political and civil rights on the grounds of the alleged unimportance of these freedoms in the hierarchy of what are claimed to be "Asian values."[67]

The former president of Singapore Devan Nair has stated, "Human rights and values are universal by any standard, and their violation anywhere is a grievous offence to men and women everywhere." [68] Wei Jingsheng, a political dissident and human rights activist exiled from China, also has argued that human rights and freedoms are universal. [69]Aung San Suu Kyi, Burmese democracy advocate and winner of the 1991 Nobel Peace Prize, has said, "Those who wish to deny us certain political rights try to convince us that these are not Asian values. In our struggle for democracy and human rights, we would like greater support from our fellow Asians."[70]

Integrative Social Contracts Theory: A Way to Avoid Ethical Paralysis?[71]

Some academics have commented that "academic moral theory is useless,"[72] and the "Asian values" debate lends credence to that view since the debate does not lead to actionable decision criteria without embracing the beliefs of one side or the other. There does not seem to any way to cut through the debate to arrive at the "truth." One is left with having either to impose one's beliefs and values on the other through coercion or by the conflicting parties agreeing to disagree.[73]

We think that it is important for managers to be able to recognize the basis for their moral and ethical decisions and to be aware, for example, if they are shifting from one theory to another as a way of avoiding tough decisions. However, global executives must make decisions and take action, and they do not have the luxury of simply debating the issue. How do they decide? How does he or she choose among these mutually conflicting moral theories?

There is no simple answer to this question. First, the MBI model from earlier in the book can be applied using these frameworks as components of the map (M) portion of the model. If you are dealing with people who use a different moral calculus, Maps (M) of the different moral philosophies provide the basis for the Bridging (B) and Integration (I) components of the MBI model to communicate across the differences and to manage them.

Another approach for resolving conflicting ethical viewpoints is Integrative Social Contracts Theory (ISCT) developed by Donaldson and Dunfee.[74] We believe that ISCT is a useful approach to resolving conflicting ethical alternatives when making decisions and determining a course of action. However, before showing how one would apply this theory, it is helpful to put it in context with the other theories previously discussed. On a continuum of extreme relativism at one end and extreme universalism at the other end, ISCT is a pluralistic theory and is closer to the relativism end of the continuum as shown and described in Figure 8.4.

ISCT essentially says that local communities and cultures can determine ethical norms for members of that society but that these norms must be based on the rights of individual members to exercise "voice" and "exit."[75] However, to be legitimate, these local norms or principles must be compatible with macro-level norms, "hypernorms," which are universal precepts. If there is a conflict, the hypernorms take priority.[76]

The challenge, therefore, is to know if a principle has hypernorm status. Donaldson and Dunfee offer 11 types of evidence that support the existence of hypernorm status.[77] The more types of supportive evidence, the stronger is the case for hypernorm status.

1 Widespread consensus that the principle is universal.
2 Component of well-known global industry standards.
3 Supported by prominent nongovernmental organizations (NGOs) such as the International Labor Organization or Transparency International.
4 Supported by regional governmental organizations such as the EU, OECD, or OAS.
5 Consistently referred to as a global ethical standard by the global media.
6 Known to be consistent with precepts of major religions.
7 Supported by global business organizations such as the International Chamber of Commerce or the Caux Round Table.[78]
8 Known to be consistent with the precepts of major philosophies.
9 Generally supported by a relevant international community of professionals such as accountants or engineers.
10 Known to be consistent with the findings of universal human values.
11 Supported by the laws of many different nations.

FIGURE 8.4   Integrative Social Contracts Theory

Theory	Position
Extreme relativism	No ethical view, regardless of source or basis, is better than any other.
Cultural relativism	No ethical view held by one culture is better than any other view held by another culture.
ISCT (Pluralism)	There exist a broad range of ethical viewpoints that may be chosen by communities and cultures. The possibility exists that conflicting ethical positions in different communities are equally valid. There are, however, circumstances in which the viewpoint of a particular culture will be invalid due either to a universally binding moral precept or to the priority of the view of another culture or community.
Modified universalism	There exist a set of precepts expressible in many different ethical languages that reflects universally binding moral precepts and that captures many issues of global ethical significance. These precepts rule out the possibility of two conflicting ethical positions in different cultures being equally valid.
Extreme universalism	There exists a single set of precepts expressed only in a single ethical language that reflects universally binding moral precepts and that captures all issues of global ethical significance. These precepts rule out the possibility of two conflicting ethical positions in different cultures being equally valid.

Thomas Donaldson and Thomas W. Dunfee, *Ties That Bind*, Harvard Business School Press, Boston, MA; 1999; p. 23. (Used with permission)

One such set of hypernorms would be the Universal Declaration of Human Rights, which can be found at the United Nations web site: http://www.un.org/Overview/rights.html.

COMPETING WITH INTEGRITY

Managers have multiple interests that they must consider because they are embedded in a complex network of relationships. The interests, goals, and values of the various actors in any situation can potentially conflict. Identifying these relationships helps in structuring an analysis. To assist in analysis and to promote rational discussion of ethical dilemmas, a series of diagnostic questions and some recommendations are presented below that we hope can serve as a guide for you in the future.

Some Guidelines to Consider

Prepare for Ethical Dilemmas

1 *Develop relationships, but with care.*

To the extent possible, enter into strong, trust-based relationships with customers and suppliers. With these relationships you will be able to assess the impact of requests that your contacts make and explain the reason for behaving the way you do. With strong relationships, your stakeholders are more likely to trust your actions, and less likely to push you into behaviors you believe are unethical or irresponsible.

Enter into dependent relationships with care. If you increase dependency on a particular customer or supplier, be certain about the relationship and make certain you retain enough power to maintain your standards.

Don't wait until you are in a crisis situation to reach out to important industry, community, regulatory, and possibly religious groups in a country. Build relationships and social capital with multiple stakeholders as early as possible to enhance your reputation and develop support, so as to increase your leverage to follow your own standards if the need arises.

2 *Get the best information possible.*

Take the time to get the facts, all of them. Avoid fuzzy thinking. Avoid using or being swayed by hearsay or unsubstantiated assertions. These are statements that have no specifics to go with them: "Everybody is doing it," "We'll lose business if we don't do it," or "It's a normal practice." When you hear statements like these, push for the analysis and details. Often, you may find that they are unsubstantiated assertions parading as analysis.

Identify the Impact on Stakeholders

3 *Identify all stakeholders.*

Remember that a company has multiple groups of stakeholders in addition to the investors in the business, and executives need to be clear about their responsibilities and obligations to all these groups. Who are the stakeholders that have an interest in or will be affected by your decision: shareholders, the home country government, host country governments, customers, suppliers, employees, unions? There are probably others that could be added to that list, but the point is to comprehensively identify the stakeholders and their interests. It can be easy to ignore some of these, particularly when they may be thousands of miles away and may not be able to stand up for their interests and rights. Ethical managers do not avoid them or pretend that they do not exist.

4 *Assess your responsibilities and obligations to these stakeholders.*

Identify the responsibilities that your organization may have to external stakeholders as well as to stakeholders (employees) in your own organization. For example, a decision about whether or not to shut down operations in a country may involve both external and internal ethical issues.

Take the situation of an insurance company that one of the authors and his colleague had some involvement with. The company was selling life insurance in Uganda during a period of civil war.[79] Years earlier, the company's operation there was nationalized and now was having its ownership restored. The branch in Uganda was not profitable, and a financial analysis showed that it should be shut down. From a profit-and-loss perspective, the decision may have been easy to make. But what were the company's responsibilities to their managers who ran the company in their interest after it had been nationalized and who were concerned about possible violence to field personnel and to themselves if the company closed its operations? And what were its obligations to its policyholders? The issue may not be whether the company should shut down, but how it should handle its responsibilities, obligations, and commitments to its employees and customers, and shareholders as it shuts down.

Assess and Select Options

5 *Identify a broad range of options.*

Some options will jump up immediately, such as pay the bribe or don't pay the bribe. Are there options that have not been identified? In trying to identify possible action, avoid characterizing decisions using false dichotomies – either/or characterizations. Alternatives and options do not have to be win/lose positions. For example, the statement "We need to pay the bribe or lose the business" portrays the situation as win/lose, but it may not be. These positions often develop because the initial analysis was not as complete as it could have been. This mind-set can limit the action possibilities open to the manager. Strive for a win/win situation. Is there a way to solve the problem that satisfies all parties and allows you to fulfill your obligations?

6 *Analyze the assumptions behind the options.*

What assumptions are being made? What ethical framework is being invoked? Whose utility is being maximized? Whose values are being used? Consider multiple (including opposing) viewpoints, but examine them carefully. Weigh the costs and benefits to all stakeholders.

7 *Select an option and develop an action plan*

If you have followed the steps above you are now in a better position to develop an action plan. Some decision criteria to consider include: do the best for all involved stakeholders; fulfill obligations; observe laws and contracts; do not use deception; and avoid knowingly doing harm (physical, psychological, economic, or social).

Consider Your Own Position Carefully   In conducting these arm's-length analyses, it is easy to take ourselves as people – the ones who make the decisions – out of the picture. Remember that there can be personal consequences associated with your decision. People have lost their jobs because someone higher in the organization needed a scapegoat, and others have gone to jail for the actions of others. Don't just think about the decision from your role as a manager. Consider your roles as community leader, husband or wife, parent or global citizen. Ask yourself if you will be acting in accordance with your own highest set of values and norms. Certainly look after the interests of your company in your role as manager, but look after your own interests, also. You may be the only one that does!

8 *Make decisions that are your responsibility.*

Do not avoid making ethical decisions on issues that are your responsibility, for example, by passing the responsibility on to someone else or waiting until the problem passes.

9 *Don't let people put the monkey on your back.*

Do not accept responsibility for decisions that are not your responsibility. Some people will try to find a scapegoat to make a particularly difficult, possibly illegal or unethical decision. Do not let them use you. How do you protect yourself? You can ask for the decision or directive in writing or suggest an open meeting with other people present to discuss it.

10 *Do not use "culture" as an excuse for not doing things the proper way.*

Just because the local company does not treat its toxic waste properly does not mean that it is acting as a role model for that culture. Also, beware of confusing culture and an individual's personality and character. If a person is asking for something that is illegal or unethical, that tells you something about that person's character, not necessarily about his or her culture.

11 *Act consistently with your own values.*

Consider the "billboard" or the "light-of-day" tests. When you drive to work in the morning, would you be happy to see your decision or action prominently announced on a large billboard for everyone to read and to know about? Or alternatively, would you be willing to discuss your actions in a meeting where you would be subject to questions and scrutiny and have to justify them? Would your actions look as reasonable in the light of day as they did when the decision was made behind closed doors?

A Final Word

As you move through your international management career, we encourage you to maintain high standards. We suggest that you follow an adage that we have modified, "When in Rome don't do as the Romans do, but rather do as the *better* Romans do."

Ask yourself, and answer honestly, if you are behaving up to your highest values and expectations of yourself. Are you happy with your answer? If not, you know what to do!

We wish you an interesting, rewarding, and enjoyable journey in your international activities and career.

Notes

1 De George, R. T., *Competing with Integrity in International Business* (Oxford: Oxford University Press, 1993).
2 Ibid., at 6.
3 Ibid., at 41.
4 Amba-Rao, S. C., "Multinational Corporate Social Responsibility, Ethics, Interactions and Third World Governments: An Agenda for the 1990's," *Journal of Business Ethics*, 12 (1993) 555.
5 "BAE faces African bribery probe," BBC News, May 28, 2001. http://news.bbc.co.uk/2/hi/business/1355838.stm (accessed November 28, 2008).

6 Doh, J. P., Rodriguez, P., Uhlenbruck, K., Collins, J., and Eden, L., "Coping with Corruption in Foreign Markets," *Academy of Management Executive*, Vol. 17 No. 3 (2003) 114–127.

7 "Sweat Shops – Inside a Chinese Sweatshop," *Business Week*, October 2, 2000. http://www.businessweek.com/2000/00_40/b3701119.htm.

8 http://www.who.int/features/factfiles/tobacco/en/index.html (accessed October 28, 2008). For a detailed analysis of the problem see *WHO Report on the Global Tobacco Epidemic, 2008*.

9 Ibid.

10 Russell, S., "Ex-Clinton Official rips White House on tobacco treaty," *San Francisco Chronicle*, February 13, 2003.

11 Representative Henry A. Waxman, "Administration Isolates the U.S. in International Tobacco Control Efforts," http://www.house.gov/reform/min/inves_tobacco/index.htm.

12 http://www.nosmoking.ws/inb5updates.htm and http://petition.globalink.org/view.php?code=fctc_de

13 Senator Richard A. Durbin and Representative Henry A. Waxman, "Letter Questions USDA Promotion of Tobacco Trade," http://www.house.gov/reform/min/inves_tobacco/index.htm.

14 US Consumer Products Safety Commission web site, http://www.cpsc.gov/cpscpub/prerel/prhtml07/07039.html (accessed November 28. 2008).

15 "Mattel apologizes to China over recalls: Firm takes blame for design flaws, says it pulled more toys than needed," MSNBC, September 21, 2007. http://www.msnbc.msn.com/id/20903731/ (accessed November 28, 2008).

16 Bapuji, H. and Beamish, P. W., "Toy Recalls – Is China Really the Problem?" *Canada-Asia Commentary*, September 2007, 1. www.asiapacific.ca.

17 See "Human Rights," *The Economist*, June 3, 1995, 58–59; and Beaver, W., "Levi's Is Leaving China,'" *Business Horizons* (March–April 1995) 35–40.

18 Beaver, "Levi's Is Leaving China," n. 17 above.

19 http://www.levistrauss.com/Citizenship/ (accessed November 28, 2008).

20 This discussion about the RugMark Foundation was taken from its web site, http://www.rugmark.org/home.php (accessed November 28, 2008).

21 http://www.rugmark.org/home.php.

22 Ibid.

23 RugMark USA, PBS Enterprising Ideas, http://www.pbs.org/now/enterprisingideas/RugMarkUSA.html (accessed November 28, 2008).

24 http://www.ikea-group.ikea.com/?ID=708.

25 Gordimer, N., "In Nigeria, the price of oil is blood," *New York Times*, May 25, 1997, E 11.

26 "Shellman says sorry," *The Economist*, May 10, 1997, 65.

27 For example in the *Globe and Mail* in Canada on November 21, 1995.

28 "Shellman says sorry."

29 Company web site, http://www.shell.com/home/content/responsible_energy/society/using_influence_responsibly/human_rights/training_tools_guidelines/training_tools_guidelines_16042007.html (accessed November 28, 2008). At this web site you also can download documents referred to.

30 http://www.state.gov/g/drl/rls/2931.htm and http://www.voluntaryprinciples.org//principles/index.php (accessed November 28, 2008).

31 "How Risky Is India?" Srivastava, M. and Lakshman, N., December 15, 2008, 25.

32 See the U.S. State Department's list of Current Travel Warnings for examples of these countries: http://travel.state.gov/warnings_list.html.

33 http://apnews.excite.com/article/20040530/D82SJSF80.html.

34 "How Risky Is India?" n. 31 above, at 24.

35 Drohan, M., "To Bribe or Not to Bribe," *The Globe and Mail*, February 14, 1994.

36 Ibid.

37   For a more detailed account of this situation see Lane, H. and Wesley, D., "Statoil Iran," Ivey case no. 9B05C036.

38   Statoil signs Iran gas deal, BBC News, 28 October, 2002.

39   This represented the first of three payments to Horton Investments. The contract was later annulled and no further payments were made.

40   "Statoil Still Afloat Despite Losing Man Overboard," *International Petroleum Finance*, October 8, 2003. Other sources of the Statoil story include Harald Finnvik Diplomatic Interview, *Azerbaijan International*, Autumn 1996; "Statoil Chief Executive Quits As Board Split On Probe," *Energy Intelligence Briefing*, September 23, 2003.

41   More information can be found at http://www.statoilhydro.com/en/NewsAndMedia/ News/2006/Pages/HortonCaseSettlement.aspx (accessed December 5, 2008).

42   This section has been adapted from the US Department of Justice web site http://www.usdoj. gov/criminal/fraud/docs/dojdocb.html (accessed December 7, 2008). For more detail about the FCPA see the web site.

43   http://www.transparency.org/index.html.

44   TI web site, http://www.transparency.org/news_room/latest_news/press_releases/2006/en_ 2006_10_04_bpi_2006 (accessed November 28, 2008).

45   Company web site, *The Spirit and The Letter*, http://www.ge.com/files_citizenship/pdf/ TheSpirit&TheLetter.pdf (accessed November 28, 2008).

46   Donaldson, T., "Can Global Companies Conform to Code?" A copy can be found on his personal web site, http://lgst.wharton.upenn.edu/donaldst/.

47   To see examples of this distinction in action in a large Wall Street firm in the 1980s, read Lewis, M., *Liar's Poker* (New York: Penguin Books, 1989).

48   Henderson, V. E., "The Ethical Side of Enterprise," *Sloan Management Review* 23 (1982) 37–47.

49   Ibid.

50   Meier, B., "Breast-feeding wisdom in question," *New York Times*, June 8, 1997.

51   This section draws on the following works: Gandz, J. and Hayes, N., "Teaching Business Ethics," Working Paper No. 86-17R, October, 1986, School of Business Administration, The University of Western Ontario; Tuleja, T., *Beyond the Bottom Line* (New York: Penguin Books, 1985); Matthews, J. B., Goodpaster, K. E., and Nash, L., *Policies and Persons: A Casebook in Business Ethics* (New York: McGraw-Hill, 1985).

52   Perry, Jr, W. G., *Forms of Intellectual and Ethical Development in the College Years: A Scheme* (New York: Holt, Rinehart & Winston, 1970).

53   In Perry's full scheme there are nine stages. The authors have chosen to use only the three major positions in the scheme.

54   Hofstede, G. H., *Culture's Consequences* (Beverly Hills: Sage Publications, 1980).

55   Gandz, J. and Nadine Hayes, N., "Teaching Business Ethics," *Journal of Business Ethics* 7 (1988) 659.

56   http://www.un.org/rights/50/decla.htm.

57   Angle, S. C. and Svensson, M., 2001, http://www.chinesehumanrightsreader.org/reader/ intros/52.html.

58   Zakaria, F., "Culture is Destiny: A Conversation with Lee Kuan Yew," *Foreign Affairs* Vol. 73 No. 2 (1994) 109–126 at 110.

59   Ibid., at 113.

60   Ibid., at 111.

61   http://www.apmforum.com/news/apmn21.htm.

62   "Mahathir warns against too much democracy," Thursday, July 27, 2000. BBC News, http:// news.bbc.co.uk/1/hi/world/asia-pacific/853673.stm.

63   Hampden-Turner, C. and Trompenaars, F., *Building Cross-Cultural Competence: How to Create Wealth from Conflicting Values* (New Haven: Yale University Press, 2000) 13. See Chapter 1 for a detailed explanation of the universalist-particularistic dilemma.

64   Fukuyama, F. "Asian Values and Civilization," The ICAS Lectures No. 98-929-FRF. ICAS Fall Symposium September 29, 1998, http://www.icasinc.org/f1998/frff1998.html.

65   See, for example, Peerenboom, R., "Beyond Universalism and Relativism: The Evolving Debates about 'Values in Asia,'" Research Paper No. 02-23, UCLA School of Law, October, 31, 2002.

66   See   http://www.hrw.org/press/2001/04/china0410.html   and   http://www.urich.edu/~vwang/ps345/art85.html.

67   Sen, A., "Satyajit Ray and the Art of Universalism: Our Culture, Their Culture," 11. http://satyajitray.ucsc.edu/articles/sen.html.

68   BBC World Service, http://www.bbc.co.uk/worldservice/people/features/ihavearightto/four_b/casestudy_art30.shtml.

69   Ibid. See also http://globetrotter.berkeley.edu/people/Wei/wei-con0.html.

70   http://www.globalization101.org/issue/culture/34.asp. See also http://www.dassk.com/.

71   We would like to thank Sheila Puffer and Dan McCarthy of Northeastern University for introducing us to ISCT.

72   See Peerenboom, n. 65, at 83.

73   Peerenboom, n. 65, at 9.

74   Donaldson, T. and Dunfee, T. W., *Ties That Bind* (Boston, MA: Harvard Business School Press, 1999).

75   Ibid., at 46.

76   Ibid.

77   Ibid., at 60.

78   "The Caux Round Table (CRT) is an international network of principled business leaders working to promote a moral capitalism. The CRT advocates implementation of the CRT Principles for Business through which principled capitalism can flourish and sustainable and socially responsible prosperity can become the foundation for a fair, free and transparent global society. At the company level, the Caux Round Table advocates implementation of the CRT Principles for Business as the cornerstone of principled business leadership. The CRT Principles apply fundamental ethical norms to business decision-making" taken from *About Us*, http://www.cauxroundtable.org/about.html.

79   Burgoyne, D. and Lane, H., "The Europa Insurance Company," Case 9-84-C049 (London: The University of Western Ontario, School of Business Administration, 1984).

CHAPTER 9

Competing with Integrity in Global Business: Corporate Citizenship

INTRODUCTION

Some writers and companies include ethics in their definitions of corporate social responsibility (CSR) but we have separated them. Our reasoning is that legal and ethical behavior, as discussed in the previous chapter, should be expected by managers in all activities.

Even though corporations may have codes of conduct specifying standards of behavior for their employees, the decision to act legally and ethically is, in the final analysis, a personal decision. As we said in Chapter 8, we are making the distinction between the decisions and behavior of individuals or a small group of people and a formal initiative of an organization that most likely uses corporate resources to achieve its ends.

In a similar vein, some include corporate governance, narrowly conceived as the corporation's relationship with shareholders – well-defined shareholder rights, effective control, transparency and disclosure, and an independent, empowered board of directors[1] – as part of CSR. We believe that the described relationship with shareholders also should be expected, although in recent years it has not proven to be the case.

In our view, "corporate citizenship" includes the broader CSR notion of aligning a company with society and more accurately describes the many formal corporate initiatives, such as helping communities in developing countries with educational or medical programs or undertaking certain "green" projects. These programs and projects are usually discretionary without necessarily having legal or ethical implications or conforming to the narrower, less inclusive, definition of governance. In this chapter we will focus on the right-hand column of Figure 9.1.

The concept of corporate social responsibility is neither new, nor is it universally interpreted in the same way. One writer has suggested that serious discussion of the

FIGURE 9.1   Global Mindset Framework Applied to Ethics and Corporate Citizenship

	Individual	**Organizational**
Self	Clarify and understand my beliefs about ethical behavior.	Clarify and understand my organization's approach to corporate citizenship.
Other	Clarify and understand other beliefs about ethical behavior in the context of other cultures and principal theories of moral philosophy.	Clarify and understand other approaches to corporate citizenship in the context of other companies, other cultures and principal codes of conduct.
Choice	Belief in and commitment to a set of ethical principles.	Belief in and commitment to an approach to corporate citizenship.

topic in North America started in 1953 with the publication of *Social Responsibilities of the Businessman* and that it turned into a debate later when Milton Friedman asserted that a company's only social responsibility was to make a profit for its stockholders.[2] Friedman said:

> . . . there is one and only one social responsibility of business – to use its resources and engage in activities designed to increase its profits so long as it stays within the rules of the game, which is to say, engages in open and free competition without deception or fraud.[3]

However, the history and ideology of corporate social responsibility as a management theme can be traced back to 1927. At that time Wallace Donham, Dean of the Harvard Business School, advocated greater corporate social responsibility as a way of "aligning business interests with the defense of free-market capitalism against what was depicted as the clear and present danger of Soviet Communism."[4,5]

According to Spector, starting in 1946, another Dean of the Harvard Business School, Donald K. David, became a "persistent and consistent voice on behalf of expanding the role of business in American society," a view also supported by the *Harvard Business Review* at the time. And there also were challenges to Donham's and David's position before Friedman's, a notable opponent of which was a Harvard Business School professor, Theodore Levitt, who in 1958, in a *Harvard Business Review* article, strongly disagreed with it.[6]

Although the social responsibility theme survived and the topic became incorporated in business schools' curricula, often only as an elective, for decades it was surpassed in the executive mindset by Levitt's and Friedman's viewpoints and encapsulated in the idea of the oft-heard phrase about maximizing shareholder wealth. Lately, however, corporate social responsibility has made a comeback and has become a much talked-about and subscribed-to idea.

In its 2005 Survey of Corporate Social Responsibility, *The Economist* observed:

> The movement for corporate social responsibility has won the battle of ideas . . . Over the past ten years or so, corporate social responsibility (CSR) has blossomed as an idea, if not as a coherent practical programme. CSR commands the attention of executives everywhere – if

their public statements are to be believed – and especially that of the managers of multinational companies headquartered in Europe and the United States.[7]

In 2008, a survey by the Economist Intelligence Unit for *The Economist* Special Report on Corporate Social Responsibility, found that "only 4% of the respondents thought that CSR was a waste of time and money."[8]

Our purpose here is not to provide a complete treatise on this topic, as there are entire books devoted it, but rather, as in previous chapters, present some ways of thinking about the issue that we have found helpful and hope that you will find useful.

Defining the Domain of Corporate Citizenship or Corporate Social Responsibility

What CSR is or encompasses is open to interpretation. Triple bottom line reporting is often a synonym for CSR, which means that companies are concerned with economic, environmental, and social outcomes. Spector states:

> CSR accepts as necessary but not sufficient the triple requirements that a corporation and its leaders act legally, meet fiduciary requirements to shareholders, and avoid harm to their communities. CSR also asks corporations to take affirmative action to ensure that a portion of the economic resources they generate is redistributed from private to public hands in a manner that is both equitable and sustainable. Further sustainability should take account of the needs of multiple stakeholders in the organization as well as the global environment.[9]

The above description, although not passive, would not be seen as proactive enough by some people. In the *Academy of Management Review*, a premier academic journal, the editors of a special topic forum took it a step further by stating that "most authors . . . are clear that corporations *should* act as social change agents.[10] The authors to whom they refer, it ought to be noted, would be academics, not necessarily managers.

The label "CSR" can have a socialistic ring about it, and CSR programs are often criticized as not much more than corporate image builders and ways to spend shareholders' money for things governments should be doing. Many companies do not like the CSR label and prefer to use corporate responsibility or corporate citizenship.[11] Ben Heineman, former Senior Vice President for law and public affairs at GE, believes that the job of a CEO is to "fuse" high performance with high integrity, which will foster corporate citizenship, which he defines in much the same way as CSR is defined:

- Strong and sustained economic performance.
- Robust and unwavering adherence to the spirit and letter of relevant financial and legal rules.
- The establishment of, and adherence to, binding global standards – extending beyond the requirements of formal rules – that are in the company's enlightened self-interest because they promote its core values, enhance its reputation, and advance its long-term economic health.[12]

The argument of maximizing shareholder wealth versus corporate social responsibility has created a specious debate, and both sides have gotten it wrong because, according to Heineman,

The basic elements of "corporate citizenship" are high performance *and* [emphasis added] high integrity that recognize the long-term interests of shareholders are advanced by responsibly addressing the concerns of other stakeholders.[13]

We endorse the high performance with high integrity orientation and have adopted the corporate citizenship label although we will use it interchangeably with CSR.

Areas of Responsibility   The areas of corporate responsibility include "the economic, legal, ethical and discretionary expectations that society has of organizations at a given point in time."[14] The first two categories, economic and legal, undoubtedly receive the most attention. These include the responsibility to produce goods and services that society wants, make a profit, and obey the laws and regulations that govern society and business. It was undoubtedly these to which Friedman was referring when he talked about obeying the rules of the game without deception and fraud.

However, companies are expected to operate and to make profits in an ethical, as well as legal, fashion. Since all of society's desired behaviors are not necessarily written down, ethical responsibilities include those behaviors not embodied in laws that also are expected of businesses. We dealt with issues of ethical behavior in the last chapter.

Finally, there is the area of discretionary responsibility "about which society has no clear cut message for business."[15] As the name suggests, activities in this area are voluntary and left to executive choice and judgement. We will provide some examples of these in a later section.

How should a company position itself regarding corporate citizenship? There is no obvious answer to that question because the factors to be considered are complex and it represents a value judgement that executives of each corporation will have to decide for themselves. Many of the issues are concerns in other countries as well; and as executives develop guidelines for addressing them, they need to keep in mind how differences in culture, values, beliefs, and practices might affect a chosen course of action.

In addition to economic, legal, and ethical responsibilities, we need to consider the philosophical orientation of companies toward corporate citizenship and specific issues, programs, and projects for which they should consider responsibility.[16]

Orientation   Companies' orientation to corporate citizenship has been described in many ways, but most commonly by a progression from a narrow set of responsibilities to more broadly conceived ones. For example, one such framework reflects a continuum from solely maximizing profits in the present to trusteeship of the quality of life for present and future generations:

- Social obligation is an approach in which responsibility is limited to benefiting shareholders, *compliance* with laws, and doing the minimum required.
- Social responsibility is a *reactive* approach to a broader group of organizational stakeholders (for example, customers, employees, suppliers).
- Social responsiveness is a *proactive*, progressive, take-the-lead approach to stakeholder and external societal interests, including environmental issues and social values.[17]

The approach chosen by a company most likely will depend on the executives' view of the relationship between business and society. Decisions about where to position a company on the spectrum are not simple ones. Managers with a view that society's moral values and business objectives are inherently in conflict, or at best totally separate domains of activity, may favor a stance that resists doing more than the minimum.[18] A paradigm in which business objectives and societal values are in harmony or are complementary will more likely lead to actions deemed as progressive or as leading the way.

The Economist has suggested another view of the CSR domain which also has three tiers or layers: the traditional base layer is philanthropy or donating money to social organizations and causes; the second tier is risk management in response to calamities such as oil spills, factories exploding, or criticism about the use of child labor; and the third, and relatively new, tier is the opportunity to use corporate citizenship in a strategic way to create a competitive advantage.[19] This structure appears to confirm the progression of a reactive, social responsibility approach morphing into a more proactive, social responsiveness one, only now with a strategic and business twist. Or, as *The Economist* described it, it represents enlightened self-interest and a shift from a moral case to a business case for behaving in a socially responsible fashion.

Issues Numerous international accords and sets of principles have been formulated, adopted, and endorsed in the last half century that provide a base for the development of a transcultural standard of corporate social behavior in a global economy.[20] These accords and principles address the following issues:[21,22]

- Employment practices and policies. For example, multinationals should develop nondiscriminatory employment practices, provide equal pay for equal work, observe the right of employees to join unions and to bargain collectively, give advance notice of plant closings and mitigate their adverse effects, respect local host country job standards, provide favorable work conditions and limited working hours, adopt adequate health and safety standards, and inform employees about health hazards. They should not permit unacceptable practices such as the exploitation of children, physical punishment, female abuse, or involuntary servitude.
- Consumer protection. MNCs should respect host country laws regarding consumer protection; safeguard the health and safety of consumers through proper labeling, disclosures, and advertising; and provide safe products and packaging.
- Environmental protection. MNCs should preserve ecological balance, protect the environment, rehabilitate environments damaged by them, and respect host country laws, goals, and priorities regarding protection of the environment.
- Political payments and involvement. MNCs should not pay bribes to public officials and should avoid illegal involvement or interference in internal politics.
- Basic human rights and fundamental freedoms. Multinationals should respect the rights of people to life, liberty, security of person, and privacy; and freedom of religion, peaceful assembly, and opinion.
- Community responsibility. MNCs should work with governments and communities in which they do business to improve the quality of life in those communities.

An accord frequently referred to, the UN's Global Compact, was formally launched on 26 July 2000 and established a set of core values in human rights, labor standards, environment, and anti-corruption.[23] Some of the supporters of the Compact, which are among the best known global companies, include ABB, BP, CEMEX, Cisco, Daimler A.G., Deutsche Bank, GlaxoSmithKline, Grupo Santander, L'Oréal, Microsoft, Nestlé, Novartis, Unilever, and Toshiba, just to name a few.[24] The Global Compact asks that companies embrace, support, and enact the core values within their spheres of influence. The 10 core values are:[25]

- Human Rights

    1 Businesses should support and respect the protection of internationally pro-
       claimed human rights; and
    2 Make sure they are not complicit in human rights abuses.

- Labor

    3 Businesses should uphold the freedom of association and the effective recogni-
       tion of the right to collective bargaining;
    4 The elimination of all forms of forced and compulsory labor;
    5 The effective abolition of child labor; and
    6 The elimination of discrimination in respect to employment and occupation.

- Environment

    7 Businesses should support a precautionary approach to environmental challenges;
    8 Undertake initiatives to promote greater environmental responsibility; and
    9 Encourage the development and diffusion of environmentally friendly
       technologies.

- Anti-Corruption

    10 Businesses should work against corruption in all its forms, including extortion
       and bribery.

A recent paper from the Corporate Social Responsibility Initiative of the Kennedy School of Government stated that the Global Reporting Initiative (GRI) has become the world's leading voluntary sustainability reporting system.[26] The reporting system covers corporate economic, environmental, and social performance indicators. GRI believes that reporting on these performance dimensions should be as routine and as easy to compare as those in financial reporting.[27] For full detail on the G3 reporting system and a listing of which companies have filed reports since January 2008, we encourage you to go to the GRI portal, http://www.globalreporting.org/AboutGRI/.

It would be naïve, however, not to acknowledge that companies can be hypocritical in their support of social responsibility and ethical behavior. Endorsing codes such as the Global Compact is easy to do, but this act alone does not mean that a company is committed to implementing them or managing by them.

Corporate social responsibility, both its definition and the management guidelines to promote it, is not only of concern to international, quasi-governmental organizations like the United Nations (UN) and the Organization for Economic Cooperation and

Development (OECD), but to some private investment companies, as well. For example, the Calvert Group of mutual funds in the United States and the Ethical Funds Company in Canada have pioneered socially responsible mutual funds in their respective countries and have created "screens" or criteria for choosing socially responsible companies.

In 1982, the Calvert Social Investment Fund™ was the first mutual fund to oppose apartheid in South Africa.[28] Calvert has since created the Calvert Social Index™, a benchmark for measuring the performance of large, US-based socially responsible companies. Companies must meet Calvert's criteria in the following areas:[29]

- Governance and Ethics
- Workplace
- Environment
- Product Safety and Impact
- International Operations and Human Rights
- Indigenous Peoples' Rights
- Community Relations

More detail on each of these areas can be found at the company's web site http://www.calvert.com/sri_647.html.

The above sets of criteria are not a comprehensive listing of all the social responsibility issues that global companies might face or need to consider, but they provide a good start. As good as the various codes and reporting systems may be, however, they do not provide specific guidance to the discretionary programs that would be considered social responsiveness.

Social Responsiveness as Enlightened Self-Interest

Social responsiveness may be viewed as a naïve ideal or as good business practice that produces a positive public image, creates a competitive advantage in selling environmentally friendly products, for example, and possibly assists in recruiting high-caliber staff looking for companies with whom they can identify.[30] Concerns about social responsiveness and good business practice are not necessarily mutually exclusive, as the following statement from John Chambers, CEO of Cisco, attests:

> We aspire to be one of the best companies in the world, and part of that goal is becoming one of the best companies for the world. [Cisco's] Corporate Social Responsibility Report offers an overview of the responsible business practices and social investments that together enable us to create long-term value for our business and for society.[31]

An example of socially responsive programs is provided by Cisco. Tae Yoo, Senior Vice President of Corporate Affairs at Cisco, in her letter in the 2008 Corporate Social Responsibility Report, stated:

> . . . Cisco collaborates with a variety of public, private, and nongovernmental organization (NGO) partners in a broad range of social responsibility initiatives, all of them enhanced by the power of networking.

. . . Future global economic growth and social progress depend on providing students with a learning environment that adequately prepares them to make a living and to contribute to their communities in an increasingly knowledge-based economy. Unfortunately, however, educational practices have not always kept pace with the needs of today's students and employers. Cisco is working in partnership with public and academic institutions to help transform education through the Cisco Networking Academy, the 21st Century Schools Initiative, and other global initiatives based on a holistic blueprint for educational reform.

Since the inception of the Networking Academy, more than 2.6 million students have participated in courses in more than 160 countries. We revamped 70 percent of the curricula over the last year and a half to stay current with new developments and learning styles, and now offer courses in all six United Nations languages and five other languages as of the end of FY08. Cisco and our partners in the Least Developed Countries Initiative have helped more than 70,000 students in over 40 countries in the developing world to obtain an IT education. Of the 18,000 students who have passed the Cisco CCNA course, 31 percent are women.

. . . Cisco and our employees are involved in a wealth of programs in partnership with public sector organizations and NGOs to improve life in impoverished and underserved communities. We invest in and support programs that not only deliver immediate benefits, but also have the potential to grow to serve additional populations. We also look for strong programs that can sustain themselves over time. And because we believe in the power of the network to improve people's lives everywhere, we focus on programs that take advantage of the Internet and web 2.0 technologies . . .[32]

Cisco is combining education improvement with its self-interest in the Internet and web technologies. Another example of enlightened self-interest is Starbucks, which has an interest in the sustainable coffee trade.[33]

In 2004, Starbucks introduced its CAFE (Coffee and Farmer Equity) Practices which were guidelines designed to encourage the growing, processing and supplying of coffee in a socially and environmentally responsible manner, regardless of the size of the producer. The guidelines focused on four areas: product quality, economic accountability, social responsibility, and environmental leadership. In 2007, Starbucks purchased 65% of its coffee from CAFE Practices suppliers, which it intends to raise to 80% in five years. In addition, it supports numerous community projects around the world.

It is not only some companies in the United States that have strong CSR orientations. Two European examples include Marks and Spencer[34] in the UK and TNT, the global logistics company headquartered in The Netherlands.[35]

Does Corporate Citizenship Pay Off? The answer to this question is not completely clear. However, there does seem to be evidence that there is at least a small benefit and, in any case, no financial downside to CSR. One meta-analysis concluded that there was a positive association between corporate social performance (CSP) and corporate financial performance (CFP) and that it "supported the validity of enlightened self-interest in the social responsibility arena."[36]

Another meta-analysis of 167 studies of corporate social performance (CSP) and corporate financial performance (CFP) found a small correlation between good corporate behavior and good financial results.[37] The authors stated that "companies can do good *and* do well, even if they don't do well by doing good."[38] On the other hand, the research did confirm that corporate misdeeds, if discovered, are very costly to companies.

We are now back to the place where we started, which is that top management must set its desired course for corporate citizenship.

Creating Sustainable Value

Most of the arguments about the issue of corporate citizenship or CSR tend to pit business against society and moral actions against profitable ones. One of the major debates is to whom and for what are the management and board of directors of a company primarily responsible – the shareholders or stakeholders. Unfortunately, this argument, much like the ones we discussed in the previous chapter, generates more heat than light.

Positioning shareholders against stakeholders creates a false dichotomy. Shareholders are stakeholders also, and management should be trying to do the best they can for both groups – aiming for the upper right quadrant of Figure 9.2.

An example in the top left quadrant might be Mattel, discussed in the previous chapter. A lack of attention to its suppliers' practices in China created the need for a large recall. The Chinese firm received value from the Mattel business, but the result took value from the Mattel shareholders. From May 1, 2007, before the recall, until a year later, Mattel's share price declined by 34.4%. Meanwhile its major competitor, Hasbro, gained 11% in the same period.

There has been a lot of attention given to executive compensation in recent years and the size of executive bonuses. In 2000, Vodafone, the British mobile telephone operator,

FIGURE 9.2 Sustainable Value Framework[39]

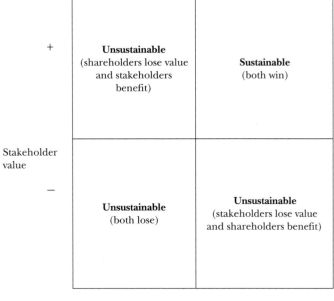

created dissatisfaction among shareholders because of a controversial incentive plan for its top management. Institutional investors, large pension plans, complained about a proposed £10 million bonus to the CEO and £4 million to two other directors to "top up their pay to reflect the work they did on the Mannesmann bid." [40] This was clearly a transfer of value from shareholders to individual stakeholders.

In the bottom right quadrant, companies that pollute the environment are presumably saving on waste treatment expenses and taking value from others who share the environment and, thus, the value transfer is to the shareholders. A listing of companies that the Political Economy Research Institute at the University of Massachusetts has identified as air polluters, for example, can be found in THE TOXIC 100.[41]

Recent examples for the last two quadrants might come from the auto industry. This chapter was being written at a time when US auto manufacturers were struggling to stay in business and had been in Washington DC looking for (some would say begging for) a bailout – and the outcome was not yet known, except for Chrysler's bankruptcy filing.

On November 19, 2008 a share of General Motors, the largest auto manufacturer in the world, closed on the New York Stock Exchange at US$ 2.79, or less than a cappuccino at Starbucks.[42] A preference for short-term profits versus a commitment to longer term innovation contributed to GM's precarious situation, as *The New York Times* observed:

> Time and again over the last 30 years, GM has spent billions of dollars on innovative ideas like its Saturn small-car company in the 1980s and the EV1 electric vehicle in the 1990s, only to then deprive those projects of further financing because money was needed elsewhere or because they were not delivering enough profit.[43]

GM's CEO admitted the company had been slow in responding to greater demand for small, fuel-efficient cars and the lead outside director on the Board stated that they were late on hybrids.[44] Thinking back to the concept of a triple bottom line, we note that, as of December 2008, GM did not score well on the financial or environmental dimensions. And its shareholders, dealers, customers, and employees all have suffered. This seems to be a pretty clear lose–lose example.

On the other hand, there is Toyota. Although its share price also had suffered in the economic downturn and financial crisis of 2008, it was still worth almost 10 times the value of a GM share. Its Prius is an example for the top, right-hand quadrant.[45] While GM is not scheduled to start selling approximately 10000 of the Volt hybrid until 2010, Toyota has sold 600000 of the Prius hybrid in the United States since 2000.[46] Prius proved to be a winner for Toyota, its shareholders, and stakeholders.

Conclusions

As we conclude this 6th edition of International Management Behavior, it is useful to recollect how much the world has changed since the original two authors started their writing about international business. The first course in intercultural management was launched at the Ivey Business School in the early 1970s. Many business executives wondered why it was being offered; several faculty colleagues remarked that there were so few differences between doing business domestically and "going international" that they wondered what would sustain more than a class or two devoted to the topic. At that time the North American Free Trade Agreement (NAFTA) wasn't on the table, China hadn't been recognized by either Nixon or Trudeau, and no one was anticipating the "Asian Century".

Although international business curricula had emerged in some business schools, when the first edition was published in 1988 there weren't many other books like this one, and we were not sure if a sufficient market existed to sustain sales and plan for a second edition. The intervening twenty-plus years have seen an explosion of international activity, even involving some dimensions of technology that didn't exist when we started our work. And we have gone from the optimism of the "end of history", which asserted that the fundamental values of liberal democracy and market capitalism had emerged triumphant to the pessimism reflected in the accusing label, "axis of evil" and the turmoil of the current global economic crisis – to the hope inherent in electing a multiracial, multicultural president in the United States!

To summarize all these changes we opened this edition with an equation that described the challenge facing global managers: Managing Globalization = Managing Complexity. We said that the complexity was reflected in increased interdependence, variety and ambiguity and that these were subject to "fast flux". And we said that dealing with this complexity started with developing a global mindset – understanding ourselves and our own organizations, and understanding a diverse set of other people and other organizations.

These *elements* of a global mindset are not different from those we faced when we wrote the first edition; but the complexity of each certainly has increased. But the tools and technologies to help us manage the increased complexity have also improved and increased. So we hope that this volume – a very *different* book than our first – will help our readers manage the complexity they face during their careers in international business. We have extended our original conceptions and knowledge, added to our own international and cross-cultural experiences of teaching and of managing, and borrowed generously from the wisdom of our colleagues and friends. What we have not changed is our excitement about the prospects for you adding to your own rich experience during your international careers and thereby increasing your abilities to contribute to the prosperity of your organizations and to the development of peace in the world. We end this 6th edition with warm and sincere wishes for success in your journey.

Notes

1   International Finance Corporation/World Bank, http://www.ifc.org/ifcext/pepse.nsf/ AttachmentsByTitle/IrresistibleCase4CG.pdf/$FILE/IrresistibleCase4CG.pdf (accessed December 4, 2008).

2   Bowen, H. R., *Social Responsibilities of the Businessman* (New York: Harper & Row, 1953) as referred to in Carroll, A. B., "A Three Dimensional Model of Corporate Performance," *Academy of Management Review* 4, No. 4, (1979) 497–505.

3   Friedman, M., "The Social Responsibility of Business is to Increase its Profits," *The New York Times Magazine*, September 13, 1970.

4   Spector, B., "Business Responsibilities in a Divided World: The Cold War Roots of the Corporate Social Responsibility Movement," *Enterprise & Society: The International Journal of Business History* Vol. 9, No. 2 (Oxford University Press, June 2008).

5   Donham, W. B., "Social Significance of Business," *Harvard Business Review* 5 (July 1927) 406–419; as reported in "Business Responsibilities in a Divided World: The Cold War Roots of the Corporate Social Responsibility Movement," n. 4 above.

6   Levitt, T., "The Dangers of Social Responsibility," *Harvard Business Review* 36 (September–October 1958) 41–50.

7   "The Good Company: A Survey of Corporate Social Responsibility," *The Economist*, January 22, 2005, 3.

8   "Just Good Business: A Special Report on Corporate Social Responsibility," *The Economist*, January 19, 2008, 8.

9   "Business Responsibilities in a Divided World: The Cold War Roots of the Corporate Social Responsibility Movement," n. 4 above, at 331.

10 Bies, R., Aartunek, J., Fort, T., and Zald, M., "Corporations As Social Change Agents: Individual, Interpersonal, Institutional and Environmental Dynamics," *Academy of Management Review*, Vol. 32, No. 3 (July 2007) 789.

11 "Just Good Business: A Special Report on Corporate Social Responsibility," *The Economist*, January 19, 2008.

12 Heineman Jr, B. W., *High Performance with High Integrity*, Memo to the CEO Series (Boston MA: Harvard Business Press, 2008) 20–21.

13 Ibid., at 6.

14 Ibid., at 500.

15 Ibid.

16 Adapted from Carroll, N. K., "Three-Dimensional Model." Although this framework was developed in the United States with domestic concerns in mind, we believe that it can be applied in international settings.

17 See Amba-Rao, S. C. "Multinational Corporate Social Responsibility, Ethics, Interactions, and Third World Governments: An Agenda for the 1990s," *Journal of Business Ethics* 12 (1993) 553–572. This article discusses conceptualizations of corporate social responsibility from a number of sources including the following, which is the primary source for the three-stage framework presented in the text, Sethi, S. P., "Dimensions of Corporate Social Performance: An Analytical Framework," *California Management Review* 12 (1975) 58–64.

18 See Barnett, J. H., "The American Executive and Colombian Violence: Social Relatedness and Business Ethics," *Journal of Business Ethics* 10 (1991) 853–861, for a description of the three models: conflict, compartment, and complementarity.

19 "Special Report on Corporate Social Responsibility," n. 11, at 4.

20 Frederick, W. C., "The Moral Authority of Transnational Corporate Codes," *Journal of Business Ethics* 10 (1991) 165–177.

21 These documents include: The United Nations Universal Declaration of Human Rights (1948), The European Convention on Human Rights (1950), The Helsinki Final Act (1975), The OECD Guidelines for Multinational Enterprises (1976), The International Labor Office Tripartite Declaration of Principles Concerning Multinational Enterprises and Social Policy (1977), The United Nations Code of Conduct for Transnational Corporations. The Caux Roundtable formulated its Principles for Business; the OECD developed its Guidelines for Multinational Enterprises (http://www.oecd.org); and in 1997 the Global Sullivan Principles were created. The Caux Round Table (CRT) (http://www.cauxroundtable.org/) is an international network of principled, senior business leaders working to promote a moral capitalism. The CRT advocates implementation of its code through which principled capitalism can flourish and sustainable and socially responsible prosperity can become the foundation for a fair, free, and transparent global society. In 1977, Reverend Leon Sullivan developed the Sullivan Principles, a code of conduct for human rights and equal opportunity for companies operating in South Africa. The Sullivan Principles are acknowledged to have been one

of the most effective efforts to end discrimination against blacks in the workplace in South Africa, and to have contributed to the dismantling of apartheid. To further expand human rights and economic development to all communities, Reverend Sullivan created the Global Sullivan Principles of Social Responsibility in 1997. (http://www.globalsullivanprinciples. org/index.htm.htm).

22 Frederick, "The Moral Authority of Transnational Corporate Codes," n. 20 above, 166–167.

23 http://www.unglobalcompact.org/AboutTheGC/TheTenPrinciples/index.html (accessed December 4, 2008).

24 http://www.unglobalcompact.org/ParticipantsAndStakeholders/search_participant. html?submit_x=page&pc=10&pn=0 (accessed December 4, 2008).

25 Ibid.

26 Brown, H. S., de Jong, M., and Lessidrenska, T., "The Rise of the Global Reporting Initiative (GRI) as a Case of Institutional Entrepreneurship." Corporate Social Responsibility Initiative, Working Paper No. 36. Cambridge MA, John F. Kennedy School of Government, Harvard University, 2007.

27 http://www.globalreporting.org/AboutGRI/ (accessed December 11, 2008).

28 http://www.calvert.com/sri.html.

29 http://www.calvert.com/sri_647.html (accessed December 2, 2008).

30 Decant, K. and Alumna, B., "Environmental Leadership: From Compliance to Competitive Advantage," *Academy of Management Executive,* 8, No. 3 (1994) 7–27.

31 Cisco 2008 Corporate Social Responsibility Report, http://www.cisco.com/web/about/ ac227/csr2008/index.html (accessed November 29, 2008).

32 Ibid.

33 http://www.starbucks.com/aboutus/csr.asp (accessed December 5, 2008).

34 http://www.marksandspencer.com/gp/node/n/43481031/279-8298838-7841101?amp; mnSBrand=core (accessed December 5, 2008).

35 http://group.tnt.com/aboutus/socialresponsibility/index.aspx (accessed December 5, 2008).

36 "Corporate Social and Financial Performance: A Meta-Analysis," Orlitzky, M., Schmidt, F. L., and Rynes, S., *Organization Studies* 24(3) (2003) 423.

37 Margolis, J. D. and Elfenbein, H. A. "Do Well By Doing Good? Don't Count on It," *Harvard Business Review* (January 2008).

38 Ibid., at 1.

39 "Expanding the Value Horizon: How Stakeholder Value Contributes to Competitive Advantage," Lazlo, C., Sherman, D., and Whalen, J., *Journal of Corporate Citizenship* 20 (Winter 2005) 67.

40 "Shareholder revolt at Vodafone," Nisse, J. *The Independent (London)* July 2, 2000; http:// findarticles.com/p/articles/mi_qn4158/is_20000702/ai_n14326618?tag=rel.res2.

41 "THE TOXIC 100: Top Corporate Air Polluters in the United States," Political Economy Research Institute, http://www.peri.umass.edu/Toxic-100-Table.265.0.html (accessed December 6, 2008).

42 On December 6, 2008 the prices of a cappuccino at Starbucks at Northeastern University were: Tall $2.80, Grande $3.35, and Venti $3.65.

43 Maynard, M., "At G.M., Innovation Sacrificed to Profits," December 5, 2008, http://www. nytimes.com/2008/12/06/business/06motors.html?hp (accessed December 6, 2008).

44 Ibid.

45 "Expanding the Value Horizon: How Stakeholder Value Contributes to Competitive Advantage, n. 39 above, at 69; and see also Porter, M. E. and Kramer, M. R., "The Link between Competitive Advantage and Corporate Social Responsibility," *Harvard Business Review* (December 2006).

46 "At G.M., Innovation Sacrificed to Profits," n. 43 above.

CASE **10**

NES China: Business Ethics (A)

By April 1998, it had been almost a year since the Germany-headquartered multinational company NES AG had first submitted its application to the Chinese government for establishing a holding company in Beijing to co-ordinate its investments in China. The application documentation had already been revised three times, but the approval by the government was still outstanding. Lin Chen, government affairs co-ordinator at NES AG Beijing Representative Office, came under pressure from the German headquarters and had to find a way to obtain approval within a month.

During the past year, Chen had almost exclusively worked on the holding company application. In order to facilitate the approval process, she had suggested giving gifts to government officials. But her European colleagues, Steinmann and Dr. Perrin, disagreed because they thought such conduct would be bribery and would violate business

Richard Ivey School of Business
The University of Western Ontario

Xin Zhang prepared this case under the supervision of Professor Joerg Dietz solely to provide material for class discussion. The authors do not intend to illustrate either effective or inef-

fective handling of a managerial situation. The authors may have disguised certain names and other identifying information to protect confidentiality.

ethics. Confronted with the cross-cultural ethical conflict, Chen had to consider possible strategies that would satisfy everybody.

COMPANY BACKGROUND

NES and NES AG

NES was founded in Germany in 1881. Over the following 100 years, by pursuing diversification strategies, NES had grown from a pure tube manufacturer into one of the largest industrial groups in Germany, with sales of US$14 billion in 1997. NES built plants and heavy machinery, made automotive systems and components, manufactured hydraulic, pneumatic and electrical drives and controls, offered telecommunications services and produced steel tubes and pipes.

NES was managed by a holding company — NES AG — that implemented value-oriented portfolio management and directed its financial resources to the areas with the greatest profit potentials. In 1997, NES AG owned NES's 11 companies in four business segments: engineering, automotive, telecommunications and tubes. These companies generally operated independently and largely at their own discretion, as NES AG was interested in their profitability and not their day-to-day operations.

NES had always been committed to move along the road of globalization and internationalization. Headquartered in Germany, NES had businesses in more than 100 countries with over 120,000 employees. In the process of globalization and internationalization, NES established a business principle that demonstrated its responsibilities not only to shareholders, employees and customers, but also to society and to the countries where it operated. As an essential part of the company's corporate culture, this principle pervaded the decentralized subsidiaries worldwide and guided the decision-making and conduct of both the company and its employees.

NES China Operations

NES's business in China dated back to 1889, when it built the flood barrages for the Canton River. In 1908, NES supplied seamless steel tubes for the construction of a waterworks in Beijing. Through the century, NES continued to broaden its presence. From the mid-1950s to 1997, NES supplied China with an enormous 5.2 million metric tons of steel tube and 1.6 million tons of rolled steel.

Since China opened up to foreign trade and investment in the late 1970s, NES's presence had grown dramatically. From 1977 to 1997, NES had completed more than 40 technology transfer and infrastructure projects. It had also set up 20 representative offices, six equity joint ventures and three wholly-owned enterprises.

In developing business links with China, NES adhered to its business principle. Most NES enterprises in China had highlighted this principle in their codes of conduct in employment handbooks (see Exhibit 1). These codes required employees to pursue the highest standards of business and personal ethics in dealing with government officials

EXHIBIT 1   Excerpt From The Employment Handbook Of One Of The NES's Enterprises In China

Article 3 Employment and Duties

3.1   The Company employs the Employee and the Employee accepts such employment in accordance with the terms and conditions of the Employment Contract and this Employment Handbook.

3.6   The Company expects each Employee to observe the highest standards of business and personal ethics, and to be honest and sincere in his/her dealings with government officials, the public, firms, or other corporations, entities, or organizations with whom the Company transacts, or is likely to transact.

3.7   The Company does business without favoritism. Purchases of materials or services will be competitively priced whenever possible. An Employee's personal interest or relationship is not to influence any transaction with a business organization that furnishes property, rights or services to the Company.

3.8   Employees are not to solicit, accept, or agree to accept, at any time of the year, any gift of value which directly or indirectly benefits them from a supplier or prospective supplier or his employees or agents, or any person with whom the Company does business in any aspect.

3.9   The Company observes and complies with all laws, rules, and regulations of the People's Republic of China which affect the Company and its Employees. Employees are required to avoid any activities which involve or would lead to the involvement of the Company in any unlawful practices and to disclose to the proper Company authorities any conduct that comes to their attention which violates these rules and principles. Accordingly, each Employee should understand the legal standards and restrictions that apply to his/her duties.

3.10 All Employees are the Company's representatives. This is true whether the Employee is on duty or off duty. All Employees are encouraged to observe the highest standards of professional and personal conduct at all times.

Article 13 Discipline

13.1 The Company insists on utmost discipline. The Employee's misconduct or unsatisfactory performance will be brought to the attention of the responsible Head of Department or Member of the Management when it occurs and will be documented in the Employee's file.

13.2 Some offences are grounds for immediate dismissal and disciplinary procedures will apply to other offences.

13.3 Offences which are grounds for immediate dismissal include: (i) Breach of the Company's rules of conduct.
      (j) Neglect of duties, favoritisms or other irregularities.

Source: Company files.

and business customers, and to avoid any activities that would lead to the involvement of the company in unlawful practices. Instead of tendering immediate favors or rewards to individual Chinese officials and customers, NES relied on advanced technology, management know-how and top quality products and service as a source of its competitive advantage. NES emphasized long-term mutual benefits and corporate social responsibility. Since 1979, NES had trained more than 2,000 Chinese engineers, master craftsmen, technicians and skilled workers in Germany. It had also offered extensive training programs in China. Moreover, NES was the first German company to adopt the suggestion of the German federal government to initiate a scholarship program for young Chinese academics to study in Germany. As a result, NES had built a strong reputation in China for being a fair business partner and a good guest company.

NES Beijing Representative Office

In 1977, NES was the first German company to open its representative office in Beijing. Along with NES's business growth, the Beijing Representative Office continued to expand. In 1997, it had 10 German expatriates and more than 40 local staff in nine business units. One unit represented NES AG. This unit was responsible for administrative co-ordination and office expense allocation. The other eight units worked for the German head offices of their respective NES companies in the engineering, automotive and tube segments.

Chinese legal restrictions severely limited the activities of the Beijing Representative Office. It was allowed only to engage in administrative activities, such as conducting marketing research for the German head offices, passing on price and technical information to Chinese customers, and arranging for meetings and trade visits. Moreover, it could not directly enter into employment contracts with its Chinese employees. Instead, it had to go through a local labor service agency designated by the Chinese government and consult with the agency on almost all personnel issues including recruitment, compensation and dismissal. As a result, the German managers of the Beijing Representative Office found it difficult to effectively manage their Chinese employees. In the absence of direct employment contracts, the managers had to rely on an internal reporting and control system.

CURRENT SITUATION

Establishing China Holding Company

In early 1997, NES AG had decided to establish a holding company in Beijing as soon as possible after carefully weighing the advantages and disadvantages of this decision. Establishing a China holding company was advantageous because, unlike a representative office, a holding company had its own business licence and could therefore engage in direct business activities. In addition to holding shares, a holding company could co-ordinate many important functions for its enterprises, such as marketing, managing government relations, and providing financial support. As a "country headquarters," a holding company could also unite the NES profile in China and strengthen the good name of NES as a reliable business partner in the world's most populous country. Moreover, it could hire staff directly and thus retain full control over its own workforce. In light of these advantages, NES AG expected substantial time and cost efficiencies from the China holding company.

Several disadvantages, however, potentially outweighed the advantages of a China holding company. First, Chinese legal regulations still constrained some business activities. For example, a Chinese holding company could not balance foreign exchange accounts freely and consolidate the taxation of NES's Chinese enterprises, although this might be permitted in the future. Second, the setup efforts and costs were high. To establish a holding company, NES had to submit a project proposal, a feasibility study, articles of association and other application documents to the local (the Local Department) and then to the central trade and economic co-operation departments (the Central Department) for examination and approval. Third, there was only a limited window of opportunity for NES AG. Once the China holding company had received its business licence, within two years, NES AG would have to contribute a minimum of

US$30 million fresh capital to it. The Chinese regulations prescribed that this capital could be invested only in new projects, but otherwise would have to remain unused in a bank account. NES currently was in a position to invest the capital in its new projects, but the company was not certain how much longer it would be in this position.

Working Team

NES AG authorized the following three individuals in the Beijing Representative Office to take up the China holding company application issue:

> Kai Mueller, 58 years old, had worked for NES in its China operations since the 1970s and had experience in several big cooperative projects in the steel and metallurgical industries. He would be the president of the holding company.
> Jochen Steinmann, 30 years old, was assigned to Beijing from Germany in 1996. He would be the financial controller of the holding company.
> Dr. Jean Perrin was a 37-year-old lawyer from France who had an in-depth understanding of Chinese business laws. He would work as the legal counsel. His previous working experience included a professorship at the Beijing International Business and Economics University in the 1980s.

The trio had advocated the idea of a China holding company to NES AG for quite some time and were most happy about NES AG's decision, because the future holding company would give them considerably more responsibilities and authority than did the Beijing Representative Office.

Considering the complexity and difficulty in coping with the Chinese bureaucratic hurdles, Mueller decided in March 1997 to hire Lin Chen as a government affairs co-ordinator for the working team. Chen, a native Chinese, was a 28-year-old politics and public administration graduate who had worked four years for a Chinese state-owned company and was familiar with the Chinese way of doing business. Mueller expected that Chen would play an instrumental role in obtaining the holding company approval from the Chinese government. He also promised that Chen would be responsible for the public affairs function at the holding company once it was set up.

Chen's View of Doing Business In China

Chen officially joined the Beijing Representative Office in June 1997. She commented on doing business in China:

> China's economy is far from rules-based; basically, it is still an economy based on relationships. In the absence of an explicit and transparent legal framework, directives and policies are open to interpretation by government officials who occupy positions of authority and power. In such circumstances, businesspeople cultivate personal *guanxi* (interpersonal connections based implicitly on mutual interest and benefit) with officials to substitute for an established code of law that businesspeople in the Western society take for granted.

In building and nurturing *guanxi* with officials, gifts and personal favors have a special place, not only because they are associated with respect and friendship, but also because in today's China, people place so much emphasis on utilitarian gains. In return for accepting gifts, officials provide businesspeople with access to information about policy thinking and the potentially advantageous interpretation of the policy, and facilitate administrative procedures. Co-operation leads to mutual benefits.

Although an existing regulation forbids government officials to accept gifts of any kind,[1] it remains pervasive for business people to provide officials with major household appliances, electric equipment, "red envelopes" stuffed with cash, and overseas trips. There is a common saying: "The bureaucrats would never punish a gift giver." Forbidding what the West calls bribery in a *guanxi*-based society where gift giving is the expected behavior can only drive such under-the-table transactions further behind the curtain.

While sharing benefits with officials is normal business conduct in China, it is interpreted as unethical and abnormal in the West. Faced with their home country's ethical values and business rules, Western companies in China cannot handle government relationships as their Asian counterparts do. They often find themselves at a disadvantage. This dilemma raises a question for a multinational company: Should it impose the home country's moral principles wherever it operates or should it do what the Chinese do when in China, and, if so, to what extent?

Different Opinions On Bribery

When Chen started working in June 1997, Mueller was sick and had returned to Germany for treatment. Steinmann and Dr. Perrin told Chen that NES had submitted the holding company application to the Local Department in April 1997 and that the Local Department had transferred the documents to the Central Department at the end of that month. But nothing had happened since then. Chen felt that she had to fall back to her former colleague, Mr. Zhu, who had close personal *guanxi* with the Central Department, to find out first who had the authority in the Central Department to push the processing and what their general attitudes towards the application were.

In July, Chen reported her findings to Steinmann and Dr. Perrin:

The approval process at the Central Department is difficult. Because holding companies are a relatively new form of foreign investment in China, the officials are unsure whether they are a good idea for China. They have been very prudent to grant approval. Hence, we don't have much negotiating leverage, although we are a big company and have products and technologies that China needs. The officials say that they will consider a holding company's application within 90 days of its submission. They issue approval however, only when the application is deemed "complete and perfect" (in that all issues have been resolved to the Central Department's satisfaction). The Central Department is under no real obligation to approve any holding company application. They can always find some minor issues. So the approval procedure may be lengthy. The legal basis for establishing holding companies is provided by the Holding Company Tentative Provisions, Supplementary Rules and some unpublished internal policies. This provisional and vague status allows the officials to be flexible in authorizing a holding company. In such circumstances, maintaining close connections with the responsible officials is absolutely critical.

Chen suggested:

> The quickest and most effective way to build such connections is to invite the responsible officials to dinner and give gifts. It won't cost the company too much. But what the company will gain in return — efficiency in obtaining approval and flexibility in the interpretation of the wording within the scope permitted by law — is worth much more.

Upon hearing Chen's report and suggestion, Steinmann was shocked:

> That would be bribery. In Germany bribing an official is a criminal offence for which both the briber and the bribed are punished. NES is a publicly traded company with a board of directors that reports to shareholders and monitoring authorities in Germany.
>
> We have met the criteria for setting up the holding company. What we should do now is organize a formal meeting with the officials and negotiate with them. This is the way we have done it in the past, and it has always worked. I am not aware that we ever had to use bribery. NES does not have a history of wrongdoing.

Knowing how critical it was to follow China's customary business practices in tackling such issues, Chen argued:

> Yes, it is correct. NES did not have to give gifts of this kind in the past. But don't forget: virtually all of NES's projects or joint ventures in the past were approved by agencies responsible for specific industries or local governments that were very keen on having access to NES's technology. As a result, NES always has had considerable bargaining power. It is different this time: we need to found a holding company, and we have to deal with the Central Department that we have never contacted before. Even Mueller does not have relations in this department. Moreover, our contacts at the industrial and local levels won't help much because they have very limited influence on the Central Department and, hence, the holding company application issue.
>
> Moreover, you can't equate gifts with bribes. The approval letter doesn't have predetermined "prices" and no one forces us to pay. We give gifts just to establish relationships with officials. We develop good relationships, and favorable consideration of these officials comes naturally. According to Chinese law,[2] to give gifts to government officials and expect them to take advantage of their position and power to conduct illegal actions is bribery. Our intent is to motivate officials to handle our application legally but without delay. I see no serious ethical problem.
>
> In some ways it's also hard to blame officials for feathering their nest because they are poorly paid. Whether they process our application quickly or slowly has absolutely no impact on their US$200 monthly income. Then, how can we expect them to give our case the green light? They are not morally wrong if they accept our gifts and don't create obstacles for us in return.
>
> Negotiation doesn't help much. Unless we have close relationships with them, they will always find some minor flaws in our documents. After all, they have the authority for interpreting the regulations. Therefore, we have to be open-minded and get accustomed to the Chinese way of doing business.

Chen hoped that Dr. Perrin would support her, as she had a feeling that the French were more flexible and less ethically sensitive than the Germans. Dr. Perrin, however, shared Steinmann's view. Perrin said:

> We should not give officials anything that has some value, with the exception of very small objects (pens, key holders, calendars and the like) given mainly for marketing and advertisement purposes. I also think that these officials should not accept any gifts. It's unethical and illegal. If we think it is unethical, we should combat it and refrain from it.

Nonetheless, Dr. Perrin understood the importance of *guanxi* as an informal solution to Chinese bureaucracies. So he agreed that Chen could invite one of the two responsible officials to dinner through Mr. Zhu and present a CD player to this official as an expression of respect and goodwill, although he thought it went too far and was approaching bribery.

On a Saturday evening in July, Chen met the official at one of the most expensive restaurants in Beijing. At the dinner, the official promised to work overtime the next day on NES's documents and give feedback as soon as possible.

The following Monday, Chen got the government's official preliminary opinion demanding a revision of 16 clauses of the application documents. Steinmann and Dr. Perrin found it difficult to understand this. NES had drafted the documents with reference to those of another company, whose application had been approved by the Central Department a few months ago. Why didn't the Central Department accept the similar wording this time? Chen again contacted her former colleague Zhu, who told her:

> You should never expect to get things done so quickly and easily. It takes time to strengthen your relationships. I can ask them to speed up the procedure without changing too much of the wording. But you'd better offer them something generous to express your gratitude since they would consider it a great favor. RMB3,000 (US$360) for each of the two will be OK. Don't make me lose face anyway.

Steinmann and Dr. Perrin thought it was straightforward bribery even if gifts were given through a third party. If they agreed to do so, they would run high personal risks by violating the corporate business principle and professional ethics. As controller and lawyer, they were expected to play an important role in implementing strict control mechanisms in the company and keeping the corporate conscience. Moreover, they were worried that the potential wrongdoing might damage the strong ethical culture of the Beijing Representative Office and the good corporate image among the Chinese employees of the office, although it likely would not affect the whole company because NES was so decentralized.

However, Chen thought that *renqing* (social or humanized obligation) and *micmzi* (the notion of face) were more important and that NES's business ethics and social responsibility could be somewhat compromised. In Chen's eyes, Steinmann and Dr. Perrin were inflexible and lacked knowledge of the Chinese business culture. Steinmann and Dr. Perrin told Chen that she needed to learn Western business rules and values in order to survive in a multinational company.

Recent Developments

In August 1997, the vice-president of NES AG led a delegation to visit China. Chen arranged a meeting for the delegation with a senior official of the Central Department. It turned out just to be a courtesy meeting and did not touch upon the details of the holding company approval issue.

In November, Steinmann and Dr. Perrin met the two responsible officials in hopes of negotiating with them such that the officials would allow NES to leave some clauses unchanged. But the officials insisted on their original opinion without giving a detailed explanation of the relevant legal basis. The negotiation lasted only half an hour, and Steinmann and Dr. Perrin felt that it accomplished nothing.

Because of the limited window of opportunity (that is, new investment projects required an immediate capital injection), they felt that they had no choice but to modify the documents according to the officials' requirements. Modifying the documents was an administrative struggle with NES AG, because due to company-internal policies, the German headquarters had to approve these modifications. The application was resubmitted at the end of November. When Chen inquired about the application's status in December, the officials, however, said that the case needed more consideration and then raised some new questions that they said they failed to mention last time. This happened once again three months later in February 1998.

WHAT NEXT?

In April 1998, Steinmann, Dr. Perrin and Chen submitted the newest revision of the application. As NES AG could not defer funding the new projects, it demanded that the Beijing working team obtained approval within a month so that NES AG could use the China holding company's registered capital of US$30 million. Otherwise, NES AG would have to re-evaluate the China holding company and might abandon it all together. In that case, Mueller, Steinmann and Dr. Perrin would miss opportunities for career advancement. As for Chen, she was concerned about her job because the Beijing Representative Office would no longer need her position.

Being very anxious about the current situation, Mueller decided to come back to Beijing immediately. Chen wanted to be able to suggest a practical approach that would gain the co-operation of the bureaucrats while conforming to the German moral standards. Chen also contemplated some challenging questions. For example, what constituted bribery? When ethical values conflicted, which values should people follow? How could these differences be resolved? To what extent should a multinational company like NES adapt to local business practices? Should the future China holding company develop special ethical codes to recognize the Chinese business culture? The answers to these questions were very important to Chen, because she expected to face similar ethically sensitive issues in the future.

The Richard Ivey School of Business gratefully acknowledges the generous support of The Richard and Jean Ivey Fund in the development of this case as part of the RICHARD AND JEAN IVEY FUND ASIAN CASE SERIES.

Notes

1   The China State Council Order No. 20 promulgated on 1988.12.01. Article 2 Any State administrative organization and its functionary shall not give and accept gifts in activities of domestic public service. The China State Council Order No. 133 promulgated on 1993.12.05. Article 7 Gifts accepted in activities of foreign public service shall be handled properly. Gifts above the equivalent of RMB200 (about US$24) according to the Chinese market price shall be . . . handed over to the gift administrative department or acceptor's work unit. Gifts of less

than RMB200 belong to the acceptor or to the acceptor's work unit. P. R. China Criminal Law (revised edition) promulgated on 1997.03.14. Article 394 Any State functionary who, in his activities of domestic public service or in his contacts with foreigners, accepts gifts and does not hand them over to the State as is required by State regulations, if the amount involved is relatively large, shall be convicted and punished in accordance with the provisions of Article 382 and 383 of this law. (Article 382 and 383 regulate the crime of embezzlement.)

2   The China State Council Order No. 20 promulgated on 1988.12.01. Article 8 Any State administrative organization and its functionary who give, accept or extort gifts for the purpose of securing illegitimate benefits shall be punished in accordance with relevant state law and regulations on suppression of bribery. The P. R. China Criminal Law (revised edition) promulgated on 1997.03.14. Article 385 Any State functionary who, by taking advantage of his position, extorts money or property from another person, or illegally accepts another person's money or property in return for securing benefits for the person shall be guilty of acceptance of bribes. Article 389 Whoever, for the purpose of securing illegitimate benefits, gives money or property to a State functionary shall be guilty of offering bribes.

CASE **11**

Arla Foods and the Cartoon Crisis (A)

In early February 2006, Astrid Nielsen, group communications director of Arla Foods, faced the greatest crisis of her career. Tens of thousands of Muslims in cities around the world had taken to the streets to protest the publication of caricatures of Muhammad by a Danish newspaper. The caricatures, which most Muslims viewed as blasphemous and offensive, prompted some to attack Danish embassies and businesses. In several countries, protests turned deadly.

Saudi Arabia was able to avoid much of the violence seen elsewhere. Instead, consumers protested by boycotting Danish products. For Arla Foods, which owned a large dairy in Saudi Arabia, the result was nothing short of disastrous. As other countries began to join the boycott, Nielson wondered what, if anything, her company could do to mitigate the total loss of Arla's Middle Eastern business.

David Wesley wrote this case under the supervision of Professors Henry W. Lane and Mikael Sondergaard solely to provide material for class discussion. The authors do not intend to illustrate either effective or ineffective handling of a managerial situation. The authors may have disguised certain names and other identifying information to protect confidentiality.

BACKGROUND

Arla Foods, a co-operative owned by 10,000 milk producers in Denmark and Sweden, was formed in 2000 through the merger of MD Foods of Denmark and Arla of Sweden. Arla was Europe's second largest dairy company, with 58 processing plants in Scandinavia and Britain, and annual revenues of nearly US$8 billion. It enjoyed a near monopoly on domestic dairy products, with market shares of between 80 and 90 per cent in most categories. The United Kingdom was the company's largest market, accounting for 33 per cent of total sales, followed by Sweden and Denmark at 22 per cent and 19 per cent, respectively. The rest of Europe accounted for another 13 per cent.

Outside Europe, the Middle East was Arla's most important market (see Table 1). The company exported approximately 55,000 tons of dairy products from Denmark and Sweden to Saudi Arabia, and produced around 30,000 tons through its Danya Foods subsidiary in Riyadh. Local production was based mainly on non-perishable goods and included processed cheese, milk and fruit drinks. In Saudi Arabia, which accounted for 70 per cent of total Middle East sales, the company's Lurpak, Puck and Three Cows brands were market leaders in butter, cream, dairy spread and feta categories. Other important Middle East markets included Lebanon, Kuwait, Qatar, and the United Arab Emirates.

TABLE 1   Arla Foods: Middle East Key Facts

Annual Revenues	$550 million
Net Income	$80 million
Danish Expatriate Workers	20
Non-Danish Workers[1]	1200
Average Annual Growth	10-12%

Other overseas markets included Argentina and Brazil, where Arla produced cheese and whey products. Arla also exported significant quantities of Danish cheese to Japan, and milk powder to less developed countries in Asia and Latin America. In North America, Arla cheeses were produced under a licensing agreement.

THE MUHAMMAD CARTOONS CRISIS

Terrorism and Self-Censorship

In 2004, controversial Dutch filmmaker Theo van Gogh produced a short film on Islam titled "Submission."[2] The 10-minute documentary, written by Dutch Member of Parliament Hirsi Ali, featured the stories of four abused Arab women. It intentionally provoked some Muslims by showing a woman dressed in a semi-transparent burqa, under which verses from the Qur'an were projected on her skin.

After the film was shown on Dutch public television on August 29, 2004, van Gogh and Ali began to receive death threats. Then, on November 2, 2004, Van Gogh was murdered while riding his bicycle in downtown Amsterdam.[3] The assailant attached a note to his body calling for Jihad against "infidel" America and Europe and threatening a similar fate for Ali.

Van Gogh's murder created broad awareness of his film, which was subsequently rebroadcast on Italian and Danish public television and widely distributed on the Internet. In Denmark, tension was already high following another well-publicized incident in which a lecturer at the University of Copenhagen was assaulted by five Muslim youths for reading the Qur'an to non-Muslims.[4] The killing of Van Gogh only served to heighten the cultural distance between Muslim immigrants and native-born Danes. Although most Europeans decried the violence of radical Islamists, many publishers, authors, and artists were reluctant to participate in projects that could offend Muslims and invite the wrath of terrorists.

Fear and Self-Censorship

In the summer of 2005, Danish author Kåre Bluitgen decided to write a children's book on the life of the Prophet Muhammad. He had hoped that such a book would help Danish children learn the story of Islam and thereby bridge the growing gap between Danes and Muslim immigrants. Yet the illustrators who collaborated with Bluitgen on other books feared reprisals from extremists and, therefore, refused to participate.[5] They understood, perhaps better than Bluitgen, that graphical depictions of Muhammad were considered blasphemous by many Muslims.[6]

Bluitgen eventually found an artist willing to illustrate his book anonymously. However, when the culture editor of the Danish newspaper Jyllands-Posten heard Bluitgen's story, he was incensed. "This was the culmination of a series of disturbing instances of self-censorship," Flemming Rose later wrote.

> Three people turned down the job for fear of consequences. The person who finally accepted insisted on anonymity, which in my book is a form of self-censorship. European translators of a critical book about Islam also did not want their names to appear on the book cover beside the name of the author, a Somalia-born Dutch politician who has herself been in hiding.[7]

Danish Cartoons: Muhammad As You See Him

To counter what he saw as a move against free speech, Rose invited 40 artists to submit drawings of "Muhammad, as you see him." Twelve artists responded, including three members of the Jyllands-Posten staff. When the cartoons first appeared on September 30, 2005, Rose wrote in the accompanying article,

> The modern, secular society is rejected by some Muslims. They demand a special position, insisting on special consideration of their own religious feelings. It is incompatible with contemporary democracy and freedom of speech, where you must be ready to put up with insults, mockery and ridicule . . . We are on our way to a slippery slope where no-one can tell how the self-censorship will end. That is why Jyllands-Posten has invited members of the Danish editorial cartoonists union to draw Muhammad as they see him.[8]

Muslim Reaction

Two weeks after the publication of the 12 cartoons, Danish imams organized a protest in downtown Copenhagen. More than 3,000 Danish Muslim immigrants gathered to show their disapproval of the cartoons. The most offensive cartoon, in their opinion, featured Muhammad wearing a turban filled with explosives. On the turban was written the Shahādah (Islamic creed),[9] while a lit fuse emerged from the back of his head.

Another image featured a schoolboy named Muhammad scribbling a message in Farsi[10] on a blackboard. "The editorial team of Jyllands-Posten is a bunch of reactionary provocateurs," it states. Ironically, artist Lars Refn was targeted by both sides in the ensuing quarrel. He was the first artist to receive death threats, while at the same time secular free speech advocates accused him of cowardice for not drawing the prophet. In apparent defense of Refn's decision to not draw the prophet, Rose explained in an editorial,

> I wrote to members of the association of Danish cartoonists asking them 'to draw Muhammad as you see him.' We certainly did not ask them to make fun of the prophet.[11]

A few days later, eleven ambassadors from Islamic countries sought a meeting with Danish Prime Minister Anders Rasmussen to demand government action against the cartoons. The prime minister refused, noting that such a meeting would violate the principles of Danish democracy. "As prime minister I have no tool whatsoever to take actions against the media, and I don't want that kind of tool," he replied.[12]

Cartoons Circulated Abroad

Meanwhile, Danish imam Abu Laban decided to take matters into his own hands. He sent a Muslim delegation on a tour of Egypt, Lebanon, and Syria, where dignitaries, religious leaders, and journalists were shown the cartoons. The greatest stir, however, was not caused by the Danish cartoons, but by three additional images that were far more graphic and offensive than those published by the newspaper.[13] While the origin of the three additional images was unknown, within days they were circulated on Islamic websites and chat rooms, causing outrage among Muslims who thought they had been published in Danish newspapers.[14]

In December, the cartoons were circulated among heads of state at a Summit of the Organization of the Islamic Conference (OIC) in Saudi Arabia. The OIC later issued a statement calling on the prime minister of Denmark to apologize. When he refused, the OIC's secretary general for Islamic education and culture urged the organization's 51 member states to boycott Danish products until they received an apology.[15] Since the entire Middle East accounted for less than one per cent of Denmark's exports, Danes showed little concern over the threat of a boycott. Moreover, a poll conducted in late January by the Opinion Research Institute found that 79 per cent of Danes supported the prime minister's decision to not apologize for the cartoons.[16]

Outside of Denmark, the OIC found wider support. United Nations human rights commissioner Louise Arbour proclaimed her "alarm" at the "unacceptable disregard for the beliefs of others." Both the Council of Europe and the Arab League condemned the cartoons.[17]

European Media Reprint Cartoons

When the OIC called on Muslim countries to boycott Danish products (see "Arla and the OIC Boycott" below), many Europeans saw it as an attack on free speech. In protest, newspapers and magazines across Europe began reprinting the cartoons. Between the beginning of January and early February, the original cartoons appeared in more than 50 European newspapers and magazines. Prominent periodicals, such as France's Le Monde and Germany's Die Welt, displayed some of the images on their front pages.

In explaining his reason for reprinting the cartoons, the editor of Le Monde stated, "A Muslim may well be shocked by a picture of Mohammed, especially an ill-intentioned one. But a democracy cannot start policing people's opinions, except by trampling the rights of man underfoot."[18] Likewise, The Economist, which did not reprint the cartoons, stated that European newspapers had a "responsibility" to show "solidarity" with Jyllands-Posten.

> In the Netherlands two years ago a film-maker was murdered for daring to criticize Islam. Danish journalists have received death threats. In a climate in which political correctness has morphed into fear of physical attack, showing solidarity may well be the responsible thing for a free press to do. And the decision, of course, must lie with the press, not governments.[19]

For many Muslims, the reprinting of the cartoons was seen as further provocation. Some protested peacefully, while others reacted with violence. In some countries, buildings were set ablaze and shops selling European goods were vandalized. In Lebanon and Syria, the Danish and Norwegian embassies were firebombed. Elsewhere, clashes with police and security forces in Afghanistan, Pakistan, and other countries left as many as 300 people dead (see Exhibit 1). In northern Nigeria, Muslims went on a rampage, burning churches, shops, and cars belonging to the Christian minority. The violence left scores of dead and as many as 10,000 homeless.[20]

ARLA AND THE OIC BOYCOTT

At first, Arla viewed the cartoon crisis more as a security concern than an economic one. "It will be a serious blow to us if the situation becomes so grave that we are forced to withdraw our Danish workers," explained Arla Executive Director Finn Hansen.

> Our tremendous success in Saudi Arabia is thanks in large part to the fact that over the past 20 years, we've kept a number of our most talented managers constantly stationed in the country. It will hurt our credibility to pull out our Danish workers, and in the long term, it will impact sales. But I don't think things will get that bad. The Irish and Dutch dairies we compete with in Saudi Arabia are keeping their workers down there for now as well. Consumers in Saudi Arabia will continue to buy food, regardless of the terror threat. So I don't think our customer base will disappear.[21]

However, within a few weeks it became clear than Arla had underestimated the threat to its business. In Saudi Arabia, its products were featured in news stories about the boycott

EXHIBIT 1   Selected News Headlines

Prophetic insults; Denmark and Islam, The Economist, January 7, 2006

Free speech clashes with religious sensitivity: For much of last year, various squabbles have simmered over several prominent Danes' rude comments about Islam. Now a schoolboy prank by a newspaper has landed the prime minister, Anders Fogh Rasmussen, in the biggest diplomatic dispute of his tenure in office.

Denmark Is Unlikely Front in Islam-West Culture War, The New York Times, January 8, 2006

Editorial cartoons published in a Danish newspaper have made Denmark a flashpoint in the culture wars between Islam and the West in a post-9/11 world.

After Danish Mohammed cartoon scandal, Norway follows suit, Agence France Presse, January 10, 2006

A Norwegian Christian magazine on Tuesday published a set of controversial caricatures of the prophet Mohammed following months of uproar in the Muslim world over a Danish paper's decision to print the same cartoons.

Drive to Boycott Danish, Norwegian Goods Takes Off, Gulf News, January 23, 2006

Riyadh: A vigorous campaign has been kicked off in Saudi Arabia calling for boycott of Danish and Norwegian products in response to repeated publishing of offensive cartoons of the Prophet Mohammad by some newspapers and magazines in those countries.

Threats by Militants Alarm Scandinavians; Denmark and Norway feel the backlash from cartoons, Los Angeles Times, January 31, 2006

Denmark warned its citizens on Monday to avoid Saudi Arabia, and gunmen in the Gaza Strip said any Scandinavians there risked attack over newspaper cartoons of the prophet Muhammad.

Caricature of Muhammad Leads to Boycott of Danish Goods, The New York Times, January 31, 2006

A controversy over the publication of caricatures of the Muslim prophet by a Danish newspaper boiled over into a boycott.

Cartoons of Prophet Met With Outrage; Depictions of Muhammad in Scandinavian Papers Provoke Anger, Protest Across Muslim World, The Washington Post, January 31, 2006

Cartoons in Danish and Norwegian newspapers . . . have triggered outrage among Muslims across the Middle East, sparking protests, economic boycotts and warnings of possible retaliation against the people, companies and countries involved.

Danish Paper's Apology Fails To Calm Protests; Cartoons Trigger Muslim Outrage, The Boston Globe, February 1, 2006

An apology by Denmark's largest newspaper . . . failed yesterday to calm a controversy that has ignited fiery protests across the Islamic world and provoked death threats against Scandinavians by Muslim radical groups. Muslim political and religious leaders and jihadists added their voices to the fury already thundering from mosques and blaring from television and radio stations from Morocco to Pakistan.

Bomb threat to repentant Danish paper, The Guardian, February 1, 2006

The offices of Denmark's bestselling broadsheet newspaper were evacuated last night following a bomb threat — a day after the editor-in-chief apologized for publishing cartoons of the prophet Muhammad that offended Muslims.

Anger as papers reprint cartoons of Muhammad: French, German and Spanish titles risk wrath: France Soir executive 'sacked' for defiant gesture, The Guardian, February 2, 2006

Newspapers in France, Germany, Spain and Italy yesterday reprinted caricatures of the prophet Muhammad, escalating a row over freedom of expression which has caused protest across the Middle East. France Soir and Germany's Die Welt published cartoons which first appeared in a Danish newspaper, although the French paper later apologized and apparently sacked its managing editor.

EXHIBIT 1   (*Continued*)

Islamic Anger Widens At Mohammed Cartoons, The Boston Globe, February 3, 2006

An extraordinary row over newspaper cartoons depicting the Prophet Mohammed intensified yesterday, with street demonstrations from North Africa to Pakistan, threats of violence against Europeans in the Middle East, and diplomatic protests by Muslim nations.

BBC shows the Islam cartoons, Daily Mail, February 3, 2006

The BBC and Channel 4 risked a Muslim backlash yesterday by showing 'blasphemous' cartoons of the prophet Mohammed that have caused outrage in the Islamic world.

Cartoons spark Islamic rage *Europe's leaders step in as controversy escalates *More newspapers publish offending images *Mideast consumer boycott hits Danish products, Financial Times, February 3, 2006

European leaders tried to contain the controversy over newspaper cartoons of the Prophet Mohammed, as the international dispute escalated into a consumer boycott and risked the gravest cultural clash with the Muslim world since the Salman Rushdie affair.

Gaza gunmen on hunt for Europeans: Aid workers, journalists, diplomats flee in fear for their lives; protests spread to Pakistan, Iraq, Ottawa Citizen, February 3, 2006

Militants threatened yesterday to kidnap or murder western citizens, in retaliation for the publication of caricatures of the Prophet Muhammad.

Broadcasters show prophet cartoons despite Muslim rage, The Herald, February 3, 2006

British broadcasters last night defied Muslim anger when they showed cartoons which have caused a storm of protest in the Islamic world.

Danes call envoys home over prophet cartoons, The Irish Times, February 3, 2006

Denmark has summoned its ambassadors back from abroad to Copenhagen for talks today about the controversial newspaper cartoons of the Prophet Muhammad that have triggered protests in the Arab world and threats by militant Muslims.

Embassies burn in cartoon protest, BBC News, February 4, 2006

Syrians have set fire to the Norwegian and Danish embassies in Damascus in protest at the publication of newspaper cartoons of the Prophet Muhammad. Protesters scaled the Danish site amid chants of "God is great," before moving on to attack the Norwegian mission.

Danish embassy in Beirut torched, BBC News, February 5, 2006

Lebanese demonstrators have set the Danish embassy in Beirut on fire in protest at the publication of cartoons depicting the Prophet Muhammad.

Protests Over Cartoons of Muhammad Turn Deadly, The New York Times, February 6, 2006

Demonstrations against the publication of cartoons of the Prophet Muhammad by newspapers in Europe spread across Asia and the Middle East today, turning violent in Afghanistan, where at least four protesters were killed and over a dozen police officers and protesters injured.

Nigerian religious riots continue, BBC News, February 24, 2006

Violence is continuing across Nigeria where religious riots have claimed more than 100 lives this week. Some 10,000 people are still sheltering in barracks in the south-east town of Onitsha after violence there killed 80.

EXHIBIT 2   Timeline Of Key Events

November 2, 2004	Film director Theo van Gogh is murdered in Amsterdam.
September 30, 2005	Jyllands-Posten publishes 12 cartoons portraying Muhammad.
January 20, 2006	The Saudi grand mufti calls for a boycott of Danish products.
January 24, 2006	In Saudi Arabia and Kuwait Aria's products begin to be removed from 50 grocery store shelves.
January 26, 2006	Arla products were removed from 300 stores.
January 28, 2006	Arla products were removed from 500 stores.
January 31, 2006	Arla products were removed from 50,000 stores, representing 95 per cent of the market.
February 1, 2006	Cartoons reprinted in several newspapers across Europe.
February 3, 2006	Danish and Norwegian embassies in Damascus are set on fire.
February 4, 2006	Danish embassy in Beirut is set on fire.
February 6, 2006	Iran officially bans Danish products.

campaign and religious leaders across the country called on worshippers to avoid Danish goods. By the end of January 2006, Danish products were removed from store shelves, replaced with signs stating "Danish products were here." Egypt, Kuwait, Qatar, Bahrain, and the United Arab Emirates soon joined the boycott (see Exhibit 2 for a timeline of key events).

The boycott also aroused the anger of many local Muslims, some of whom threatened and harassed Arla employees as they went to and from work. In two separate incidents, workers were physically assaulted as they removed banned Arla products from store shelves. As a result, Arla provided employees with additional security escorts.

In early February, Iran became the first country to officially sever all economic ties with Denmark.[22] It made a further symbolic gesture by renaming domestically produced Danish pastries as "Roses of the Prophet Muhammad."[23] "The Commerce Ministry will not allow Danish brands or products which have been registered in Denmark to clear customs," announced Iranian Commerce Minister Massoud Mir-Kazemi.

> Iranian importers, including state-affiliated organs and companies, have three months to designate substitute products for Danish goods and then we will enforce the law. All ongoing negotiations or contracts with Denmark which are pending will also be suspended, and all signed contracts will be reviewed. The exchange of delegations between the two countries will be suspended until further notice.[24]

The rapid deterioration in relations between Denmark and the Middle East stunned Arla Foods executives. Although they had been monitoring the situation since the cartoons were first published, the boycott "was hard to foresee," Nielsen explained.

> Some of our customers are extremely influential and powerful people. One of the retailers owns a large chain of grocery stores and he is extremely religious. Everyone else looks to see how he will react . . .

We were in constant contact with our customers, and they never suggested that they were going to boycott our products. But they had to react when the religious community told them to. Even after the boycott was announced, retailers said to us, "We want to do business with you, but we can't."

The immediate impact of the boycott was extensive. "Our business has been completely undermined," Hansen lamented. "Our products have been taken off the shelves in 50,000 stores. Without a quick solution, we will lose our business in the Middle East."[25] Meanwhile, Arla was losing sales worth $1.5 million per day, or about eight per cent of the company's worldwide revenues.[26]

Other companies preemptively distanced themselves from the cartoons. Switzerland-based Nestlé bought front-page advertisements in Arab newspapers to explain that its powdered milk was "neither produced in nor imported from Denmark." French supermarket giant Carrefour went further, removing Danish products from store shelves with a notice declaring "solidarity with the Islamic community." Other signs read "Carrefour doesn't carry Danish products."[27]

European Criticism: "The Right to Offend"

In Europe, some viewed attempts by European companies to show "solidarity" with Muslim protesters as cowardice. At a Berlin rally, Hirsi Ali, who rarely made public appearances in the face of the numerous threats against her life, expressed outrage. "I am here to defend the right to offend," she proclaimed.

> Shame on those European companies in the Middle East that advertised "we are not Danish" or "we don't sell Danish products". This is cowardice. Nestlé chocolates will never taste the same after this, will they? The EU member states should compensate Danish companies for the damage they have suffered from boycotts. Liberty does not come cheap. A few million Euros are worth paying for the defense of free speech.[28]

European Union President José Manuel Barroso also felt it his duty to uphold the principles of free speech. "I have spoken with the Prime Minister of Denmark and expressed [our] solidarity," he noted.

> I want to send my solidarity to the people of Denmark as well; a people who rightly enjoy the reputation as being amongst the most open and tolerant, not just in Europe, but in the world. Our European society is based on respect for the individual person's life and freedom, equality of rights between men and women, freedom of speech and a clear distinction between politics and religion. Our point of departure is that as human beings we are free, independent, equal and responsible. We must safeguard these principles. Freedom of speech is part of Europe's values and traditions. Let me be clear. Freedom of speech is not negotiable.[29]

The Crisis and Communications Group

As the seriousness of the boycott progressed, Arla CEO Peter Tuborgh decided to convene an emergency meeting with senior executives, dubbed "The Crisis and Communications Group." Earlier in his career, Tuborgh had worked in Saudi Arabia for four years as an operations manager. He understood the seriousness of the boycott, but he also felt that the company should not stray in any way from its global mission statement (see Exhibit 3). Any action taken by Arla would need to be consistent with the company's overall vision and reflect its values.

Jens Refslund, director of Arla's production division, suggested that the company needed to act quickly to cut production to reduce costs. He explained,

> Once sales in the Middle East have come to a standstill, it will inevitably have consequences for production. A decision about what we do next must be taken within the next few days.[30]

Refslund estimated that the company would need to layoff as much as one third of the staff at a havarti cheese plant in Denmark, or approximately 50 employees. To avoid delays, negotiations with the dairy workers' union needed to begin immediately. Moreover, numerous Scandinavian dairy farmers faced a loss of some of their income if the Middle East market remained closed to Danish dairy products.

Nielsen expressed concern about the company's ability to recover from the crisis.

EXHIBIT 3 Arla Mission Statement

Our Mission is:

"To offer modern consumers milk-based food products that create inspiration, confidence and well-being"

Arla Foods' primary objective is to meet consumers' wishes and requirements. Its mission underlines the company's focus on the consumer.

"Modern consumers" covers consumers of all ages who look for inspiration, variety and innovation.

"Milk-based products" means that the products must contain milk or milk components.

Arla Foods is committed to providing consumers with inspiration by offering a multitude of ways of utilizing its products.

Arla Foods creates confidence and well-being by providing tasty and healthy products that not only meet statutory quality requirements, but also satisfy consumers' demands for "soft" values. Consumers can be assured that Arla Foods consistently demonstrates its concern for the proper exploitation of resources, the environment, animal welfare, ethics, etc. throughout the entire production process.

Our Vision is:

"To be the leading Dairy Company in Europe through considerable value creation and active market leadership"

Through its vision, Arla Foods wishes to demonstrate that its activities are designed to create value for both the company and its owners.

By using the term "value creation" instead of "results," we wish to emphasize that our objectives are based on the long-term rather than short-term financial gains.

To become the world leader in value-creation within the dairy sector, Arla Foods must be:

*Northern Europe's preferred dairy group among consumers, customers and milk producers
*Northern Europe's market leader within all types of dairy products with a broad range, strong brands and a high degree of consumer confidence
*Represented in Southern Europe with a selected range of cheese and butter
*Represented in a number of markets outside Europe through a range adapted to individual markets

One billion customers have rejected our products because it has suddenly become a synonym for the insult to the Prophet Mohammed. What can we do? We can't edit newspapers, we can't comment on government actions, we can't get involved in politics and we certainly can't address religion.

Nevertheless, Finn Hansen, who had responsibility for the Middle East, remained hopeful. He believed that in order for Arla to recover, it had to communicate with the individual consumer.

Arla has been producing dairy products in Saudi Arabia for so long that we believe the authorities consider us a local dairy. It is not enough to persuade the supermarket chains to put our products back on the shelves. We should take our message directly to the consumer.

Notes

1   Most of Arla's non-Danish staff was comprised of Muslim migrant workers from less developed countries. Many entered Saudi Arabia as Hajj pilgrims and remained in the country at the end of their pilgrimage.
2   Submission is the English translation of the word Islam.
3   Gunman kills Dutch film director, *BBC News*, November 2, 2004.
4   Overfaldet efter Koran-læsning, *TV 2 (Denmark)*, October 9, 2004.
5   Allah und der Humor, *Die Zeit*, January 2, 2006.
6   Not all Muslims agree on the interpretation of Muslim scholars who have issued fatwas against images of the prophet Muhammad. Some argue that Islam has a centuries-old tradition of paintings of Muhammad and other religious figures. The more famous of these continue to be displayed in palaces and museums in various Muslim countries, including Iran. Source: Bonfire of the Pieties: Islam prohibits neither images of Muhammad nor jokes about religion, *The Wall Street Journal*, February 8, 2006.
7   The Dutch politician refers to Hirsi Ali, who collaborated with Theo Van Gogh on the film Submission. Why I Published Those Cartoons, *Jyllands-Posten*, February 19, 2006.
8   Translated from Muhammeds ansigt, *Jyllands-Posten*, September 29, 2005.
9   The Shahādah is the declaration of belief in the oneness of God and in Muhammad as his messenger. Recitation of the Shahādah is considered one of the Five Pillars of Islam by Sunni Muslims. In English the Shahādah reads: "There is no god but God and Muhammad is his messenger."
10 Farsi is a Persian language spoken in Iran, Afghanistan, and several other Middle Eastern countries.
11 Why I Published Those Cartoons, *Jyllands-Posten*, February 19, 2006.
12 The Danish Cartoon Crisis: The Import and Impact of Public Diplomacy, USC Center on Public Diplomacy, April 5, 2006.
13 Anatomy of a Global Crisis, *The Sunday Herald (Scotland)*, February 12, 2006.
14 Child's tale led to clash of cultures, *The Guardian Unlimited*, February 4, 2006.
15 Muslim organization calls for boycott of Denmark, *The Copenhagen Post*, December 28, 2006.
16 OIC Demands Unqualified Danish Apology, *Arab News*, January 29, 2006.
17 Prophetic insults, *The Economist*, January 5, 2006.
18 France's Le Monde Publishes Front-Page Cartoon Of Mohammed, *Agence France-Presse (AFP)*, February 2, 2006.
19 Cartoon wars, *The Economist*, February 9, 2006.

20 Although the latest hostility was sparked by the cartoon crisis, ethnic violence has been part of an ongoing conflict that has claimed 10,000 lives in Nigeria since 1999. Source: Nigerian religious riots continue, *BBC News,* February 24, 2006.

21 Terror threaten dairy exports, *The Copenhagen Post,* January 7, 2006.

22 EU warns Iran over boycott of Danish goods, *China Daily,* February 8, 2006.

23 Iran targets Danish pastries, *Aljazeera.net,* February 17, 2006.

24 Iran bans import of Danish products, *Islamic Republic News Agency (Iran),* February 6, 2006.

25 Muslim protest spreads to Danish butter, *The Sunday Times,* February 3, 2006.

26 Danish Companies Endure Snub by Muslim Consumers, *The New York Times,* February 27, 2006.

27 Carrefour JV with MAF in Egypt halts sale of Danish products, *AFX News Limited,* February 3, 2006.

28 From a speech titled "The Right to Offend" given in Berlin on February 9, 2006.

29 EU President Barroso's Statement On The Issue Of The Cartoons Of Prophet Muhammad, *Press and Public Diplomacy Delegation of the European Commission,* February 15, 2006.

30 Arla dairy sales crippled by Middle East boycott, *Dairy Reporter,* January 31, 2006.

CASE **12**

The Credit Suisse Christian Values Fund

Annie Hildebrandt had always shown concern for human rights. In high school, she joined the Amnesty International Student Group. After she graduated from college, Hildebrandt spent two years in Tanzania as a school teacher for Vitas Humanis Africa, a Catholic charity that provided support to refugees.

When she returned to Switzerland, Hildebrandt landed a well-paying job as a Public Relations specialist for a multinational food corporation. Over the years, she was able to save a considerable amount of money. Most of the funds were invested in bonds and money market instruments. However, she wondered if she could be earning better returns by investing in the stock market. Newspaper ads lauded the high returns of equity mutual funds.

However, Hildebrandt was reluctant to let a mutual fund manager control her money, which could end up in the hands of companies that produced weapons. Too often, such weapons found their way to developing countries, where they compounded the suffering caused by civil wars and ethnic strife. Hildebrandt had seen the results of that first hand, and she wanted no part of it.

This case was written from public sources by David Wesley under the direction of Professor Alexandra Roth for the purpose of class discussion. The authors do not intend to demonstrate either effective or ineffective handling of management situations.

Recently, Hildebrandt came across an article in a Swiss newspaper that talked about "ethical investing." She was intrigued to find out that a new breed of mutual funds not only avoided weapons companies, but also supported environmental sustainability. Additionally, their returns far exceeded anything she was earning.

One of the banks mentioned in the article was Credit Suisse. Since Hildebrandt already had an account with the bank, she decided to find out what they had to offer. When her investment advisor produced a list of ethical funds, Hildebrandt was surprised to find one called the "Christian Values Fund." In addition to avoiding companies that made weapons, tobacco, and other harmful products, the fund sought to follow "Christian values" and had the backing of the Catholic Church. Although Hildebrandt did not always agree with the Church on issues such as the use of contraceptives, she considered herself to be pro-life, and supported the Church's role in advocating for greater human rights. At the end of her meeting, the investment advisor promised to send her prospectuses for the Christian Values Fund and a couple of environmental funds. In the meantime, she planned to do some research on the Internet to learn more about the fund and to see how its returns compared to her current investments.

When Hildebrandt went online, she found numerous websites and articles devoted to ethical investing. Some articles mentioned the Christian Values fund, and one site included a short video interview with Philipp Röh, the fund's portfolio manager.[1] However, Hildebrandt's online queries raised more questions than they answered. Ultimately, she decided that the best way to find answers to her questions was to speak directly with her investment advisor.

SOCIALLY RESPONSIBLE INVESTMENTS (SRI)

Socially Responsible Investments included a broad range of funds that made investment decisions based on criteria that included social, environmental and/or religious values. SRI funds used two types of screening, positive and negative. Positive screening involved actively seeking out companies that participated in socially desirable activities, such health care, education, and alternative energy. Negative screening focused on avoiding companies that were thought to be engaged in harmful activities, such as human rights violations, war profiteering, and nuclear energy. The actual criteria used to screen assets varied from fund to fund depending on the personal values and beliefs of clients.

Although contemporary SRI investments typically fell into four main categories, namely human rights, peace, environmental protection, and religion, most funds used several categories to screen their holdings. Nearly all contemporary SRI funds avoided investments in tobacco (96%), alcohol (83%) and military equipment (81%). The majority (80%) also used some form of environmental screening. Human rights and abortion were criteria in only 40 percent and 25 percent of SRI funds, respectively.[2]

Religious Values

Since the middle of the 20th century, the world has seen a rise in traditional religious beliefs and values. According to a special report in *The Economist*,

The proportion of people attached to the world's four biggest religions—Christianity, Islam, Buddhism and Hinduism—rose from 67 percent in 1900 to 73 percent in 2005 and may reach 80 percent by 2050. Moreover, from a secularist point of view, the wrong sorts of religion are flourishing, and in the wrong places. In general, it is the tougher versions of religion that are doing best—the sort that claim Adam and Eve met 6,003 years ago.[3]

At the same time, a study by the Pew Research Center in Washington, DC discovered that "wealthier nations tend to place less importance on religion."[4] Based on these findings, an *Atlantic Monthly* editorial criticized *The Economist's* predictions.

Breathless warnings about rising religious fervor and conflicts to come ignore two basic facts. First, many areas of the world are experiencing a decline in religious belief and practice. Second, where religions are flourishing, they are also generally evolving—very often in ways that allow them to fit more easily into secular societies, and that weaken them as politically disruptive forces.

To be sure, while religion was often blamed for wars and civil strife, most religious devotion was peaceful, particularly in more prosperous countries. And it was in such countries where the ranks of the devout created opportunities for companies poised to offer products and services catering to their spiritual needs.

Although the first ethical mutual funds were not publicized as belonging to any specific religious denomination, most were guided by religious (and specifically Protestant) principles. Even funds that promoted non-religious causes, such as peace and human rights, often had religious backers.

Islamic Funds

Among religion-based ethical funds, Islamic funds were the most significant. Islamic banking and finance (IBF) sought to offer investment products grounded in Shari'a (Islamic law). In the 1990s, a growing cadre of American and European banks began to recognize the potential value in attracting Muslim clients, not only from oil-rich Middle Eastern countries, but from Europe, North America, and Southeast Asia. Chase Manhattan Bank, Citibank, and HSBC were among the better known brokers to set up Islamic desks. By 2006, the number of Islamic funds had grown to 250 worldwide with combined assets totaling $300 billion.[5]

The most important principle guiding the majority of Muslim investors was the avoidance of interest. Interest in any form was often interpreted as a form of usury and therefore prohibited under Islamic law. Consequently, companies that were included in Islamic funds were required to have a debt to equity ratio of less than 33 percent. Complete avoidance of interest was impossible. Therefore, Islamic funds underwent a "purification" process that involved donating any income generated by interest to Islamic charities.[6]

Islamic investments also could not participate in or support the production and distribution of proscribed goods and services. Companies that produced or distributed alcohol, pork, and pornography, for example, were automatically excluded. Hotels, grocers, and meat plants were automatically excluded because of the probability that these companies were engaged in prohibited activities.

Islamic investments were approved by Shari'a councils of qualified religious scholars who were also trained in finance and economics. Any lay person who, in good faith, followed the recommendations of a qualified scholar would be considered blameless in the eyes of God, even if the recommendation was given in error.

Christian Funds Christianity was often cited as the root of the modern SRI movement. As early as 1928, the first socially responsible mutual fund company, Boston-based Pioneer Investments, was created based on the Christian principles of its founder, Philip L. Carret. For 50 years, Pioneer used a "sin screen" to avoid companies that "profited from the sale of alcohol, tobacco, and gambling products."[7]

Contemporary Christian mutual funds were almost exclusively an American phenomenon. The largest Christian funds, such as the Lutheran Brotherhood's Thrivent Financial, eschewed any form of religious criteria, choosing instead to operate in much the same way as secular funds. Consequently, the total value of mutual funds based on strict Christian principles, commonly known as faith-based funds, was considerably smaller than the amounts often reported in the popular press (see Exhibit 1).[8]

EXHIBIT 1[9] List of US-based Christian Mutual Funds

Plan	Religious Affiliation	Year Founded	Assets ($ million) 01/31/2008	5 Year Average Annual Return (%)
MMA Praxis Intermediate Income B	Mennonite	1994	21.2	3.6
MMA Praxis International A	Mennonite	1999	45.2	16.9
MMA Praxis International B	Mennonite	1997	20.1	15.6
MMA Praxis Core Stock B	Mennonite	1994	49.6	7.2
New Covenant Balanced Growth Fund	Presbyterian	1999	326.7	8.9
New Covenant Balanced Income Fund	Presbyterian	1999	112.1	6.8
New Covenant Growth Fund	Presbyterian	1999	897.7	11.9
New Covenant Income Fund	Presbyterian	1999	536.0	3.9
Schwartz Ave Maria Bond I	Catholic	2003	10.0	N/A
Schwartz Ave Maria Bond R	Catholic	2003	35.3	N/A
Schwartz Ave Maria Catholic Values	Catholic	2001	233.4	13.8
Schwartz Ave Maria Growth Fund	Catholic	2003	111.6	N/A
Aquinas Value Fund	Catholic	2005	36.1	N/A
Aquinas Fixed Income	Catholic	2005	9.4	N/A
Timothy Plan Small Cap Value A	Evangelical	1994	62.5	13.3
Timothy Plan Small Cap Value B	Evangelical	1995	7.4	12.5
Total Assets			2,514.3	
S&P 500[10]		Market Index		12.0
S&P Nat. Municipal Bond Index		Market Index		4.7

Source: SocialFunds.com

The largest faith-based family of funds in the US was New Covenant with nearly $1.9 billion in assets. New Covenant limited "investments in companies involved in gambling, alcohol and firearm related issues," and a portion of the funds management fee was used to support "ongoing gift development" for the Presbyterian Church."[11]

Mennonite Mutual Aid sought to promote peace and human rights through its Praxis funds. Praxis primarily served "people and groups within the Anabaptist family of churches," namely Baptists, Amish, Mennonites, and Evangelicals. Like most faith-based funds, it also avoided investments in "companies materially engaged in alcohol and tobacco production and in the gaming industry."[12]

The Ave Maria Catholic Values Fund offered an investment alternative for American Catholics by avoiding investments in companies that provided products or services that were considered "contrary to core values and teachings of the Roman Catholic Church."

> The Catholic Advisory Board sets the criteria for screening out companies based on religious principles. In making this determination, the Catholic Advisory Board's members are guided by the magisterium of the Catholic Church and actively seek the advice and counsel of Catholic clergy. This process would, in general, encompass two major categories of companies: first, those involved in the practice of abortion, and second, companies whose policies are judged to be anti-family, such as companies that distribute pornographic material or whose policies undermine the Sacrament of Marriage.[13]

The most conservative faith-based fund was the Timothy Plan, which included "a family of mutual funds offering individuals a biblical choice when it comes to investing." Founder and President Arthur Ally explained his company's objectives,

> We are concerned with issues like abortion and pornography, the non-married lifestyle, and the homosexual agenda. We are not homophobes, but we will not own shares in companies that are promoting the agenda.[14]

The Timothy Plan refused to invest in most entertainment companies, which were seen to be aligned with the interests of the gay community. It also avoided pharmaceutical companies that manufactured drugs that could be used to perform abortions.

US Christians, however, held diverse views on issues such as abortion and homosexuality, and many disagreed with the values advanced by faith-based mutual funds. Some chose instead to invest in secular SRI funds, while others continued to invest in traditional mutual funds.

Jewish Funds   The fact that "the history of SRI goes back to the ethical precepts embodied in Jewish law,"[15] and was enshrined in the fundamental beliefs that informed both Islamic and Christian investments, was not lost on advocates of Jewish funds. "Judaism and its ancient sources do provide ample basis for the principles under which a Jewish-based ethical fund could be established," they argued.

> Such a fund would maintain a unique perspective on minority-share holders, and the general principles of this fund could be categorized under seven headings: abiding by Jewish law; abetting; justice and goodness; abiding by contracts; preserving life; settlement of the world; and Sabbath, festivals and Kosher food.[16]

Nevertheless, the only US-based Jewish mutual fund, the B'nai B'rith Growth Fund of Israel, closed in 1997 due to "the Fund's failure to attract sufficient assets."[17]

Performance

According to conventional wisdom, funds unfettered by the limits imposed by SRI criteria should outperform those motivated by non-financial concerns. However, historical data demonstrated that many SRI funds outperformed the market by a significant margin, while others performed close to market averages.

A case in point was the Pioneer Fund. One thousand dollars invested in the Pioneer Fund in 1928 would have grown to nearly $6 million in 1997, while the same amount indexed to the S&P 500 would have grown to less than $1.2 million. Similarly, the Ave Maria and Timothy Plan funds have consistently outperformed the market.[18]

These results supported the findings of a KPMG Consulting study, which concluded that financial returns and risk levels were "not affected negatively by adding SRI-criteria."

> Since SRI funds first appeared, the sophistication of stock selection techniques has increased markedly. In particular, the decreasing importance of negative screens and the rise of positive stock selection using environmental and social criteria focusing on best-in-class companies in each industrial sector, has allowed SRI fund managers to more easily marry financial and social performance requirements.[19]

THE CREDIT SUISSE CHRISTIAN VALUES FUND[20]

Credit Suisse believed that sustainability themes, such as ethics and environmental issues, would be among the more important financial trends in the coming years. Constant media attention and political campaigning helped to raise public awareness, and more people began to seek ways to limit their impact on the world around them. In 2006, the demand for SRI products in Switzerland increased by 56 percent over the previous year.

The bank's research had shown that the use of ethical screening had no detrimental effect on performance. It noted that "for the three year period ending 31 July 2006, the Ethical Investment Sector delivered an average return of 49.7 percent."[21]

> Our research suggests that ethical investors are investing for the long term. Over the long term, they can anticipate superior investment returns by avoiding industries in decline, such as the oil industry and tobacco. Instead, they should consider investing in growth areas of the economy such as healthcare, which will benefit from an ageing population, and companies with innovative solutions to environmental challenges or those involved in renewable energy.[22]

The idea for the Christian Values fund was first raised by Prince Mariano Hugo Fürst zu Windisch-Grätz, a dignitary of the Holy See and descendent of the Austrian aristocracy.[23] Launched in Luxembourg in July 2007, the fund was targeted to investors who wished to invest in companies that did not violate their moral convictions. (For the returns of the Christian Values Fund, see Exhibit 2).

EXHIBIT 2   Credit Suisse (Lux) Christian Values Fund – Fund Performance[24]

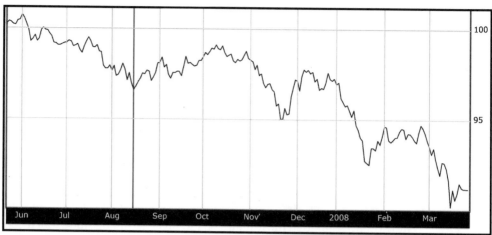

Currency: EUR

52-Week High	52-Week Low	Assets (Mil EUR)	Returns (YTD)
100.76 (06/01/07)	90.20 (03/17/08)	43.68 (03/31/08)	-6.25 %

To ensure conformity to Christian values, the fund was audited by two Catholic organizations, the Pontificium Regina Apostolorum University in Rome, and the Westchester Institute for Ethics and the Human Person.[25] Both organizations were run by the Legion of Christ, a Roman Catholic religious congregation founded in Mexico City in 1941. The Legionaries mission was "to extend Christ's Kingdom" and bring "Jesus Christ's saving and redeeming message to all hearts."[26]

The Legion of Christ was known for its conservative values and for its tendency to minister to wealthy and powerful Catholics. Among its benefactors was Carlos Slim, a Mexican business magnate who for a time was the wealthiest man in the world. In Latin America, the Legion ran a large number of elite schools and clubs for the families of wealthy business leaders, bankers, and politicians. Members were expected to adhere to strict Catholic principles or face social exclusion. In some places, membership in the group was seen as a prerequisite to career advancement. Consequently, critics of the group often referred to it as the "Millionaires of Christ."[27]

The Legionaries developed a list of Christian ethical criteria that Credit Suisse used to select stocks for the fund. The criteria followed strict and absolute rules, such as excluding companies that engaged in the production or sale of alcohol, tobacco, and gambling. In the selection process, securities belonging to standard market indices were first screened using the exclusion criteria. The result was a restricted list of companies that did not violate any of the negative selection conditions. From this list of candidates, Credit Suisse analyzed the remaining companies to determine their desirability according to positive selection criteria. The fund also invested heavily in government bonds (see Exhibit 3).

Selecting companies using inclusion criteria was far more complex than filtering out undesirable investments. Therefore, Credit Suisse employed "specialist support." The Christian Values Fund first used inclusion criteria developed by the Legionaries of Christ to rank investments (see Exhibits 4 & 5). It then employed data provided by the

EXHIBIT 3 Credit Suisse (Lux) Christian Values Fund Investment Mix[28]

Unit Class

Category B
(capital growth)

ISIN	LU0293559083
Bloomberg ticker	CRSCVLB LX
Net asset value (NAV)	93.85
1 Year High	100.76
1 Year Low	92.52

Asset Types in %

Fund currency	Money Market Fund	Money Market BM	Bonds Fund	Bonds BM	Real Estate Fund	Real Estate BM	Equities Fund	Equities BM	Others Fund	Others BM	Total Fund
EUR	0.77	-	49.64	-	-	-	9.41	-	-	-	59.82
USD	2.30	-	-	-	-	-	11.84	-	4.12	-	18.26
GBP	-	-	4.36	-	-	-	2.68	-	-	-	7.04
CHF	-	-	-	-	-	-	6.02	-	-	-	6.02
JPY	0.77	-	-	-	-	-	2.51	-	-	-	3.28
CAD	1.06	-	-	-	-	-	1.08	-	-	-	2.14
NOK	-	-	-	-	-	-	1.34	-	-	-	1.34
DKK	0.01	-	-	-	-	-	0.87	-	-	-	0.88
SEK	0.09	-	-	-	-	-	0.63	-	-	-	0.72
MXN	0.01	-	-	-	-	-	0.49	-	-	-	0.50
Total	5.01	-	54.00	-	-	-	36.87	-	4.12	-	100.00

Maturities in years

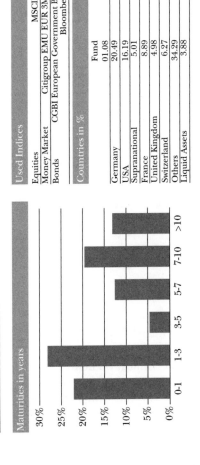

Used Indices

Equities	MSCI Word (NR)
Money Market	Citigroup EMU EUR 3M Euro Dep.
Bonds	CGBI European Government Bond Index - Bloomberg SBEUEU

Countries in %

	Fund 01.08	Fund 02.08
Germany	20.49	17.32
USA	16.19	13.86
Supranational	5.01	11.26
France	8.89	8.96
United Kingdom	4.98	7.04
Switzerland	6.27	6.02
Others	34.29	30.53
Liquid Assets	3.88	5.01

Top Holdings

	Coupon %	Maturity	as % of assets
EIB	3.875	15.10.16	4.46
Hellenic	3.500	20.04.09	3.46
Austria	4.125	15.01.14	3.45
BTAN	3.000	12.07.08	3.41
Ireland	4.600	18.04.16	2.43
Belgium	7.500	29.07.08	2.37
Italy	4.250	01.08.13	2.31
KFW Intl. Fin	3.250	25.04.08	2.30
DEPFA Bank	4.375	15.01.15	2.28
LD Baden W	4.000	08.02.11	2.26

EXHIBIT 4   Exclusion Criteria[29]

Exclusion criteria	Explanation
Violation of human rights	Failure to respect the Convention on Human Rights or the International Labor Organizations' minimal conditions for employees
Weapons	Companies that generate earnings from the production or sale of weapons
Money laundering	Companies with a proven involvement in this illegal activity
Disregard for environmental protection	Companies whose failure to comply with internationally accepted environmental standards has been proven
Violation of the right to life	Production of contraceptives, abortive pills or other products that deny the right to life
Negative leadership	Activities that contradict the values and anthropological vision of this initiative
Pornography	Companies involved in the production or distribution of pornographic material
Countries with political/religious intolerance	Companies from countries that contradict the values and anthropological vision of this initiative
Alcohol, tobacco and gambling	Companies that generate more than 5% of their revenues from the production or sale of these goods

EXHIBIT 5   Inclusion Criteria[30]

Inclusion criteria[31]	Explanation
Respect for human dignity	Companies that assign humans priority over other productive factors
Development of creativity and intelligence	The continued training and development of employees
Solidarity	Companies that develop models to promote cooperation among their employees and interest groups
Cultural and religious respect	Companies that respect the different origins and beliefs of their employees
Quality and value of products and services	Companies with production processes that respect public resources
Support for the family	Companies with family-oriented practices and rules (paternity/maternity leave, protection of marriage)
Ecological awareness	Production processes which comply with standards that go beyond legal requirements
Social responsibility	Companies that take part in charitable projects
Moral leadership	Top managers with strong moral beliefs, which they apply to their decisions and actions

Global Ethical Standard, a service developed by GES Investments of Sweden, to cross reference the activities of specific companies to each inclusion criterion.

The two most important reports offered by the Global Ethical Standard were "GES – Controversial" and "GES – Risk." GES – Controversial focused on weapons, tobacco, alcohol, pornography, and gambling. The analysis consisted of three steps.

1   Each company was classified according to the general risk level for its industry relatively to the criteria.

2   If there was a risk of association to any criterion, this was clarified through an analysis of company information and other sources of relevance for the criterion.

3   Any remaining uncertainties were followed up with the company and additional sources.[32]

GES – Risk focused on the environment, human rights and corporate governance. Each company was given a ranking from A to C indicating the "general risk level in the company's industry." The rating was supposed to show "the company's ability to deal with the general risks that concern the type of activity and to comply with international norms and procedures."[33]

Since the historical data that GES provided to clients like Credit Suisse were not always current, it tried to keep clients abreast of new developments through a weekly "alert service." GES attempted to report any recent incidents or allegations of violations of "international norms on Environmental, Social and Governance issues" before they were reported in the mainstream media.

CRITICISM

Despite its laudable objectives, Socially Responsible Investing was not without its critics. According to detractors, funds were only able to achieve high returns by not adhering to their own investment criteria. In the UK, for example, one study found that the majority of environmental funds made large investments in well-known polluters. According to the report,

> Most funds' top ten holdings are surprisingly mainstream, with names like Vodafone and Royal Bank of Scotland occurring again and again. Some hold BP, Shell and even Total. Very few funds have companies which are directly tackling climate change in their top ten holdings.[34]

In the United States, the situation was no different. Environmental funds like the Sierra Club Stock Fund and the Pax World Fund invested in oil companies, large retailers, and other known polluters. According to environmentalist Paul Hawken,[35] the problem was a lack of oversight. "The international SRI mutual fund industry," wrote Hawken, "has no standards, no definitions, and no regulations other than financial regulations."

> Anyone can join; anyone can call his or her fund an SRI fund. Over 90 percent of Fortune 500 companies are included in SRI portfolios. The term "socially responsible investing" is so broad it is meaningless. If a fund doesn't own companies involved with gambling and pornography, it can be called socially responsible. Never mind that it owns Halliburton and Monsanto."[36]

Even more narrowly defined terms were open to interpretation. Although it might be straightforward for a Catholic fund to avoid companies that produced contraceptives, funds promoting "social justice" and "environmental sustainability" could easily modify the selection criteria to fit within the broad meaning of such terms. The assumption was clear: only by manipulating the screening criteria could fund managers match the returns of conventional funds.

Hawken believed that, while investors wanted to promote ethical practices, they evaluated funds based on financial, rather than social, performance. "Investing can be an emotional and stressful experience," he observed.

> Most small investors cannot afford to lose the money that they have saved, as it represents a future down payment on a house, college funds, and/or retirement security. There is tremendous pressure on financial managers to perform. Financial anxiety experienced by investors as well as competition in the industry has induced asset managers to focus on achieving the highest rate of return.[37]

In Hawken's opinion, the desire to realize exceptional returns explained why the Sierra Club, considered one of the foremost environmental organizations in the world, invested in large retailers like Best Buy and Costco, instead of companies that promoted organic foods and alternative energy. "There is not a single company in their portfolio that addresses the environment in an innovative or proactive way," he complained. "There is no company that measures its ecological footprint. There are no alternative energy companies."[38]

Similarly, the Pax World Fund, founded in 1971 by Methodists opposed to the Vietnam War, was one of the oldest and most respected SRI funds. Yet its holdings violated nearly every one of the Funds investment principles (see Exhibit 6). Even so, Pax was one of the better funds. SRI "peace" funds were found to have invested in Raytheon, a defense contractor, while "green" funds invested in companies like Dow Chemical, Monsanto and ExxonMobil.

In the first study of its kind on "Socially Responsible Investing," the National Capital Institute (NCI) found that almost everywhere in the world, SRI funds did little to address the concerns of investors. (For the total number of SRI funds by region, see Exhibit 7). In fact, the combined top 30 holdings of global SRI funds were virtually indistinguishable from the top holdings of conventional mutual funds. That report noted that "even though the increase in global greenhouse gas emissions is the number one environmental problem, SRI funds hold stock in every car company in the world. Only two bicycle companies are held, one in a small fund in Luxembourg and the other by a handful of UK funds."[39]

Occasionally, investments in companies that violated a fund's ethical principles could be justified. For instance, through shareholder activism, individuals and organizations could motivate companies to change their business practices. Shareholder activism took many forms, including proxy battles, publicity campaigns, shareholder resolutions, litigation, speaking out at annual meetings and negotiating with management. Yet, according to the NCI study, SRI funds were rarely involved in such activities.

> The question is then: What effect do monies placed in these funds have on large-cap companies? The fair answer is a little, sometimes, depending on whether the company is getting feedback or pressure from non-investor groups . . . With few exceptions, SRI mutual funds are not activists. They see their primary duty as being a fiduciary and their number one goal as shareholder return.

EXHIBIT 6 Pax World Fund Principles vs. Holdings[40]

Principle	Examples of Securities Held	Associated Products and Services	Alleged Violation
Environmental Stewardship	Fluor Corporation	Builds refineries, oil and gas production, chemical plants	Facilitates well known polluters
Green, not Greed	Microsoft Corporation	Software	Antitrust violations
Treat Toxic Waste	UGI Corporation	Natural Gas and Coal Power Generation	Generates pollution
Reduce, Reuse, Recycle	Pepsi	Soft drinks	Large amounts of plastic bottle and metal can waste
Prevent Pollution	General Motors	Vehicles	Poor fuel efficiency in vehicles such as the Hummer
Clean air, clean water, clean energy	DPL, Inc.	Coal fired plants	Generates pollution
Equal Opportunity	Apogent, Nokia, Comcast	Communications	Under-representation of female managers
Diverse Independent Boards	Chesapeake Energy Corporation, Tidewater	Oil and gas	Exclusively white male members of boards
Conserve resources	Baker Hughes	Oilfield services	Resource depletion
Restore Ecosystems	Corn Products Intl.	High fructose syrup	Corn production destroys topsoil and pollutes rivers
Encourage alternative energy	Apache Corporation	Oil and gas exploration	Promotes fossil fuels
Equal pay for equal work	Bed, Bath, and Beyond	Retail	Sells products produced mainly through low cost labor in China

EXHIBIT 7 International SRI Funds[41]

Region	Number of identified funds	Number with complete holdings confirmed	Number with partial holdings confirmed	Number with no holdings data confirmed	Number with no information available
Africa	3	2	0	1	0
Australia & NZ	45	19	2	16	8
Canada	40	40	0	0	0
Europe	367	215	70	13	69
Japan	12	11	1	0	0
South America	2	2	0	0	0
Asia (exc. Japan)	8	2	0	0	6
United States	109	108	1	0	0
Middle East	16	0	1	0	15
Total	602	399	75	30	98
% of Total		66.3	12.5	5.0	16.3

To NCI, the problem was clear. As long as ethical funds continued to compare their returns to conventional funds, they would be incapable of addressing the social concerns of investors.

> The obsessive drive to compare SRI funds with conventional funds should cease. The difference in yield is largely irrelevant. What is relevant is what a company does, how it does it, and then, and only then, is yield relevant.[42]

The Christian Values Fund

The Christian Values fund attracted its own critics, which included members of the Catholic clergy. One such critic was Father Albert Ziegler, a Jesuit priest and lecturer in business ethics at Zurich University, who did not believe that the banks "worried about ethics."

> They are simply providing funds targeted toward a customer segment that is concerned about ethical issues. Although such offerings are certainly not unethical, they are less likely to arise from ethical motives than from marketing considerations. The banks respond by saying that as long as ethics is important to customers, it is their job to fill that customer need. The customer should be able to choose whether or not to invest in ethical sectors. Our top business priority is not ethics, but customer freedom.

Ziegler felt that such a position was disingenuous, because the banks themselves were not bound by the ethical positions proposed to their customers.

> The credibility of Credit Suisse's "Christian Values" fund is based on trust. As such, banks should view ethical funds as more than just a modern marketing tool, but as an opportunity to challenge themselves to behave more ethically.

Ziegler also questioned the blanket criteria used to select "ethical" investments. For example, was the production of weapons, condoms, or oral contraceptives always immoral? "Perhaps only a papal university would make such an assertion," he remarked.

> But what if such a company produces its products in an environmentally friendly way, provides maternity and paternity benefits to its employees, and has a carbon neutral footprint? Can it be a better investment than a manufacturer of solar panels that is only concerned about producing its products in way that meets the [minimal labor and environmental] regulations?[43]

Suzie Kemp, a UK-based fund manager for Credit Suisse, agreed that one of the greatest challenges in SRI investing was determining what should be considered ethical. "What is ethical to one person may not be to another," she observed.

> Take, for example, genetically modified organisms. It is possible to make strong ethical arguments for and against investing in companies involved in genetic modification. Throughout the

Third World, there are benefits from genetic modification technology, as we see in India where it is now possible to grow rice that will protect people against waterborne diseases that cause blindness. However, some people might take the view that by growing fields of genetically modified rice, we might be changing the balance of the ecosystem with potential longer-term consequences. One of the most interesting things about doing this job is that the issues are ever-changing and so are the criteria of the fund.[44]

In Germany, one commentator questioned the Christian Values fund's "passive strategy." Although Credit Suisse excluded obvious violators of the fund's ethical principles, it did not look deeper. Instead, the fund purchased government bonds and other relatively safe securities, he noted.

One can easily place a seal of approval on such a fund, when it mainly invests in government bonds, and Credit Suisse is following this pattern to a T. However, a little ethics is probably still better than none at all.[45]

UNANSWERED QUESTIONS

In the past few days, Hildebrandt had learned a great deal about ethical investing. Although not all of what she learned was positive, the concept still appealed to her. After seeing the video of Philip Röh discussing the Christian Values fund, Hildebrandt decided to make some phone calls. With her questions in hand, she began dialing.

Notes

1   investchannel.ch/instrumente/Anlegen-mit-dem-Segen-des-Vatikans.aspx Accessed April 11, 2008
2   Investing for Good, *Bank Investment Consultant,* December 2007, p. 39
3   In God's Name, *The Economist,* November 1, 2007
4   One exception was the United States. According to the Pew study, the US had twice as many religious people per capita as Canada and five times as many as France. Americans, the study concludes, were "closer to people in developing nations than to the publics of developed nations." Source: *Among Wealthy Nations, U.S. Stands Alone in Its Embrace of Religion,* The Pew Research Center for the People & the Press, December 19, 2002 (pewglobal.org/reports/pdf/167.pdf Accessed March 3, 2008)
5   Profit versus the Prophet, *The Los Angeles Times,* February 10, 2008, Part M, Pg. 11
6   Purification by Charity, *Muslim Investor,* June 19, 2001 (muslim-investor.com/mi/purification.phtml accessed February 27, 2008)
7   Cory, Jacques; *Business Ethics: The Ethical Revolution of Minority Shareholders,* Springer; New York, 2004, p.49
8   For example, CNN reported that assets held by Christian mutual funds grew from $2.4 billion in 2000 to $15.9 billion in 2006. Source: Investors bet on their faith, *CNNMoney.com,* March 23, 2006 (money.cnn.com/2006/03/23/markets/religious_funds/index.htm Accessed March 3, 2008)
9   The table excludes faith-based funds created after 2006.
10 S&P data to January 31, 2008 Source: standardandpoors.com
11 Source: www.socialfunds.com, accessed February 27, 2008

12   mmapraxis.com/stewardship_investing/core_values.html Accessed March 3, 2008

13   Ave Maria Mutual Funds Prospectus, Schwartz Investment Trust, May 1, 2007, p.3

14   Christian Investors Put Their Beliefs Into Practice, NPR Morning Edition, November 14,
     2006 (npr.org accessed February 27, 2008)

15   Is Your Money Where Your Heart Is?, *Common Ground,* October 2004, pp. 14–17

16   Schwartz, Mark et. al, Capital Markets and Jewish Teachings, p. 3 (www.kayema.com accessed
     February 27, 2008). Mark S. Schwartz, Meir Tamari, Daniel Schwab (2007) Ethical Investing
     from a Jewish Perspective, Business and Society Review 112 (1) , 137–161

17   The only U.S. mutual fund investing in Israel is closing, Washington Jewish Week, April 11, 1997

18   Ethical funds that bear fruit, *Investment Adviser,* January 14, 2008

19   Screening of Screening Companies, MISTRA, The Foundation for Strategic Environmental
     Research, October 2001 (www.ecnc.nl Accessed March 6, 2008)

20   Except where noted, the text for this section was summarized from "Credit Suisse Fund
     (Lux) Christian Values – Q&A for media inquiries," distributed by Credit Suisse, July 2007

21   Credit Suisse: Investing with Conscience, *The Credit Suisse Multi-Manager Ethical Fund,* October 6,
     2006, p. 2 (uk.csam.com/uk/documents/cs_ethical_4pp.pdf Accessed April 4, 2008)

22   Investing with a Conscience, *Credit Suisse e-magazine,* April 20, 2006 (emagazine.credit-suisse.
     com Accessed April 4, 2008)

23   Fonds religieux : investissez sans pécher, Le Figaro, July 27, 2007, p. 19

24   Source: Bloomberg.com Accessed April 1, 2008

25   Ibid.

26   regnumchristi.org/english/quienes/index.phtml accessed February 29, 2008

27   With elite backing, Catholic order has pull in Mexico, *The Wall Street Journal,* January 23, 2006

28   Source: csam-europe.com/dss/factsheet/fs_csfl_chrval_b_ch_eng.pdf Accessed April 1, 2008

29   Source: "Credit Suisse Fund (Lux) Christian Values – Q&A for media inquiries," distributed
     by Credit Suisse, July 2007

30   Source: "Credit Suisse Fund (Lux) Christian Values – Q&A for media inquiries," distributed
     by Credit Suisse, July 2007

31   The criteria were not weighted in any way. Each category was given equal consideration during
     the selection process.

32   ges-invest.com/pages/?ID=71 accessed February 29, 2008

33   ges-invest.com/pages/?ID=69 Accessed February 29, 2008

34   *Guide To Climate Change Investment,* Holden & Partners, February 29, 2008
     (holden-partners.co.uk/documents/Guide_To_Climate_Change_Investment.pdf   Accessed
     March 3, 2008)

35   Paul Hawken was the head of the Natural Capital Institute, an environmental advocacy
     organization that published the World Index of Social and Environmental Responsibility
     (WISER).

36   Is Your Money Where Your Heart Is?, *Common Ground,* October 2004, pp. 14–17

37   Hawken, P., *NCI Socially Responsible Investing,* The National Capital Institute, October 2004
     (responsibleinvesting.org Accessed March 5, 2008)

38   Ibid.

39   Hawken, P., *NCI Socially Responsible Investing,* The National Capital Institute, October 2004
     (responsibleinvesting.org Accessed March 5, 2008)

40   Based on holdings as of June 2003. Adapted from: Is Your Money Where Your Heart Is?,
     Common Ground, October 2004, pp. 14–17

41   This list was compiled by the National Capital Institute includes all known SRI funds in the
     world as of April 30, 2004. Source: NCI Socially Responsible Investing, responsibleinvesting.
     org Accessed March 5, 2008.

42   Ibid.

43   Translated from the original German. Eine Gefahr für die eigene Glaubwürdigkeit, *NZZ Online,* December 17, 2007 (nzz.ch/nachrichten/startseite/eine_gefahr_fuer_die_eigene_ glaubwuerdigkeit Accessed April 2, 2008)

44   Investing with a Conscience, *Credit Suisse e-magazine,* April 20, 2006 (emagazine.credit-suisse. com Accessed April 4, 2008)

45   Translated from the original German. Ethik-Fonds Geldsegen von ganz oben, *Süddeutsche Zeitung,* July 26, 2007 (sueddeutsche.de/finanzen/artikel/516/125329/ Accessed April 2, 2008)

Index

Index compiled by Terry Halliday